PARTISAN AESTHETICS

SANJUKTA SUNDERASON

PARTISAN AESTHETICS

Modern Art and India's Long Decolonization

STANFORD UNIVERSITY PRESS
STANFORD, CALIFORNIA

Stanford University Press
Stanford, California

Printed in the United States of America on acid-free, archival-quality paper

Library of Congress Cataloging-in-Publication Data is available upon request.

ISBN 978-1-5036-1194-8 (cloth)
ISBN 978-1-5036-1299-0 (paper)
ISBN 978-1-5036-1300-3 (electronic)

Cover design: Kevin Barrett Kane
Cover image: Somnath Hore, *Wounds* (c. 1977). Courtesy Akar Prakar Gallery.
© Artist's Estate
Typeset by Motto Publishing Services in 11/15 Adobe Caslon Pro

To Mamma, Baba, Poppy.

CONTENTS

ILLUSTRATIONS

PREFACE

Partisan Aesthetics develops out of, and at the juncture of, many crossings: of the disciplines of history and history of art; of questions that are at once national, global, and distinctly locational; and of associations, encounters, and (at times) blind trails. Such crossings, spurred by whims, serendipities, and old and new convictions, have generated questions that will exceed the limits of this book. They have also produced the distinct method and scope of *Partisan Aesthetics.*

This book reads art *as archive*, and understands artistic form as and via entanglements of art and history itself. Its protagonists are not key artists or institutions of twentieth-century Indian modernism but rather the granular histories of an aesthetic field formed through convergences of art and politics during late-colonial and early postcolonial India. Decolonization read in its *longue durée,* as the book will show, made such histories gain particular configurations—what I am calling *partisan aesthetics.*

The book will echo my training in social, cultural, and intellectual history, for which I am indebted to my teachers, Madhavan Palat, Majid Siddiqui, Neeladri Bhattacharya, Rajat Kanta Ray, and Subhas Ranjan Chakraborty. It will also carry questions that have emerged along my graduated crossing into visual art, as well as the negotiations between pulls of the historical and the aesthetic. In its earlier stages, this work was enriched by the cross-disciplinary drifts that came from some early commentators: I am grateful to Christopher Pinney, Clare Harris, Jyotindra Jain, Partha Mitter, Raminder Kaur, and Tapati Guha-Thakurta for some of their early provocations and nudges. My historian's fixations were both harnessed to and liberated by the terms set by art and by the question of *form* itself. Without the rigor and generosity of my former doctoral mentors, Andrew Hemingway and

Natasha Eaton, what became a fruitful crossing of art and history in the work would not have been possible.

Formative to the book are the friendships, critiques, and generosities of Iftikhar Dadi, Kamran Asdar Ali, Lotte Hoek, and Sonal Khullar, and the conversations we have had on histories and cultures of the postcolonial left. Even in its closing hours, the book continued to benefit from the insights of an expanding world of rather generous peers: I am grateful to Aditi Chandra, Diana Campbell, Elizabeth Giorgis, Harsana Rambukwella, John Tain, Ming Tiampo, Samina Iqbal, Simon Soon, and Simone Wille for ever-new conversations around archives, worldings, and contextualities of art—in South Asia and across resonant geographies of the Global South.

"Hometown," to me, has always meant more alienation than comforts of familiarity and, ironically, has offered a looking *from within* that remains still uncontained: Calcutta—in its histories, contradictions, and dis/locations in (postcolonial) historiography itself—has become, without an initial intent, the subconscious subject of *Partisan Aesthetics*. I am thankful for the help I have received, in this both baffling and promising city: I recall with gratitude the generosity of the late Arun Ghose at the Bhupesh Bhawan Library, the cartoonist Chandi Lahiri, Asim Dasgupta at the National Library, Kamalika Mukherjee at the Centre for Studies in Social Sciences, Sandip Dutta at the Little Magazine Library; the staff members at the Bangiya Sahitya Parishat; the Government College of Art and Crafts; the Rabindra Bharati University; the Rammohan Public Library; and the family library of the veteran scholar Nikhil Sarkar—known as Sripantha to many. Many of the archives in this book are private papers, at times collated somewhat, by a market-driven private art gallery world, but often simply untethered to any collection (or order). I am thankful to the artists and artist families who gave me time and rare resources to enable me to write this history in its formative stages: I recall with gratitude the son of artist Atul Bose—Sanjib Bose; the son of the artist Nikhil Biswas—Debabrata Biswas; the son of artist Gobardhan Ash—Nirban Ash; the daughter of artist Gopal Ghose—Deepa Bose; the sons of artist Rathin Maitra—Riten and Romain Maitra; the late artists Bijan Choudhury and Rabin Mondal; the collector Rubi Pal Chowdhury; the art critics Pranab Ranjan Ray and Sandip Sarkar; and the archives of the Society of Contemporary Artists in Calcutta. I am grateful also for the help I received from Tapati Guha-Thakurta and Hari Vasudevan in the early stages of my research in Calcutta. In this book, as is evident already, I will stick to the city's old name, as was current for the book's purview, rather than the new name, Kolkata, which has been used since 2001 (the same will apply for Bombay over Mumbai, altered since 1995).

Foundational archival work for this book was done in New Delhi, my adopted city of much love: in the modest plenty of the P. C. Joshi Archives of Contemporary History at Jawaharlal Nehru University (JNU), New Delhi; amidst trunks and suitcases of files (and utility bills) furnished by Pradeep Dasgupta, son of the sculptor Prodosh Dasgupta; and the ever-shifting yet consistently kind staff at the documentation division of the Delhi Art Gallery (DAG). The reluctant archivists of Lalit Kala Akademi and the National Gallery of Modern Art could be balanced out, most of the time, with their more pliable staff members at the library. Amba Sanyal, daughter of the artist Bhabesh Sanyal, has offered me generous sources on the artist and his worlds in Delhi, the full richness of which I will be returning to in my future work.

My early (albeit brief) conversations with Ashish Anand of DAG and Neville Tuli at Osian's (Mumbai) in 2007 around the rare works of the artist Chittaprosad triggered my interest in an artist both missing from the art world of postcolonial India and yet, unbeknownst to me, on the verge of a significant art-market revival in the late 2000s. The book itself ended up weaving the wider political and intellectual histories that contained Chittaprosad's appearance in the early 1940s, his erasure (somewhat self-steered) from the 1950s through the 1970s, and a belated salvage from relative obscurity of the 1990s.

Partisan Aesthetics has benefited at various points from generous research support: I am grateful to the UK-India Education and Research Initiative, the British Council; the Central Research Fund of the University of London; the Graduate School Bursary of University College London; the European Commission's Marie Curie Career Integration Grant; and project and publication grants I received from Leiden University's research profile Asian Modernities and Traditions. It has also benefited in its closing stages from my participation in thinking through transnational pedagogies of art and politics, under the Getty Foundation's Connecting Art Histories initiative "Modern Art Histories in and across Africa, South and Southeast Asia," steered by Cornell University's Institute for Comparative Modernities, the Dhaka Art Summit in Bangladesh, and the Asia Art Archive in Hong Kong. For the images in this book, I am grateful for the generosity of the Akar Prakar Gallery in Calcutta; DAG, the NGMA, and the P. C. Joshi Archives of Contemporary History at Jawaharlal Nehru University in New Delhi. Most significantly, I am grateful for the archival documents I received from artists' personal collections of albums, catalogues, and diaries.

A world of friendships has sustained me along and despite each crossing. This is the perfect place to note in joy and gratitude (and in diligent first-name alphabetical order) some fellow travelers of varying spells, from a couple of continents and an island: Aditya Pant, Barry Watt, Bindu Menon, Bodhisattva Kar, Damayanti Sarkar, Ditipriya Chattopadhyay, Emilia Terracciano, Mandakini Devasher, Mahesh Gopalan, Maggie Gray, Mark Edwards, Onni Gust, Paramita Bramhachari, Partha Pratim Shil, Rachna Singh, Rohan Deb Roy, Rose Vickridge, Shaila Bhatti, Shinjini Das, Shipra Nigam, Sohini Dasgupta, Sraman Mukherjee, Steve Martin, Warren Carter, and Zirwat Chowdhury. To Aditi Sengupta and Uditi Sen, I remain indebted, in a nutshell.

Joining Leiden University in the Netherlands and finding myself within what was to me a new world of area studies has been both enriching and challenging—perhaps not much unlike the crossings I noted at the start. Worlds of colleagues and friends overlap at Leiden in ways most reassuring and mirthful. I have benefited over the years from those who have sustained me socially and intellectually, have commented on the texts in progress, and have borne with the ups and downs and absences of my writing process: I can only mention in gratitude (and remaining with the alphabetical drift) Ajay Gandhi, Anna-Isabelle Richard, Ben Arps, Carolien Stolte, Carolyn Nakamura, Crystal Ennis, Cyrus Schayegh, David Henley, Eftychia Mylona, Erik de Maaker, Ethan Mark, Henrietta Lidchi, Kiri Paramore, Limin Teh, Fan Lin, Maghiel van Crevel, Nell Crawford, Nira Wickramasinghe, Noelle Richardson, Priya Swamy, Radhika Gupta, Ra'id al-Jamali, Roshni Sengupta, Sandrien Verstappen, S. Suryadi, Tom Hoogervorst, Tsolin Nalbantian, and Wang Jue. A special note stays reserved here for Nira Wickramasinghe, who has spurred the momentum of this project in more ways than she will know. I recall fondly, too, the wonderful yet fleeting presences in Leiden of Aarti Kawlra, Antonella Fiona, Anup Grewal, Britta Ohm, Carola Lorea, Debjani Bhattacharya, Eva Ambos, and Gwen Bennett. My sincere thanks go to Tom Aldrich, for his keen editorial eye and the work of indexing for this book, but most importantly, for humoring the pace of the manuscript. Leiden's scattered yet sustaining forums have often given a backbone to my at-times-unfolding plots and drafts: I am thankful to the company I have received from the History Workshop, the Global South Seminar, the MENA Region and Global Aesthetics collective, and the reading group, Utopias.

The larger world of my Dutch family has remained a generous and patient companion in this book's writing-up years. I thank Ans and Simon Boven, Chaya, Guido, and Yaëla Boven for humoring me in these years of ever so scurrying time.

It would have been a joy to share this book with my grandparents, but for senility and mortality. I wonder how they would have recollected the histories I write here, as they had lived them in the city, in their neighborhoods.

My parents, Ranjit and Ruma Sunderason, have been present for each day of this journey, in support, conversations, and freedom itself—to think and write, and respect what stays non-spectacular. I owe my instincts to them.

Martijn Boven has driven and lived with the *becoming* of this book. To him I raise here a toast, for keeping our shared worlds adequately tangible, and delectably absurd. His mind refreshes my writing and all that it entails.

The publication of *Partisan Aesthetics* has survived academia's at times baser instincts. I am thankful, *en fin*, to my field, and to my editors at Stanford University Press for trusting and steering the work.

Sanjukta Sunderason
The Hague, December 2019

PARTISAN AESTHETICS

INTRODUCTION

PARTISAN AESTHETICS

Configurations

IN 1992, Somnath Hore, a noted artist and former Communist activist, exhibited in Calcutta (Kolkata since 2001) a series of figurative drawings, abstract white-on-white paper-pulp prints (this book's cover image, for instance), and bronze sculptures. Titled *Wounds*, the exhibition was a compendium of Hore's works on a theme he had been pursuing obsessively since the 1970s; the "wounds" were, as he noted in an autobiographical piece accompanying the exhibition, "intimations of only one subject matter—the helpless around us, the rejected, the hungry [. . .]—a *wound that would not heal* (emphasis mine)."[1] Wounds, Hore wrote, were the memories he himself carried from the 1940s, when as a young artist-reporter of the Communist Party of India (CPI), he sketched victims of the notorious wartime Bengal famine in 1943–44 that had displaced and decimated millions from rural Bengal. Wounds were also marks of the visceral violence the artist saw around him in the 1970s—the far-left political agitation of the Naxalite movement in Calcutta, the genocide across the borders with the birth of Bangladesh in 1971 (from what had become the eastern wing of Pakistan after Indian and Pakistani independence and partition in 1947), the horrors of the Vietnam War. As Hore wrote, "The ruts left on the road by wheels, the cut from the axe on the side of the tree, the injuries on the human body left by weapons."[2]

Hore was also writing under the shadow of a dissolving Soviet Union. The closing pages of his brief autobiography rang melancholic, as he reflected on the memory, forms, and destiny of the left that he himself had been a part of since the 1940s, despite his formal dissociation from the CPI in the late 1950s:

> Against the background of the socialist movement and in the context of events in the Soviet Union, dreams and aspirations received a shattering blow. Yet dreams are not all untrue. Poets, artists, writers, even scientists, have discovered truths through the medium of dreams. Socialism was both truth and dream for many of us. And its culture has not yet been made entirely grimy. Socialism remains the only answer to ruthless oppression. The one thing that has become noticeable, however, is that if the methods employed are wrong, many attempts are doomed to fail. [3]

In the early 1990s, while Hore's *Wounds* were citing—as memory, trace, and metaphor—intertwined histories of left-wing cultural initiatives, of famines, genocides, and wars that trailed the global footprints of twentieth-century decolonization, his former comrade, mentor, and friend Chittaprosad—another Communist artist—was being recuperated from comparative oblivion by a fledgling private art market in India. Known for his iconic drawings of famine victims and socialist resistance in the pages of the CPI's national organ, *People's War* (*People's Age*, post-1945), Chittaprosad had pioneered communist visual reportage in the 1940s as a new artist-cadre of the CPI. Unlike Hore, however, he remained both a self-proclaimed outsider to the art world of postcolonial India and a figure almost erased from the narratives of Indian modern art. After his dissociation from party circles in the late 1940s and until his death in 1978, few people noted his legacy at a national level, beyond his former friends and comrades, and some vernacular "little magazines" in Calcutta that sporadically published his letters, essays, and poems through the 1970s and 1980s. In the 1990s, however, Chittaprosad was to undergo an ironic retrieval by a booming art market and private commercial galleries, despite his lifelong rejection of the commercialized art world. Steered by the Delhi Art Gallery (DAG) and Osian's in Bombay (Mumbai since 1995)—private art galleries and auction houses—Chittaprosad's corpus of drawings, sketchbooks, prints, letters, puppets, and manuscripts was brought into the public eye and onto the auction circuit. Nestled now amid a vibrant pastiche of cultural paraphernalia from twentieth-century India that Osian's and DAG exhibited through the 2000s in centers across New Delhi and Bombay, Chittaprosad's socialist art seemed poised to join the canons of Indian modernism, affirming at the same time a left-wing nostalgia for what CPI activist and chronicler Sudhi Pradhan had in the late 1970s documented as the "Marxist cultural movement."[4]

As exhibitions and retrospectives of left-wing artists like Hore and Chittaprosad have grown steadily through the 2000s, they have responded to multiple demands from the contemporary art world. Since the 2010s, such left-wing iconography has begun to enter international biennales and art summits, framed under a new global curatorial and art historical interest in global modernisms, artists from the Global South, and art during decolonization. For instance, at the 2017 documenta 14 at Kassel, Germany, Chittaprosad's works from the Bengal famine of 1943 were displayed alongside the works of another iconic artist of the famine—Zainul Abedin, who had migrated to East Pakistan after Indian partition, becoming an artist-pedagogue and the national artist of Bangladesh. As curators cite the momentous histories of war, famine, and anti-imperial movements that these artists inhabited, they frame artists like Chittaprosad, Hore, and Abedin within new curatorial configurations of the emerging field of mid-twentieth-century "Third World" aesthetics.[5] While such directions respond to calls for the expansion of historiographical attention to art from the Global South, or postcolonial modernisms, they are also opening up, I argue, a new narrative space *shared* by visual art, the left, and the politics of decolonization in its *longue durée.*

This dynamism in the curatorial gaze has, in most instances, not been matched in history writing around the art and artists of decolonization. While art historians have occupied themselves with retrieving figures of modern art from non-Western contexts, as a justifiable counter to the Eurocentric canons of modernism, they have too often remained close to iconic figures, biographical modalities, and celebrational impetuses. Historians, meanwhile, continue to be absorbed in studying the political ruptures of decolonization, with little attention to the cultural field where the scopes of postcolonial freedom itself were being negotiated. Studying the entangled field of visual art, the left, and the long decolonization in the Indian subcontinent demands a historiographical agenda that is attuned to both art and politics, and the very *forms* of such entanglements; and that connects *as methodology*—dispersed and disparate stories. A curatorial vision, I propose, must guide the historical eye: art must become archives, and artists must enter histories as constituents or protagonists, beyond becoming, for instance, symbols of national or global or postcolonial modernisms.

Hore's metaphor of the wound and Chittaprosad's belated salvage, as well as the curatorial grids of "Third World aesthetics" in our times, animate histories of the "political" in visual art under the shadows of India's long decolonization. Such histories emerge out of the late-colonial decades of heightened mass politics and displacements in the 1930s and 1940s, and grow within the long shadows that the climactic ruptures of the 1940s cast in the cultural memory and artistic forms through the postcolonial decades. Modern art and India's long decolonization thus constitute an intertwining of artistic form and historical time itself. We encounter here not only politically committed artists such as Hore and Chittaprosad, who drew hunger and resistance, but also their comrades, critics, and fellow artists, who sought to make sense of the turbulent and transitional times they inhabited, with or without professed (left-wing) political commitments. Pursuing them reveals lines of alignment, affiliation as well as dissociation that escape and exceed stable determinisms of ideology and commitment. They present to a historian (of art) a dialectical field of the political—with dispersed, fragmented, and at times contradictory histories.

Partisan Aesthetics is my endeavor to conceptualize and write this field. I am laying out here what "partisan aesthetics" connotes as a conceptual frame, what historical work it can do with the artistic field of mid-twentieth-century India as my archive, and what it can lend—methodologically—to an ever-expanding field of global and transnational art histories of the twentieth century.

THINKING CONJUNCTURALLY

In 1943, in the heart of the imperial war effort in late-colonial India, a famine descended upon rural Bengal. Widely acknowledged as "man-made," the famine's causes were as multipolar as its very temporality. While some scholars date the famine back to a cyclone that ravaged the Midnapore district of southwest Bengal in the autumn of 1942, aggravating an already depleted rural economy, its more immediate causation was steeped in the wartime strategies of the imperial government. With the entry of Japan into World War II and the fall of Burma in early 1942, Bengal had become the easternmost front of the Allied forces. To quell the approach of the Japanese army, the colonial British government had implemented a scorched-earth strategy. Throughout 1942, the Allied forces burned, confiscated, and eliminated from the market massive stocks of rice, and sank thousands of boats to cut off the riverine economy and infrastructure on the eastern frontier of the province along the Burmese border. Persistent denial of food scarcity by the colonial government aggravated the already mounting rural hunger. Beginning under the shadow of the cyclone, the famine became stark along the eastern frontier of the war in Chittagong, which was exposed to Japanese bombing in January 1943.

The Bengal famine has been described as notoriously man-made, triggered not only by official apathy and the forced extractions of the war, but also by wartime profiteering, maladministration of food, aberrant market conditions, hoarding, and a "moral collapse."[6] Contradicting the "food availability decline" hypothesis of the Famine Enquiry Commission (the Woodhead Commission) of 1944, for instance, the economist Amartya Sen has argued for "failure of exchange entitlement" to explain the crisis of 1943, arguing that the cause of the famine was not food shortage but unequal "access" to food among certain sections of the rural community who were entirely dependent on the market by late-colonial times—the most badly hurt among them being agricultural laborers, craftsmen, and fisherfolk.[7] As it spread, the famine ravaged villages and displaced millions, who trekked to suburban and urban Calcutta in search of food. By July 1943, Calcutta and other semi-urban towns were filled with rural refugees uprooted from their villages. While the famine was essentially a rural phenomenon, decimating entire villages, its particular modality of urban destitution was what made it iconic, as refugees inhabited city streets, struggled for survival in food queues, and died of starvation.

Ian Stephens, the editor of Calcutta's noted English daily *The Statesman*—one of the earliest to break the news of the famine through photographs of Calcutta streets—recollects in his memoirs the gradual "arrival" of the famine to Calcutta: it arrived unnoticed, he wrote, there being "little strikingly unusual about the appearance of Calcutta streets till well on into the summer of '43. The hot weather passed, the rains began before it was evident that famine had come."[8] Stephens points to the particular quality of the rupture in the urban landscape that registered the reality of the famine: "Death by famine lacks drama . . . horrid though it may be to say, multitudinous death from this cause looked at merely optically, regarded without emotion as a spectacle, is until the crows get at it, the rats and kites and dogs and vultures, very dry."[9]

For the common man in the city, "knowing" the arrival of the famine came from "seeing" the changing sights on the streets, a dramatic transformation beyond the usual sights of urban poverty. The *natun bhishuk* (new beggars), wrote the Bengali daily *Anandabazar Patrika*, were easily distinguished as *grihasthas* (peasant householders from the villages) who were forced to swarm to the city in search of food; in contrast to the "professional beggars," the "new" ones did not nag, nor did they lose their temper if alms were denied—"they merely went away with dimmed faces," a fatalism that marked the famine victims as well as their representation. From July onward, the city streets bore macabre sights of starvation deaths, piled-up dead bodies on street corners, men and dogs fighting over morsels from city bins. The death toll (recorded) of destitute people rose from 100 a day in late July to as many as 1,300 a week in August, with almost 11,000 dead in Calcutta alone between August 1 and October 30.[10]

The middle-class gentry witnessed these scenes of death in the streets with dismay, and contributed aid by their own means, through relief work or funds collection, while also giving cultural forms to their outrage in a corpus of literature—novels, short stories, plays, poetry—

and songs produced during 1943 and 1944. The famine was given "social," "political," and "emotional" values by becoming what Gennifer Weisenfeld has called a "visible evidence" of colonial and capitalist extraction.[11] While the Bengal famine left its trail in the official and political literature of journalistic surveys and statistical records,[12] in the domain of cultural representation it triggered radically new terms and dynamics of visuality and representation. By late 1943, hunger and destitution became shared content in the palpable cultural production that emerged around the famine, the image of the starving rural migrant appearing in literature, plays, painting, and sculpture. The famine also spawned a genre of (visual) reportage that combined journalistic texts and statistical surveys and data, as well as paintings, drawings, or photographs of famine victims. Artists across the board responded to the famine: there were adherents to the orientalist "Indian style," who had till then portrayed lyrical mythological subjects or idealized rural genre paintings; there were those trained in European academic realist styles, who through the 1930s had been turning toward urban subjects but were now forced to rethink figurations of the grotesque; and there were new formations, like the Calcutta Group of artists formed in 1943, who saw in the famine an urgent need to imagine a new modernist idiom via social realism. Representing famine required a dramatic overhaul of figurative tropes and active experimentation with the possibilities of realism. Under the shadow of the famine, realism became a radical tool in the visual arts, and the Communist Party of India (CPI) its keen and active patron.

The famine marked the consolidation of cultural platforms that the left had been developing since the mid-1930s. The CPI had been banned by the colonial state of British India since 1934, and operated underground through the 1930s, informally entering political and cultural forums like the dominant political party, the Indian National Congress (INC), the newly formed peasant congress, the All India Kisan Sabha (AIKS, formed in 1936), or the All India Progressive Writers' Association (AIPWA or PWA, also formed in 1936). It was only in 1942, following the German attack on the Soviet Union, when the CPI went against the tide of the nationalist movement by pledging support for the imperial war effort for the cause of the Soviet Union, that it was legalized. Even as the CPI began establishing new cultural forums like the Friends of the Soviet Union (1941) and the Youth Cultural Institute (1941), which became the Anti-Fascist Writers' and Artists' Association (AFWAA, 1942), it was the famine of 1943 that gave the party a new mission in the cultural field, as it distanced itself from anti-imperial *direct* political agitations. Through relief work and famine awareness campaigns, the CPI found a new legitimacy in the political field that it had been lacking during the high noon of the Quit India movement of 1942. Under CPI General Secretary P. C. Joshi, artists, writers, and activists were brought together to "represent" the famine; the party organ, *People's War*, and its regional counterparts like *Janayuddha* (in Bengal) were transformed into visual scapes where a new genre of famine reportage was being generated. Artist-cadres like Chittaprosad and, soon after, Somnath Hore, were key contributors. The famine also triggered the foundation of the Indian People's Theatre Association (IPTA, 1943), which sought to introduce "new revolutionary motifs"[13] to cultural production. Visual reportage in the pages of *People's War* and its regional organs, touring famine exhibitions, and IPTA performances held across the country at peasant congresses and anti-fascist cultural congregations were foundational to what has been memorialized as the "Marxist cultural movement."

A famine, it has been argued, is less an "event" than a "continuum"[14]—of gradually growing scarcities as well as lingering afterlives of destitution and mortality. Scholars have sought to "delink" the famine from 1943, arguing rather for the *longue durée* footprints of it, dating not only back to the British exploitation of colonial subjects of this frontier province as the war front but also, and more significantly, forward to the peculiar "time pattern" in the persistence of the famine post-1943/44, seen in growing mortality rates over the following years.[15] While the famine reveals a shadow narrative in which Europe's colonies were indeed the little-acknowledged theaters of WWII,[16] its embeddedness within the momentum of the closing decade of anticolonial struggle kept its own histories marginal to the national narratives of struggle, partition and the arrival of freedom. The famine was followed soon after by communal riots, genocide, and partition of the province in 1947, on the eve of India's independence and the formation of Pakistan, prompting a new spate of refugee influx to Calcutta. The Bengal famine, it has been argued, had "brutalized the consciousness"[17] of the population, and was a "psychological prelude" to the riots that scorched Calcutta in August 1946, a year before the partition of India.[18]

By predating the genocide and displacements of 1947, the famine in fact set the terms through which the region could enter the "promise" of freedom: the moment of arrival into freedom for Bengal, one could argue, was also the moment of multiple displacements. Such displacements were, on the one hand, structural and socioeconomic: the refugee exodus from the famine of 1943 accelerated post-partition with fresh spates in 1947, and further through the 1950s through the 1970s, while the region negotiated porous borders, political turbulence, and new civil wars across the border in East Pakistan—the pre-partition East Bengal—as it fought for its own liberation from (West) Pakistan in 1970–71. On the other hand, displacements were also ontological: in Hore's *Wounds*, for instance, hunger and destitution could be seen as becoming metaphors for the region, entering artworks (and cultural imaginaries, particularly in films and literature) from the region as obsessive content and, indeed, the *vernacular form* of (postcolonial) modernity itself. Decolonization cast a long shadow here, and dis/placed the region vis-à-vis the new "national-modern" imaginary of postcolonial India under the new prime minister, Jawaharlal Nehru.

The relatively few studies of post-1940 art in Bengal repeat the trope of "politics in art and the politics of art,"[19] identifying the famine as a blanket cause for a social realist turn in art,[20] or over-determining this art by a left-wing cultural momentum.[21] Yet rather than being an overarching cause for political art, the famine activated multiple and contesting forms of art *becoming* political. The 1940s—with war, famine, genocide, and partition at the arrival of independence—created, in the words of Antonio Gramsci, a "conjunctural terrain." Beyond being art's new "content," this conjuncture became a ground upon which multiple "forces of opposition"—social, political, and aesthetic—were organized.[22] A conjuncture, as Stuart Hall has noted, following Gramsci, is a moment of "crisis" during which multiple contradictions "come together to give it a specific and distinctive shape" —they "condense" and trigger radical "change," though "the nature of their resolution is not a given."[23] A conjunctural reading of the Bengal famine, as attempted by historian Janam Mukherjee in recent times,[24] opens up new possibilities for studying art via entanglements of (artistic) form and history, art and politics. The question of "representation" itself becomes conflicted here, putting under pressure the assumed idealism of seeing the nation as a site of abstract beauty, or from the position of an idealized rural quotidian as has been dominant in the Indian modernist canon.

Thinking conjuncturally, according to Hall, "involves 'clustering' or assembling elements into a formation," tracking divergences rather than "adding up[s]." The conjunctural need not reside in a "simple unity" nor in a "single 'movement,'" but rather may be found in artworks and practices tied together in "fused but contradictory dispersion"—in the ways in which artists of the same generation (or period) do different kinds of work, shift their trajectories over time, return to where they began, or follow a style or a subject obsessively "long after its 'moment' has passed."[25] The circular potential of Hall's decentered notion of the conjunctural drives the afterlives—concrete as well as metaphoric—of the famine, and helps to rethink the conjuncture *beyond* the period of crisis—through memory, obsessions, and also, along the echoes of Hore's concluding note in his autobiography, a left-wing melancholia. If melancholia, as Enzo Traverso has suggested, "resides in imagination, not doctrine,"[26] aesthetic form, as we will encounter it in the course of the book, can allow wider participatory histories of the cultural left that are both tied to and independent from the rationalities and histories of the political left. They also remain attuned to recurring conjunctures that echo historical pasts *within* the *longue durée* of decolonization. The status of the "event" or a disaster in art—often frozen in tropes of representation—when retrieved and read via recurrence as metaphor or metonym—or the "vexed and asymmetric space of hindsight"—generates radical historiographical possibilities.[27] Seen through the singularity of the event and the circularity of its afterlives, the Bengal famine and the region's experience of the 1940s at large offer clues for writing conjunctural histories of art, the left, and the long decolonization in South Asia, opening up, as for my project in this book, the historical question of the *political* in art.

The contradictions within Hall's conjuncture, when read along with Pierre Bourdieu's view of the "field of cultural production" not as one of coherence or objective consensus, but of "struggle" with "all the contradictions it engenders"[28]—take us closer to the idea of the political. Struggles and "position-takings," which constitute and hold together the system of the artistic field, also provide, Bourdieu rightly noted, its temporal dimension, its historicity.[29] Such historicity thus comprises rhetorical acts—agendas, projections, manifestos, and counter-propositions, of both affirmation and negation—and generate, in effect, the political content of the artistic field. The question of artistic style becomes central to this dynamic of the political *as* art's historicity; styles become fronts, as Susan Sontag has noted, behind which "other issues, ultimately ethical and political" are debated.[30] Pursued more closely, this question of style, and the aesthetic conflict around it, can reveal critical possibilities for destabilizing the often-assumed symbiosis between art and nationalism in the post/colony, or for rethinking modernity in postcolonial art *beyond* modernism's affirmations.

The Bengal famine played a critical role in such destabilizations. Via its ruptures—sensorial, imaginational, and discursive—new negotiations between self and society, nation and locality, were identified. The famine ruptured the sensorial domain and attached new values to visualities and new vocabularies to the discourses on vision, the nation, and the modern. For cultural production in Bengal in the 1940s, aesthetics—in its spatial, sensorial and ethical regimes—framed in the words of Reinhart Koselleck, the "space of experience," and continued to cast shadows over the "horizons of expectations"[31] that the region could envision in postcolonial times; aesthetics became also what Paul Ricoeur has called the "site of initiative"—a productive ground for both observation *and* action—more than experience and imagination, and providing in effect a participatory and potentially partisan space.[32] Aesthetics—the question of vision and the values of beauty itself—

shaped the historicity and historiography of the region, and thus lies at the core of understanding the conjunctural terrain of decolonization.

THE AESTHETIC DIMENSION

Modern art in the post/colony tends to be read through the lens of nationalism or postcolonial nationhood; questions of artistic modernity are mediated via their representations of the "nation-form" and the national-modern imaginary. Such has been the dominant trope in reading art from Bengal, where the early twentieth-century "Indian-style" aesthetic, steeped in mythological and precolonial revivalism, was framed time and again, as the authentic national-modern idiom. The Bengal School—as the Indian-style movement came to be known—was steered by the master-artist Abanindranath Tagore and his students at the colonial Government School of Art, where he served as vice-principal in the 1910s, as well as by a cohort of critics, patrons, and institutional networks he created. The Bengal School stood in opposition to the practitioners of European academic realism in Calcutta, who were rebuffed and marginalized as "denationalized" and "deracinated"[33] pursuers of "western-style" art, thriving through "apathy and ignorance of the country's inheritance and tradition."[34] An "aesthetic conflict" had been growing between artists trained in western-style academic realism and adherents of the orientalist mythological revivalism of the Bengal School, as was noted by Percy Brown, the incoming principal at the Government School of Art in Calcutta in 1917.[35] Atul Bose, a veteran realist artist and one of the key organizers of the academic realist artists, would later write of this in his memoirs as the climate of "*ghat-pratighat*" (counter-attack)—a dialectical shadow contestation between values of the mythological revivalism of Indian-style and western-style academic realism practiced by artists like himself[36] in which any proposed assimilation of both styles was often snubbed as "incongruous."[37]

Steeped in idealism, the notion of the national in the paintings of the Bengal School was an idea abstracted from the political ruptures of a surging anti-colonial movement. In his early polemical text, *Es-*

says in National Idealism (1909), Ananda Coomaraswamy, the patron critic of the school, noted that the "real significance" of Indian nationalism lay in its formulation of an "idealist movement" and its withdrawal from the "political reality;"[38] international reviewers of exhibitions of the school noted its apparent banishment of "every kind of struggle," and "the abolition of the temporal" with no concern for the present.[39] As art historian Tapati Guha Thakurta has observed in her exhaustive study of the nationalist aesthetic of the Bengal School, the "avowedly nationalist yet consciously depoliticised" character of Indian-style painting was indeed its central paradox.[40] During the 1920s and the 1930s, this internalized and insulated aesthetic rooted in the past would transform through new pressures of the *external* and the *present*, as art became a ground for negotiations between the self and society, the national and the contextual. There were palpable shifts—among followers of both the Indian style and the western style—from the imaginary and the literary to the lived, the contemporary, and the sensorial, captured in the shared idea of the "everyday"—what art historian Partha Mitter has read under the broader idiomatic umbrella of "Indian primitivism."

Primitivism operated, Mitter has argued, through artistic romanticism and idealization of the tribal body and the simplicity of the tribal everyday—a cultural reaction rooted in a ruralist critique of urbanism as well as a nationalist trope of claiming a rural nation.[41] However, a rising discontent with revivalism was more complex and differentiated. Contemporaneity—the turn toward the rural and the everyday—while being a shared value, was *seen* and *framed* differently by artists following the orientalist style and those committed to academic realism. What Mitter sees as a "paradigm shift" toward shared directions of artistic primitivism—I will argue both in addition to and a departure from his seminal work—was less a paradigmatic shift toward a shared consensus of *what* to paint (the *content* of art) than a series of conflicted and conflictual positions around *how* to paint (the *style* in which to paint). It is in the domain of artistic style that new artistic and political values, as well as local and global scales, would become entangled. Ideological harnesses of otherwise shared artistic subjects and values were going to become increasingly different through the 1940s, before being realigned along fresh crosscurrents in early postcolonial India.

I will argue that during the transitional decades of late-colonial and early postcolonial India, artistic primitivism presented an ambivalent aesthetic field: its scopes were not necessarily limited to tribality or indigeneity; it accommodated, appropriated, and collapsed in its folds various "perceptions" of the "non-urban" and the "contra-urban." The peasant, the *adivasi* (alluding to indigenous communities), the rural, and the tribal imaginary overlapped in what I see as a site and spectrum of pliable alterity—an "otherness" that was both plural and malleable. Primitivism became an ambivalent resource that found multiple *uses*—across nationalist, Gandhian populist, left-wing, and nation-statist rationalities. Such uses involved not only valorizations of premodern sites, practices, or peoples remote to modern, urban temporalities (as has often been argued), but generated also *material* encounters, assimilations, reproductions. This productive materiality is significant for the uses I will be pursuing in this book.

For Indian-style artists, the turn toward the everyday had begun in the 1920s, when Nandalal Bose—a favorite pupil of Abanindranath Tagore and a staunch advocate of the Indian style—relocated to Kala Bhavan, the new art school of the experimental ruralist university at Santiniketan set up by the poet Rabindranath Tagore in 1919. Tagore's own pedagogical idealism sought to bring to aesthetic education a "social ethics" and an "organic connection" between learning and the "complete life of the people—economical, intellectual, aesthetic, social and spiritual."[42] Bose assimilated Tagore's ruralist universalism—which was a transnational aesthetic during the interwar period—into the pedagogical triad of "Nature-Tradition-Originality" from the Japanese aesthete Okakura Kakuzo, to generate a new sensibility of national-modern art rooted in the rural and tribal everyday.[43] New landscape studies, drawings of flora and fauna, drew their material from the rural everyday, and murals embedded rural environs within university walls.[44] For Bose, formulation of art pedagogy went hand in hand with formulating "aesthetic experience," steeped in what he called "empathy"—a new ethics of seeing, through which the artist and the subject of their contemplation and experience coalesce and become one.[45] The production of the rural place at Santiniketan was consciously organic: an "implacement," in Edward Casey's words, that assimilated discourses around art with experimental cultural processes that accumulated ingredients from the natural world—"bodies or landscapes or ordinary 'things'"—an "acculturation" that is in itself "a social, even a communal act."[46] Through the 1920s and 1930s, Bose's aesthetic pedagogy steered the mythological idealism of the Bengal School toward rural materialities in art; however, "nature" as well as the tribal subject despite an "added strength of ruggedness" was idealized in his resolutely anti-realist style to reconnect with the mystical gaze of the Bengal School.[47] The tribal and peasant figures betrayed a strong pastoral romanticism staunchly removed from the lived everyday of rural poverty.[48] It is here that the everyday, while being a shared idiom for artists across stylistic boards, became a complex node of both convergence and difference, even *within* Kala Bhavan, where Bose's insistence on combining the rural with a classical figuration and a steadfast rejection of realist sensibilities persisted in the face of opposition.[49]

For academic realist artists in Calcutta, a similar turn toward the everyday transformed the urban space into a site for new artistic imaginations of materiality, and a new aesthetic of ugliness and grime.[50] From naturalist verisimilitude, academic artists in the 1920s sought to move toward a figuration of the social underbelly, the urban and a subaltern everyday, even as they struggled to find exhibition space and patronage to support this new direction. New and young entrants to the field in the 1930s, like Gobardhan Ash, Zainul Abedin, and Abani Sen, along with senior academic artists like Hemendranath Mazumdar, Debiprasad Roy Choudhury, and Atul Bose, strove time and again to form new collectives to support realism in art, and claim a modernity for realist art that had been denied to them thus far by the Bengal School.[51] In 1931, they formed the modest and short-lived Young Artists' Union, whose exhibitions were noted for original themes that fell outside both mythology and academic exactitude. Soon after, in 1933, they formed the Art Rebel Centre, issuing a brief manifesto that called for retrieving art from the clutches of tradition and turning toward the concrete: "Our aim is to create an art that is strong, bold, virile and antisentimental, fearless in its desire for new adventures—a powerful advance-guard, which alone can save art in India, now threatened by traditional conservatism and the habitual indifference of the public."[52] Such shifts were early tendencies toward a social realistic style that would emerge more strongly in the 1940s.

The first exhibition of the Art Rebel Centre featured oil paintings and watercolors of dilapidated huts, dockyards, city streets, and profile studies of subjects taken from the poor fringes of the city, its laboring and squatting underbelly.[53] To the reviewer from the modernist journal *Four Arts Annual*, the aim of the group seemed to be the search for art's "true perspective," "to pay particular attention to realism in spirit."[54] Gobardhan Ash, Abani Sen, and Zainul Abedin, among others, represented this turn toward addressing gritty social components from the urban everyday. Reviewing their works in 1936—most notably Ash's award-winning oils like *Scavenger's Cart*, *City Outskirts*, and a series on construction sites, as well as Abani Sen's head studies and ink drawings of animals—a critic described them as the new "modern school" in Bengal,[55] steeped in new values of portraying the margins of society and urban themes, drawing art from the demands of the contemporary. To Gobardhan Ash, this was a personal language of realism, what he called "subjective realism."[56] By the late 1930s, such values of realist art were already beginning to question the idea of the nation-form: *how* and *from where* must the nation be visualized?

To the critic Jaminikanta Sen, artists like Ash, Abedin, and Sen were depicting the changes in the rural landscape, altered by industrialization—the impingement on the picturesque by mechanical forms associated with electricity, such as water pumps and engines, or the famished villagers and their actual living conditions. For academic artists, there was indeed a nascent and at times active demand for transforming the aesthetic framing of the everyday, and rethinking in the process the visualization of the nation as an idealized site—whether rooted in a remote mythological past or in romanticized visions of a rural quotidian. While such exhibitions in the mid-1930s were consolidating new values of realism within spaces of the modern, they were also triggering new values of nationalism in art. The question of beauty was central to this critique. Noting the "unreal" tendency of Indian artists to create images of untarnished beauty, unmediated by contextual representation, Sen commented that such imageries of myth and fancy were "bereft of the reflection of the motherland." While literature had made the transition into realism, he wrote, the plastic arts too needed to portray the harsh "truth of contemporary reality" instead of seeking refuge in mythology; what was required in art was a new *satya-bodh*—a "sensibility of truth" in an era of "new nationalism" that would recognize the changing landscapes and sites of the nation.[57]

Sen's appeal to "new truths" in art reveals, on the one hand, new demands for thinking aesthetically about the city and, on the other hand, new values of portraying ugliness in art, as opposed to sustaining an idealized nation-form. Discussing the question of "beauty" in early twentieth-century writings on Calcutta, historian Sudipta Kaviraj has noted that the insistence on "beauty in the narrow sense produced a crisis of sorts in writing about the city," for the modernity of this notion of beauty could not accommodate "the teeming, disorderly, ungainly modern city of Calcutta" that "was not by any definition a beautiful theme."[58] Apart from the works of academic realist artists, a shift toward capturing the margins and "disorderly and ungainly" sites of the city in art had been detectable also in the works of Indian-style artists working in Calcutta; the writer and reviewer Pulinbehari Sen references a range of realistic subjects in varied styles, including huddled passengers in a third-class railway waiting room, city masons at work, alleys and urban thoroughfares, docklands, and the interiors of film studios.[59] Yet there persisted a tendency among these artists, wrote Nirad Chaudhuri—who became a renowned author in his later years—to remove "all traces of actuality," until pictures of the rural everyday resembled "excerpts from folk-tales."[60] The "concern for the everyday," according to Chaudhuri, while commendable, needed to resist transmuting everyday sights into idyllic images of pristine beauty, or a sterile adherence to archaic revivalism bereft of contemporary resonance. What was required, he argued, was the rejection of hackneyed mythological themes that were current in art schools at the time, and a re-casting of technique in art making, to record "greater contact with actuality," not necessarily to make modern Indian art realistic or purely representational, but to reveal a "greater directness of inspiration."[61] Such critiques called not only for altering the *constituencies* of the national-modern form (a shift in subject), but also for rethinking the *values of beauty* in art (a shift in aesthetics).

Nationalist imagination in colonial India, as historian Dipesh Chakraborty has noted in discussing the poet Rabindranath Tagore, carried two "different and contradictory ways of seeing the nation": the "adoring eye" that hailed its beauty and the "the critical eye" that probed its defects.[62] The difference between these ways of seeing is both aesthetic and political. It is also foundational to the contesting values of beauty, tradition, commitment, form, and freedom that inhabited the practices and discourses of modern art in India. Indeed, friction between these two ways of seeing the nation is one of the core problems I am setting out to identify and pursue in *Partisan Aesthetics*. While an "adoring eye" could produce an idealized space, sociopolitical ruptures like that of the famine pushed a new modality of seeing and showing cities; aesthetics became a modality for inhabiting and re-producing to the uncanny—as experience as well as active initiative as I noted earlier. By displacing the rural into the urban *as destitution*, the famine can be seen to represent a "collapse of the primal shelter"[63]—the idealized rural as the site of production and (urban) sustenance collapsing into the bare life of hunger. The famine victim assumed an allegorical role that combined the critique of colonial extraction with that of the inadequacy of a nationalist vision of the nation as an idea and an ideal.

Through the late 1930s and the 1940s, such aesthetic shifts generated new cultural vocabularies like the social, the real, the people, and the progressive; as these vocabularies interacted with political visions and agendas, a new field opened up in which aesthetics and politics could act upon each other. This field was not one of propaganda art or of stable political commitments in art, but a *becoming political* of the artistic field. The transitional decades of decolonization are key to studying this being and becoming political. The idea of the political—

as it relates also to the artistic—is worth unpacking here. While politics relates to concrete political events, Chantal Mouffe argued, the political is the ontological basis on which the society, and as such, a system is constituted. Following Ernesto Laulau, Mouffe sees the political as a context of conflict—as a *dimension of antagonism*.[64] The political-as-antagonism captures my reading of the political as contradictions within a conjuncture, or struggles and aesthetic conflict within an artistic field. To understand the political in art, the demarcation between politics-as-theory and politics-in-practice remains important. Artists' interfaces with politics in practice happened only when "unexpected political events"—or conjunctures, as I call them—drew artists out as activists.[65] Beyond such political determinism of conjunctures, or an "emergency,"[66] as artists go beyond topicality or pamphleteering, the question of the political becomes internalized by the logic of form itself.[67]

"The critical function of art, its contribution to the struggle for liberation," Herbert Marcuse has noted, resides in its "aesthetic dimension"—"not by virtue of its content (i.e., the 'correct' representation of social conditions), nor by its 'pure' form," but by the "*content having become form* (emphasis mine)."[68] In Marcuse's reading, art incorporates as well as sublimates reality, and historical conditions appear in artworks in multiple forms—as a background and horizon of possibilities, in imagery and in language of discourse. The perfect aesthetic form both intertwines with and transcends political tendencies;[69] as art becomes "reality's own Form," the artist must participate "as artist rather than as political activist."[70] In the unstable ground of late-colonial and early-postcolonial India, where multiple ideological forces were at play, being and becoming political captures not only the multiple modalities of the political at play, but also the historical undulation itself that animated the political.

BEING AND BECOMING POLITICAL

The aesthetic turn toward the everyday in late-colonial India paralleled a growing populism in politics through the interwar period, beginning with the emergence of Gandhian mass politics with the noncooperation movement, and the gradual beginnings of left-wing politics that expanded through the 1920s and the 1930s. The Communist Party of India (CPI), formed abroad in 1924, did not establish organizational roots until the early 1930s. The party was banned by the British colonial state in 1934, but gained membership through the following decade via underground networks and liaisons with the Socialist Party within the Indian National Congress (INC). The expansion of popular politics found new impetus with the Government of India Act of 1935, which gave increased electoral powers to the provinces, introducing new modes of locational participation in imagining the nation. At the Lucknow Session of the INC in 1936, a series of developments made the convergence between political and aesthetic populism more active. As Gandhi announced a new stage of "rural congresses" at Lucknow, a new cultural drive was emerging, for foregrounding the rural in political congregations as the "popular "and the "new national." In visualizing this new national-popular imaginary, Gandhi drew on board Nandalal Bose, who decorated the grounds of the INC annual conferences with idealized vignettes of rural quotidian and labor for three subsequent years (1936 through 1938) at Lucknow, Faizpur, and Haripura.[71] With such convergences of the artistic and political spheres, the abstract notion and value of the nation developed concrete and material locational forms. These also became new texts for materialization of global thought, discourse, and currents of interwar ruralism beyond the strict rationalities of the nation and nationalism.

In the 1920s–1940s, art and politics converged at three main intersections of multiple transnational discourses that were current in mid-twentieth-century India, and more specifically in Bengal. The first is the intersection between interwar ruralism that celebrated "back to the land" ideologies and late-colonial romantic pastoralism (in the art of Santiniketan, for instance), and nationalist populism (which had both Gandhian and Communist affiliations in these decades) that sought to bring politics to "village India." The second intersection is that of anti-fascism and anti-imperialism, which often materialized in forums and travels around interwar peace movements and the circulation of anti-fascist imageries in print and reproductions. The third intersection is between social realism and the more ideologically streamlined *socialist* realism (upheld in the Soviet Union in the early 1930s), the slippages between which would produce new political dialectics in postwar aesthetics. Across this plural field of intersecting global and local discourses grew new concepts that become for historians potential nodes for tracking the dialectics of the global, the local, and the national.

One such nodal concept is that of the "people" and the "popular"—shared and contested by cultural apparatuses of both anti-colonial nationalism and global left-wing politics, each committed to reimagining and representing an expanding scale of political constituencies. Realism and the ideas of the "people" or the "popular" (as pertaining to the people, and popularization of politics and art) became natural allies during this period, forming the core aesthetic of the cultural resistance that the left built around anti-fascism and socialist internationalism. Writing in the late 1930s, Bertolt Brecht viewed realism as "an issue not only for literature" but also a "major political, philosophical and practical issue [that] must be handled and explained as such—as a matter of general human interest."[72] This call for new forms to imagine new times was both political and aesthetic, and resonated across intersections of political and cultural discourses during the interwar decades—in metropolitan Europe under the shadow of fascism, and in the colonies, where anti-fascism developed in dialogue with anti-colonial sensibilities.

In art, the people and the popular remained plural, ambiguous, and malleable categories. Their plural meanings revealed configurations of "social, material and political developments" whereby political processes sought to "produce" their own "subject."[73] The correlation between the political constituency of the "masses" and the cultural imagery of the "people," Jacques Rancière has noted, is not a given, but is constructed, interpreted, staged, or acted out—an intimate link has existed historically, he argued, between *people's theater* and the *people as theater*, with history as the stage.[74] The "inherent difference" within categories like the people is a site for "political inventiveness" and a "stage" where the "play" introduced by this difference opens up possibilities for transformations of meaning.[75] This reading resonates with the particular histories of cultural and political coproductions of the people that I am pursuing in this book. In the artistic field, the people as a political and cultural value produced new vocabularies of "art for the people," "popularization of art," or "people's artist" that were shared across stylistic and ideological lines. Yet differences in artistic visualizations of the people—not in subject, but in style, as I have suggested earlier—became sites for registering political difference. Increasingly through the late 1930s, the idea of the rural everyday in art lent itself to notions of "revolutionary popular" imagination and agency. These journeys of art "into the rural," while being parts of a wider middle-class intellectual celebration of a "pure" non-urban other, also became parts of a distinctly left-wing rhetoric of radical popular agency that would reframe the nation-form via revolutionary, iconic potentialities of the subaltern. This radical visualization from the left questioned the romantic pastoral gaze of nationalists that framed the rural as the unchanging "essence" of India's resilience despite the perceived enslavements of colonial modernity. It staged in the process, a new resurgent "folk" idiom—a politically activated rural culture—that was to become the cornerstone of a new communist resistance and its cultural movement.

Populism in late-colonial India carried both nationalist and socialist accents, being closely aligned with the momentum of Gandhian populist politics as well as Communist popular mobilization. Yet the political agencies of these visions of the people were different. Through the late 1930s, both the INC under Gandhi and the still-underground CPI under P. C. Joshi took active interest in combining populism in politics with the popular in art, thus absorbing current aesthetic idioms and practices of pastoral romanticism, ruralist idealism, and the folk revival in art, and (in the last case) producing new dimensions of a revolutionary folk with distinctly left-wing connotations: hence the ambivalent overlaps between the vocabularies of the people and the popular common to both Gandhian and left-wing discourse, and hence also the tendency across Gandhian and left-wing forums to identify artists like Nandalal Bose—or, as we will see in the following chapter, Jamini Roy—as "people's artist[s]," and, further on, the idiom of Gandhian "village congresses" being picked up and reconfigured in a Communist discourse around peasant congresses in the 1940s.[76] By that time, an entanglement of the values of artistic realism and the popular produced in art discourse shared and ambiguous vocabularies of critical realism, social realism, and socialist realism. Looked at closely, an active fluidity of such vocabularies affirms not the uniqueness of these terms, even in their conjunctural use, but an ambivalence that was *equally conjunctural.*

The rise of cultural populism in late-colonial India reflected the rhetorics of the Popular Front period of the Communist International after its Seventh World Congress (1935);[77] this initiated anti-fascist political and cultural coalitions that thrived through an "enculturalization of politics," which had also asserted the primacy of the "conjunctural and the particular." Realism and the popular came together in new modes of "concrete analysis of a concrete situation" that would harness art and aesthetic experience to the "demands of social transformation," making art a part of (and partisan to) "the broader concept of cultural praxis."[78] Realism during these years increasingly connoted not verisimilitude of perspective but social truth, critical social address, and political engagement, at once ideological and open to a collaborative ethic of "uniting the politics of the people with an aesthetic for the people."[79] This element of "social extension," as Raymond Williams has observed, was a feature shared by all realisms, alongside the insistence on everyday life, the non-elite, the contemporary or the near-contemporary, and a valorization of the secular over the mystical.[80] A new national agenda of political transformation was being developed around these shifts in the 1930s, and more concretely in the 1940s. This revolved around the production of the new national-popular aesthetic through the conscious fusion of popular imaginaries with a national agenda, and a mélange of the "cultures" of the peasantry, the proletariat, and the intelligentsia.[81] In the 1940s, the ambivalent interfaces of real/rural/popular entered the socialist realist drawings and prints of artists on the left like Chittaprosad and Somnath Hore, and their fellow artist-cadres. Even after the 1940s, when the cultural movement of the left had petered out and such artists themselves steered away from the party, they kept returning to the theme through formal experiments, with or without active harnesses to an avowed Soviet socialist realist aesthetic, revealing little-explored, post/colonial modalities Soviet Socialist Realism "without shores."[82]

The ambivalent meanings that grew up around overlapping notions of the real and the rural, and the new aesthetics of the national-popular, produced new nodal terms for the artistic field, which were seized on by new artists' groups in their manifestos. "Progressive" art in the 1930s and 1940s was one such node where such conjunctural vocabularies of realism, the people, and the popular entangled. Often collapsed with the Progressive Artists' Group (PAG), formed in Bombay in 1947, the vocabulary of progressive art had critical longer histories, both tied to the intellectual precedence set by the Progressive Writers' Association and embedded in the artistic formulations around the Bengal famine. As histories in this book will show, progressive art was meant to be primarily figurative, committed to realism and designed for taking art "to the people," as its specifically left-wing connotation of the period suggested. The category of progressive art in the 1940s became a melting pot accommodating a range of artistic impulses and discursive concerns—from a projected organic integration of the artist with community life, to a distinctly urban repertoire of rupture and angst, to a site for dialogue between realism and modernism, and to a complete embrace of modernist internationalism free from determinisms of nation and tradition. The idea of progressive art concretized the needs of vision both in style and in rhetoric, and produced genres and vocabularies of visual reportage, art as testimony, and aesthetic forms that assimilated, for a while, cultural production to social activism and political partisanship. It also became a ground for the play of multiple vocabularies of a transnational left, and of symbols of "transcolonial affiliations": an "economy of recognition among the colonized and the 'semi-colonized' of the earth."[83] The artistic field constructed around the intersections and ambivalent vocabularies of realism, the popular, and progressive art—from nationalist discourses as well as global left-wing discourse—produced the "ecumen": a "field of symbols" of dynamic thought-worlds inhabited and shared by artists and intellectuals in India and from different sites worldwide.[84]

The ambivalence in such vocabularies was historically necessary in order for collaborations across ideologies in late-colonial India to occur. Such ambivalences also came into play in multiple projects, appropriations, and dissolutions under altered political and ideological milieus. Ambivalence is what gives the concept of what I am calling "partisan aesthetics" its historical densities, allowing for the play of participation as much as that of alienation and dissociation. This ambivalence would become particularly active in *implicit* ways in early postcolonial India, where the collaborative patterns of the interwar decades as well as the radical harnesses of the 1940s would have to negotiate multiple displacements—of ideologies and solidarities as much as of populations and nations. In the dialectic between the industrial complexes and rural hinterlands of a new post-independence Nehruvian nation-state committed to development, the rural everyday was to be transformed anew into mythic resource material for national-modern nostalgia, not too distant from its late-colonial imaginaries. The political unconscious of Indian modern art during the subcontinent's long decolonization, I will argue, lay in these plays of the aesthetic with the overlapping and contradictory pulls of nationalist, socialist, as well as consciously apolitical or depoliticized "humanist," ways of seeing and framing. The overlaps among ideas of realism, the people, the popular, or the progressive—despite their differences—produced the peculiar artistic field of decolonization, which I will develop through the chapters that follow as "partisan aesthetics." Histories of the cultural left as well as of modern art in the post/colony are deeply rooted in the dialectical temper of this field, and its miscellaneous-ness when it comes to thinking about the political.

Pursuing the word's military origins, Carl Schmitt has argued that the "partisan" is a "marginal" figure and an "irregular" fighter, operating outside the "classical regularity" and "containments" of state-war.[85] A partisan is active particularly during "revolutionary times,"[86] and is often a "non-conformist," even a "self-consistent individualist," who fights on their own account.[87] A partisan thus potentially both rejects hegemonic structures, in a commitment to margins and fragments, and remains malleable to irregular forms of political engagement. Such notions of the partisan are useful in combining questions of temporality with those of participation—political actions in conjunctural times that are steered not only by ideological zeal and affirmations but, significantly, through irregular affiliations and activations of marginality. The idea of the partisan is intrinsically tied to the historicity of artistic struggles and the conjunctural reading of art itself. Partisanship in art, Arnold Hauser wrote, lies in its "thoroughly social character," as art "always speaks for somebody to somebody and reflects reality from a particular social standpoint so as to be seen from that standpoint."[88] To the committed left-wing Indian auteur Ritwik Ghatak, partisanship is built in (artistic) action itself: "[N]othing happens without politics, everybody is in it, including people who claim to remain outside it. There is nothing called apolitical. You are always a partisan, for or against something."[89]

Rather than simply describing particular artists or critics as partisans, I am more interested in understanding in what forms and through what terms a particular aesthetic *became* partisan, and what the partisan itself meant in its particularities and contradictions. Partisan aesthetics is not an attempt to define "political art" or to pursue its usual suspects—propaganda imagery, political posters, calendar art—studied often under "visual culture."[90] Neither do I tie it to key artists, art movements, or singular genres that lend themselves to synchronic narratives of twentieth-century modern art in India. Partisan aesthetics is an effort to think through a dialectical field, where art and politics interact in forms that are not ideologically predetermined, but rather are irregular, locational, ambiguous, or unresolved. The partisan, as I hope to show in this book, potentially reveals the ways in which the political enters the artistic field through aesthetic forms—of seeing, writing, or contesting. The political can be imagined by artists not (necessarily) involved in political agendas, or projected upon artists by critics/academics without defined ideological affiliations. It can be implicated in artists' grappling with what their "commitment" should be, with more-tentative or irregular affiliations than dominant ideological convictions. The political can also manifest in active negations of politics, or of the rhetoric of art as "weapon." In effect, partisan aesthetics is an effort to make visible the forms through which art bears testimony to and produces the political, or becomes haunted by the memories of displacements.

CONFIGURING PARTISAN AESTHETICS

The term "partisan" has appeared time and again in discourses on Indian cultural practice, used consistently for instance, by the noted art critic Geeta Kapur. For the now famous exhibition *Place for People* from 1981, in which a set of artists primarily from the art school of M. S. University in Baroda exhibited a bold new genre of narrative art, Kapur wrote a critical introduction titled "Partisan Views on the Human Figure."[91] In it, she lauded the artists—of whom she was a patron critic—for bringing a political sensibility to modern art, for lifting art above "conventional polarities of Indian and Western idioms" and for thrusting forth "new options—of sensibility and ideology" by imparting to the human image a "contemporary purpose."[92] Kapur's own partisan position implicates her *in* the histories that I draw in this book; indeed, the methodology driving my formulation of the partisan aesthetics historicizes, and in doing so disperses, some of the conceptual certainties that Kapur's otherwise foundational writings have sustained. For instance, the "place for people" in twentieth-century Indian art was not particular to the political exigencies emerging out of the national Emergency of 1975–1977 declared by Prime Minister Indira Gandhi, from which Kapur develops her key theorizations of the political. Places for people had, as chapters in this book will hopefully show, *longue durée* histories that hark back to late-colonial and early postcolonial India, histories of Indian modern art being deeply entangled with ways in which notions of the people and the popular were grappled with during the long decolonization—if not through concrete consolidations, at least in the textured and conflicted negotiations themselves.

To some extent, Kapur remains alert to alternative possibilities around the "partisan," as it appears in her writings on the auteur from Bengal, Ritwik Ghatak, iconic for his partition films,[93] or on the writer-critic-patron associated with the cultural left, Mulk Raj Anand.[94] But in each case, she seems to use the concept to align the subject with history, which for her remains almost always that of the nation. To Kapur, the artist is the protagonist in a symbiosis of national belonging and modernist imagination—a "national/modern" aesthetic, and an "embodied consciousness that most persistently tries to articulate the self into history"—what she has repeatedly referred to as the "national allegory."[95] While in reading Ghatak's films on the displacements of Indian partition, Kapur is alert to the auteur's denial of the unifying cultural impetus of a national allegory,[96] in her writings on visual art, the dense, non-national, and contradictory histories of the people or the popular, and indeed the "partisan" itself, remain lost or at best marginal or hasty. Kapur's reflections—while of immense historical importance for being one of very few theorizations of the political in Indian art—appear inadequate if we begin questioning the fundamental coherences within notions of the national and the modern, particularly during decolonization. While figures like Ghatak and Anand are connected by their participation in the left's cultural movement and in conjunctural aesthetics, the history they inhabited was in itself more fragmented and their modes of participation irregular. Histories of such participations lie *in excess of* the recognizable iconic figures; it is in modalities of participation, I suggest, that the political is produced and partisan aesthetics structured.

The left-wing cultural movement in the 1940s, while having concrete platforms in the field of literature (the All India Progressive Writers' Association from 1936, and the Anti-Fascist Writers' and Artists' Association from 1941) and performance (Indian People's Theatre Association from 1943), had a curious relationship with visual art. There were no dedicated forums, manifestos, or even art critical support options for artists affiliated with the CPI. Visual art has remained marginal within appraisals of the cultural movement,[97] or has been significantly dehistoricized in narratives of twentieth-century Indian modernism. The rhetoric of progressive art, unlike that of progressive literature, was also late in arriving in visual arts. It was hardly visible until the mid-1940s, and thereafter it sat uncomfortably with the modernist agenda of post-independence artist collectives, most notably in the vehement denial of the alleged "Communist" tag of progressive art from artists of the iconic Progressive Artists' Group (PAG) in Bombay after 1947. Yet it is in the field of visual art, I will argue, that a particularly critical history of left-wing aesthetics can be traced, one that draws out the contradictions within the cultural movement as much as across the multi-textured politics of decolonization in South Asia.

Archives of such shared histories of the cultural left, visual art, and decolonization lie not in individual biographies or institutional sites, but in a decentered field of sources that are potentially both marginal and informal. I have sought them, for instance, in a range of periodicals—both vernacular and in English—spanning art, performance, literature, and politics, as well as in private papers—often scattered across dusty folders and reedy albums, or in obscure trunks in abandoned apartments. From this dispersed field, I have drawn concepts and vocabularies that were active during the long decolonization. Not only do these documents reveal the Foucauldian discursive system—the "enunciative possibilities and the impossibilities"—of the period under scrutiny, and differentiate the "discourses in their multiple existence,"[98] but they *are* at the same time archives *by chance*—the becoming archive of a random assortment of documents, images, and newspaper clips. This miscellaneous-ness lends the conceptual and narrative backbone to my reading of partisan aesthetics. These archives have steered me to make connections between artists, writers, forums, and vocabularies. They have revealed that the political participation in visual art resides in rejections as much as affiliations, in absence as much as assertions, and that connections between aesthetic forms and ideologies are often left to the historian's craft rather than being found in recognizable or consistent artistic commitments. In the chapters that follow, I have tried, as much as possible, to bend with such archives, or the lack thereof.

Artists in this book are its archives rather than its protagonists, and the absences—of some of the period's most commonly known or iconic artists—are constitutive of the histories that this book seeks to draw. Such histories involve artists, critics, writers, academics, and political activists, whose friendships, agendas, and anxieties are integral to the ways in which I conceptualize modalities for partisan aesthetics. Rather than tracking the biographical vectors of individual artists or pure iconographic analyses, I am interested here in the choices that artists and critics made as they negotiated and grappled with the structures that they found themselves in or outside. I have benefited immensely from the expanding body of art historical literature that in the past three decades has built and nuanced studies of South Asian modernism.[99] I have also drawn from a thoroughly informative corpus of vernacular literature, on visual art in Bengal, for instance,[100] as well as from locational and, at times, partisan studies of the left-wing cultural movement. These resources have provided me, on the one hand, with their diligent chronicling of figures and narratives that remain elusive in the more national and global literature,[101] and have alerted me, on the other, to the foibles of writing on the cultural left *from* a commitment to (and hence, celebration of) the political left. Rather than modernist imaginations in the post/colony or narratives of promise and construction, or even key institutional sites of the postcolonial modern, this book is alert to non-formal, less visible sites, and even to failure, with its diverse and contradictory connotations, symbolic charges, and cultural roles.[102]

In five chapters, I mark the multiple stages and modalities through which art and politics entangled through late-colonial and early postcolonial India. Two themes structure the narrative:

The first, Dialogues and Dissonances, studies the trajectories of the left-wing cultural movement between 1936 and 1953 to draw out the particular modalities that the left took vis-à-vis visual art during the critical transitional decades of decolonization. I unpack here a narrative of left-wing culture that is often assumed to be a unitary story of political solidarity and "social consciousness" in art (and hence, in counternarratives, of inadequacy), and identify instead, three modalities that reveal the formations of partisan aesthetics between the 1930s and the 1950s. In Chapter 1, I have focused on a series of reviews and essays on the artist Jamini Roy written by members and affiliates of the Parichoy circle that grew around the Bengali critical review quarterly *Parichoy*. While interpreting the folk modern idiom of Roy through sociological and quasi-socialist vocabularies, these writings generated, I argue, discursive space for a new progressive art and art criticism through what I have called a *passive participation* of art in the political mobilization of culture. Here, modernist writers, socialist fellow travelers, and cultural workers of the still-underground CPI could come together through friendships and social associations before and without the more concrete post-1942 consolidation by the CPI. Chapter 2 studies the artists committed to the CPI during war, famine, and popular resistance in the 1940s, and the *active authorship* of socialist visual reportage that they pioneered. As artist-cadres of the party like Chittaprosad and Somnath Hore visually documented the Bengal famine, peasant movements, and party conferences through the 1940s, the party developed a complex and contradictory cultural policy: it deployed its artist-cadres as collectors of raw material, while seeking to assimilate artists outside the party fold within an expanding scope of socialist realist art. This process arrested not only the formation of a politically committed avant-garde within midcentury Indian modernism, but also the modernist potential of subversive partisan iconographies of party artists like Chittaprosad. In Chapter 3, I focus on an artist collective outside the party fold that the left sought to draw in. The Calcutta Group of artists came into being during the famine years, with a self-proclaimed mission of developing a modern idiom of art rooted in social reality. In its decade-long tenure, the group both aligned with and deviated from the left's rhetoric of socialist art, while carving out a new dialogical field of modernism and realism. These *vacillating affiliations* to the social and the socialist, along with the shifting art discourse, particularly after Indian independence in 1947, reveal both the left's anxious trysts with modern art, and, as I argue, subtexts of the deradicalization of the vocabularies of progressive art at the arrival of Nehruvian political modernity.

The second theme in the book—Postcolonial Displacements—follows the afterlives of the conjunctural decade of the 1940s in postcolonial India, and asks how aesthetics in the post/colony captured the displacements—social, ideological, and epistemic—that marked the transition to independence in 1947. In Chapter 4, I follow the afterlives of left-wing political art in Nehruvian India in order to ask: what happened to the visual rhetorics of left-wing radical aesthetics once the anti-imperial struggle was transformed? And what forms did socialist art take once the high noon of the 1940s cultural movement had passed? In the late 1940s, as the left-wing cultural movement itself dissipated under a change of the guard within the CPI, art discourse in Nehruvian India was reformulating the radical vocabulary of socialist art into new, deradicalized values of democratic consciousness in art. At its center now stood the image of "Man," as the sovereign citizen-subject outside the shadows of ideology, yet at the core of a new national-modern sensibility. In Chapter 5, I return to Calcutta as the new postcolonial site, where the displacements of decolonization were not only socioeconomic, sustained by refugee influx and inadequate rehabilitation, but also political, cultural, and epistemological. Embedded in visualities of post-partition Calcutta, where social displacement, economic stagnation, and volatile everyday politics had destabilized the modernist promise of the post-independence nation-state, artists negotiated the "city-form" through obsessive treatments of recurring visualizations of hunger and destitution, or in their own struggles with the city's marginalized status in the post-independence art world in India. In the expressionistic and surrealistic iconography that they produced, an alternate *tamashik rasa*—an aesthetic of darkness, or a tragic consciousness—can be identified that challenges the contained national-modern aesthetic of early postcolonial India.

Rethinking displacement through these two directions in the artistic field is also a way of understanding the ideological shadows of postcolonial modernism, whose celebration of the nation-form and the citizen-artist brought with it a nuanced ideological flattening of subversive art. Mobilizing the possibilities of difference—not simply to affirm the eclecticism of Indian modernism, but to activate the contradictions within—can reveal new political densities of postcolonial modernism. Such differences complicate both the apparent homogeneities of anti-colonial nationalism in art and the cultural politics of the post/colony—long before the political ruptures of the 1970s under the Emergency, which have often been seen as the high point of political art in post-independence India. More importantly, reading modern art vis-à-vis the politics of the long decolonization generates complex configurations and unique possibilities of understanding partisanship. It raises questions not only of what affiliation or commitment in visual art has meant historically, but how such meanings create irregular histories, and hence carry deep historiographical resonances.

DISCORDANT GEOGRAPHIES, IRREGULAR HISTORIES

Since the early 2000s, a surging art historical scholarship on South Asia has addressed formations of Indian modernism in a wider turn toward critiquing Eurocentric art histories. In a set of interventions in *Art Bulletin* in 2008, for instance, art historians argued for moving toward "a more heterogeneous definition of global modernism,"[103] with attention to "particular art histories, the context of their ideologies, contradictions, and fractures in their engagement to modernity."[104] A call was issued to move beyond the binaries of centers and peripheries, or horizontal expansions of the canon of modernism through inclusion of the "non-Wests" and the "not-yets" and to study, rather, the "extremely complicated and contradictory histories, agents, and objects of modern art" in its spaces "elsewhere" and its "out-of-sync moments."[105] Yet despite the felt need to nuance what the "periphery" is, scholarship has remained largely inattentive in research to the politics of the periphery—particularly in nuancing the dissonances that lie *within* the postcolonial nation-states. Peripherality is both a location and a political position; if the field of modern and contemporary South Asian art is to turn toward nuancing peripheries, and to begin looking for *particular* art histories—complete with contradictions and fractures—what might the narratives look like? Does the study of "peripherality" actually require completely different questions? More importantly, has the pursuit of postcolonial modernisms carried with it an intrinsic impulse for looking at triumphs, signposts, and icons—the discursive "other," one could argue, of peripherality?

The debate is currently entering a new phase—one in which the nation as a category is being nuanced. In Sonal Khullar's *Worldly Affiliations* (2015), for instance, the notion of "affiliation" in colonial and postcolonial art is used to release the "nation" from the shadow of what was seen as "Indian-ness": affiliations, Khullar has argued, allow artists to embrace nuanced worldliness in their art while being rooted in national dynamics. As a mode of "transnational exchange and critique," affiliations generate "historical processes by which a national art world came together and became conjoined with an international art world."[106] Such affiliational networks surpass the binaries of "centre and periphery, or origin and derivation, and their corollaries domination and resistance, or inclusion and exclusion," and turn instead to "other worlds imagined by artworks and their makers and preservers."[107] Subscribing to this concept of affiliation rather wholeheartedly, I would like to push its scopes further, to rethink the global from my own interest in deeply locational formations.

Speaking from within the archives of what I have called here partisan aesthetics, the trope of affiliations becomes alive in what is a very chaotic field—of artists, critics, texts, and debates, as well as dreams, disappointments, and alienations—constituting what can be seen as deep intellectual histories of twentieth-century art in India, ones that are free from the constraints of the "nation" or are at least dialectically tied to it. For the artists represented in this book, the nation was hardly an active frame in their work, but neither were they committed—in simplistic ways—to a non-Indian idiom. What persisted in them, rather, was the question of how to navigate the pressures of context, and in particular how to appeal to universal notions of realism, the popular, and eventually humanism. Realism, in its multiple stylistic and ideological registers, was active in their works, as was a framework of *being political*—a commitment, at the least, to addressing the social, even when deeply mediated via formal abstractions. In studying such aesthetics, the tropes of East/West, and even tradition/modernity appear rather sterile. More active is the dialectical relation of this aesthetic to the idea of a national art, and its affiliations to transnational as well as sub-national aesthetics.

Recent scholarship in South Asian art has sought to understand the transnational from within and vis-à-vis the spaces of the national. Iftikhar Dadi, in particular, has marked this turn toward located intellectual histories of artistic modernism in South Asia. The transnational,

Dadi argued, does not bypass the particularities of context and located histories. The "specific intellectual and processual trajectories" within which art and art histories of the non-West are located, and "the considerable labor its intellectuals and artists have undertaken to articulate their place in modernity" are foundational ingredients to their histories, he has noted. Understanding of tradition, as well, is often mediated by transnational affiliations rather than unchanging and assumed national pasts.[108] The idea of transnational affiliations, I will suggest, echoing Dadi, is a route into what Andreas Huyssen has called "alternative geographies of modernism" that would read the "transnational" through dialogues among the local, the national, and the global, keeping in mind their "temporal inscriptions" and "constitutionally different formations of artistic subjectivities and strategies of representation."[109] Such a study, Huyssen noted, would attend to "temporal and spatial differentiations" and the "deep histories and local contingencies" that produce a "dialectics of modernism" that is "locally-mediated and historically conditioned." This attention to the local as a site of intersections and reconfigurations is a step toward understanding dissonances and contradictions within the apparent homogeneities of the nation-state. At the same time, it is a demand, along Huyssen's lines, for "new kinds of comparisons that go beyond clichés of colonial versus postcolonial, modern versus postmodern, western versus eastern, center versus periphery, global versus local, the West versus the rest." [110]

Histories in this book animate echoes of the global via deeply locational forms and negotiations. Outside such locational particularities, the global, one can argue, remains disembodied and dehistoricized; locality itself can be seen here to work as a historical agent. Locality, as Arjun Appadurai has argued, is a "relational contextual" idea, rather than scalar or spatial; the local carries, he noted "complex phenomenological quality," which is expressed in certain kinds of agency, sociality and reproducibility.[111] The local, hence, is potentially a site of production as well as difference—where the global is both received and transformed, and where hegemonic "national" narratives themselves can be destabilized, or reconfigured through sub-national imaginaries. A "specialized knowledge about sub-national settings" plays a critical and strategic role in developing "knowledge about the global," Saskia Sassen has suggested: "It is knowledge about the nation-state as an all-encompassing formation that loses capacity to explain the global, but not knowledge about the sub-national." [112] My vantage point *from locality* in this book is hence also a bid to understand other modalities of the global and of alternate internationalisms as deeply embedded in particular locations and locational histories. While I stand on the foundational critiques of Eurocentric art histories that have foregrounded new histories of Indian modernisms or postcolonial modernisms,[113] I am seeking to move beyond modernist studies steered by national or even transnational frameworks: the locational is my bid for turning toward excavating the more granular histories of artistic modernity itself, as produced by the dreams and displacements of decolonization.

While the transitional period from late colonial to postcolonial India gets overdetermined by narratives of the euphoric arrival of the new Nehruvian nation-state, the "anti-imperial" consensus of the pre-1947 period, as historian Sekhar Bandopadhyay has argued, did not naturally morph into a postcolonial "Nehruvian consensus"[114]; "divergent visions of freedom led to different imaginations of the enemy," thus shaping the polyvalent politics in the post/colony. While the transition from the colony to the post-colony was a dialogic process of the colonial past and a postcolonial present, the production of a "hybrid political modernity" that accommodated and celebrated "difference, and also pluralism,"[115] carried a political mechanism as well—what Timothy Mitchell has called the "discipline of historical time" that "reorganizes discordant geographies into a universal modernity."[116] In postcolonial nation-states, the nation as an "allegorical meta-text" uses tropes of both belonging and commitment as well as institutional structuring of cultural production and identities.[117] Such meta-narratives flatten not only dissonance but also confusion and negotiations, denying, as it were, the "ambivalent margins" and "narrations of nation-states."[118] Yet, as Raphael Samuel argued, there are, justifiably, "wildly different versions of the national past on offer at any point of time," depending on the optic adopted.[119] Even as the Indian nation-state stumbled into imagining its modernity in the 1950s and 1960s, there were asymmetries in its imaginations of national modernity—often marked by the asymmetries of decolonization itself. The politics of narration and postcolonial history-writing itself is the issue at stake here.

The retreat of empires and the arrival of freedom in the new postcolonies carried multi-textured and multi-polar politics. They generated social and cultural negotiations that often spilled outside nation-state-driven histories—collecting not so much in Raymond Williams's "wide margins of the century"[120] as in the crevices and shadows of hegemonic histories—nationalism being one, globalization being the other. How can decolonization be retrieved as an analytical field for the post/colony, beyond the harnesses of the nation-states? For the processes of decolonization were *longue durée* and irregular, marking localities rather than the abstraction of the nation. Nation-statist historiographies read decolonization through the transfer of power from the colonial to a postcolonial state, while scholarship driven by postwar international politics tends to foreground the "retreat of empire" and Cold War configurations. However, decolonization was not a "coherent process,"[121] its incoherence being not merely global but also internal, *within* nation-states. The post-colony, rather, is a "necessarily clumsy, complicated, and inherently incomplete (that is, fragmentary)" site,[122] an "imaginary institution" riddled by the "state of contradictions."[123]

In subaltern studies scholarship, this fragmentary character of the post/colony has been raised time and again. Nations, as Partha Chatterjee has argued, are not bound by what Benedict Anderson called "homogeneous empty time," but through the "heterogeneous time" of modernity;[124] uses of "the fragmentary, the local, and the subjugated" unmask, he has argued, "the will to power that lies at the very heart of modern rationality" and decenter the "epistemological and moral subject."[125] The view from the locality offers that site of heterogeneity and the fragmentary that, as Gyan Pandey argued, resists the "drive for a shallow homogenization and struggles for other, potentially richer definitions of the nation and the future political community."[126] In the fields of visual art and cultural histories, however, such fragmentations continue to be overridden by the historiographical needs of salvaging a national-modern art history, to enter the canons of a global, postcolonial modernism. What histories of art and decolonization emerge, one could ask, from the vantage point of specific locational experiences beyond national and nation-statist frames?

Viewed from the locational vantage point, Bengal offers a curious perspective in fragmenting this hegemonizing gaze of the nation-form, and national-modern art. While the province has often acted as a surrogate for "the nation" in histories of anti-colonial nationalism in India, post-1940s, its marginalization offers, I will suggest, a new politics of locality, with hitherto untapped historiographical potentials. In post-1940s Bengal (West Bengal after partition in 1947), the trails of decolonization—in famine, war, and communal genocide—persisted in quotidian hauntings, where the specific experiences of displacement produced particular forms of marginality and vernacularity. These were locally rooted and defined, and in a contradictory relation to the nation-form, rather than being sites of simple regional diversity within the hegemonic vision of the nation-state. Vernacularity is not merely a valorization of the local—active in twentieth-century India as celebration of the rural and living traditions; it speaks, rather, to "the heterogeneity of postcolonial idioms and forms of experience."[127] Unlike the "subaltern," which speaks exclusively to a position of subordination within a given power relation, rendering itself vulnerable to romanticization, the "vernacular" can be "simultaneously subordinate within one set of power relations and dominant in another."[128] Bengal, in its twentieth-century histories—both as the frame for anti-colonial nationalism and in its ironic displacement from the national-modern imagination of the post-colony—is critical for understanding the wider politics of the "vernacular modern," a provincialization, as it were, of the national-modern imagination in art history writing.

Provincializing the modern is a demand for "heterotemporal" experiences of history, ones that will be written from narratives of located modernities and inscribed by the particularities of locational experience, discourse, and politics. This will challenge not just the universalistic impulse of Eurocentric narratives of modernity,[129] but the rationalities of meta-narratives and canons as well.[130] While tracing the transnational routes of non-European modernisms or salvaging the legitimacies of multiple modernities will reveal new "densities" of the modern, as Elizabeth Harney has argued,[131] it is by identifying the political unconscious of the postcolonial modern in itself, I argue, that new dialectical histories of art from the Global South can be written—both in dialogue with and in contradiction to canonizing tendencies of national or modernist or global art narratives. While I explore in this book a broad set of national artistic and political processes, my focus on locality and region is a mode of activating such contradictions.

"Partisan aesthetics," in effect, is a proposition to both historicize and conceptualize such contradictions via the textured histories of the political in twentieth-century aesthetics in India. As I enter here what I identified at the beginning as a participatory field of visual art, the left, and the long decolonization, I will elaborate such contradictions—both through the dialectical ways in which art and politics interacted on the ground and in the differential aesthetics *from below* that refracted homogenizing discourses of postcolonial modernity.

Part I
DIALOGUES AND DISSONANCES

CHAPTER 1

"POLITICAL POTENTIALITY"

Jamini Roy and the Formations of Progressive Art Criticism

IN SEPTEMBER 1937, Jamini Roy, already noted in Calcutta's art circuits for his experiments in the flat, linear "folk" styles of *pats* (the narrative scroll paintings of eastern India), exhibited a large number of his works at the Indian Society of Oriental Art in Calcutta. With almost two hundred paintings on display, the exhibition showcased Roy's entire artistic oeuvre from the 1910s to the 1930s. It included oil paintings from his earliest academic naturalist training and his impressionistic watercolors, his gradual shifts into the minimalistic linear charcoal sketches of the late 1920s, and his more recent compositions in the free-flowing bold lines and flat color-planes of the *pat*s of rural Bengal. Inaugurated by Fazlul Haq, prime minister of the newly formed provincial government in colonial Bengal, the exhibition was attended by the city's politicians, artists, writers, bureaucrats, and social workers. Newspaper reviews hailed the event as a "triumph of technique," and Jamini Roy was lauded as the "People's Painter."[1]

The year before, at the April 1936 session of the Indian National Congress at Lucknow, a similar title had been given to the artist-aesthete and principal of Kala Bhavan in Santiniketan, Nandalal Bose, by none other than M. K. Gandhi, to applaud the artist's "display" of rural India at the INC conference grounds. Bose became for Gandhi the true "artist-craftsman," a "people's artist."[2] While Bose decorated the grounds of the Lucknow Congress in 1936, Roy was limited to a modest decoration of the Congress president's chariot—a cow-drawn cart symbolic of rural transportation—that remained marginal to the artistic initiatives around the congregation.[3] Unmarked by institutional lineages, pedagogical address, and least of all, political patronage, Roy's ruralist aesthetic was still somewhat marginal to the national-modern discourse in the early 1930s. While his exhibitions attracted in the urban connoisseurs, he continued to be framed as an "urban *patua*"—an urban artist of rural narrative scrolls—his art hailed often by critics as an "improvement upon the traditional art of Bengal."[4] The 1937 exhibition at the Indian Society of Oriental Art would change this perception in ways that both included and *exceeded* Roy's own art. As the dramatist and later IPTA activist Sachin Sengupta already noted in his review of this exhibition, Roy's art carried more "intellectual appeal" than "emotional appeal," and thereby called for a seasoned eye (fig. 1.1).[5] This drift was captured, in more ways than one, in a set of writings that were to follow.

Soon after the 1937 exhibition, Shahid Suhrawardy, then the Bageswari Professor in Art at the University of Calcutta, wrote a lengthy review of Roy's works—"The Art of Jamini Roy"—in his volume of collected essays, *Prefaces: Lectures on Art Subjects.*[6] This piece became the first in a series of essays and reviews on Roy that were to emerge between 1937 and 1944. In 1939, the modernist poet Sudhindranath Datta wrote another extensive study of Roy's artistic career, "Jamini Roy and the Tradition of Painting in Bengal," which was reprinted in 1943 in the *Longman's Miscellany.*[7] In 1944, a third lengthy essay on Roy came from the poet and, by then, key figure in a fledgling left-wing cultural movement, Bishnu Dey, who coauthored the piece with an ardent patron of Roy, John Irwin—a civil servant and aide-de-camp to Richard Casey, the governor of Bengal.[8] Shahid Suhrawardy, Sudhindranath Datta, and Bishnu Dey were writers and poets with a defined modernist disposition, who gathered around the critical-review journal *Parichoy* (modeled after T. S. Eliot's *Criterion*), edited by Datta himself. Two further pieces on Roy from the spaces of the *Parichoy* circle need to be mentioned here: in 1938, Dhurjatiprasad Mukhopadhyay—writer,

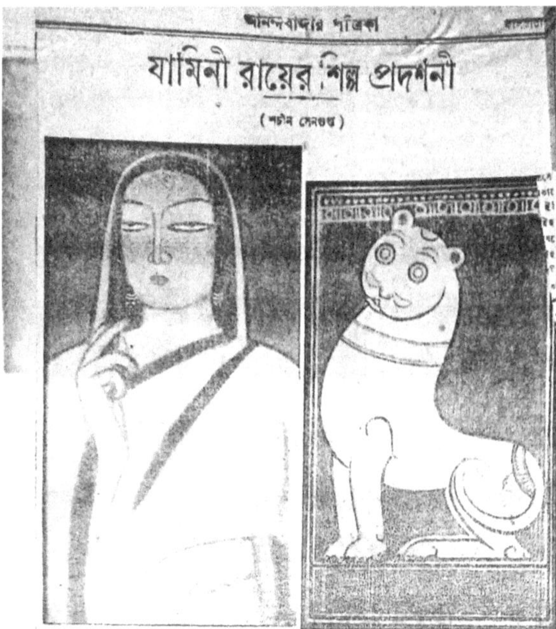

আনন্দবাজার পত্রিকা

যামিনী রায়ের শিল্প প্রদর্শনী

(শচীন সেনগুপ্ত)

Ananda Bazar Patrika

গগনেন্দ্রনাথ ঠাকুরের অন্ত্যেষ্টিক্রিয়া

বিশিষ্ট ব্যক্তিদের যোগদান

FIGURE 1.1. *Sachin Sengupta, "Jamini Ray-er Silpa Pradarshani." Anandabazar Patrika, undated, possibly from September 1937. Source: Album of newspaper reports. Courtesy of Archives of the Indian Society of Oriental Art, Calcutta.*

sociologist, and member of the newly formed Bengal chapter of the Progressive Writers' Association (PWA)—explained the social roots of Jamini Roy's art in his broad sociological analysis of Bengali painting, "Social Background of Contemporary Painting in India, with a special reference to Bengal," published in the PWA organ *New Indian Literature.*[9] And in 1944, Mulk Raj Anand—writer and founding member of the PWA—reviewed Bishnu Dey and John Irwin's essay in *Our Time*, a communist cultural journal in London. Anand, though not directly associated with *Parichoy*, shared the collective's general platform, visiting the group as early as 1938 during the second annual session of the PWA held in Calcutta, in which they played a significant organizational role. Bishnu Dey, by far the closest to Roy, served as a bridge between the artist and the literary and left-wing circles and continued to write about Roy, with two significant pieces published in 1948 and 1955.[10]

These art-critical pieces on Roy were produced not by art critics but by academics, writers, and poets (echoing also the dramatist Sachin Sengupta's reading of Roy's intellectual rather than emotional appeal). Even as the political alignments of the writers themselves remained divergent, or at least dissonant, shared sensibilities were being developed that sought actively to connect the local "folk" idiom of Roy with global discourses on an artistic modernity drawn from ruralist idioms. The social spaces of the *Parichoy* circle, or the political resonances of left-aligned literary forums like the PWA, make such essays refract along multiple historical interpretations and positionings—of both Roy's own work and the grids of discourse that contained or sought to contain him. Three intertwined aesthetic ideologies current in the period stand out in particular: modernist formalism, social realism, and socialist humanism—each marking a fluid discursive field around Roy and prompting new dialogues between the social and the formal values of art, as well as the aesthetic and the ideological affiliations of artists and critics. The ambiguities and contradictions in these essays around ideas of the social signification of art, as I will go on to show, were in fact converging grounds for two critical streams of art discourse in late-colonial India: first, the wider questions of form and technique that had been sharpening since the early 1920s, primarily as reactions against the mythological revivalism of the nationalist Bengal School of painting; and second, the beginnings of the left's cultural movement, with its rhetoric of taking art "to the people"—which had by the late 1930s generated new vocabularies of "progressive art."

In these essays, I argue, a *passive participation* of the aesthetic in the political can be identified, one that posed its own modality of partisanship in art. This involved a shadow engagement of art with a less-defined leftist politics, where critics were keen on identifying the political "potentiality" of artistic form rather than its active political commitment. This passive participation was conditioned by two factors: first, the Communist Party itself was underground between 1934 and 1942, and its political actions or mechanisms could appear in cultural action only as shadow processes—less visible, more informal, and often dispersed; and second, artists and critics associated with *Parichoy* were often not interested in active political participation, but were committed rather to exploring potential relations between aesthetic form and historical experience, and indeed between scopes of the modern and the popular in visual art. Their engagement with political vocabulary in art, while indirect and without defined ideological affiliations, was spurred by located celebrations of folk art as vestiges of "living traditions," untarnished by colonial modernity and providing new sites for national identities.[11] The rhetoric of "progress" (*pragati*, in Bengali)—translated and repeated across the writings on Roy—was in itself multi-scalar, firmly harnessed to an interwar internationalism that sought to address both anti-colonial nationalisms and anti-fascist front-making, the "people" becoming both shared value and rhetoric. Such writing echoed particular transnational cultural values *in motion*, the most critical being the collaborative political and cultural ethos of the Popular Front period of the Communist International that encouraged left-wing activists in India to seek new liaisons, albeit ambiguous, between cultural modernity and "the people" in the 1930s, before its more concrete ideological streamlining by the CPI in the 1940s. The *Parichoy* circle is a key protagonist in thinking through this particular character of what can be seen as a "vernacular" communist culture of the interwar 1930s that grew independently from the political destinies of the CPI.

In this opening chapter, I follow conversations and discourses that constituted this passive participation of art in politics, and the production of "political potentiality" in art discourse. At the same time, I draw out, the ideological consolidations of the Communist left *within* the milieus of progressive art criticism around Roy, which transformed this passive participation into more active authorship of socialist art by the early 1940s.

JAMINI ROY AND THE *PARICHOY* CIRCLE

By the mid-1930s, Jamini Roy had covered a wide trajectory. His social exposures in Calcutta had always been plural. In 1903, when he was barely sixteen, Roy came to Calcutta from his native village of Beliatore in the Birbhum district of Bengal. His father, a staunch social idealist, had quit his government job to pursue cultivation, growing his own crops, rearing animals, and spinning cotton.[12] When Roy joined the Government School of Art in Calcutta in 1903, he became one among the first batch of students to be taught by Abanindranath Tagore, who had become the new vice-principal of the school and, by the 1910s, was beginning to lay the groundwork for what was to become the Bengal School of painting. Yet Roy never entered Tagore's coterie of students, followers, patrons, and critics, who formed the social and discursive body of the revivalist art movement of the Indian style; he preferred, rather, an academic naturalist training. As a migrant in the city, Roy trained as an artist while doing an array of odd jobs—ferrying parcels for his brother's bookshop in the city, painting business cards for a Jewish trader, assisting an old lithographer in north Calcutta, painting bamboo frames for engravings, manning a garment shop in the evenings, painting sets for theater companies.[13] At the art school he became a favorite of the new principal, Percy Brown, who arrived in the mid-1910s. So pleased was Brown with Roy's use of perspective and color that he apparently granted the young student the freedom to attend classes at any level and at any time, without fees or routine.[14]

By the 1920s, Roy had excelled as a prominent portrait painter earning a fair living. At that point he decided to move away from the academic realist tradition to seek alternative forms in his art—to capture, as he noted, the essence of "Indian" art without relapsing into classicism or academic naturalism. In the mid-1920s, he withdrew to his native Beliatore to dedicate himself to the search for pure form, hoping to be inspired by the regional folk art and craft styles. While acute financial stress plagued this renunciation of lucrative portraiture commissions in the city, Roy strove assiduously to economize his form, shifting increasingly toward minimizing lines and naturalistic details, defining contours through heavy colors. The dialectic between perspective and plasticity in art was in a way ideally played out in Roy's work, given his parallel habitation of orientalist idealized figuration and western academic realism throughout his early years. A genealogy of Roy's linear abstraction can be traced through his gradual distillation of linear structure from academic naturalist figuration. It paralleled his assimilation of the visual ethics of rural terra-cotta pottery and narrative scrolls, and followed his new subjects drawn from tribal figures, domestic themes such as mother-and-child motifs, epic and mythological characters from the *Ramayana*, the Krishna legend, as well as religious icons like Christ and his disciples.

Roy's turn toward stylized linearity was noted right away at the first exhibitions of his new style in 1929–30: first in 1929, when the Government School of Art hosted a solo exhibition of Roy's work, exhibiting his Santhal (tribal) paintings as a part of the ex-students' exhibition series;[15] and second, soon after at the 1930 exhibition at the Indian Society of Oriental Art, where reviewers already noted a "primitive, spontaneous, robust" mood of the artist graduating from his "subtle, pensive and mystical" works of the previous years.[16] This exhibition introduced Roy's new interpretation of the folk idiom of narrative scrolls. In twenty large tempera studies of mythological characters outlined in sweeping brushstrokes, the artist was seen to have introduced a mysticism of a "primitive, naive character."[17] The explanation of the new mood of the works, the report duly noted, lay in Roy's seeking inspiration from "traditions of medieval Bengali art—the painter craftsman of the Bankura district of West Bengal."[18] At the exhibition, this was amply illustrated by the display of three panels in which village artists, invited for the show, painted domestic scenes in an "unsophisticated, lively style," two of which were "completed" by Roy himself.[19] Through the 1930s, Roy developed this distillation of essential form from folk motifs by foregrounding the essence of linearity and the use of earthy colors that would echo a ruralist aesthetic, exhibiting his works twice a year in his modest residence in a narrow alley in north Calcutta. These exhibitions were noted for the ambience of idealistic rural tranquility that Roy consciously designed with archetypal forms and motifs from village Bengal, complete with ritual votive lamps, earthenware, and wooden stools, while his own scrolls hung as tapestries enshrining this idealized space.[20]

Jamini Roy's primitivistic art, as Partha Mitter has argued, was indeed providing a robust aesthetics of "crude rigour" that on the one hand challenged the "cloying figures of oriental art," and on the other recast a modernist self rooted in local identity "in opposition to the Pan-Indian historicism of the Bengal School."[21] Yet Roy's reception in Calcutta's art circuits was mixed through the 1930s and 1940s. His new style was noted widely, with some commending him for a brave departure from the dominant classicism of the Bengal School, but others marking him as a mere *patua* (a village scroll-maker) who repeated artisanal motifs mechanically with no painterly imagination or scientific basis of artistic anatomy. An indirect indication of this distrust of Roy's "flat technique" can be found in an excerpt from an interview with Nandalal Bose, dated June 4, 1932, in reference to Gurusaday Dutt, the civil servant and patron-scholar of folk crafts of Bengal, where Bose noted tacitly:

> It's my feeling that Mr. Dutt is giving the *pats* much more than what they deserve. Though certain artists have been able to express their feelings through the *pats*, one cannot be too enthusiastic about such originality. It is only *arbitrary work, without scientific basis* [emphasis mine]. Therefore it cannot last. The *pat* gives a flat treatment. We are familiar with several such modes of flat treatment. But the *patuas* who do not have any scientific basis cannot be a source of inspiration for any other artists.[22]

It is worthwhile to note that Jamini Roy's exhibition in 1931 at the Indian Society of Oriental Art, juxtaposing his *pat*-style works with those of rural *patuas*, was followed by Gurusaday Dutt's exhibition of his own collection of folk crafts, which included wooden works, *pats*, and textiles. Bose's unstated allusion to Roy here remains unmistakable. A similar critique would later echo in what Bose's student and colleague, the iconic artist Benodebehari Mukherjee, called Roy's "mannerism" and lack of "originality" in repeating the "external decorativeness" of the folk art of *pats*.[23]

Roy's experiments, exhibitions, and the mixed reviews he received paralleled his constant search for intellectual dialogues with and affirmations from fellow artists and writers. He had friends in the Kallol Group, a modernist collective of writers and poets, and was a regular at the gatherings of the Four Arts Club, Kallol's predecessor. In the late 1920s, Jamini Roy's paintings had been published in *Kallol* magazine in monochrome or halftone prints.[24] Alongside these occasional forays into modernist spaces, Roy had close social ties with his friends in the academic realist circuits in Calcutta, with whom he had forwarded the cause of giving visibility to struggling realist painters of the city in the 1920s. His new paintings in the 1930s were also earning him new patrons among the connoisseurs of folk art, riding high on the ruralist turn of the interwar period. By 1937, however, Jamini Roy had not only emerged as a celebrated modernist but had also acquired the iconic status of the most "progressive painter," his new patrons being a new generation of modernist poets and writers, intellectuals, and academics in Calcutta, some of them with defined Marxist orientations.[25]

The 1937 exhibition with which we began is noteworthy in affirming this turn in Roy's career, not just for introducing his art to the intellectual circuits but more importantly, for generating a specific discourse of art criticism. For the first time, this genre of art discourse highlighted Roy's intellectual labor and struggle with form—his "modernist" intervention into traditional materials and motifs, as Shahid Suhrawardy argued, or, in Sudhindranath Datta's words, his "integrated design" of combining modernist simplification with indigenous craft practices. These new writings on Roy paralleled his social dialogues with the *Parichoy* circle. Since the mid-1930s, he had been a regular at the weekly Friday gatherings around the journal, usually at the residence of the editor, Sudhindranath Datta.[26] Between 1937 and 1940, Roy featured in these gatherings frequently, either in person or through discussions of his work. During these years, *Parichoy* became a space for the critical patronage of Roy's art and a site for both discourse and sociality around emerging values and vocabularies of progressive art.

Roy himself was far from being a communist; he was rather more of a Gandhian, much unlike the political temper of the *Parichoy* circle. He saw himself as a craftsman, repeating his motifs, even allowing copies of his works to be made by his son, and integrating his whole household in the making and copying of the paintings, erasing artistic signature entirely in some cases. Having familiarity with different techniques of craftsmanship and different tools, Roy had the ability to employ a wide variety of materials—dolls, glass painting, scrolls, and modeling. Speaking to Bishnu Dey, he asserted the centrality of technique in his art—it was the construction of form that was fundamental, not the subject.[27] Yet it was this image of the artist as artisan, and the potential for an organic integration of the two, that drew him into an emerging left-wing cultural criticism during these years. The association of the artist with the craftsman, the interfaces of intellect, craft, and the process of production itself opened Jamini Roy's art up to potential Marxist readings, where a more structural dialogue of the formal and social values of art could be captured. While excusing the lack of realism, this body of writing around Roy created a wider social base and frame for art criticism through a broad cohesion of modernists and left-wing intellectuals.

Parichoy had begun in 1931 as a critical-review quarterly. After the first five years, it became a monthly and developed into a platform for new writing and a collective of modernist writers, poets, and intellectuals in late-colonial Calcutta. The editor, Sudhindranath Datta—one of the stalwart modernist poets in the post–Rabindranath Tagore generation—was the fulcrum around which the new literary culture of the 1930s was growing, *Parichoy* being a successor of a kind to the Kallol Group. Datta had returned to India in 1930 after a year-long visit to the

United States and Europe, accompanying Rabindranath Tagore during his voyage to America. Upon his return, he and some of his new associates in the city founded the review journal. *Parichoy* grew through personal networks of like-minded writers and poets who, although diverse in their political inclinations, nonetheless shared a disposition against cultural revivalism, while some of them had overt leftist sympathies. In the 1930s and 1940s, *Parichoy* functioned not simply as a critical portal in literary reviews, but more importantly as a literary club and social site for new modernist discourse. Its scope was eclectic, an active ground for the production of new scales of transnational cultural conversation, the term "parichoy" itself connoting the sense of "making acquaintance." Its first issue, in 1931, explained the purpose of the review as "a rendezvous through literary discourse," one that would bring about transnational conversations through literary analysis, translation, commentary, and criticism.

Over the next decade, *Parichoy* became a forum for internationalist discourse, publishing series on the Russian Revolution, the Soviet Union, and fascism in Europe, its early issues setting the tone with reviews of current leftist international literature like Maurice Thorez's *France Today and the People's Front,* Leon Trotsky's *The History of Russian Revolution,* and André Malraux's *Days of Contempt.*[28] The genre of reviews in *Parichoy* became a critical transit for local-global conversation, and for developing a new perspective of engagement. Amiya Dev, Datta's biographer, argued that the culture of reviews in post-Rabindranath literature of the 1920s and 1930s provided a whole new style, "a new philosophy of writing and in most cases a new *solidarity* [emphasis mine]. . . . A review meant a new manifesto bearing the whole group's signatures, however distinct they may later develop as writers in their own rights."[29] Introducing the review to the western world in 1936, Humphrey House, then a professor of English literature at the University of Calcutta and a regular at the *Parichoy* gatherings, noted in the *Times Literary Supplement* that "*Parichoy* marks the definite passing of Indian literary criticism into the modern world. . . . [I] t has set itself far above anything else in Indian periodical literature, in catholicity, range, intelligence and freedom from prejudice." A typical *Parichoy* number of 1936, Edward Shils noted, carried "a long analysis of Fascism and detailed articles on the Chinese renaissance, certain Hindu minor philosophical texts, the poetry of Hugh MacDiarmid and R. C. Trevelyan and a detailed analysis of T. S. Eliot's *The Rock* and *Murder in the Cathedral*."[30] Gandhism held little attraction for the *Parichoy* circle, the majority of its members being drawn to Marxism and socialist thought. Most of the reviews (of books of history, economics, and politics) had a Marxist bias, as Datta's biographer Amiya Dev observed, "not because the editor himself was a Marxist, which he probably was not, but because the reviewers often were." Datta's choice of writers and reviewers was rather consistent, Dev wrote, showing "not simply his loyalty to friends but a liberalism that regarded Marxism as a scientific solution to social issues."[31]

Jamini Roy's association with *Parichoy* and the new post-Rabindranath generation of literary modernists, it can be assumed, came through Bishnu Dey, with whom he shared a close personal friendship. Writing on Roy in 1944, Dey noted the critical importance of new patronage networks for artists, which were necessary to appreciate and support new art initiatives that diverged from both the western portraiture patronized by the affluent aristocracy and the mystical Indian-style paintings of the neo-orientalists. The new intelligentsia of modernist writers, poets, and critics in Calcutta, Dey observed, were ideally located to recognize the work of Jamini Roy, for "despite their lack of means, [they] were nevertheless the only group in society which preserved its own standards of integrity."[32] Buddhadeb Bose, another modernist poet and an early associate of Roy's, echoed this when he wrote that modernist poets and writers like him were best situated to appreciate Jamini Roy, as they themselves were fighting the same battles, albeit in literary form, through the modernist encounter with an "indigenous tradition."[33] Jamini Roy acknowledged his association with the *Parichoy* collective as one of mutual understanding. *Parichoy*, he noted, provided a space for him to test his ideas and gain clientele for the work of his new style of paintings.[34] The *Parichoy* circle also became the new buyers of Jamini Roy's art, long before the development of the much-discussed wartime Allied Forces clients for his works.[35]

As members of the *Parichoy* circle started writing about Roy after his 1937 exhibition, albeit in a dispersed manner rather than in concerted forms, a new art-critical turn was being charted. This turn, not programmatic but attentive to a new agenda, was one that would seek to forge dialogues between modernist form and the social rootedness of art—in itself a partisan project. This discursive moment came about not through clearly articulated manifestos or organized action, but rather in the form of scattered essays and reviews. These pieces revealed multiple configurations of aesthetics and ideology, and a dynamic interplay of modernism and realism animated by friendships and affinities, dissonances and lapses, rather than concrete ideological affiliations. The overlaps of social space and discursive space that formed around the essays on Jamini Roy from the *Parichoy* circle suggest a peculiar conjunctural dynamic, critical to understanding not only the left-wing cultural movement in India but also its transnational resonances. They reveal, as we will see in subsequent sections, new vernacular forms of the ethic of sociopolitical alliances of the Popular Front period of the international left, where collaborations and dialogue within the broad ideological rubric of anti-fascist cultural solidarity allowed curious political possibilities of art to consolidate.

A politics of friendships and associations was as important here as the imagination of progressive form was. In the words of Raymond Williams, this early discourse of progressive art can be seen as a "cultural formation"—"simultaneously *artistic forms and social locations* (emphasis mine)."[36] Explaining the constitution of the cultural front in America in the 1930s, Michael Denning, echoing Williams, distinguished two notions of the politics of art under the Popular Front: first a "cultural politics," i.e., the politics of the allegiances and affiliations that form the cultural field, and second, "aesthetic ideologies," i.e., the politics of form. If allegiances and affiliations represent the "social consciousness" of the cultural front, then the works produced by the artists and intellectuals on the left embody, Denning argued, a "political unconscious," the notion of the cultural front itself being "an attempt to theorize the relation of culture to politics."[37] Such are indeed the frames through which one might approach the material here.

VISION, DESIGN, AND "INTEGRATED DESIGN"

Shahid Suhrawardy's 1937 essay on Roy, "The Art of Jamini Roy," located the artist firmly within the cultural circuits of Calcutta. An art critic, linguist, dramatist, and professor of English literature, Suhrawardy commanded a wide knowledge of contemporary art movements. Upon his return to India in 1932, after spells at Moscow University and the League of Nations in Paris, he became a regular at the *Parichoy* gatherings through his close association with Sudhindranath Datta. His essay on Roy is significant in its intellectualizing of Roy's art, not in the manner of a eulogy but with a more academic approach. He offered a systematic analysis of the integrated aesthetic potential of Roy's art, the stylistic connections between various stages of his work and between his art and his habitat—his native village of Beliatore. Refusing to label Roy as a "mere" *patua*, or his art as simplistic or decorative, Suhrawardy denounced criticisms of Roy as a crank, a rebel against the Bengali revivalist movement, or a fanatic in vain pursuit of originality. Rather, he upheld the monumentality of Roy's works, which he saw as rooted in the intellectual pursuit of form and not in a popular pleasure in the visual. His vindication of Roy's formal experiments carried a critique of the taste of "Indo-Anglican coteries" that failed to extend patronage to Roy's art. Instead, he claimed Roy to be truly an "artist's painter," incapable of being appreciated by the layman. He highlighted Roy's artistic labor, his protracted struggle with form-making marked by a lack of patronage, and the "concentrated seclusion" of the artist in his native village.[38]

Suhrawardy compared Roy's withdrawal from Calcutta to Beliatore to Cézanne's withdrawal to his native Provence, though Roy's flight, he wrote, led to his conscious apprenticeship with the village artisans, not the distant gaze of the outsider. This subjective encounter of an artist trained in urban environs with his rural roots and artisanal traditions was, to Suhrawardy, a personal reflection as well as an anthropological excursion into the collecting and documenting of folk art and crafts; it was, as he argued, a modernist intervention upon tradition. Suhrawardy admitted that Roy's adoption of the indigenous idiom resulted in a change of palette, incorporating more traditional local methods of preparing color and composition. Yet, it was necessary, he argued, to differentiate Roy from the *patuas*, for his intervention was not merely a continuation of a folk repertoire: "Folk art, by its very nature and function, apart from the simple technique and the resultant easy communion with it, must teach many useful lessons to creative artists in search of basic forms"—the most important being a concentration on the object with its laws of line, light, and volume, "undisturbed by the picturesque."[39] While Jamini Roy adopted his style from the *patuas* and was not claiming originality there, his more sustained intervention, claimed Suhrawardy, lay in his outline drawings in rhythmic minimalist lines, which he saw as Roy's "most characteristic and felicitous manner, strongly individual, reminding one of modernist pencil drawings of Europe and at the same time of the Kalighat pats of some fifty years ago."[40] Jamini Roy's art, he asserted, was "justified by modern, if not modernistic, art theories" that were dominant in the West, much to the ignorance of the proponents of the European academic style in India.[41] To Suhrawardy, Roy's sense of structural design and compositional integrity, or his discovery of "the possibilities of plasticity in the apparently rigid forms," made him more than a decorative painter. Though these images "may incidentally serve a decorative purpose," he wrote, they were "pure realizations of form executed to fulfill a disciplined artistic intention with a high sense of artistic responsibility."[42] The panel drawings shown at his 1937 exhibition (see, for example, fig. 1.1) were held up by Suhrawardy as Roy's most mature compositions, monumental in their structural harmony of rhythmic free flowing lines. He compared Roy to the European post-impressionists in his "rigid selectiveness . . . an austere elimination of the unnecessary" as well as his incapacity "to leave the representational for the schematic," though he differed from the post-impressionists, as Suhrawardy noted, in his "unabating love for surface and outline," without broken brushwork or surfaces.[43]

Suhrawardy's essay imparted to Roy's art a formalist exclusivity—a "totality of aesthetic experience" and a "tenacious aesthetic will"—shorn of any topical or illustrative content. He placed Roy above the cultural preoccupations of contemporary India, in the domain of "timelessness," seeking "the inherent idea of the object distilled from its concreteness."[44] More importantly for the contemporary artistic field, Suhrawardy pitched Roy opposite his contemporary master painter from Santiniketan, Nandalal Bose, placing Roy in the domain of pure formal consciousness, while celebrating his obstinate and consistent pursuit of "fundamental problems of art," and "expressive form, shorn of uncoordinated irrelevancies." [45] The relative significance and comparison of the works of Roy and Bose were, in fact, regular features at the *Parichoy* gatherings, as Shyamal Krishna Ghosh has noted in his published diary entries on the *Parichoy* evening gatherings.[46] In such conversations, Jamini Roy is noted to have argued that Nandalal Bose and Abanindranath Tagore could not become great artists because, despite intellectual preparation and finesse, they followed the "wrong technique." When a fellow member of the gathering argued that technique was inconsequential if the subject matter was *mohot* (signifying "mighty" or "noble"), Sudhindranath Datta retorted that such paintings were but examples of "Literary Art" and not true form,[47] while Roy explained that technique alone mattered, and carried within it a mix of truth and imagination.[48]

While it is widely acknowledged that Shahid Suhrawardy's essay marked Roy's sudden prominence and widespread popularity, it could be argued that this essay, more than increasing his popularity, introduced Roy *into discourse*. It planted him firmly in narratives around modernity in Indian art, informed as they were with questions of locality, tradition, artistic subjectivity, and formalism. This was a new kind of art criticism, one invested in expanding the dialogical scales of modern art. The essay also projected a modernist self-reflexivity on Roy and emphasized his personal struggle with form-making, which was paralleled with struggles for the emergence of an integrated modernism. This modernist subjectivity was immersed in folk sensibilities, as Suhrawardy demonstrated by consciously foregrounding Roy's appropriation of indigenous idioms in his aesthetic struggle with form.

Interestingly enough, in his bid to foreground the intellectual value of Roy's art, Suhrawardy placed Roy's work above "popular approval": Jamini Roy, he asserted, could not be easily grasped by laymen, "particularly as the entire trend of his life, both as an artist and a man, has been in the direction of evading popular approval."[49] This position was in direct contrast to the interpretations of his fellow critics from the *Parichoy* circuit, Sudhindranath Datta and Bishnu Dey, who were eager to project a popular consciousness onto Roy's art. In Suhrawardy's text, an intellectualization of Roy's formal experiments paralleled his conscious distancing from the popular, marking the first step toward creating an exclusive aesthetic value for Roy, a modernist subjectivity that would later become, in the essays by Datta and Dey, defined by Roy's commitment to the popular and the folk roots of his iconic forms. Suhrawardy's modernism was, however, mediated via the social rootedness of art, or the "organic integration" of content and form that the English critic Herbert Read upheld during these years. Shahid Suhrawardy shared a close friendship with Read from his student days at Oxford, and through Suhrawardy, Read's ideas could have become available to critics in Calcutta, particularly his earlier works, *Vision and Design* (1920) and *Meaning of Art* (1931). The significance of Read's works for this body of writing cannot be underestimated. Suhrawardy would have been familiar with Read's work through the 1930s, including "*What Is Revolutionary Art?*" (1935), *Art Now* (1933), and *Art and Society* (1936). Both he and Sudhindranath Datta would later invoke Read in their essays. As Read's fundamental interest was in understanding the relation of the individual to the collective society, it is likely that his understanding of an "avant-garde creativity emanating from the soil of its native culture" would have shaped the new art writings that sought to explain Jamini Roy's organic assimilation of living traditions of his village.[50]

When Sudhindranath Datta wrote his extensive and erudite essay on Jamini Roy, he not only offered a vindication of Roy's modernist intervention but posited a deep social significance in his art. "Jamini Roy and the Tradition of Painting in Bengal" was written in 1939, following Roy's 1938 exhibition at the British Indian Street in Calcutta, at the studio of the painter Kshitish Roy, showcasing his most significant works from the 1930s in the new "flat" technique, his new series of biblical themes, and subjects from Santhal life.[51] Datta began by breaking the image of Roy as a "slothful simpleton," attributing to the epithet "decorative" a new intellectual edge. Unlike Suhrawardy, who resisted the decorative label, Datta tried to vindicate a critical agency in the construction of decorative motifs by introducing into the essay notions of "integrated design" or "significant design." In a "cohesive community," he wrote, art becomes a necessary part of an "organic system," legible and accessible to the community.[52] Going beyond Suhrawardy's intellectualization of Roy's modernist intervention in folk forms, Datta sought to vindicate the decorative as a social tool with a cohesive value for the community. His conceptualization of the "organic" sought to root iconography in shared community aesthetic values. Following Clive Bell, he noted that for the artist to construct "significant form," the discovery of patterns was required, which would hold both social and formal relations that constitute images. Roy's subject matter, to Datta, was inconsequential in this selection of form, since "neither subject matter nor treatment determined the nationality of a picture as much as technique generated by a particular type of vision."[53] For Datta, the question of the "nationality" of art—its Indian-ness in this case, was thus inseparable from the mode of visualizing and imaging, an argument that made him locate the question of style in the realm lived every day, thereby connecting the modern with the popular, and form with context, without fetishizing either. A picture was "not a patchwork quilt of motley hues," Datta wrote, "but a tapestry of uniform materials, and while fidelity to local color was a commendable virtue, it did not preclude unity of conception, accomplished through logical systematization of flat tints to replace harmonious development of light."[54] This is at once a critique of a monolithic subscription to indigenous tradition, and a vindication of the freedom in form-making.

To Datta, Jamini Roy's withdrawal to his native village was more complex than a European artist's romantic retreat from the urban conundrum to primordial roots. Neither was it a return to his childhood initiation into folk art. Jamini Roy's relation to the folk, Datta maintained, was complicated in itself. Noting the difference between folk form and modernist drawing, he highlighted the incapability of folk art to distinguish between vision and design. It was the significance of vision, he argued, that gave a structural monumentality to drawing and made Roy's formal intervention a critical exercise. Datta critiqued the weak contours, lines, and color of the Indian style of the Bengal School for its dearth of instruction in draftsmanship. He saw an essential continuity between Roy's early training in European draftsmanship, his distancing from the weak lines of the Bengal School, and his search for a bold linearity and more solid use of flat primary colors. Roy's return to his village, Datta noted, began as a "disinterested curiosity, free from the least thought of profit," and it was only after completing this full circle that he could see similarities between his treatment of mass and that of the contemporary European masters.[55]

Sudhindranath Datta's description of the most mature stage of Roy's work is evocative of the final triumph of realized form, utterly non-representational and completely "indigenous." Roy's friezes of the mid-1930s, all exhibited in the 1938 annual exhibition, brought out a use of primary colors that was, Datta wrote, no less than revolutionary within the art circuits in Calcutta; the new medium of tempera and handmade colors from native seeds, flowers, and stone restored an Indian-ness hitherto absent in Indian art:

> [D]ark green and Indian red, golden yellow and mandarin blue . . . never shading into one another, nor allowed to suggest the least likeness with natural colours of the objective world . . . all applied uniformly, the very brush strokes being completely obliterated in order to destroy every suspicion, or perhaps shadow of actuality; and thus indigo trees leaned against scarlet skies and green girls stood or sat in sculptural poses, offering white leaves and black flowers to absent gods.[56]

To Datta, Roy thus provided an affirmation of "collective consciousness" as much as a firm denial of "actuality"—a popular art without the trappings of realism, a new entry of the "objective world" and "sense experience" into art "without artifice."[57] In experimenting with, and exceeding, the *pat* technique, Roy was thus no mere craftsman, or "plagiarist cribbing from actual peasants," but an artist attuned to both the "everyman" and the "purity" of form: "Jamini Roy's present problem was to make concrete the generalities that constitute an event rather than the metaphorical presentation of some Crocean experience that is immutably self-expressed the moment it comes into existence."[58] While to Datta, Roy's art reflected similarity with Matisse, it was in Picasso that he saw Roy's closest comparison.[59]

In the essay, Datta's concern about the social in art was more implicit than overt. He identified the social signification of Roy's art in its integration of vision and design, what he saw as the "organic" roots of decorative form. His treatment of modernist abstraction in Roy's art projected a defined materialism on his aesthetic. This was harmonious with the Indian pictorial tradition that necessitated abstract form-making from the concrete sensation: "These were surely abstractions, but abstractions that had not forgotten their concrete basis"; Roy's art was therefore at once eminently non-pictorial yet "rich in humanity and full of such insight into character."[60]

It is interesting to draw parallels between Datta's stress on an imperative formal logic in Roy's art and his own modernist treatment of verse. Datta's conceptualization of integrated design, pictorial abstraction, and social cohesion resonates with his subjective, literary interface with form and material, which stressed values of both congruity and artistic abstraction. The inaugural issue of *Parichoy* in 1931 had emphatically set out this disposition. Datta's article "Kabyer Mukti," translated and reprinted later as "The Emancipation of Poetry," had already hinted at this potential convergence with Roy's aesthetic, where he noted, "Art [. . .] brings about a congruity between man and the world around him. It is true that art cannot survive in antagonistic social circumstances; but unless it ultimately rises above its environment, it is futile."[61] Stressing (poetic) form's imperative to distill essentials from reality, Datta noted, "The emancipation of poetry lies in acceptance. If the poet wants anything from eternity he cannot afford to be factitious. He must move through the dark alleys of the city with a begging bowl in his hand, asking for what is left after the feast is over—there is no other way."[62]

Sudhindranath Datta's essay on Roy brought visual and literary modernism closer together in discourse, introducing at the same time a discursive terrain where the vocabularies of literary and artistic modernism, and of art's formal and social values, could converge and interact more closely. This convergence was also embedded within a wider turn toward the social signification of art that was brought about from the platforms of the PWA. The PWA resonated within the modernist literary circuits in Calcutta, most notably in the *Parichoy* circle, more than among artists. The *Parichoy* circle took up a key position in the second PWA convention held in Calcutta in 1938. In "Whiggism, Radicalism and Treason in Bengal," Datta's address at the gathering, he foregrounded the significance of the "foundation of tradition" that was guarded not by the "introspecting intellectuals" but by "the enduring masses" who were the "directors" of progress itself: "[W]hatever be the calibre of the experimenter, unless he passes the pragmatic test of his people, the facts he would fondly establish are febrile dreams and the truths he would loudly proclaim are a maniac's fancies."[63] A staunch opponent of romantic-sentimental-idealist tendencies in literature, Datta was far removed from the rhetoric of popularization and populism that dominated the political and cultural firmament in the 1930s. Yet his participation in a forum such as that of the PWA, and his intellectualization of the mass resonance of art and tradition, added credibility to the development of the progressive movement within Calcutta. It also animated the notions of the popular and progressive within the spaces of modernist experimentation, beyond, as he was conscious in stating, the "narrowly nationalist" channels. Jamini Roy, he noted in the closing sections of this talk, was "the most progressive painter," whose intensely Bengali technique could break through nationalist preoccupations to craft a more universal language of art, for "he alone among his contemporaries understands that the traditional artist, being more natural than the experimental one, has, paradoxically, the greatest affinity with the Universal Man who, whether in fact he exists or not, must at least be imaginatively rediscovered in every living art."[64]

Speaking from the platforms of the Progressive Writers, Datta foregrounded the class character of the "crisis in culture" and charted the directions that progressive art should take to address what he vaguely formulated as the "regeneration in the people who are permanently outside class and thus eternally outside crisis."[65] His remarks, with their projection of critical agency on Jamini Roy, were characteristic of these years in introducing a new discourse around the popular and the progressive in art, one that foregrounded questions of both radicalization of tradition and the social signification of form. In both, Jamini Roy became the point of focus, consolidating a still embryonic Marxist art discourse, as well as a modernist celebration of formal abstraction in art. Sudhindranath Datta would consciously place himself outside Marxism or even a rhetoric of progress, as he would admit to his friend, associate, and fellow poet Bishnu Dey.[66] Yet his concerns, as his speech at the PWA conference of 1938 showed, lay in harnessing the local with the universal, the experimental with the popular, and in connecting aesthetics and politics more actively.

Although Datta's article was written in 1939, it was not until 1943 that it was published in *Longman's Miscellany*. While in Datta's modernist framing, Roy's art received a more structural grounding in collective lives and popular traditions, in the texts of Dhurjatiprasad Mukhopadhyay, Bishnu Dey, and Mulk Raj Anand, it was to become more directly implicated in fostering a left-wing aesthetic. Together, these critics associated with the *Parichoy* circle and the PWA served, albeit indirectly, to bring modernism and socialism closer together in art discourse. What is significant in this alignment is the balance struck between elite modernism and social commitment in art, an ambivalence that persisted throughout the formulation of progressive art in the 1940s and beyond. These writings on Jamini Roy revealed the early conversations around the "popularization of art," and the place of political movements in cultural action that had been developing since the formation of the PWA in 1936.

TOWARD "PROGRESSIVE" ART

The 1930s saw a gradual consolidation of socialist vocabularies in the cultural field. The idea of the progressive was central to such formulations. This idea already had *longue durée* associations with the international peace movement and disarmament conferences in the interwar years, which sought to attract progressive-minded intellectuals to the anti-fascist cultural resistance. It picked up socialist connotations in the

1930s, as a familiarity and affinity with socialist ideals grew within the cultural field in Bengal, particularly after Rabindranath Tagore's serialized "Letters from Russia"—published regularly in the *Modern Review* during 1930, and in book form in 1931 as *Russia-r Chithi*—hailed the revolution in its overthrow of oppression.[67] Tagore's *Letters*, complemented by Maxim Gorky's *Mother*—translated into Bengali in 1933—helped to encourage a palpable enthusiasm for the Soviet state amid the young generation.[68] After his trip to the Soviet Union in 1930, Tagore also drew his abstract composition titled *Spirit of Russia*, lauding the resurgent masses, which was later reproduced in Sudhi Pradhan's collection of the documents of the Marxist cultural movement.[69] By 1934, the English translation of the *Letters* was banned in India, the same year as the banning of the Communist Party of India, although Tagore's letters, from his tours of both Russia and China, continued to appear in the *Modern Review*. In 1934, Soumendranath Tagore—by then a key Indian figure in the international communist presence, and soon to be the founder of the breakaway group the Communist League (later the Revolutionary Communist Party of India)—wrote the first Bengali book on fascism, shortly after writing his *Hitlerism or the Aryan Rule in Germany*. Already a regular in the Kallol Group, Soumendranath would also have been a regular at modernist niches like the *Parichoy* circle.

When Hiren Mukherjee, an activist of the underground CPI, inaugurated the Bengal chapter of the Progressive Writers' Association in 1936, the idea of the progressive was given concrete form in two critical publications. The first, *Towards Progressive Literature*, published the collected documents of the first PWA conference of 1936, including the manifesto and resolutions—a model it shared with the publication of papers from the Soviet Writers' Congress of 1934.[70] The second, a 1937 anthology of anti-fascist literature jointly edited by Surendranath Goswami and Hiren Mukherjee, *Pragati* (*Progress, An Anthology of Anti-fascist Literary Movement*), staged the idea of progressive culture via its international, national, and regional resonances. It included, for instance, translations of André Gide, T. S. Eliot, E. M. Forster, a report from Spain by the journalist Claude Cockburn (alias Frank Pitcairn),

("Madrid: 1936"), and the work of renowned regional novelists and poets Bibhutibhushan Bandopadhyay, Manik Bandopadhyay, Premendra Mitra, Dhurjatiprasad Mukhopadhyay, Buddhadev Bose, Sudhindranath Datta, Samar Sen, and Bishnu Dey.[71] In 1939, following its second session, held in Calcutta in 1938, the PWA published its first official journal, *New Indian Literature*, in which the idea of the progressive was expanded further, and for the first time in relation to visual art.

In the first volume of *New Indian Literature*, Dhurjatiprasad Mukhopadhyay, a sociologist, novelist, and a regular at the *Parichoy* circle, provided a concrete Marxist perspective on visual art, which one could argue was the first of its kind in an Indian context. His essay, "On the Social Background of Contemporary Indian Painting (with particular reference to Bengal)," drew connections between art practice, partial economic development, and disjointed social relationships. In India, he argued, the artist and the artisan were not separate entities; both were craftsmen, anonymous and non-naturalistic in their art. In opposition to this "medieval Indian tradition," he noted, art in Bengal had developed as "Fine Art," divorced from crafts, the artist claiming independence for his own technique, his subject poetically displayed. The decay of feudal patronage, and the inability of the new propertied class in colonial Bengal to become entrepreneurs, increased the social rupture between the artist and the artisan. In the absence of a "genuine rapport between the artist's life and that of the community," Jamini Roy could be seen to have "rejected all trappings decreed by attitudes of the hour and clung to the basic verities of painting."[72] In upholding Roy as the most "sincere artist," Mukhopadhyay highlighted a rebellion in Roy's art, one that Roy pursued not through direct social commentary or revolutionary imagery but through the purely formal painterly devices of construction and composition. Preempting the tenor of Sudhindranath Datta's article, which was to be written the next year, Mukhopadhyay viewed social content in Roy's art not in representational motifs but within its formal, architectonic structures. Even when coming from a Marxist writer like Mukhopadhyay, this discourse of what is progressive remained closely associated with the question of structural and formal elements, which were derived from an organic integration of the social relations from which the artist emerged. This was a far cry from the overtly realist ethic to be upheld by critics within the communist left from the mid-1940s on, as we will see in subsequent chapters.

By the mid-1940s, writings on Jamini Roy were beginning to pick up clearer socialist accents, particularly in the contributions of both Bishnu Dey and Mulk Raj Anand, who invoked Sudhindranath Datta's exhaustive essay on Roy. In 1944, Bishnu Dey, Datta's friend and fellow poet from the *Parichoy* circle, coauthored the aforementioned catalogue essay on Jamini Roy with John Irwin. Dey shared an intimate association with Roy, an enduring friendship that was sustained through correspondence and regular visits to the artist's studio. Accompanying a pictorial album on Jamini Roy that was released by the Indian Society of Oriental Art, this essay is perhaps the most quoted text on Roy. Dey wrote it as an account not only of the artist's modernist idiom, but also of his subjective interface with the folk, the popular, the progressive, and most importantly, the socialist idiom in his art. Like Suhrawardy and Sudhindranath Datta before him, Dey foregrounded the formal elements in Roy, invoking at the very start Henry Moore: "to feel shape simply as shape ," and Cezanne: "When colour has its richness, form has its plentitude" (fig. 1.2). Dey's text, however, moved swiftly to connect Roy's "pure and vital intensity of creative expression" to his "close organic relation to the soil." Opening with Roy's drawing of a tiller at work, Dey connected Roy's form to a detailed study of the landscape, political history, and local culture of his native village, Beliatore. Rural myths soon gained in Dey's drift the political potential of folk forms.[73]

Dey idealized Beliatore as a site of syncretic tradition that retained a medieval economy due to its geographical seclusion, where the artisan combined the functions of both the artist and the craftsman, and where art was never outside the domain of the necessary: "when it is not religious, it is functional."[74] To Dey, Beliatore served as an ideal site for the proliferation of a rich folk tradition, with the "revolt and assimilation" of pre-Aryan customs and practices within the local culture. He attached to this folk tradition a "political potentiality," a character of protest that became the means of defying the upper-class ethic, "but always in the guise of a rich humanism."[75] It is interesting to probe

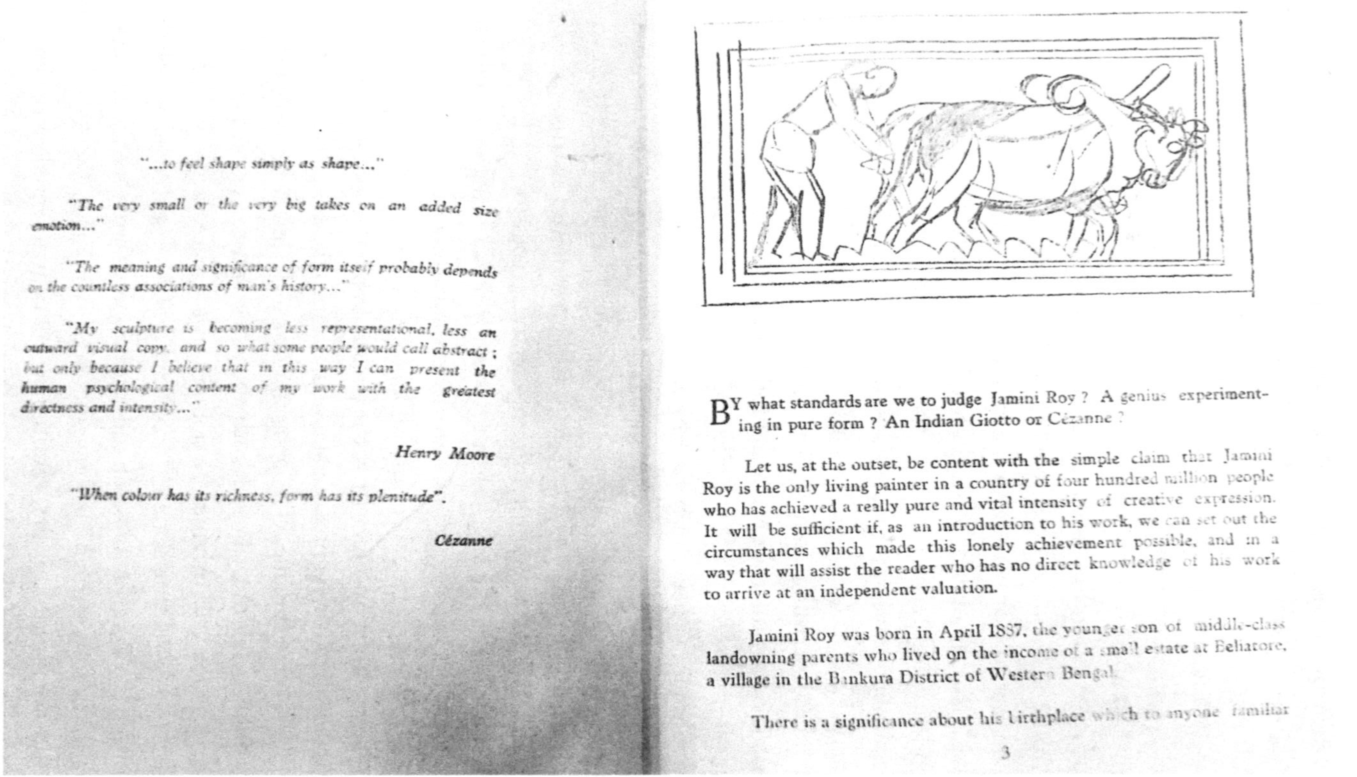

"...to feel shape simply as shape..."

"The very small or the very big takes on an added size emotion..."

"The meaning and significance of form itself probably depends on the countless associations of man's history..."

"My sculpture is becoming less representational, less an outward visual copy, and so what some people would call abstract ; but only because I believe that in this way I can present the human psychological content of my work with the greatest directness and intensity..."

Henry Moore

"When colour has its richness, form has its plenitude".

Cézanne

BY what standards are we to judge Jamini Roy ? A genius experimenting in pure form ? An Indian Giotto or Cézanne ?

Let us, at the outset, be content with the simple claim that Jamini Roy is the only living painter in a country of four hundred million people who has achieved a really pure and vital intensity of creative expression. It will be sufficient if, as an introduction to his work, we can set out the circumstances which made this lonely achievement possible, and in a way that will assist the reader who has no direct knowledge of his work to arrive at an independent valuation.

Jamini Roy was born in April 1887, the younger son of middle-class landowning parents who lived on the income of a small estate at Beliatore, a village in the Bankura District of Western Bengal.

There is a significance about his birthplace which to anyone familiar

3

FIGURE 1.2. *Title page, Bishnu Dey and John Irwin, Jamini Roy. Source: Catalogue of Indian Society of Oriental Art (Calcutta: ISOA, 1944).*

the notion of politicality in Dey's treatment of Roy's art, a selection of which, primarily rough drawings and sketches, was reproduced in the essay. For Dey, Roy's cohabitation with the rural, and his close observation of and formal abstraction from the rural everyday or familiar iconic forms (for instance, Roy's signature image of Radhika, the consort of Krishna, a household god of rural India), as exemplified in the sketches, became a way of arriving at the structural social integration in Roy's art.

Dey's projection of Roy as truly the "people's artist" paralleled his characterization of Roy's artistic form as revolutionary—a resurgent folk idiom that, he wrote, emanated directly from Roy's native Bankura district. By assimilating the rural and the everyday within the schema of the "popular" form in art, Dey was trying to invoke the leftist cultural movement's program of the "popularization" of art, which by the early 1940s carried a clear objective of taking art "to the people." At the time, Dey was a key figure in the fledgling cultural movement that the left patronized—both through inchoate associations between artists and intellectuals and in an expanding visibility of the Communist Party, particularly after its legalization in 1942, which ended a decade-long ban. Apart from his involvement with the PWA, Dey was active in left-wing forums like Friends of the Soviet Union, the Anti-Fascist Writers' and Artists' Association, and the Indian People's Theatre Association. He was, more interestingly, a point of contact between the party and the writers and artists who were outside the party fold.

Yet, although Dey was located firmly within the left-wing cultural movement during these years, his vindication of a socialist idiom in Roy was not tempered by any valorization of a realistic aesthetic, which by the mid-1940s was becoming sharper in left-wing discourses of progressive aesthetics. Rather, Dey imparted a potential for resistance to folk art itself: "a healing and direct attitude to life, an earthiness dynamically related to the unseen, and in the art itself a certain self-assurance and vitality patterned against a hostile world."[76] Roy's decision to move away from the European tradition, Dey noted, reflected his search for a communion with the social significance of the tradition in which an artist tries to paint. The equipage of an artist was not enough without the artist's conscious engagement with "the deeper sources of creativeness," he noted, and Jamini Roy drew his resources from the "life and culture of the people," "not as an outsider but as one who had an intimate knowledge and understanding of the living experiences of the people where lay the roots of the folk culture itself."[77] Dey placed this proximity to and intimacy with myths and living traditions at the heart of the question of form and abstraction in art: "It is only within the *social patterns of culture that abstractions of form achieve significance as symbols* [emphasis mine]. The purer the form or abstraction the more it must depend upon a background of myths if it is to carry content or pictorial value."[78] For Bishnu Dey, the socially cohesive role that Shahid Suhrawardy or Sudhindranath Datta spoke of took on a socialist character, facilitating a more explicitly Marxist discourse on art and society. Indeed, when he argued that art must integrate a "new way of life under socialist humanism, which will acquire its new myths," he was harnessing the organic integration between art and collective life, captured in Roy's art, to the revolutionary potential of popular art itself.

When Mulk Raj Anand wrote about Jamini Roy for the first time, in 1944, he was introducing Roy to a left-wing readership in Britain and also expanding on Bishnu Dey's projection of socialist humanism onto Roy's art. Jamini Roy's return to his own native village, Anand noted, made his encounter with the folk traditions different from that of "modern primitivism," as well as from the "return of a middle-class Bengali artist from the world of 'fashionable' painting to the folk tradition." Echoing Bishnu Dey and John Irwin, Anand reasserted that Roy's location was not that of an outsider, and he was shorn of the sentimentalism that often marked a western artist's journey into primitive cultures in search for purer forms. Yet, Roy's insider location did not make his creative integration with "traditional" sources simple or easy; his success as a painter, observed Anand, lay in the "struggle" he negotiated with those traditions to arrive at his own individual expression: "Jamini Roy never had to pursue Gauguin's far-away search for equivalence and symbolism, nor was it necessary for him to study the painting of Matisse in order to develop an 'integral vision.'" The indigenous world to which Roy returned, Anand noted, was not "by itself" what was attractive to him; rather, the attraction came from the artist's realization that "much excellence lies in inheritance, as in the conquest of environment, and that the artist *transforms* his material." Roy's work was "tantamount to a revolution" in Indian art, for he "restored to the picture not only the state of mind of the indigenous artisan, but he consciously revived that respect for the quality of line which is an Indian specialty."[79]

By describing Roy's art as a conquest of environment, Anand was once again locating him outside contemporaneity, in the realm of the "timelessness" that Suhrawardy found in Roy's modernist idiom. However, Anand view, similar to Bishnu Dey's accent on socialist humanism, was also insistent in evoking, and even projecting, a critical realist agency in Roy's art: "In his satirical pieces and cartoons, he was already, before the war, aware of the clash of social forces: moneylenders and landlords, with the heads of beasts of prey, were symbolic of the emergence of peasant struggles, as the dream-birds were haunted by the sense of malevolent spirits gathering on the horizon."[80] For Anand, projecting a social agency onto Roy's art was a mode of locating him within the trajectory of critical realism, beyond a purely formalist or primitivist idiom—a direct resonance of Anand's own location as one of the key articulators of the realist ethic of the PWA during its still-early years. While Anand admitted to a literary "bias" in looking for messages in pictures, he felt nonetheless that Roy's imagery posed a conscious questioning of social crisis; Roy, he wrote, was not simply "seeking peace in the abyss," as argued by some of his detractors; he was seeking "form through stress and strain."[81]

This intellectual and artistic struggle with matter and form as the marker of revolutionary socialist art echoed Anand's familiarities with international left-wing art criticism from the 1930s. In his London days, Anand had been a close associate of Randall Swingler, a key poet affiliated with the Communist Party of Great Britain (CPGB) and editor of the *Left Review*, the mouthpiece of the Writers' International in Britain (1934–1938).[82] Through Swingler, Anand and his PWA fellow-founders, most of them students in London in the early 1930s, would have come across the cultural wings of the anti-fascist Popular Front period of the Communist International, like the Ralph Fox Group, or the Left Book Club. Anand's closeness to left-wing, anti-fascist forums in Britain also drew him to the new art criticism from the likes of Herbert Read. Read's ideas seem to echo in Anand's writings on Roy, both in his plea for a strong social language in art and, before Anand, in Suhrawardy's distinctly modernist agenda. In his brief essay "What Is Revolutionary Art?" (1935), published in the heyday of the Popular Front, Read had defended neither Soviet art nor Communist views on art, stressing rather the revolutionary potential of so-called "abstract art," not of naive celebrations of "folk-art, peasant pottery, madrigals and ballads," but "something tougher, something more intellectual and 'difficult'"[83]—a point that resonates, as we can see, in Anand's reading of Roy. Within the Read-ian framework, Anand's and the other left-wing framings of Roy can be viewed as consciously integrating Roy's political aloofness with the socialist resonances or potential of his art, idealizing his views on *production* itself. This defined intellectualization was an effort by these writers to rescue his art from the comfortable labels of "folk art" *into* a space of a robust socialist modernism. Roy's own framings of his struggle echo here. Speaking to Mary E. Milford, Roy is heard noting in 1944, "Peace is not good for an artist, art is born of experience, of stress and strain, wrestling with problems, intellectual and physical."[84] It was this rhetoric of struggle and transformation that had made Roy critical to the incipient socialist art-critical vocabulary since the early 1940s.

Anand had previously introduced the rhetoric of "Marxist materialism" in art in 1938, when he spoke at the Calcutta convention of the PWA. In his inaugural speech, he invoked the epistemology of Marxist materialism in "psychological" terms, and not in the language of political "dogma," to uphold what he saw as an active determination of consciousness by the experience and cognition of social reality, "reality in this signification being not only the data which is actively noticed at any given time but the whole gamut of the seen, felt and remembered experience."[85] Anand's speech had sought to situate "progressive criticism" not in the writer's class but by relating their art with the "history of the time in which the writer lived," and "the intensity of his realization of the social reality of the time."[86] This was a language of intellectual opposition that posited a role for the artist as an activist, an engaged and critical role for art in society, and, most importantly, a political logic to guide the artist. In Jamini Roy, left-wing writers like Dhurjariprasad Mukhopadhyay, Bishnu Dey, and Mulk Raj Anand can be seen to search for (and find) a dialectical potentiality between content and form, and between social cohesion and modernist abstraction, that did not conflict with Roy's lack of active political engagement. The activism that these writers managed to project on Roy was a formal one. Indeed, the whole discourse of art criticism generated around Jamini Roy was one that was against representationalism or pictorial realism.

Yet contemporaneity remained a persistent concern in these essays from the *Parichoy* circle. Sudhindranath Datta's liberal politics did not stop him from critiquing Roy's "purblind Gandhism," which he felt sustained in Roy revivalist dreams and an aloofness from the contemporary scene:

> He seems to find themes with evident rhythm rather than create order out of chaos by a supreme act of will. Why otherwise should he be attracted by the traditional dignity of the dancing Santhals and repelled by them when they were drunk and disorderly, fascinated by the primordial peasant and appalled by the industrial worker, or lyrically moved by the praying muslims and revolted by their riotous frenzy?[87]

If Roy could only "enlarge his sympathy," Datta continued, "the demonstrations of organized labor should present him with fewer formal difficulties than the excesses of a *kirtan* procession," for "the turmoil of our cities is by now firmly rooted in our soil as the stillness of our plains and the majesty of our hills."[88] Datta's closing lines in his essay on Roy are remarkable: "Since Jamini Roy's ambition in life has been to lose himself in the identity of his people, he must not turn away from them when they are on their pre-destined way. Of all men I can think of, he is best fitted to become their representative and give shape to their aspirations."[89] By the mid-1940s, the concern with contemporaneity also became stronger in Bishnu Dey, as he lamented:

> Jamini Roy's triumph has been the unity of head and hand. But if as we say, the development is to continue, this unity has constantly to achieve fresh organic integration. If only the hand comes to function and if there remains only an air of facility, the reason is not in an atrophy of the mind itself but in a failure of the mind to re-adjust itself to the objective world which is various and changing.[90]

In visual art, this growing concern with the contemporary converged with wider debates over contextuality and the social signification of art practice, which, by the mid-1940s, hardened notions of the progressive in art at many levels—from modernist rejection of sterile mythologism to new forms of critical realism in art practice, from a new rhetoric of social commitment and ideological commitment to active party-political agendas of "popularizing" art. A concrete turn toward realism was increasingly apparent in the left-wing cultural circuits, much unlike the social roots of abstraction that Suhrawardy, Datta, or Dey had explored in their earlier writings on Jamini Roy. Post-1943, the changing tenor of art criticism within these circles could be heard more sharply, both in the cultural forums and vocabularies and in the composition of *Parichoy* itself, as the consolidation of realism as art's social and political value reflected ideological lines in art criticism drawn more visibly.

The writings on Jamini Roy from the *Parichoy* circle, with their shared concern with an organic aesthetic, could sustain an ideological fluidity while at the same time lending ground to a gradual consolidation of socialist terminologies in art practice. As ideas of progressive culture were developing in such discursive forms, new shifts were pushing this rhetoric toward sharper socialist idioms. The early 1940s became a critical period of transformation, when a series of international events, together with locational developments, began shifting the mechanisms of cultural front-building within a growing left-wing cultural movement. The German attack on the Soviet Union in 1941 shifted the collaborative equations of the Popular Front period; as the hitherto-banned CPI pledged to join the Allied war effort in defending the Soviet Union, the British colonial government legalized the party, and thereafter, a more "visible" communist presence in cultural forums could be noted. A growing socialist accent in the writings around Roy can be traced through the early 1940s, a period during which the composition of *Parichoy*, too, was changing.

SHIFTING FRAMES

Shyamal Krishna Ghosh, an archivist of the *Parichoy* gatherings during the late 1930s, observed an increased presence of Marxist thought in *Parichoy* after 1938. The entry of political activists of the underground CPI like Hiren Mukherjee and Surendranath Goswamy, as well as the formation of the PWA, Ghosh noted, facilitated a more pronounced Marxist accent, with circulating memberships of the Left Book Club and an uptick in reviews of left-wing literature in *Parichoy*.[91] Both Mulk Raj Anand and Sajjad Zaheer, founding members of the PWA, were active participants in *Parichoy* gatherings in 1938.[92] The rise in communist rhetoric in cultural contexts—which was current transnationally—was also observed by the colonial government, which was anxious to curb the communist underground presence. In 1937, a review of communist activities prepared by the Intelligence Bureau, Home Department, Government of British India, reported the growth of "Intellectual Communism" in India, which deployed strategies "for a few convinced and trained Communists to establish contacts with all sorts of organizations and societies having interests in intellectual, cultural and social contacts, with the object of spreading communistic ideas and gaining converts."[93] In this report, bodies like the PWA, the Civil Liberties Union, Friends of the Soviet Union, the Spain Aid Committee, and the League against Imperialism—all established since 1936—were viewed as enclaves of Intellectual Communism. The report also noted the proliferation of a large number of study circles and youth leagues associated with the CPI, particularly in the United Provinces and Bengal, which aimed "to infuse communist ideals not only among students but in all walks of life, utilizing the essential Communist system of 'cell' working."[94] As a caveat, the report added that while many members of such forums might be unaware of possible Communist connections, that fact only revealed the insidious mechanisms deployed by the Communists in penetrating the ranks of the intelligentsia. Anxieties expressed here around structures of Communist cell working and political liaison with intellectuals seem valid if one follows the mechanisms by which culture was being turned into a "front" for anti-imperialist, anti-fascist resistance by the underground CPI through the late 1930s.

Between 1936 and 1944, a *passive participation* in the political found in writings on Jamini Roy offers an early political history of what would be consolidated as progressive art from the late 1940s. This history grew through vernacular forums that localized a global conversation around socialist aesthetics, not just through manifestos circulated in national platforms (of which there were hardly any in visual art), but also through located conversations—formal, informal, even marginal. This locational discourse sought to assimilate folk imagery with the modernist subjectivity of an artist like Roy, using ideas of "organic integration" between art and society, *without* participating in idioms of socialist realism that had already taken root in global left-wing cultural circuits. In the writings on Roy, a socialist reading such as that of Bishnu Dey could be advanced without either apparent conflict with a social realist aesthetic or any direct reference to the very different model of art prevalent in the USSR.

This phenomenon was widespread on an international level; while there were increasing constraints on artistic practice in the USSR beginning in 1934, at a tactical level the parties of the Communist International permitted considerable pluralism within the front organizations they set up. Thus, while Bishnu Dey's 1944 essay on Roy echoed a left-wing conception of a resurgent folk art, his parallel associations with modernist literary collectives—like the Calcutta Group, which we will encounter later in this book—sustained in him a formalist consciousness, increasingly excused in the new crop of left-wing cultural writings since the mid-1940s. More-active CPI workers also reflected this open-endedness. For instance, Hiren Mukherjee, in his 1943 edited volume *Us: A People's Symposium*, published for the Anti-Fascist Writers' and Artists' Association, could maintain a relatively un-doctrinaire approach even while asserting that the soundest way of aligning with progress was through socialism, without which art itself would become "increasingly false."[95] Progressive criticism, as another commentator wrote in the same volume,

> does not glibly ask for hallelujahs to the dirt and the dross, the dust and the scum of the earth . . . does not prefer photographic naturalism, which can tell the truth about life only in exceptional circumstances, in revolutions and often also in wars; does not cherish the illusion that new culture brings full-bodied realism into existence at the word of command. Progressive criticism realizes that the richer and deeper the emotional life, the more slowly it changes its nature, and even so, this is largely an intangible change generated in the very process of living.[96]

This fluidity would gradually harden. The notion of the popular would also undergo a transition; from a Gandhian ideal of contained, pure rural resilience, untarnished by colonial modernity, as idealized in Nandalal Bose's Haripura posters or in nationalist celebrations of "folk traditions," the people would now gain a "resurgent folk" identity. The CPI would increasingly direct cultural efforts toward harnessing existing nationalist investments in folk culture to revolutionary national politics. A new "national-popular" aesthetic with active socialist realist framings was to emerge through the transformational mid-1940s. This was captured in new art writings from the left with new actors and critics. When the Indian People's Theatre Association (IPTA) was formed during the famine year of 1943, its first bulletin, *People's Theatre Stars the People*, observed the dearth of realism in art, asserting the need for combining realism with the use of "revolutionary motifs" in painting and dance, and for representing the real "*in its revolutionary significance* (emphasis mine)"—an active echo of the Soviet rhetoric of socialist realism.[97] A key tension would emerge now around the ideological harnesses of the vocabularies of popular, progressive art.

In 1943–44, Sudhindranath Datta handed over the editorship of *Parichoy* to the Bengal committee of the Anti-Fascist Writers' and Artists' Association (AFWAA), officially managed by the PWA. *Parichoy* came to be edited by the historian Susovan Sarkar, and soon after, by Hirankumar Sanyal and Gopal Haldar, both active CPI members and cultural front organizers.[98] From 1943 on, *Parichoy* became, indeed, the unofficial organ of the AFWAA and the PWA in Bengal, under the direct ideological control of the CPI.[99] According to Amiya Dev, Sudhindranath Datta's biographer, that *Parichoy* should pass entirely over to the left after Datta's departure was probably not an "accident," nor was the "allegation" that Datta's *Parichoy* had been a nursery of Marxism in Bengal an "exaggeration."[100] In the 1930s, the *Parichoy* gatherings attracted a wide range of scholars, writers, aesthetes, and poets, some of them left-oriented and some of them members of the underground CPI. Among the artists and art critics visiting *Parichoy*, apart from Jamini Roy, were Atul Bose, Satish Sinha, O. C. Gangooly, and Amiya Ganguli. The renowned communist leader M. N. Roy, too, was known to attend the gathering in the late 1930s.[101] Dev called the circle "modernist" rather than "technically Marxist"; the shared concerns of the collective included new forms in literature and art, anti-revivalism, and anti-fascist political and cultural resistance. This reaffirms the fluidity of the new writing on art, and its social roots in the *Parichoy* group during Sudhindranath Datta's time as editor; while sharing a social consciousness with platforms such as the PWA, these writings nonetheless remained far removed from advocating social realism, still less so the more ideologically driven socialist realism. Indeed, between 1936 and 1942, realism in left-wing discourse can be seen as a "less specific"[102] aesthetic than it was later to become, the ambiguity of the style and its ideologies stemming from the fluidities of social associations.

Gopal Haldar's editorship defined the deepening Communist hardline in the magazine. Jamini Roy's name continued to be mentioned in the meetings of the Bengal Progressive Writers' and Artists' Association in the early 1940s (associated with the Anti-Fascist Writers' and Artists' Association),[103] but in art criticism generated from within the cultural movement, the tenor of ideological critique was sharpened. While Gopal Haldar introduced a regular art section in the *Parichoy* magazine itself, it became a forum for a direct avowal of socialist realism. While Jamini Roy continued to be celebrated, the strain of art criticism combining socialism and formalism did not continue. Writing on Roy's exhibition in 1945, Haldar rejected the modernist vocabularies of "abstract qualities" or "significant form," and even those of "rules of art," "nationalist consciousness," or "artistic subjectivity." Rejecting also what he saw as the anxieties of Roy's bourgeois "intellectual" patrons around his repetitive idiom, he upheld instead the "purely folk quality" in his art that would be truly accessible to "the people"—not a quality, he was careful to note, with a demand for photographic realism, but committed instead to making the "beauty of national form accessible to the common man."[104] Within a new formulation of a resurgent revolutionary popular art—a socialist aesthetic veering increasingly toward an idealized popular idiom—Jamini Roy could be assimilated only via the mediations of a "national-folk" idiom, as defined by Haldar, which was soon to become unable to meet the demands of the more direct "mobilizational" presence of the party in cultural production. Apart from Bishnu Dey, no left-wing cultural critic wrote on Jamini Roy's modernist idiom in the 1940s, as he became coopted within the left's "national-popular" rhetoric or critiqued for his rejection of the social turbulences that marked the decade.

The writings on Jamini Roy from the *Parichoy* circle, despite their growing socialist vocabularies, reveal the peculiar impulses of the Popular Front period of the international left—in India, the United Anti-Imperialist Front period inaugurated at the Lucknow Congress of 1936—where fronts were built *despite* ideological differences along the lines of progressive, anti-fascist, or people's art. A *passive* partisanship in a growing left-wing rhetoric characterizes these writings on Roy from the *Parichoy* circle, where a less-defined, diffused cultural front-building allowed a commitment to both modernist form-making and a humanism with varying degrees of socialist accents—a political potentiality, rather than political content in art. This mechanism was particularly suited to the underground years of the CPI, when alliances were being developed not along party lines but through shared activist values. The writings around Roy capture this aesthetic of "fellow-travelers," as distinguished from active affiliation with the CPI. The idea of the left-wing fellow-traveler—central to the colonial government's specter of Intellectual Communism—is, as David Caute has argued, "someone who accepted part of the public programme of the Communist Party, but who was not a member."[105] Further, Caute's "Western fellow-traveller" is "anti-rationalist, anti-urban, anti-modern, anti-western and in love with the peasantry," but also a true product of the Enlightenment, a "firm believer in the doctrine of 'Progress.'" Romantic primitivism, social idealism, and humanist progressivism are thus only a few of the markers of a fellow-traveler—a constitutionally fluid social alignment that involves "commitment at a distance which is not only geographical but also emotional and intellectual."[106]

This combination of participation and distance is part of the curious formation of a partisan aesthetic that can be seen in the critics writing on Jamini Roy from the spaces of the *Parichoy* circle or the PWA. Among Roy's interlocutors from the *Parichoy* circle were staunch modernists, humanists, radical socialists, and plain skeptics; their romance with the peasantry bound them in a broad ideological engagement with the "folk," but, more importantly, their affinities with the left-wing cultural movement were crafted, enacted, and sustained through both a shared distrust of the romantic nostalgia celebrated in nationalism and a shared faith in an "integrated" future. While a critic like Shahid Shuhrawardy had no socialist sympathies, his text on Roy became the first radical intellectualization of Roy's art, locating him firmly in modernist art discourse and within a concept of the progressive associated with literary modernism in Bengal since the late 1920s. The participation of a figure like Sudhindranath Datta in the PWA, and the common ground he could find with communists and fellow-traveling writers and critics around the "popular" in art, foregrounds a key feature of progressive art criticism during these years—one rooted in a transnational aesthetic of anti-fascist cultural action and concretized in the United Front in Indian politics, with its groundwork of social associations, political alignments, and ideological ambiguities. This assimilation of differences and fellow-travelers within a growing cultural front during the period between 1936 and 1944 was critical in forming the social base of what became a Marxist legacy in radical cultural activity. This collaborative-partisan ethic and aesthetic also produced a set of values—the idea of the progressive, for instance—that would form the crux of new cultural debates in the subsequent decades.

Elaborating on the nature of the progressive cultural movement, Mulk Raj Anand had noted in 1936 that instead of regarding political movements as static forms dictated by singular leaders with singular ideologies, intellectuals must think in terms of critical collectives, coming together in the face of danger, but not necessarily with uniform ideologies or sensibilities.[107] While disavowing implications that the PWA was a clique or a coterie, Anand called for writers, artists, intellectuals, and people of the country at large to align themselves with the vanguard of the Indian struggle for political and economic emancipation, "as ordinary persons, as political persons in the day-to-day work."[108] This was an agenda for the "popularization of culture"—"preparing people to understand and respond to the new cultural renaissance," to "arm our people intellectually," so that they are responsive to this "new humanism."[109] It was also the stirring of a new kind of artistic subjectivity, one that was actively engaged in the fusing of cultural action with political participation. It was a new direction toward a partisan aesthetic.

The movement of individuals among different platforms such as the PWA, the *Parichoy* circle of Calcutta, and the anti-fascist cultural organizations had often resulted from personal ties of an ill-defined, essentially pluralistic ideological and political nature, combined with a conscious engagement with an emerging left-wing discourse. It is important to follow the persona of Bishnu Dey here, not only in the development of the cultural front in Calcutta, but also in the entry of the pictorial arts into a movement otherwise dominated by literature and theater. Bishnu Dey's initiation to Marxism dated back to his graduation days and was reinforced in the mid-1930s, particularly after his association with his then-colleague at Ripon College, Hiren Mukherjee.[110] Mukherjee had recently returned to India after completing his law studies in Britain, and had become involved with the then-illegal Communist Party of India and the developing cultural front of the left. When the PWA was formed, Hiren Mukherjee was one of the collective's close associates, some members of which he had known from his student days in London. His principal concern in these years was to facilitate the expansion of the cultural front, and when the Bengal chapter of the PWA was formed, he became an integral part of the initiative. He drew in with him Bishnu Dey, by then a regular contributor to the *Parichoy* circle and a close associate of Sudhindranath Datta, and, through him, a cross section of intellectuals from different political affiliations. During this time, Bishnu Dey worked closely with both Mukherjee and P. C. Joshi, the new general secretary of the Communist Party of India, whom he met around 1936, along with the Communist leaders Muzaffar Ahmad and Philip Spratt.[111] Bishnu Dey's significance, recalls Hiren Mukherjee in his memoirs, lay in his facilitating the entry of more active Communist writers and intellectuals into the *Parichoy* gatherings, as well as in drawing non-Marxist writers and artists to the cultural movement that the Communist Party was increasingly trying to patronize.[112]

The dialogue between Marxist thought and the language of modernist formalism that was initiated in these early writings of Roy was marginalized within the official left movement from the mid-1940s. Rather than laying out a concrete Marxist agenda, this discourse had pointed toward simultaneous and intertwined affinities between modernist formalism and the social signification of form, making the left-wing rhetoric in these years not only inchoate but fluid in its political harnesses to progressive art. Political potentiality in Roy's art gave modernist writers the opportunity to bring closer *in discourse* rhetorics of the formal and the social around the vocabulary of progressive art. Thus, Sudhindranath Datta, a complete outcast in left-wing circles by 1944, could still close his commentary on Jamini Roy thus: "As it is, he is the most satisfying artist I have ever known: we both look back at the same past and are confronted by the same future."[113] And Bishnu Dey, writing as late as 1948, in the course of his own disassociation with the Communist Party that had by then assumed a fully socialist realist aesthetic, could still assert the Marxist core of the "dialectic of development" in Roy's stylized purity of form, which while assimilating the "'conscious' creativity of the artist with the 'habitual' craftsman was still the basis in which any modern movement in art [could] have its beginning."[114]

THE SCATTERED ART-CRITICAL PIECES on Jamini Roy, from a time when the left had hardly assimilated the visual arts, and which were produced not by art critics but by academics, writers, and poets, invite us to rethink the concept of progressive art that came to dominate narratives of Indian modernism after 1947. From these essays on Roy, I am drawing three propositions that will historicize this narrative of the progressive in visual art.

First, the notion of the progressive in visual art had its lineages on the cusp of the discourses around form and content, and between a transnational modernist formalism and left-wing realism.

Second, its vocabularies were furnished not by artists alone but by a crisscrossing social world of literature, art, and political activism.

And third, its often ambivalent articulations, agendas, and anxieties through the 1940s, and their eclipse thereafter in post-independence India, necessitate all the more a keen attention to dissonance rather than coherence, while navigating this discourse of art and (left-wing) politics in twentieth-century India.

I continue to follow these threads—around dialogues and dissonances—between art and an expanding political rhetoric in the cultural field, in the chapters that follow.

CHAPTER 2

"AS AGITATOR AND ORGANIZER"

Socialist Realism and Artist-cadres of the Communist Party of India

CONSIDER THE OPENING IMAGE HERE (fig. 2.1)—a full page from a September 1944 issue of *People's War*, a national political organ of the Communist Party of India. Titled "Life behind the Front Lines," the piece, like many other serialized reports in *People's War* and its regional variations, was written and illustrated by Chittaprosad, a young artist who had been recruited to the CPI in 1941–42. In 1943, Chittaprosad was one of what can be called the "artist-cadres" of the CPI—a party member and a political and cultural organizer. His sketches, cartoons, and illustrated reports appeared regularly in CPI publications across India, circulating from the party headquarters in Bombay, where he had relocated. By late 1943, Chittaprosad had become famous for his visual reportage around hunger and displacement. Throughout the 1940s, alongside fellow artist-cadres including Somnath Hore and Debabrata Mukhopadhyay, Chittaprosad developed new figurations of the body politic, in iconic sketches of the wartime Bengal famine of 1943 and postwar images monumentalizing labor and resistance. Whether in sketches, cartoons, or photographs, such images were more testimonies than journalistic data, steeped in the rhetoric of the artist "as witness" and the CPI as vanguard political front. Visual reportage combined text and image, within the didactic and activist role that the party played.

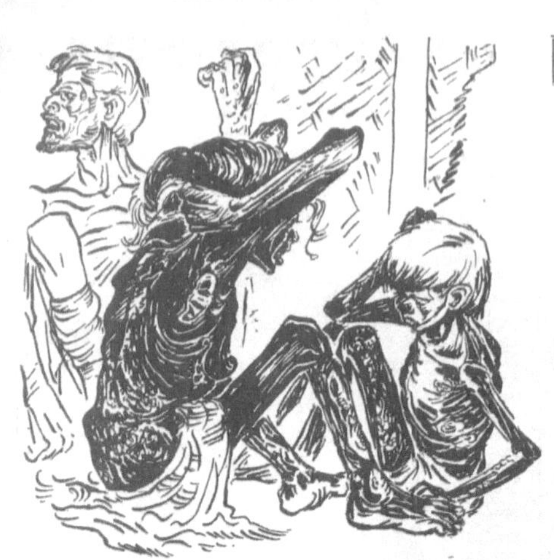

VISIT TO COX'S BAZAR

LIFE BEHIND THE FRONT LINES

by Chittaprosad

COX'S BAZAR is the southern Sub-Division of Chittagong district. It is the main Allied base for operations against Arakan. I knew the area, I had lived there as a boy. I went there this time to see what difference famine had made to the life of the people.

BEFORE the war rice used to sell at 20 seers a rupee. During last year's famine it sold at half a seer a rupee, and when the winter crop came to the market, rice became one and a quarter seer and in July when I visited the place the price was three quarters of a seer for a rupee. In other words, for over a year rice has been beyond the reach of the poor. The local people put the whole situation in one pithy sentence, 'North has become South and the South, North,' when they describe how their life has gone all topsy turvy. What they mean is that formerly the South used to supply rice to North Chittagong and now they have to wait endlessly for the same to come from the North.

Before the war, the district of Chittagong used to be free from malaria and Cox's Bazar area was considered a health resort for the whole of East Bengal. From what I saw now my own old memories of the place did not seem to have been ever real but yet came back to the mind like some ancient fairy tale. The contrast was beyond words. There is not one famine-disease that did not play havoc with the people of Cox's Bazar.

●

The area is inhabited by the Moghs and the Muslims. Moghs are a Buddhist tribe. Most of them were artisans, engaged in weaving, carpentry and cigar-making and some were traders. After the fall of Burma they lost their market and also the source of raw materials. When they saw the endless stream of evacuees pass through their area, they sold off all they had at any price they could get and waited for orders to evacuate which never came. Not being agriculturists, famine hit them hardest; they had to sell off their tools and became labourers in the army camps.

Be it said to their credit that their sense of tribal solidarity has saved their women's honour and their families from disintegration. They offer their labour in groups and come back to their villages in the evenings so that family life remains intact. Their women used to wear silks, gold mohurs round their necks and champak flowers in their hair. All that is gone. They labour together and share the suffering by helping each other. Thus damage to them has been less than to their Muslim neighbours.

The Muslims were the agriculturists in this area. A large part of their lands has been commandeered for building roads, camps, aerodromes and also as training grounds. The majority of their cattle died off through epidemics or were bought by the army contractors. During the famine days of 1943, seed and agricultural implements were sold off. Ever since 1943 the starving peasants have been too weak physically to put in any sustained labour on their farms. Thus in the granary of Chittagong, farming itself has gone to pieces.

●

How has all this worked itself out in the life of the Muslim peasantry? They leave the village in quest of jobs, come to town and stand in long queues before the army contractors. If they are not already too weak to labour, they may get a job on a daily wage of 12 As. to Rs. 2 as per physical strength and skill. The peasant brings malaria with him from the village itself and works as an army labourer in the grip of fever. He breaks down in a couple of weeks. If some other member of the family is yet strong enough there is some hope of survival. But then he too falls ill.

The next stage is begging for food by the road-side till the voice becomes too weak to speak and the legs too weak to totter along. And then it is pitiful death, with no will left even to struggle against it.

What I saw in the verandah of the Civil Supply godown is the last stage of the journey. I have tried to portray it with my brush in the two sketches given on this page.

In the verandah—six yards by one—6 men, 12 women and 8 children had taken shelter. The place stank of unwashed bodies and rags, nightsoil and rotting open wounds.

Above in the centre is Amina Khatun. Her husband had four acres of land and a sampan (boat), a pair of bullocks and a cow. The land and the boat were sold off to carry on through the famine. He left her a year ago in search of a job in the Army Labour corps. The bullocks and the cow died off in the cattle-epidemic, but her elder brother was there to help. He too left a month ago and like her husband earlier, nothing was heard of him either. Then she too had to leave her home-village Moishkali together with her little brother and joined the labour corps.

As I could guess from the syphilitic ulcers all over her body, she had to sell not only her labour but her body as well. Now she was too weak to work and of no use to any scoundrel. The skin of her little brother was covered all over with scabies which had become foul ulcers.

●

In the background sat Abdul Rehman of Chakoria village. He could not move about, because of ulcerous wounds in the feet. His only child, a six-year old girl, with fever, had gone out to beg and bring some food for the starving father.

I asked Amina Khatun why she had not gone to the Government Destitute Home at Khuruskul or the Relief Hospital at Kalatali. She screamed out:

"Even brothels are better places; in the brothels no one treats you as a vermin, but there they do that. And who told you they give food and medicine there? They don't. They too are goondas and butchers like the rest. They hate us. To them we are bitches and not humans."

The way she said it is in the sketch. As she spoke, Rehman looked away, the little brother cast his eyes down and tried to hold his drooping head with his lean hands.

I had visited the Destitute Home myself and life there looked no better than what I was seeing in front of me.

●

In another corner of the verandah another woman started crying bitterly as I was talking to Amina. I turned aside to sketch her. She was muttering something in between her sobs which interrupted the flow of her words and I could not catch them. She did not answer me at all. Some one said she too came from Moishkali and her husband was a Muslim peasant. She had now gone mad. She had lived for a while in the Government Destitute Home but could not stick it out. She was now only skin and bones, had ulcerous wounds below her breasts and not even a rag to cover her shame. My head reeled as I saw what hunger and humiliation had done to our mothers and sisters of Chittagong and I had to summon every ounce of my strength to be able to continue sketching.

The boy in front looked a horrible sight, with scabies all over and an unduly enlarged spleen, as he went on crying the more I tried to soothe him. He was old enough to be able to tell about himself, yet he could not. The normal wit of a growing child had gone due to what he had suffered. He could beg and he could cry but he could do nothing else. Another destitute told me that his widow-mother had left him in the market place and run away. I was foolish enough to ask, why? I was told in simple words; "Which mother can see her child starve?"

I found not less than 200 destitutes, in a little better or a little worse state than Amina Khatun and Abdul Rehman. I also saw no less than 500 famine-orphans, just like the kids in these sketches, hovering round the military barracks to pick up whatever food was thrown away or whatever charity the soldiers would give.

I was told half a dozen underground brothels are being run by a gang popularly known as 'women-suppliers.'

●

I saw a boy lying dead in the court premises the evening before I left. Enquiries revealed that he was not the first victim of the second famine. Some 20 persons had died of starvation and disease within the municipal limits of this small town, during the last one month alone. And this boy's was the second death I saw in my three days' stay in Cox's Bazar.

I summoned up courage to ask some of the Muslim elders what they proposed to do about the disintegration of life around. They pretended not to understand me.

Shame cannot be the subject of talk with strangers as per bhadrelok code of good manners. I began describing what I had seen with my own eyes.

●

Their talk revolved round two themes, the sinfulness of war-rich contractors and the rottenness and corruption of the Government officials.

But then I would ask point-blank: "Do not the common people, you and me have a duty to help and save our neighbours, our own flesh and blood?" They would become speechless and try to look away, as Rehman did when Amina spoke out. People had stopped thinking. Those who were not yet driven into the Labour Corps or into the ranks of the destitutes had put on blinkers to be able to live their own individual lives without getting a splitting headache thinking of the human misery all around.

At Cox's Bazar, I saw what happens to national morale in conditions of crisis and suffering when an alien Government rules and the patriots only find fault with each other as has been happening in the country ever since the war broke out. People's morale collapses, even civilised social instincts become dull if not dead.

Chittaprosad 24 July 44 Cox's Bazar

REGD No.B. 4677

People's War

FIGURE 2.1. *Chittaprosad, "Life behind the Front Lines," leaf from People's War, 24 September 1944. Source: P. C. Joshi Collections. Courtesy of Archives on Contemporary History, Dr. B. R. Ambedkar Central Library, JNU, New Delhi.*

In a short piece titled "Chhobir Sankat" ("Crisis of Art"), which appeared in the CPI periodical *Arani* in October 1943, soon after the publication of the IPTA bulletin, Chittaprosad described art as the carrier of the social mind and a weapon for society, which, he noted, must become society's "agitator and organizer."[1] The artist as agitator and organizer carried the distinct air of Stalin's call for writers and artists to become the "engineers of the soul,"[2] Chittaprosad himself alluding to this statement in his (unfinished) autobiography as "the most valid and most well defined definition of an artist's responsibilities and his scope in human history."[3] Chittaprosad's rhetoric also resonated with an ethics of anti-fascist cultural renaissance and a critical realism sharpened with the new ideologically accentuated vocabularies of the CPI circulating in its periodicals and reports—culture as *front*, art as *weapon*, artists as *cultural workers*, and touring collectives of performers as *cultural squads*. Years later, in the early 1940s, Chittaprosad would reassert this mission as a Communist artist: "I was forced by circumstances to turn my brush into as sharp a weapon as I could make it . . . not only my weapon or not only artists [*sic*] self-expression, but fundamentally . . . a weapon of his whole society, which includes himself, self-expression of his fellow beings to whom he belongs."[4]

Chittaprosad's expressionistic sketches of hunger, alienation, and resistance echo a host of twentieth-century graphic art that grappled with the horrors of war, famine, and resistance. Collated without accompanying texts, such images of hunger and displacement could have been the wordless woodcut novels of an artist like Frans Masreel[5]; laid side by side, they could resemble the expressionistic march of war and destruction in Li Sewen's epic post–World War II visuals in *The Parade*.[6] Chittaprosad himself saw in his works echoes of Francisco Goya, Georges Rouault, and Käthe Kollwitz.[7] The socialist realist accent in Chittaprosad's works not only distinguishes them from those of his contemporaries in India, but suggests, more importantly, a radical (re)-framing of socialist realism in the colony.

While works of artist-cadres like Chittaprosad displayed an indelible Communist *partiinost*—the socialist realist value of what is "tendentious art," or party-ness[8]—the patronage of socialist realism in the colony carries its own paradoxical form. Socialist realism, as György Lukács had noted, "is a possibility rather than an actuality."[9] As a "revolutionary romanticist" aesthetic, socialist realism was meant to capture both "the pathos of creating a new society and what urges them on," the artist being able to, in effect, "perceive the beauty and poetry of that reality."[10] If socialist realism is about the promise and beauty of a socialist future, how is this page from *People's War* socialist realist? In its portrayal of disintegration, it suggests more expressionistic realism from Weimar Germany than a Soviet realism of an idealized future "in its revolutionary development," as Maxim Gorky had described at the Soviet Writers' Congress in 1934.[11] This tension is, however, a peculiar feature that constitutes "socialist realism across shores" as much as the circulation of communist ideology or political imperatives in the late-colony.[12] Though this idiom would change after the war, in Chittaprosad's own works and in those of his fellow artist-cadres, it is worthwhile to note here this late-colonial nuance in socialist framing, where a peculiar *refraction* of global concepts takes place through located triggers, in this case the Bengal famine.

To understand socialist realism in Indian art, and trace its peculiar formations of partisanship, one needs to rethink the global via the localizations of "located imaginations." Socialist revolution was an imaginary space, a "horizon of expectations" in Reinhardt Koselleck's terms,[13] and pages from *People's War* and *People's Age* were unique in both reflecting and constructing these horizons. The scales of the local, the national, and the global were consciously brought together within such frames of visual reportage, to produce a sense of struggle and solidarity *across frontiers*. This new visual scape of internationalism emerged through reporting from "multiple fronts"—the war, anti-fascist resistance, peasant congresses, famine victims, and cultural tours of the communist fronts—as well as creating multiple fronts for "seeing" resistance. There was a production of a conscious partisan subjectivity in artists, and what can be seen as their *active authorship* of socialist self-fashioning—not in manifestos but in field notes, diary entries, and eventually (fragmented) autobiographies. Such socialist subjectivities were also new modes of transnational affiliations, *beyond* the limits of nationalism, and carried particular forms of negotiations with the category of (political) art itself. I turn here to the structures that contained and defined this "active partisanship" of artist-cadres like Chittaprosad.

AS "AGITATOR AND ORGANIZER"

When P. C. Joshi became the general secretary of the CPI in 1935, he had to face the task of consolidating different factions of the left in order to establish the credibility of the party in national politics. Despite the official ban of the CPI in 1934, the party under Joshi used its underground years to build up connections at the grassroots level and through direct association with socialist elements within the national movement. After the German attack on the Soviet Union on June 22, 1941, Communist politics in India was rocked by a dilemma, caught between support for the Allied war effort in defense of the Soviet Union and the compulsions of national politics that demanded resistance to the imperial war effort. By December 1941, the CPI had ruptured the 1937 Anti-Imperialist United Front with the INC to pledge support for the Allied war effort under the new political rubric of "People's War." In 1941–42, Japanese bombing on the eastern borders of Bengal made anti-fascist resistance a political reality, and the CPI set about mobilizing the peasantry through the activists of the All India Kisan Sabha (the peasants' congress formed earlier in 1936) and local cadres of the party, much along the lines of the Chinese model. In June 1942, the colonial government legalized the CPI, although it remained under government vigil for its advocacy of peasant militancy, with the government accusing the Communists time and again of misusing the right to function in public.[14]

By declaring the war to be the people's resistance against international fascism, Joshi sought to connect India's struggle to larger international currents, and the journal *People's War* became a forum for the circulation of news on worldwide anti-fascist movements, featuring the People's Republic of China, the Soviet Union, Bulgaria, France, and others, with widely circulated pamphlets like "The Indian Communist Party, Its Policy and Work in the War of Liberation" attempting to collapse anti-imperialism and anti-fascism into one.[15] In July 1942, Joshi had launched *People's War* (the regional edition in Bengali was *Janayuddha* or *LokYudh* in Hindi) as a forum for popularizing the new party line. In national politics, the People's War line did not go down well with a people charged with anti-British nationalist sentiments, particularly explosive after the Quit India movement launched by M. K. Gandhi in August 1942.[16] The party earned considerable unpopularity when it abstained from supporting the Quit India movement, and its pro-Soviet policies, attacked as anti-nationalist, had to be defended and popularized to sustain a national role for the Communists.

Yet, despite this difficult political positioning, CPI membership soared, from only 4,000 in 1942, to 15,000 in May 1943, 53,000 in mid-1946, and more than 100,000 at the time of the Second Party Conference in February 1948.[17] This result reflected the effectiveness of alternative strategies that the party developed to increase its social reach and motivate its grassroots cadres still working with nationalist sentiments of the United Front days before 1941. Historians have observed a "locality-specific," three-pronged strategy: in East Bengal, where the threat of Japanese attack was strongest, the party followed a defined anti-fascist line; in the Midnapore district, which had been a nationalist stronghold since the early 1900s, the CPI abstained from a direct pro-war mobilization; and in north Bengal, where the party had already gathered a support base through the grassroots anti-*hattola* (taxes levied by landlords in weekly markets) movement, particularly among sharecroppers and small peasants, the mobilization for land reforms continued.[18]

The political logic of combining anti-imperialism with anti-fascism in a new rhetoric of "cultural front" was critical to the party's visibility and popular outreach. It served to create an alternative national forum wherein the CPI could harness the anti-fascist, pro-Soviet sentiments of the intelligentsia—despite many of them remaining non-Communist—and orchestrate a cultural resistance that became integral to its politics in the 1940s. The anti-fascist program of the party also became a recruiting ground for "cultural workers," among them the new artist-cadres, pursued by Joshi most actively between 1942 and 1948.

Both Chittaprosad and Somnath Hore came from Chittagong, an

eastern district that was exposed directly to the Japanese bombing in 1941. In their memoirs, both mention that their first exposure to the CPI came through their political involvement as students, or their association with revolutionary terrorists in Chittagong or the activists of the Bengal Provincial Kisan Sabha. The connection that these artists and the CPI shared with political extremists at the grassroots level is significant. In Bengal, disillusionment with both Gandhian nonviolence and a culture of political extremism had brought within the party's fold many erstwhile Gandhites and revolutionaries who had ties to both the National Congress and grassroots peasant networks. As a graduate student, Chittaprosad had been involved with student activism and had friends among the revolutionaries of the Chittagong Armoury Raid.[19] In 1941–42, he became associated with the party in Chittagong through his early apprenticeship in making anti-fascist posters. In his autobiography, he recalled the "red-letter day" when an underground peasant volunteer demanded of him "primarily as an artist . . . in the name of freedom and progress, an active support in rousing and uniting the people against the Jap-invasion."[20] His recollection of this first encounter with the party carries a zealous affirmation of his "call" to turn his brush into a "mighty weapon," a romantic avowal of the political mission of art that stayed with him all his life.[21] Asked by the party to make posters for a future peasant conference, Chittaprosad noted that he did not "write" the posters, but instead painted them in "tempera and wash . . . with words and letters playing all [*sic*] insignificant or even no role in some cases"; these carried "his experiments in form and style," and formed his new "Indian Art" with "themes of horrors of war and fascism and of valor and heroism."[22]

Chittaprosad's posters were exhibited in traveling exhibitions in the villages surrounding the Arakan Road linking Chittagong with the borders of the Arakan, and became a part of "Anti-Fascist Volunteer Units of peasants and villagers for self-defence,"[23] and also the "All-India Defend Chittagong" campaign week from June 19 to 25, 1943, for which he made anti-Japanese resistance posters for *The Student*, the mouthpiece of the All India Students Federation (AISF) in Chittagong. Such posters were often displayed alongside subversive

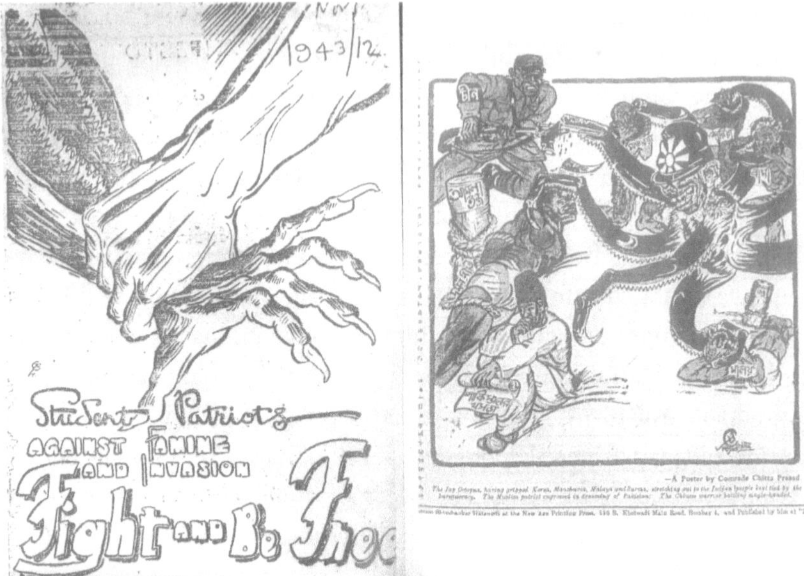

FIGURE 2.2. *Chittaprosad, Antiwar cartoons published in political pamphlets of the CPI. Source: P. C. Joshi Collections. Courtesy of Archives on Contemporary History, Dr. B. R. Ambedkar Central Library, JNU, New Delhi.*

works of peasant artists, like decorated ritual plates with new motifs of peasants' houses and families being destroyed by Japanese bombing[24] or sharecroppers killing landlords, instead of the traditional images of gods and goddesses.[25] His posters were particularly critical in the modes in which he combined the food crisis of 1942–43 with imperialism and capitalism, merging activism around the famine with the anti-invasion politics that preceded it. In particular, he would develop complex metaphors for making "visual connections" between imperialism and fascism—war and hunger—in ways that were not possible in political action. See, for instance, the tableau (fig. 2.2) with two such posters featuring anthropomorphic imageries: "Jap Octopus—Hindus and Muslims of Chittagong unite to resist the Japs" (in the May 23, 1942, issue of *People's War*, before he had formally joined the party), and the pamphlet cover for the manifesto of the All India Students Federation held at Bombay, November 25–30, 1943: "Student Patriots against Famine and Invasion—Fight and Be Free."

Chittaprosad was soon noticed by the police, and on a few occasions his posters were torn down and he was asked to leave Chittagong; he also recalls being sheltered from the police in these years of volunteer work by the "peasants and village folk" of the bombed regions. When his posters were displayed at a peasants' conference at Dhalghat Rangamati, Joshi took note of them and soon after that, Chittaprosad was absorbed into the party office in Calcutta. He joined the CPI formally in 1942. Within the next few years, he would become an integral part of the Anti-Fascist Writers' and Artists' Association, the Indian People's Theatre Association, and the official organs of the party in Bombay and Bengal. In 1943, he was taken to the headquarters of the Communist Party in Bombay.[26] The Bombay office was the center of the cultural front, with an entire staff of artists, performers, photographers, and writers assembled by Joshi. Chittaprosad became the artist-reporter, probably the first in India to combine on-the-ground research, political reporting, and visual arts. As a CPI cultural worker, he would go on extensive tours of the country, documenting peasant movements, workers' strikes, peasant conferences, political agitations, and most important of all, the wartime Bengal Famine of 1943.

Somnath Hore, beginning with a similar trajectory of making posters for local party cadres, came in touch with the CPI in 1940–41, when the party was still underground. In his brief autobiographical piece, Hore, younger than Chittaprosad and later his apprentice in the party, mentions how in Chittagong a whole generation of anti-British terrorists turned communist, "full of wonder at what the Russian Revolution accomplished."[27] Connections between the party and erstwhile revolutionary terrorists went back to the mid-1930s, boosted by the release of many of the revolutionary fighters from prison. Hore's early anti-fascist posters were handwritten in ink and brush, and put up by party workers in various parts of Calcutta, including its industrial outskirts. Forced to leave Calcutta under economic duress, he remained in close contact with the party cadres in Chittagong, and his posters were hung regularly, in marketplaces, shops, and trees, to create awareness of the imperialist war and later of the party's new slogan, "People's War."[28] During the Bengal famine of 1943, his ties with the CPI were consolidated, and he was made a full-timer overnight, working under Chittaprosad to document and report on the famine from the afflicted areas.

In 1945, Hore was spotted by P. C. Joshi, and at Joshi's behest was admitted to the Government School of Art in Calcutta, where he came under the mentorship of the academic realist artist Zainul Abedin, who in the early 1940s had become one of the youngest instructors at the art school (and would go on to be the most iconic artist of post-partition East Pakistan). It was as a graduate novice from the art school that Hore was sent by the party to North Bengal in 1946 to document the peasant struggle for *tebhaga* (demand of the sharecroppers for two-thirds of the crop produce in place of the usual one-third), the result being his *Tebhaga Diary* (*A Diary from Tebhaga*, 1946).[29] Other artist-cadres, like Mani Roy and Surjo Roy, were art school students expelled for being members of the Communist Party, who went on to work with front organizations like the Youth Cultural Institute (later the Anti-Fascist Writers' and Artists' Association) and later joined the traveling famine exhibitions of the IPTA Cultural Squad.[30] For another life-long communist artist, Debabrata Mukhopadhyay, working on such visual reportage for the party was a continuation of his fascination with traveling across the country and sketching people at work.[31] During the early 1940s, the party was also attracting artists from the district committees who would complement "the more famous images of Com. Chittaprosad, pictures brought from the Soviet Union."[32]

In Calcutta, the People's War line of the CPI was popularized through a network of periodicals that were either CPI organs or informally tied to the cultural movement. The ideological transformation of the critical review journal *Parichoy* under the new pro-CPI editors, Hiran Sanyal and Gopal Haldar, made it a forum for discourse around the left-wing cultural movement. However, *Parichoy* was limited to the publication of reviews of books and essays, and while it carried a regular cultural review section, written mainly by the party cultural theorist Gopal Haldar, there were none of the illustrations that had come to dominate party organs like *People's War* and *People's Age* (or the Bengal edition, *Janayuddha*). Somnath Lahiri, the party secretary in Bengal, started the Bengali periodical *Swadhinata* directly after the Second World War[33] and built up a team of young journalists and artists who were asked specifically to develop the emotive content behind peasant movements like the Tebhaga struggle.[34] While *People's War* and *People's Age* carried sketches and reports by artist-cadres like Chittaprosad, a periodical like *Arani* (1942–48), under the editorship of the journalist Satyendranath Mazumdar, featured new activist writings on art and socialism, emphasizing art's political commitment to *ganasilpa* (people's art), as well as detailed reports on various "fronts" of the movement—the war, students' movement, workers and peasants' congresses and strikes, as well as the cultural conferences of the Anti-Fascist Writers' and Artists' Association.

The famine provided a critical juncture for the political role of the CPI, particularly during a period of relative unpopularity due to the pro-war party line. Since the party was unable to launch a direct offensive against the colonial government because of its official support for the imperialist war effort, cultural opposition to capitalist accretion and profiteering—which were seen as active causes of the famine—was politically crucial for the party. Indeed, the famine of 1943 should be seen as the single determining factor in the integration of visual imagery with the development of left-wing cultural activism in India. For the CPI, it became the front line for mobilizing support, membership, and social action through relief work. The CPI founded the People's Relief Committee (PRC), not only as a significant agent in the party's relief work but as a harness to bind relief efforts and cultural activism together. The IPTA, formed alongside the PRC, provided an active mobile resonance, with the "IPTA cultural squads" ("central squads" after 1945) traveling to villages, factories, and small towns.

Famine relief was intertwined with the rhetoric of grassroots popular heroism, and famine reportage generated layered narratives that combined journalistic text with performative and visual representations of hunger, rural displacement, and destitution in the streets of Calcutta and the suburban towns. *People's War* became a forum for commissioning the artist-cadres and party photographers to produce visual reportage from the famine-affected districts. In a unique step undertaken by Joshi, an appeal was issued by the party organs inviting sketches and photographs of the famine, which would be published or exhibited by the party to create platforms for generating popular consciousness and relief funds. Mani Roy, for instance, was commissioned by the PRC to tour Dacca and Mymensingh and send back images of his encounters with famine victims.[35] In 1944, Chittaprosad was operating out of the CPI headquarters in Bombay, and under his tutelage younger artists such as Somnath Hore were also being trained as artist-reporters of the famine. Alongside artists, photographers like Sunil Janah were active documenters of the famine, with the more immediate and radical truth quotient of disaster photography; sharing broadsheet space with Chittaprosad's sketches, photographs, and drawings, Janah's photo documentation of the famine produced a visual agenda for famine activism.[36]

With his detailed reports from the affected districts, Chittaprosad was evidently the prime artist-reporter of the party, although Mani Roy and Somnath Hore also contributed occasional sketches. Alongside images by these artist-cadres, CPI organs like *People's War* and *Janayuddha* also contained drawings and linocuts from art-school artists like Sudhir Ranjan Khastagir, Muralidhar Tali, Rathin Maitra, and most importantly, the intensely moving famine drawings of Zainul Abedin, which we will arrive at in the following chapter. This was part of a conscious drive by the party to invite famine works by "non-party" artists, which can be seen as an effort to create artistic linkages across ideological lines. The *People's War* volumes of 1943–44, in particular, carry works by non-party artists, accompanied often by features *on* the artists themselves, and never under reportage—much unlike the artist-cadres themselves.[37] Zainul Abedin, for instance, was championed by the party as an itinerant famine artist; the party organized his first exhibition of famine sketches in 1944, and Chittaprosad wrote a feature on him in *People's War*.[38]

The images produced by artist-cadres from the 1940s were, in fact, directly connected to the party agenda from the People's War phase (1941–45), and thereafter to its renewed involvement in anti-imperialist, anti-capitalist mass movements after the war, when the CPI actively propagated and programmed "popular" art, as reflected in the post-1945 socialist realist iconography of Chittaprosad. In approaching the corpus of imagery generated by the artist-cadres in the 1940s, two distinct periods can be identified: the first, between 1942 and 1945, corresponded to the wartime People's War policy of the CPI and the famine of 1943; the second, between 1945 and 1948, corresponded to the party's postwar return to agitational politics, when it actively participated in popular resistance, such as the peasant struggles in Tebhaga and Telengana, and industrial strikes.

ART "BEHIND FRONT LINES"

Chittaprosad was commissioned to tour famine-affected districts of Bengal in the summer months of 1944, and his investigative reports form some of the earliest ground reviews and grassroots reportage on the famine in the Indian press. Throughout 1944 and 1945, he produced a substantial body of sketches on the trail of the hunger, displacement, and pestilence that the famine unleashed across rural Bengal. His visual work, published in serialized weekly reports in *People's War* beginning in the summer of 1944, was populated by uprooted villagers, deserted villages, parched landscapes, hospitals, orphanages, and relief kitchens, as well as hoarders, black marketeers, and relief workers. The landscapes he drew bore marks of the recent cyclone and accompanying flood, with villages turning into disintegrating ruins. His reportage from the "front lines" (see fig. 2.1) was steeped in a resonant critique of greed, hoarding, black marketeering, government incompetence, and political mismanagement. In 1944, twenty-two sketches from Chittaprosad's tour in the Contai subdivision of the Midnapore district were published along with the journal he kept during the tour. *Hungry Bengal: A Tour through Midnapore District by Chittaprosad, in November 1943* was the first instance of the genre of visual reportage by a political artist in India. Five thousand copies of *Hungry Bengal* were burned by the British government soon after.[39]

Hungry Bengal begins with the image of teeming destitution thronging the streets of Calcutta—"famished, helpless, living skeletons that once formed Bengal's village society, the fishermen, the boatmen, potters, weavers, peasants, whole families of them"[40]—a rupture in the social fabric of rural Bengal, which spilled over into the streets of Calcutta, curdling into sights/sites of hunger, displacement, depravity, and death. Chittaprosad's journey traces the routes of hunger and destitution from the city streets back through the sub-divisional towns and into the famine-hit villages. His narrative is built up with reports and interviews. All along his bus journey, he recorded huddled, destitute families along the road, shelters for the homeless, and makeshift hospitals being constructed. He encountered profiteers, black marketeers, politicians, and bureaucrats, along with uprooted villagers, emaciated orphans, prostitutes, the robbed, the dying, and unattended corpses. He reported from clusters of displaced families in the towns, from the village markets selling everything but rice, from the crowded stalls of goldsmiths and brassware with long queues of villagers selling off their belongings, even sacred idols, and from the equally crowded stalls of the District Sub Registrar Office, where hundreds of land transfer deeds were being registered daily in exchange for paddy. These reports were matched with parallel sketches in black ink, including extensive notes on his subjects and locations scribbled in the margins or on the reverse side.[41] The diary also mentions the considerable difficulties he had to face as a "Communist reporter"; these trials were emblematic for him of the efforts of the party's grassroots work and commitment. While *Hungry Bengal* forms a part of a corpus of famine literature, it also comes to us as a representative document of Communist politics during the famine years, steeped in the visual ethic that the party instituted around famine reportage.[42]

Chittaprosad's famine victims were, however, not an undifferentiated mass of victimhood merely illustrating the textual corpus on the famine. He annotated his characters, giving active identities to his subjects, the text and the image working together to produce a new kind of visual reportage with an active corporeal identity. The singularity that he carved out for his individual subjects comes through, for instance, in a sketch from June 1944, where the artist describes his subject—a starving villager from the district of Hooghly:

> This is hungry, disease-ridden and almost naked Rabi Raut, a kisan boy of Kadamdanga village, Balagor, Hooghly district. He has three younger brothers and a sister, all bed-ridden through malaria, scabies and cough, and a father, who is in a dying condition, also through malaria. The mother begs for the entire family—they go without food two or even three days in a week. One old man said to me about them: "They can neither sit nor sleep, only keep standing—there is the nuisance of flies, having hardly rags to cover themselves with. Formerly these young kids could cry, but now they cannot even do that."[43]

This sensibility of destitution and suspended subjects is key to Chittaprosad's famine sketches. What these sketches capture is not only the moment of complete erasure but also the shock of dislocation. In his autobiography, Chittaprosad reflected on the minds of the victims he encountered—uprooted villagers thronging relief camps, hospitals, orphanages, and streets in the towns and in Calcutta, fully conscious of not being beggars till being forced by hunger to sell their land, their possessions, their bodies: "and they died . . . one and all of them, with a firm hope that they would survive the onslaught and return to their old life at the end."[44] The drawings were made in thick, concave lines that mark out fissures and furrows in emaciated bodies. The artist captures the postures and gazes of his subjects, at times interviewing them, and the annotated images reveal this rawness and immediacy of his drawings. A physiognomy of hunger and depletion emerges through such images, as well as the aura of the loss of human dignity. The psychological element in the drawings integrates artistic imagination and empathy with investigation, moving beyond the immediate denotative element of journalistic illustration.

In its sheer visual resonances, the Bengal famine of 1943 impacted artists and writers in Bengal like no previous event, resulting in a substantial body of literary and art works. While artists across the board responded to the famine in their compositions, what makes the location of an artist like Chittaprosad interesting is his commission as the party reporter, a part of the artist-cadres that traveled with IPTA cultural squads. The drawings made in the course of his travels were done in ink on cheap paper, in stark contrasts of black and white that not only supported speedy execution but also brought out the ragged edges and ruptures that marked bodies wrecked by hunger and displacement. On some occasions, he would have to fill in the drawings with color at the party office, but more often than not, the images remained black and white. Responding to his immediate project of active documentation, an artist-reporter like Chittaprosad is left with little room for significant stylistic experiments: the form had to be realistic, the appeal popular, and more importantly, the process of production brisk. Operating within the evident technical limitations of journalistic drawing, he pushed his drawings of emaciation toward a new figuration of grotesque realism, aware as he was of his specific location as an artist-cadre, charged with a conscious voice of representing the famished, as well as transforming the identity of art itself. His famine drawings, he would note later, made him realize the significance of graphic techniques, which he had started picking up alongside his proficiency in the medium of pen and ink and the practical usefulness of swift pencil sketches.[45]

The famine years formed the core of an aesthetic radicalism that the CPI was adopting in its cultural intervention in the 1940s. Officially supporting the Allied war effort, Communist critique of the British government in India was couched in a policy of "no-strikes," and could express itself chiefly through relief work and famine activism rather than active revolt. This was to change in the postwar years, when liaisons of culture and politics could be fleshed out with sharper political edges. Post-1945, the party was geared for rapid action not only in the popular movements but also in cultural production, where the audience and viewership that had been harnessed during the famine years could now be accessed to develop a vocabulary of protest art. As the freedom struggle in India was entering its final phase (1945–47), the CPI articulated a policy of direct resistance, supporting mass movements, strikes, and popular rebellion to the fullest. In a review of the political character of the postwar period, the Resolution of the Central Committee of the CPI, passed at its meeting in December 1945, stated the programmatic slogans of the party in the changed context.[46] Championing the urge for freedom in the "common people" in the "final bid for power," the CPI sought to present itself as the organizer and the agitator of the masses irrespective of sectarian politics: "The main strength of the party derives from its being the organizer of whatever working class and peasant movements exist in our country, which are the living embodiments of the joint organizations of Hindu and Muslim masses and constitute the mass democratic base of the party."[47]

The projected targets were now the colonial government, the British and national bourgeoisie, the profiteering merchants and black marketeers, as well as feudal structures in the countryside. This political agenda of the CPI as the custodian and organizer of the "popular" is a necessary backdrop to studying the repertoire of images generated by artist-cadres between 1945 and 1947. The rhetoric of direct contact and grassroots reportage also changed, as artist-cadres were encouraged to actively accommodate and address revolutionary agency in the masses.

In 1946, this shift in the cultural line of the CPI was evident, particularly when the Tebhaga movement began in north Bengal, followed soon by the Telengana struggle in Andhra Pradesh. Somnath Hore was a second-year graduate student at the Government School of Art in Calcutta when he was asked by the Communist Party to visit Dinajpur and Rangpur—districts in northern Bengal where the Tebhaga movement was brewing. The Tebhaga issues had to do with the recurring demand of the *adhiars* (sharecroppers) to retain a two-thirds share of the produce, and thereby to gain a reduction in the rent that they paid to the *jotedars*—a class of rich farmers who claimed rights on one-half to one-third of the sharecroppers' produce. The movement has been described as the "outgrowth of left-wing mobilization of the rural masses . . . the first *consciously* attempted revolt by a politicized peasantry in Indian history."[48] Traveling to North Bengal with a Kisan Sabha activist, Hore observed the movement through the eyes of a young cadre full of enthusiasm and faith in the promise of revolution; the diary he kept, *Tebhaga Diary*, is representative of the shift in the party line during the postwar period. In his sketches, it is clear that he is grappling with the visualization of a "revolutionary folk," portraying individual sharecroppers, peasant activists and comrades, peasant congregations and processions, collective harvesting, and, more importantly, the landscape of protest—paddy fields strewn with the red flags of the CPI and with *lathis* (bamboo sticks) as symbols of peasant resistance—resounding with a collective euphoria of harvesting and resisting the landholders' appropriation. Together, these images evoke an artist-reporter drawing out a revolutionary landscape, populated with agents and activists. Sketched on the spot, they reveal not merely visual "facts" through direct contact, but also the grassroots presence and visibility of the party. The significant part of the reportage was the equation it drew between the revolutionary agency of the sharecroppers and the CPI cadres and volunteers present in the region. The disillusionment that would surface with the suppression of the movement at the turn of the year is not visible in this 1946 diary, which remains even now a document of revolutionary mobilization.[49] A similar repertoire can be seen in Hore's *Tea-Garden Journal*, where the artist sketched grassroots resistance in the tea gardens of north Bengal.[50]

Aware of their primary responsibility as artist-reporters, Chittaprosad and Somnath Hore shared a high level of political commitment in their art practice. While in terms of Communist ideology, such commitment in the 1940s could have been half-baked for an artist like Hore, who was still a novice, what remained pronounced was a deep critical engagement with the human predicament, an empathy that was integrated by the party in generating this genre of iconography. Through Chittaprosad's encounters with his subjects during his famine tours over the course of two years, the act of sketching itself became a mode of "participating" in their struggle, his memoirs recalling his sense of empathy and commitment to recording their experience. It can be argued that the rhetoric of "direct contact" was drawn from the example of Chinese anti-Japanese resistance, regular reports of which were visible in the pages of *People's War*. In May 1942, speaking at the Yenan Conference on the problems of art and literature in China's Liberation War, Mao Zhedong, the Communist leader of Liberation China, had urged the cultural workers of the party "to participate in the actual struggle of the workers, peasants, and soldiers; and to portray and educate them." Mao's speeches at Yenan, reproduced serially in *People's War*, stressed the need for "real" contact, echoing his call "to investigate, to observe, to study, and to analyze the various personalities, the different classes, the various social groups, and the various active forms of life and struggle."[51] The method of weaving grassroots experience into art production—the integration of the "study process with the creative process"—was an active pedagogical, as well as visual, ideology set in motion by the party through these documentation commissions to artists.[52]

The genre of famine reportage, as well as commissions like Somnath Hore's *Tebhaga Diary*, circulated a rhetoric of reporting "truth" through images, with an evidentiary status and impulse of emotive mobilization, drawing the reader into the scene as an indirect witness of the truth of misery. While famines in colonial India had been depicted visually from the early nineteenth century onward in documentary, illustrational, and satirical pieces in periodicals, they were mainly captured in official government photographs, drawn by European artists, or produced by British officers in colonial anthropological works such as the *People of India* series. The pages of *People's War* were different. They created an entirely different optic, that of an artist and a colonial subject walking the famine-struck streets of urban Calcutta. The traveling artist became the projected image of a committed worker in quest of the "true" representation of reality. These marked at the same time a radical shift from art's social content to a "socialist" content, framed *within* the ideological grids of party organs like *People's War* and *People's Age*, or their vernacular editions across India. Direct contact and artistic commitment were actively intertwined in the practice and discourse around these images, combining realism and politics more vividly than ever, and adding a connotative element to their otherwise documentary roles. The "form" of socialist realism in the late-colony needs to be read within this political and moral landscape of visual reportage, where expressionist imageries of hunger shared space with mobilization of grassroots, both charting in their own ways the raw trails of late colonialism—in its reality as well as its potentiality. Those who, like Chittaprosad, served as both artists and reporters experienced a split sense of practice and commitment, creating a tension between the dual roles in which they were engaged; as he commented, "I started for a wide sweep of a tour round all the districts of Bengal, beginning with Chittagong, of course; and I started it with the full awareness of the urgency and responsibilities and problems including my own limitations of my primary purpose as a reporter of the famine; but I was fully self-conscious as an Indian artist too."[53]

Chittaprosad noted being aware of the possibilities of developing a fresh iconography of cultural activism outside the "moral and formal abstractions" or the "individual formal mannerisms" of his contemporaries, "particularly those who could avoid any *direct contact* [emphasis mine] with the famine victims."[54] In his critique of the reduction of the grotesqueness of the famine to an "idea," his reference, albeit unnamed and indirect, to Nandalal Bose's iconic famine painting of an emaciated Shiva—the Hindu god of destruction—dancing as his goddess consort holds up the world's bowl of rice, cannot be missed. While the technical mastery of the artist concerned still brought critical acclaim to this painting, Chittaprosad felt that such artists were reducing famine victims to "performers of ghastly and ridiculous tricks," often in a zeal for social realism, while succumbing to the "very elementary weaknesses which must be consciously overcome by artists who desire to succeed as social realists in Art."[55]

Yet it is this conflicted situation of being both an artist and a political worker, engaged at once in direct documentation and contemplated form-making, that sharpens the historical location of these artist-cadres. In the postwar period, Chittaprosad charted a new genre of political art, one that was removed from the documentary tropes of famine reportage and was keen on experimental figurations of labor, resistance, and utopic revolutionary socialism. The new phase matched a defined shift in the political mandate of the CPI. Chittaprosad began exploring more "aestheticized" embodiments of resistance—activated not merely by direct contact but by conscious artistic explorations into visualizing a body politic—producing an active political figuration hitherto unseen in Indian art. This was a new stage of socialist figuration, one that developed in dialogue with nationalism, but transcended its boundaries in multiple internationalist affiliations—harnessed to Afro-Asian anti-imperialist solidarities as much as to transnational working-class resistance.

A sketchbook by Chittaprosad, made in 1943 and published by the Delhi Art Gallery, illustrates this distinct global self-staging. With a frontispiece carrying the slogan "Freedom, Peace, Progress," "Presented to the Commune NHQ, CPI" on the occasion of "Lenin Day" in Calcutta, the book contained simple sketches of Communist figures.[56] What is striking, however, is the range; starting from Marx, Lenin, Engels, and Mao Zhedong, Chittaprosad seems to have created visual profiles spanning the Comintern: party general secretaries, generals of the Red Army, poets, as well as figures of the left in Britain, France, and Spain, alongside his own comrades and friends within the CPI. This was a visual scape of the transnational horizons of left-wing internationalism, a sign of the more concrete socialist affiliations of his art post-1945.

ART "NATIONAL IN FORM, SOCIALIST IN CONTENT"

The art that brought artist-cadres like Chittaprosad to public attention was one of rupture, hunger, and destitution, yet in the postwar period there was a shift in these artists' work toward revolutionary and utopic visions of labor, plentitude, and resistance, which introduced a definite idiom of socialist realism in Indian art, and a new figurative form attuned to visualizations of labor *in action*. In a series of charcoal sketches, linocuts, posters, and political cartoons from the post-1945 period, Chittaprosad depicted strikes, peasant movements, popular agitation, and official repression. In a mélange of the nationalist populism and anti-fascist artistic realism of the Popular Front era, these images express a full-bodied socialist realism with a new visual ethic of utopic revolutionary figuration, which had been suggested by the manifestos and speeches from the platforms of the Progressive Writers' Association in the late 1930s, but never fully realized in visual art until the mid-1940s.

The artistic method of socialist realism had been introduced officially in 1934 at the Soviet Writers' Congress, presided over by Maxim

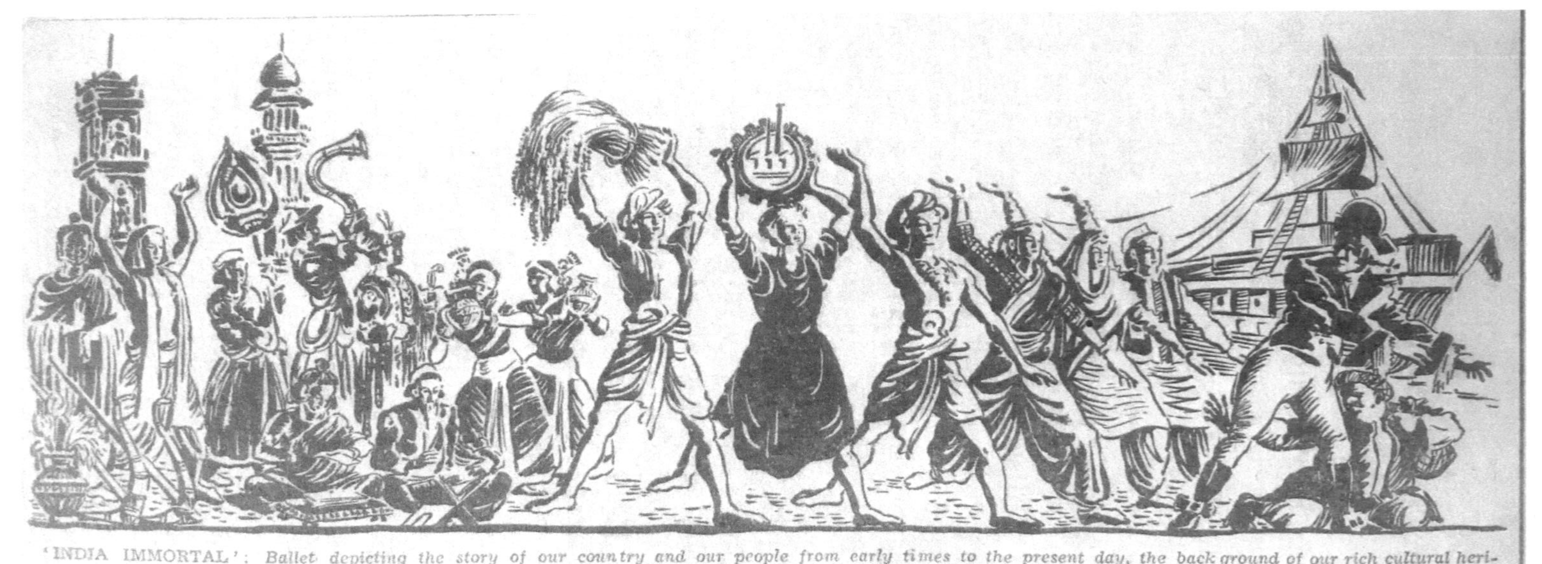

FIGURE 2.3. *Chittaprosad, Panel for India Immortal, People's Age, 6 January 1946. Source: P. C. Joshi Collections. Courtesy of Archives on Contemporary History, Dr. B. R. Ambedkar Central Library, JNU, New Delhi.*

Gorky, A. A. Zhdanov, and Karl Radek. It demanded of the artist "a true and historically concrete depiction of reality in its revolutionary development," which should then be combined with "the task of educating the workers in the spirit of Communism."[57] In India, where the Communist Party was marginal, and operated under the dominant platform of anti-colonial nationalism, the visual forms and routes of socialist realist art were curious in their *difference*. The celebratory rhetoric that such images embodied and circulated was not only framed by Chittaprosad in mere naturalistic narrative illustrations of revolutionary hope, but also manifested in new modes of expressionistic figuration, with greater attention to the development of politicized bodies than had been possible in his famine images. For Chittaprosad, figuration became a formal tool for creating icons of resistance and resilience, foregrounding the revolutionary potentiality of figures themselves.

In the postwar years, the CPI was formulating, under Joshi's guidance, a cultural vocabulary of a "national front" of revolutionary communion of workers and peasants, Hindus and Muslims, against the imperial British government in India. Chittaprosad echoed this in artistic forms, visualizing the revolutionary agency of the workers, peasants, and cultural workers of the party, in their resistance against not only foreign exploitation but also indigenous merchants, profiteers, and black marketeers. These idioms become active in a poster panel he made for an IPTA ballet, *India Immortal* (fig. 2.3),[58] where he fused symbols of India's cultural diversity and traditional past with the "new national form" of a resurgent popular. *India Immortal* was a part of the annual tour of the Central Dance Troupe of the IPTA, which traveled to Bombay, Calcutta, Asansol, Patna, Kanpur, Delhi, Lahore, and many other smaller towns. Published along with the report of the Central Cultural Squad, Chittaprosad's poster here is a tableau, with three distinguishable spatial divisions. The left corner carries images of Buddha, a Vaishnava saint, a Hindu, and a Muslim priest, with their respective holy texts open in front of them, and behind them, a celebrational procession and women in traditional attires, dancing with the sacred *kalash* (a ritual pitcher, an item that has auspicious symbolism in India). In the far-right corner are two figures almost pushed out of the frame:

a crouching *bania* (traditional Indian merchant class) with a sack and an Englishman, attired in the manner of an East India Company merchant. In between, at the center, forming an interface between the two extremes of the frame, is a row of six men and women, in an almost avant-garde forward movement, poised in a harmonious union; sturdy and confident, one of the men carries a sheaf from the rice harvest, another an emblem of a factory; the three women are reminiscent of cultural performers. Together, their postures are evocative of a ballet; in forward advance, they seem to thwart the activities of the merchants. The background is marked on the left by a traditional chariot (*ratha*)—characteristic of the eastern coast of India—and a mosque, while at the right is the image of a ship, behind the English merchant, probably symbolic of the west coast. This image is, in fact, a plastic counterpart of ideas of the popular that were circulated by the cultural movement in the 1940s. It forms a visual embodiment of what the cultural movement aimed to achieve—a fusion of the national and the popular, with culture at the vanguard. Chittaprosad was the designer and draftsman for IPTA performances. IPTA's *First Bulletin* carried the IPTA logo made by Chittaprosad: a heroic image of a drummer, beating a colossal drum, summoning the people in the villages to come forward and join the ranks of the people's theater.[59] He also designed costumes and composed some of the IPTA songs. While the *First Bulletin* claimed to reinvent art as "a potent force for the creation of [the] future," and addressed directly the "divorce between arts like dancing and painting and the revolutionary *motifs* and attitudes of the masses,"[60] Chittaprosad's sketches and posters for the IPTA ballets and plays like *Spirit of India* and *India Immortal* became plastic versions of the "people's spirit" that IPTA claimed to foster and represent.[61]

In the immediate postwar period, Chittaprosad's sketches in *People's Age* combined socialist imagery with an expressionistic style that towered over the political fault lines of the period. The national/colonial or Hindu/Muslim binaries, for instance, were countered by radical new imageries of worker-peasant, *Mazdoor-Kisan* solidarity. When strikers of the Royal Indian Navy staged a mutiny against the colonial government in Bombay between February 18 and 23, 1946, and the

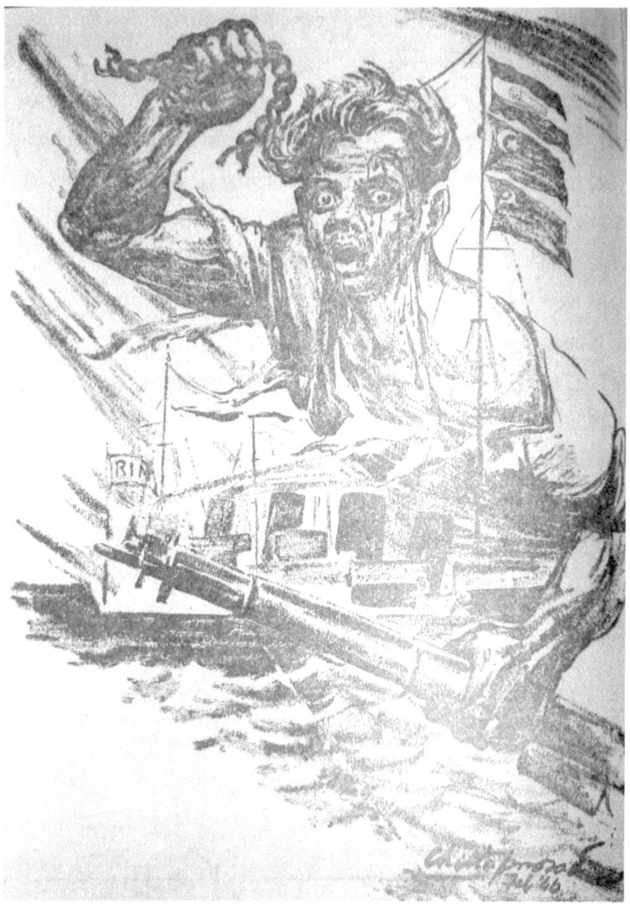

FIGURE 2.4. *Chittaprosad, Wounded Striker, Royal Naval Mutiny (1946), People's Age, 3 March 1946. Source: P. C. Joshi Collections. Courtesy of Archives on Contemporary History, Dr. B. R. Ambedkar Central Library, JNU, New Delhi.*

CPI organized strikes in Bombay and Calcutta in support of the mutiny, Chittaprosad made a set of six sketches, one of which, reproduced in *People's Age* (fig. 2.4), exemplified his new socialist expressionism: a wounded striker, wielding a rifle, rising like a leviathan over the image of the royal navy. The image of the striker's turbulent rise, shattering his fetters, brings forth an element of expressionistic horror, as well as an outburst of popular fury.

Unlike the *Hungry Bengal* sketches, this image is not one of resignation; instead, it captures a moment of revolutionary upsurge. The use of figuration in this and similar images shows the artist developing a corporeality of resistance by evoking a tense fury, embodying agitation not in simplistic illustration but in an accentuated, grotesque realism, evidently expressionistic in tone. Chittaprosad moves beyond the genre of caricature and cartooning in such images, combining satire with the revolutionary address. The projection of a revolutionary utopia in the visualization of working-class resistance in the context of the 1940s in India, particularly through the muscular, angry image of the worker, is significant. It conveys a sense of an uncontained, unrestrained labor in the form of active resistance, and introduces an overtly socialist trope into visual imagination, which in the 1940s had a distinct Stalinist currency—particularly if we consider the enormous influence that the victory of the Red Army had on socialist and communist circles in India. In fact, it is Stalin's idea of an art "socialist in content, national in form" that was pursued by the CPI in its own forays into cultural production during this period.

Central to formulations of socialist realism, noted C. Vaughan James, were principles of *narodnost* (people-ness), *partiinost* (party-ness), and *klassovost* (class-ness), all developed under *ideinost* (an overarching ideological unity)—of communism.[62] Socialist realism was an art of promise that actively combined tropes of productivity, progress, and the heroic triumph of labor. In India, the combination of anti-colonial, anti-imperialist nationalism with the utopic faith in revolutionary socialism that the left-wing cultural movement generated forged a convergence of the notions of the nation and the people, the national and the popular, whereby the vision of the nation's future was reconfigured in terms of popular resurgence and a triumphant populism. In understanding the socialist realist resonances of the works of an artist-cadre like Chittaprosad, this revolutionary potentiality of laboring bodies is noteworthy, particularly in how he transformed an otherwise common genre of portraying a rural everyday, which had been well established since the 1930s. In more "contained" forms, this visualization of the popular was already evident in the Gandhian conceptualization of rural resilience, vivid artistic portrayals of which were seen in Nandalal Bose's Haripura Posters, which celebrated vignettes of everyday life from rural India, apparently unaltered by colonialism. Although this trope recurs in Chittaprosad, what evidently demarcated the two visualizations of the popular were not figurative idioms or even ideological differences between the Gandhian Nandalal Bose and a Communist artist, but the rhetoric of popular agency. In Chittaprosad's works, rural bodies join those of the urban resistance and working-class struggle to generate a new active popular consciousness in art.

This sense of *narodnost*—an active agency of the people, often in its utopic dimensions—was combined in the works of artist-cadres with the language of "uncompromising realism" that the PWA had called for in the late 1930s, albeit primarily in literature. It resonated with "progressive" demands for developing a specific approach to the portrayal of the masses, one that would convey material content in all its "ruggedness without embellishments and unnecessary insistence on form and technique"—a direct valorization of content *sans* artistic romance.[63] For Raghupati Sahai ("Firaq"), an Urdu poet in the PWA, Gandhian politics had already discredited an earlier notion of culture as "emotional, mystic, intellectual," in favor of "the concrete, the actual, the realistic." [64] The pulsating presence of the masses at the forefront of political action sought to introduce "new content" and a materialistic, realistic emphasis in culture. Firaq saw in this regeneration a "new renaissance" of Indian art, "a new creative simplicity, marked by mass character, mass content and mass purposiveness"—one that would be "socialist in content, national in form,"[65] with the entry of the people into political and cultural frames. By the mid-1940s, during a wider turn to a more concretized socialist ideology, this popular consciousness transformed itself into a utopic figuration, the *partiinost* and the *ideinost* taking over the visualization of the "people" more actively.

This change was sharper in the utopic images of popular resistance that Chittaprosad produced for *People's Age* during 1946–47, where a defined folk turn in figuration marked the visualization of a utopic future. In his *India in Revolt* series of twelve panel sketches, made for the Independence Day issue of *People's Age*, this stylized imagery unfolded not in the realist idiom but in a folk-ornamental figuration with the illustrational function of depicting various stages of promise, struggle, and triumph in the popular rebellions from 1920 to 1946.[66] This stylized radical popular iconography becomes sharper in Chittaprosad's series of drawings on the Telengana movement, where rural productivity and the greener pastures of the future were as active as figures of protesting peasantry, despite impending repression of the movement in the post-independence period. Chittaprosad's 1947 works were striking in how they combined the euphoria of independence with a critical eye to its limits, asserting the wider and continuing struggle of the working classes in India, Pakistan, and the Asian and Arab worlds at large, against both bourgeois nationalism and the persistence of imperialism (figs. 2.5 and 2.6). The socialist accent of these images grows stronger as they reassert, like his anti-war images of the early 1940s, the nexus between the nationalist elite, the native bourgeoisie, princely states, and a retreating empire. It is not coincidental that in the late 1940s, *People's Age* was increasingly being brought under censorship for thrusting forth radical rejections of both empire and the false promises of freedom.

This socialist imagery resonated with a transnational circulation of socialist realist iconographies. Party artists were exposed, for instance, to socialist prints from China, the Soviet Union, and Germany. In particular, images from *Life* magazine were reprinted: for instance, in April 1945, when *Life* published a feature on Chinese resistance—scenes of Chinese peasants resisting Japanese crop thieves, "Woodcuts help fight China's battles" and "Woodcuts show wartime life"—the images were reprinted in *People's War*, with the titles "Civilians and soldiers fighting side by side in wartime China" and "Peasants defending their grain," both by the artist Yeng Han (for reproduced woodcuts in People's War, see fig. 2.7).[67]

A transnational socialist imagery would be made visible also in the conference grounds at exhibitions of the Kisan Sabha or the gatherings of the Friends of Soviet Union (FSU). There were, for instance, references to Mayakovsky's posters being circulated[68] and, at the Kisan Sabha annual sessions of 1945, a prototype inspired by Vera Mukhina's monumental 1937 sculpture of worker-peasant union, *Worker and Kolkhoz Woman*, was displayed, though here the figure of the peasant

ASIA MUST UNITE FOR BATTLE AGAINST IMPERIALISM!

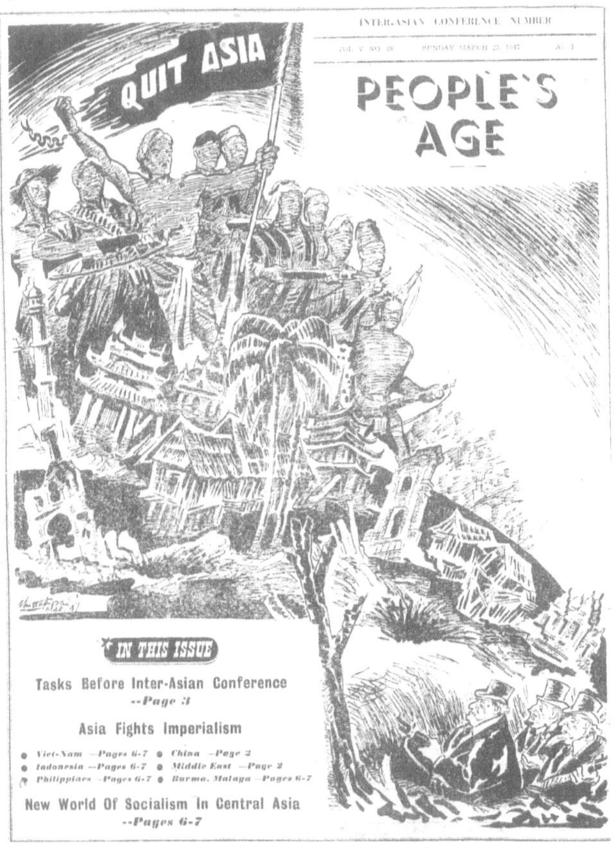

INTER-ASIAN CONFERENCE NUMBER

PEOPLE'S AGE

IN THIS ISSUE

Tasks Before Inter-Asian Conference
--Page 3

Asia Fights Imperialism

- Viet-Nam —Pages 6-7
- China —Page 2
- Indonesia —Pages 6-7
- Middle East —Page 2
- Philippines —Pages 6-7
- Burma, Malaya —Pages 6-7

New World Of Socialism In Central Asia
--Pages 6-7

FIGURE 2.5. *Chittaprosad, "Inter-Asian Conference," People's Age, 23 March 1947. Source: P. C. Joshi Collections. Courtesy of Archives on Contemporary History, Dr. B. R. Ambedkar Central Library, JNU, New Delhi.*

rather than the worker was singled out (fig. 2.8).[69] In an exhibition of Soviet posters in Calcutta in 1945 organized by the FSU, works on display included socialist realist propaganda art, euphoric images of the army and the navy, political leaders, cultural organizations, and so on.[70] The IPTA acted as a coordinating body for the import and dissemination of Soviet and Chinese texts and films. There were reports of posters being "brought from the USSR,"[71] and in its Bombay Provincial

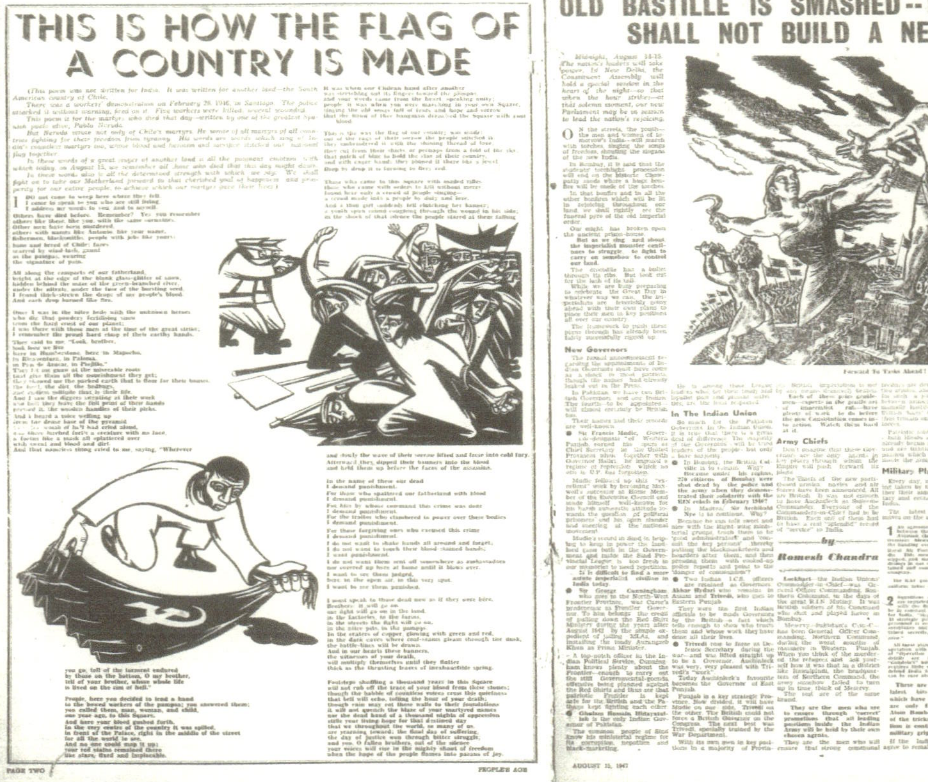

THIS IS HOW THE FLAG OF A COUNTRY IS MADE

OLD BASTILLE IS SMASHED -- IMPERIALISM SHALL NOT BUILD A NEW ONE

Forward To Tasks Ahead!

New Governors

In The Indian Union

Army Chiefs

Military Plans

Economic Control

by Romesh Chandra

PAGE TWO

PEOPLE'S AGE

AUGUST 15, 1947

PAGE THREE

FIGURE 2.6. *Chittaprosad's drawings for People's Age, 15 August 1947. Source: P. C. Joshi Collections. Courtesy of Archives on Contemporary History, Dr. B. R. Ambedkar Central Library, JNU, New Delhi.*

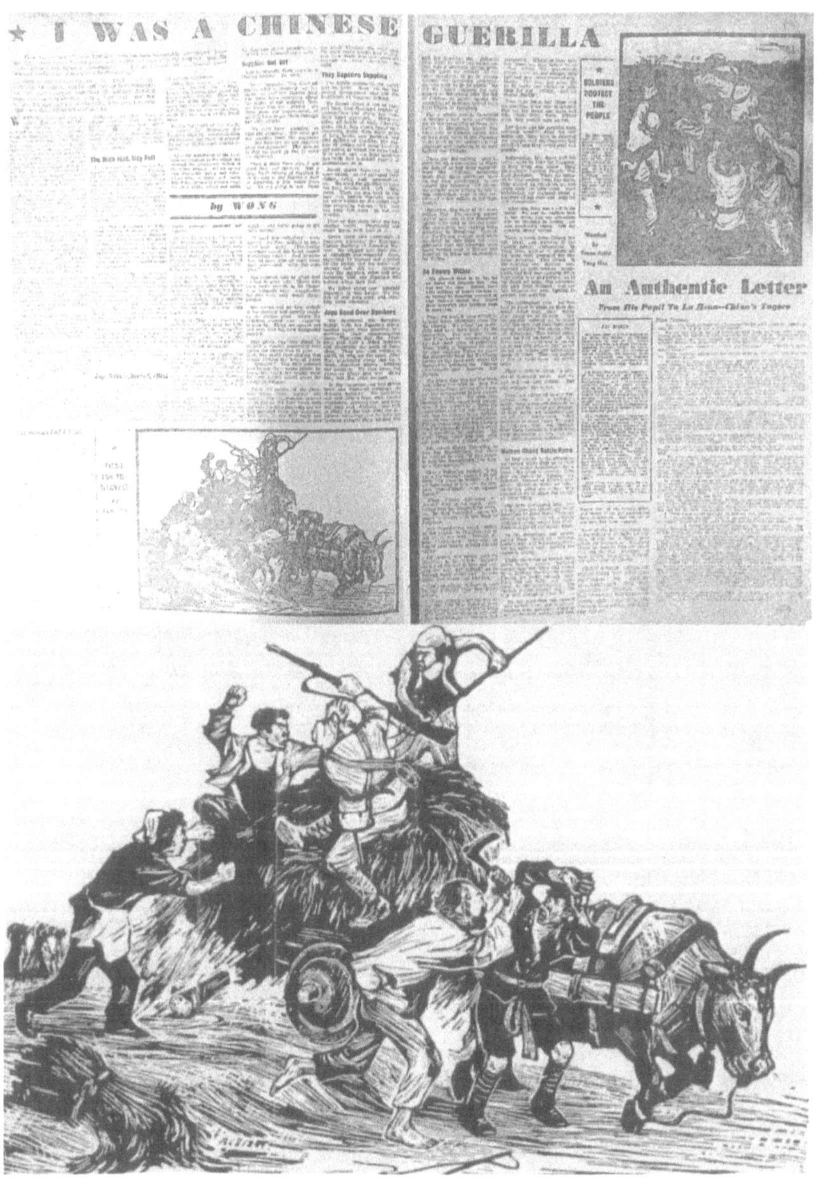

★ I WAS A CHINESE GUERILLA

by WONG

SOLDIERS PROTECT THE PEOPLE

An Authentic Letter

FIGURE 2.7. *Reproductions of Yenan woodcuts, People's War, 2 September 1945. Source: P. C. Joshi Collections. Courtesy of Archives on Contemporary History, Dr. B. R. Ambedkar Central Library, JNU, New Delhi.*

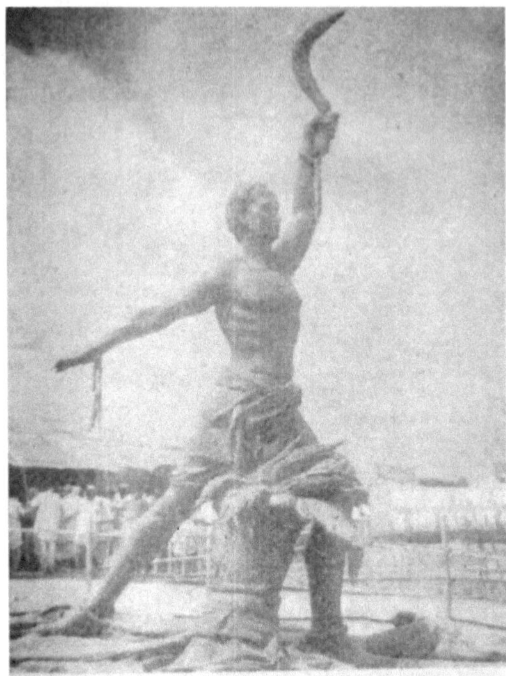

FIGURE 2.8. *A clay model visibly inspired by Vera Mukhina's famous 78-foot-high 1937 steel sculpture, Worker and Kolkhoz Woman, at the Ninth All India Kisan Sabha Conference. People's War, 6 May 1945. Source: P. C. Joshi Collections. Courtesy of Archives on Contemporary History, Dr. B. R. Ambedkar Central Library, JNU, New Delhi.*

Report, IPTA mentions contacts with the Society for Cultural Relations (VOKS) in Moscow, and also with Chunking, from which books, plays, and films were imported to India. Socialist realist iconography of agrarian promise and the rural everyday was thus common in the posters displayed by the CPI or the FSU in rural areas, where the viewers were often illiterate. The images of hunger and destitution, or those of a prosperous peasantry and vibrant laborers, were addressed primarily to the peasantry and industrial workers, or used in strikes and processions.

The works of the artist-cadres were connected also with the distinct pedagogical economy within which the CPI operated in the 1940s. These works suggest a radical use of the graphic medium, which artists like Chittaprosad and Somnath Hore would take up more strongly in the following decades, as a mode of communicating "moral and political" values in art. For Chittaprosad, the graphic medium came from his fascination with folk arts, such as the Chinese and Japanese prints and the ink drawings or woodcut prints of Nandalal Bose at Santiniketan.[72] It is in this confluence of the popular, the political, and the pedagogical that the aesthetic agency of these images can be located. Significant to the visual culture of the CPI in the 1940s were the decorations of the conference grounds, sites that in themselves became central to the assimilation of art, activism, pedagogy, and propaganda—the visual providing new potentials for attracting the semiliterate or illiterate rural population. Examples of this practice included the sites of the national congress of the Communist Party,[73] or those where anti-fascist writers and artists congregated.[74] Such gatherings provided scopes for exhibitions, which during the famine years formed the core of the CPI's cultural activism. "Bhooka Bengal (Hungry Bengal)" exhibitions were organized throughout the country, aimed at gathering relief across political planks. One such exhibition, held in Bombay, attracted particular attention. *People's War* called it "not just an art exhibition—though some of the exhibits, sketches in black and white or colored caricatures or photographs, could justifiably lay claim to be placed in any art salon"; neither was the exhibition a "mere presentation of Bengal's miseries and horrors." Rather it was a mission to "convey, through facts, figures and [a] set of photographs, how this manmade famine in Bengal has come about; what part the bureaucracy, the hoarders and the patriotic parties inside Bengal have played; and what we, the people in other parts of India, can and should do to see that the tragedy of 1943 is not repeated in 1944."[75]

The Bhooka Bengal exhibition offers a typical example of the pedagogical thrust of a CPI famine exhibition. The *People's War* report noted three broad sections in the exhibition hall at Khetwadi in Bombay. The first carried a series of photographs by Sunil Janah, "the young camera-artist from Bengal"; the themes were the price rise, hoarders taking over the market, the disappearance of the entire crop into the black market, the trek of refugees uprooted from the villages onto the city streets, from relief kitchens to the cremation ground, and the heroic efforts of famine relief workers. The second section consisted of black-and-white sketches by Chittaprosad, made in the course of his extensive travels in the famine-affected regions of Chittagong and Midnapore. The third section carried colored cartoons by R. M. Jambhekar and M. Bharatan from the Bombay Friends of the Soviet Union. The exhibition, noted *People's War*, illustrated "the politics behind the man-made famine—how the bureaucracy gave free rein to the hoarder and how the factional strife amongst the patriotic parties of Bengal let the hoarder within each part get away, with the people's food."[76] Such exhibitions would receive high publicity, with previews arranged for press representatives and the public turning out in huge numbers.

The Cultural Squad of the IPTA played a central role in circulating the works of party artists. As the chief organizer of the Fine Arts Sub-Committee of the Anti-Fascist Writers' and Artists' Association, the party artist Mani Roy carried exhibitions of famine sketches to various parts of India along with the traveling IPTA Cultural Squad. Roy circulated a set of ninety cardboard-mounted pictures in the "Save Bengal" exhibitions that were organized all over the country.[77] The Cultural Squad toured provinces in India to collect contributions for the Famine Relief Fund, in the course of which sketches by Chittaprosad were auctioned, with ever increasing demands.[78] However, this circulation could not be sustained due to lack of funding from the party.[79]

In the mid-1940s, the Kisan Sabha annual conferences—the Eighth Annual Session of the Kisan Sabha, held at Bezwada in Andhra Pradesh during the famine year of 1944, and the gathering held the following year at Netrakona in eastern Bengal—carried extensive famine works of the CPI artists. At Bezwada, a volunteer corps of four thousand Kisan boys and girls was gathered and trained for the occasion, a township was built on the conference grounds, and propaganda squads of almost 450 people covered more than two thousand villages. Throughout the conference, cultural performances representing folk art of various provinces and peoples were organized. These performances would often depict a variety of topics of interest to the peasants, thus becoming a very effective tool of Kisan Sabha propaganda.[80] The Bezwada conference also adopted a new kind of propaganda; a big *prabha* (a two-walled moving exhibition on a bullock cart) of posters toured the village of West Godavari, calling all Kisan families to hurry to the conference. Women in some villages created new forms of *rangoli* (auspicious designs drawn in front of thresholds), incorporating conference scenes and slogans, as documented by Chittaprosad for the richly illustrated brochure of the Bezwada congress.[81] Joshi had visualized the peasant congress along the same lines as the congress annual sessions of the late 1930s; the Kisan Nagars, townships now constructed to accommodate the conference, bore a resemblance to the vast Congress Nagars that had been seen earlier. A report on the Bezwada conference mentioned that "over thirty thousand people passed through the exhibition stalls," and the images "made almost every visitor put a coin in the collection box before he left."[82] A still grander layout came in the Ninth Session of the Kisan Sabha, held April 5–9, 1945, at a Kisan Nagar constructed on the outskirts of Netrakona, a town in the Mymensingh district of Bengal. Attended by 642 delegates from sixteen provinces, this Kisan Nagar grew into a small township dominated by an enormous bamboo platform for cultural performances by the IPTA Cultural Squads. The Netrakona conference included an exhibition of numerous picture posters and charts, many of which were drawn by a band of artists under the guidance of Mani Roy.[83] Two dance dramas were particularly notable: *Amara Desa* (My Country) and *Bharater Marmabani* (The Spirit of India), which accompanied the conference's "cultural displays," featured posters and panels by Chittaprosad.[84]

These apparently unpolished, allegedly propagandist images by artist-cadres embodied, nevertheless, a critical agency in visualizing bodies and landscapes of resistance while also developing a figuration of trauma. Such images lay at the interfaces of image and ideology, art and propaganda, culture and politics, and they activated questions of subversive and pedagogical iconography, as well as the socialist currents in Indian visual art. The socialist idiom in itself was a distinctly locational reconfiguration of the idealizing gaze of the classical Soviet socialist realism that projected revolutionary futures, with the contextual dynamics of social realist and expressionistic imageries of hunger, trauma, and destitution in the late-colony. It is in these experimentations in the socialist realist idiom and their localized figuration through a national-popular iconography, despite immediate functional constraints, that a historical appreciation of the works of artist-cadres can be initiated. Among the questions that arise: How was the fundamental *partiinost* of these images accommodated, if at all, within the cultural movement's rhetoric of progressive art, which had been developing in dialogues with non-party cultural alliances through the late 1930s? More specifically, how were these prints and sketches positioned vis-à-vis those of artists outside the party fold, whom the CPI actively patronized from the early 1940s? And how do notions of art's social signification and its political role interact within the broader commitment to realism that the famine concretized?

PARTIINOST AND THE POLITICS OF DISPLAY

The images by artist-cadres were produced with minimal financial support and often in a characteristic economy of journalistic drawing. Moreover, they carried an indelible *partiinost*, being displayed on a regular basis at CPI conferences, strikes and rallies, fund-raising exhibitions, and in party organs or pamphlets. Such partisan production shaped the artistic value of this genre of visual reportage and political iconography, putting it on uneasy terms with the institutional and discursive spaces of high art. The mechanisms of display and circulation, as well as the discursive parameters of left-wing aesthetics in the 1940s, doubly marked this corpus of imagery: on one level, the CPI affirmed and utilized such images in its larger project of "popularizing culture," or taking art "to the people"; on another level, a distinct reductive functionalism prevented party critics from elevating or developing this iconography into a larger art movement, thus re-inscribing their topical status and marginality in the narratives of modern Indian art. Moreover, artist-cadres like Chittaprosad became the subjects of a paradoxical cultural policy of the CPI; while sustaining a collective of young artists committed to party assignments, the CPI sought to develop close associations with practicing artists outside its fold, and to promote and patronize them through an expanding discourse of social commitment in art. This politics of assimilation, however, marginalized its own artist-cadres, in the process arresting not only the formation of a politically committed avant-garde within midcentury Indian modernism, but also the modernist potential of subversive political iconographies.

The production and circulation of the works of the artist-cadres derived from the political agenda of the CPI, and this largely determined their visibility in the public domain. Infrastructures available to these party artists were minimal. There was reportedly a "den" of the CPI in central Calcutta, where artists like Chittaprosad would try their hands in litho-printing, without a litho press. From her interview with Somnath Hore, Anuradha Roy writes: "They used to place wet paper on stone, press the paper with a wooden block, then keep jumping on the block for quite some time. . . . The Tebhaga Movement was going on at that time and a large number of posters were needed."[85] While the CPI is known to have held classes on art instruction, providing training to artists from the provinces in poster-making (one such report mentioning Mani Roy as the instructor),[86] the economies of circulation that marked the works of artist-cadres reflected not only their journalistic use but also their "artistic value." Their exhibitions, for instance, were hardly ever organized outside the party fold or the political framing of the cultural movement in the 1940s. In all probability, this affected the way critical reviews of these works could be produced, contributing to a dearth of critical recognition. A constant circulation and visibility in party organs also added to their topical and contingent character. A politics of display thus needs to be considered in order to understand the scarcity of commentary on the CPI artists in the 1940s, and the eventual marginalization of this protest art in narratives of Indian modernism.

The works of the artist-cadres often seem to lack aesthetic finesse, due to their documentary character and the organizational preoccupations of the artists themselves. Thus, a trained art school student like Mani Roy, who traveled extensively to visually document the famine and to exhibit famine posters, could not develop his art beyond the overtly functional frames of the party. Even Chittaprosad's works from the 1940s remained largely limited to party commissions, with hardly any time for his own aesthetic pursuits, a grievance he shared with fellow artist Debabrata Mukhopadhyay.[87] These images, which in the 1940s would have been familiar to a large cross section of people, have occupied a somewhat uncomfortable place in the implicitly hierarchized matrix of modern Indian art. Ignored in narratives of postcolonial Indian modern art, these political imageries remained restricted to the spaces of political iconographies in niche activist circuits, surfacing sporadically during the tense political atmosphere of Naxalite politics in Bengal and the national Emergency of the 1970s. Curiously enough, even art critics within CPI circles in the 1940s failed to see beyond the immediate, transitory use of the works. While in literature and performance, the left's cultural agenda of taking art to the people was more pronounced, the posters and sketches of the party artists were mainly reduced to their functional and propaganda quotient. When it came to the plastic arts in the cultural movement, we do not see manifestos like the IPTA bulletin for painting, although that ethos was shared and reflected in the works produced during the period. The art critics of the left in these years did not encourage stylistic experimentations in the work of the artist-cadres. Instead, their plaudits remained limited to artists who were officially outside the party fold.

Two distinct patterns can be identified in the official CPI approach toward non-performative visual arts in these years: the first was an art-critical frame within which artists operating in folk or social realist idioms were actively promoted; the second, a purely functional pattern, was geared toward an economy of propaganda and grassroots mobilization. Within the first frame of reference, party critics engaged with the works of established artists like Jamini Roy, and those of art graduates who, in the famine years, formed the modernist collective of the Calcutta Group—a subject we will turn to in Chapter 3. The CPI not only highlighted the works of these artists in art reviews of leading left-wing periodicals like *Parichoy* and *Arani*, or as artists-in-focus in the CPI organs; it also organized exhibitions, including the first exhibition of the Calcutta Group, which the IPTA took to Bombay.[88] In contrast to the critical space given to these artists, the artist-cadres occupied the second category of an overtly functional role within the cultural movement. This binary opposition between the critical and the functional was by no means absolute, as many of the young artists within the Calcutta Group were also actively connected with stage decoration and poster-making during the Kisan Sabha conferences, serving purely documentary roles. Nirode Mazumdar and Rathin Maitra, two of the founding members of the Calcutta Group, which was formed in Calcutta in 1943, were involved in decorating the conference grounds of the Netrakona session of the Kisan Sabha, while others, like Zainul Abedin, were also members of the Anti-Fascist Writers' and Artists' Association, which served as a major link between artists and the party. However, these artists' concerns were hardly political, and they were neither formally integrated in the party apparatus or commissions, nor destined to sustain their association with the CPI beyond the famine years. As independent artists, both Maitra and Mazumdar stayed outside the CPI and thus beyond its journalistic and documentary demands; this position distinguished them from the artist-reporters of the party, who had to operate within an essentially functional, mechanistic idiom. The functional role of the artist-cadres within the cultural discourse of the party is evident in the exhibition displays of these imageries.

The invisibility of the artist-cadres in art-critical writings published during the 1940s is also stark. Apart from the documentary works in *People's War* or *People's Age*, and their various regional counterparts, artist-cadres like Chittaprosad found no discursive support; there were no writings on them in the left-wing journals. A journal like *Arani*, for instance, while heavily laden with anti-fascist rhetoric derived from Soviet Russia and China, carried almost no engagement with the works of artist-cadres of the CPI apart from Chittaprosad's own writings as an early correspondent, when he published two extensive pieces on the role of art in contemporary society, including his most significant piece on using art as "weapon."[89] As his famine commission introduced him to the art circuits of Calcutta, to which he had had no previous access,

Chittaprosad seems to have been engaged in thinking about the challenges and potentials of revolutionary art. He noted the absence of a narrative of resistance in the art of the Bengal School; its idealism, he asserted, was grounded in a mistrust of popular rebellion. Its idealization of the rural was an escapism fostered by the socioeconomic frustration of the upper classes in the face of colonialism; the negation of the urban as the site of struggle resulted in a romantic imaginary of the pastoral ideal. In Nandalal Bose's art, he noted, the idealistic was undoubtedly grounded in the contemporary, but the terms of association with the context itself continued to be "imaginary"—though these "ties," as he maintained, were real, resilient, and full of potential.[90] However, such deliberations on art and the popular, and the scopes for a revolutionary aesthetic in the visual arts, remained unrealized in the 1940s, even as party critics began writing about political art.

The mid-1940s saw a growing body of art-critical literature from cultural activists of the CPI, among which a notable figure was the writer, journalist, and CPI loyalist Gopal Haldar. In 1944, Haldar took over the editorship of *Parichoy* and introduced a serial "cultural section" in the journal. Around this time, he was also emerging as a key voice in theorizing the CPI's art policies. Haldar translated the 1935 Artists' International volume from London, *What Is Revolutionary Art?*, which had included articles by the likes of Herbert Read, Francis Klingender, and Eric Gill.[91] The contributors to this volume, though not all Marxists or advocates of socialist realism, had nonetheless commented on modes of integrating art with society. In his new bilingual translation, *Revolutionary Art: A Symposium*,[92] Haldar transformed the original collaborative ethic of this Popular Front publication, and gave the volume a more pronounced socialist connotation through his extensive foreword to the edited Indian edition. The "philosophy of historical materialism" in art, Haldar argued, would yield answers only for those who could forge the "connection between history of the people and the history of their art, and knew the relation between 'structure' and 'superstructure' of social life"; in other words, the study of the national peoples was required in order to develop "a Marxist reading of Indian art." Haldar's foreword activated a direct Marxist rhetoric for art. Aesthetic theories and art criticism, he asserted, needed to be seen in the "proper historical perspective," and required what he highlighted as the "examination of the socio-economic interpretation or of the 'class' explanation of arts in the concrete."[93] This conscious ideological lexicon accommodated both the popular and the pedagogical, and the artist-cadres were implicated within this rhetoric as "providers" of truth, the suppliers of "raw material" for higher artistic pursuits.

Haldar's voice is important in getting closer to the ways in which artist-cadres like Chittaprosad continued to be seen within the party apparatus. In a 1944 article, "Culture O Communist Dwaityo" ("Culture and Communist Responsibility"), addressed to cadres of the CPI, Haldar charted the "cultural responsibilities" of party workers. Overtly didactic in tone, the article, which circulated widely among party cultural workers, invoked culture as a form of political action, a forum for harnessing the support of intellectuals in creating a "democratic culture"; art would be made "for the people," by enlisting the artist as producer and adopting a socialist use of stylistic technique.[94] Explaining the role of artists within the party, Haldar noted that party artists belonged to a "lower order" (*chhotodor-er silpi*) compared to the "higher-order" (*borodor-er silpi*) artists and writers outside the party, and as such, their cultural role as party workers was to prepare the ground for higher goals of art practice by furnishing "truths" to the non-party artists and intellectuals. The party artists were also required to "rise above mere sloganeering" and remain committed to "sincere understanding" and "accepting the responsibility" in society, appreciating the "unity of purpose with the intellectuals" and "supplying the content to the intellectuals" for cultural production.[95] While Haldar admitted that the "larger gain" of this reaching-out lay in loosening old ideas on art and literature by generating an awareness of culture among the people (the Cultural Squad supplying proof of Communist intervention in the field of culture), he saw the primary role of CPI artist-cadres as being within the essentially functional repertoire of grassroots mobilization, as facilitators and providers of content and raw material for further artistic pursuit. This reductive logic, common to party critics, not only dovetails with the stunted patronage extended to the artist-cadres but also glosses over a curious moment of critical realism in Indian art.

Haldar's formulation of the instrumentalist role of "lower order" artist-cadres is symptomatic of the larger theorization of Communist intervention in cultural action in the 1940s. Marxist historian K. N. Panikkar has argued that two approaches could be observed in Marxist cultural perspectives in India: "instrumentalist" and "transformatory." While instrumentalism no doubt benefited the advancement of radical politics, its imprint on the dialogue between politics and culture was nonetheless restrictive, a largely one-way response that lacked "an inter-penetrative process." In the 1940s, Panikkar noted, the party's cultural initiative remained rooted in the party's immediate political needs, and hence in instrumentalist imperatives that eventually thwarted its transformatory potential.[96] The artist-cadres were no doubt framed by this limited mobilizational rhetoric, but their historical location and artistic agency need to be evaluated both through their location within the artistic field of the 1940s and vis-à-vis the complex trajectory of the left during the conjunctural years of political transition in the late 1940s.

Independence altered the cultural politics of the left at a national level through rifts within the party that mirrored international shifts within the Cominform, particularly the hardening of the Soviet line under the shadow of the Cold War. The Second Congress of the Communist Party, held in Calcutta in February 1948, called for armed struggle against the new nation-state, declaring the idea of a "national front" of the Seventh Congress of the Comintern from 1935 null and void. This period saw the consolidation of Zhdanovism—a stringent cultural doctrine adopted in 1946 by Andrei Zhdanov, secretary of the Central Committee of the Communist Party of the Soviet Union, declaring socialist realism as the official aesthetic of Stalinist Soviet Union and demanding ideological and aesthetic conformation from artists, writers, and cultural workers. P. C. Joshi's disagreement with the new party line resulted in his suspension in January 1949 on the charge of bourgeois reformism. In India, Joshi's exit led to a considerable dissipation of the cultural movement, particularly its cohesive national-popular aesthetic that had harnessed both nationalist and socialist affiliations in the 1940s.

The apathetic attitude of the new incoming general secretary, B. T. Ranadive, to cultural action contributed to the waning spirit of the cultural workers, and many artists left the party over the next few years. Chittaprosad largely dissociated himself from the party by 1949, retiring to Bombay, where he lived in abject poverty in the city's outskirts, with little financial support and few commissions from the party. His association with the CPI remained fraught. Hailed as a "Joshite," he had clear ideological differences with the new party leadership; and yet, as his letters to his former comrades reveal, he remained a firm believer in Communist politics and the revolutionary potential of art—a point I will return to in a later chapter. Somnath Hore entered mainstream art practice in the 1950s, becoming one of India's ace printmakers and sculptors in subsequent years; his association with a humanist repertoire continued, although he did not renew his party membership after 1956. Other artist-cadres, like Debabrata Mukhopadhyay, continued in the role of party activists all along, producing occasional posters and woodcuts for student activists. For all these artists, their work from the 1940s remained foundational, arising as it did from the political impulses and ethos of the time. Each lamented a lost spirit, and the inability of the party to give direction to cultural action, with artists like Hore actively denouncing Communist associations in later years.

THE WORKS OF the artist-cadres, with their rhetoric of political "commitment," point toward a distinct tension within the visual mores of the 1940s in general and, more specifically, within the frames of the radical aesthetic patronized by the CPI during these years. A point in question is to locate this genre of political imagery, with its definite socialist realist notes, within the wider turn toward the "social" that marked this period, a turn made more pronounced by the Bengal famine, which drew the attention of artists across stylistic and ideological boards to a rhetoric of politically committed art.

Social realism, a sensibility and visual idiom explored by artists extensively during this period, had a curious dialogue with this genre of socialist art—both styles shared a commitment to the contemporary, to a ruptured everyday that the famine brought forth within the urban space itself; both styles shared space with the leftist cultural movement, with artists from both camps frequenting the cultural and political gatherings patronized by the CPI and forming a broader social cohesion around the movement. Yet, the active partisan commitment of artist-cadres attributed a distinct location—exhibitionary as well as discursive—to their practice, shaping also the stability of artistic realism during these years. It is here, in the question of *commitment*, that a tension between a social and a socialist framing of art can be identified, marking the location of artist-cadres as distinctly different from that of artists outside the party fold, no matter how frequent the association of the latter with the party might have been.

In Chapter 3, I turn to such internally split visual ideologies of the social and the socialist in a group of artists that the CPI sought to patronize, and who grappled in their turn with the fault lines and ambivalences within realism as a style during the transitional decade of decolonization in midcentury India.

CHAPTER 3

"CONCRETE CONTEXTUALITY"

Realism and Its Discontents in the Art of the Calcutta Group

BURIED DEEP on the rusty shelves of the Government College of Art and Craft in Calcutta (the erstwhile Government School of Art) is a scrapbook titled "Famines of Bengal," with cutouts dating from the wartime famine years of 1943–44.[1] It features cover pages of contemporary publications on the famine, with images—photographs, drawings, cartoons—that reveal the visual culture of the famine years. A cartoon (fig. 3.1) from this faded volume is a useful entry point for this chapter. The cartoon shows an exhibition of art titled *Modern Bengal*, as catalogues piled on a table suggest. From a gilded portrait, the noted nationalist poet Dwijendralal Roy, a composer of celebrated patriotic songs in colonial Bengal, gapes in horror at the paintings on display. Around his portrait are paintings of destitution, vultures, piles of rotting bodies, and graves. Bewildered, the poet seems to be tearing apart his own famous elegy to the motherland—*dhana dhanye pushpe bhara, amader ei banshundhara* (a song hailing the bounty of the motherland and its pastures of plenty). The contradiction between an idealized motherland and a ruptured reality cuts through the cartoon, as it asks: "*Tumi ki shudhui chhobi, shudhu pote likha?*" ("Are you a mere portrait, conjured on canvas?")

This cartoon points to contradictions between the two kinds of "vision" with which I began the book—an "adoring eye" and a "critical

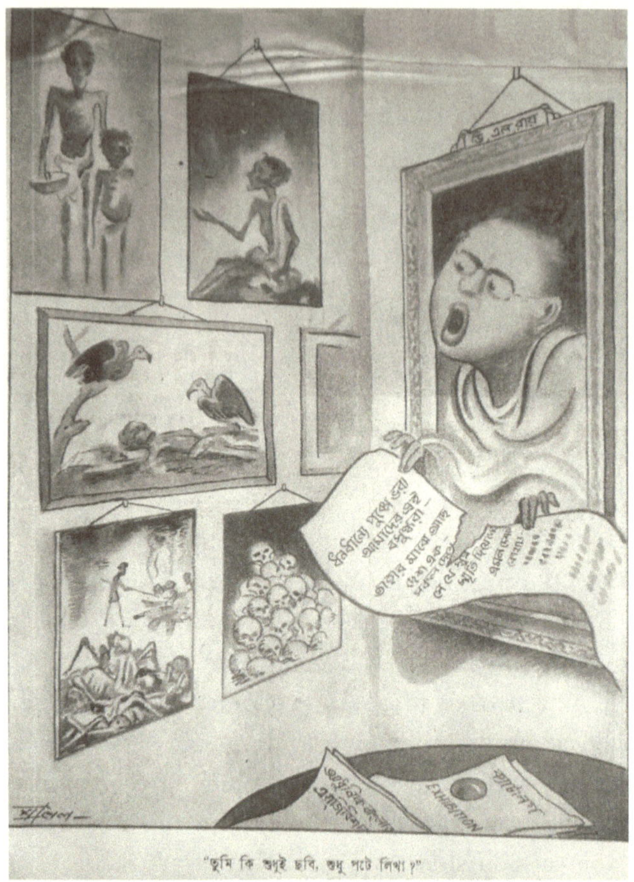

FIGURE 3.1. *Tumi ki shudhui chhobi, shudhu pote likha? Untitled cartoon. Source: Album of famine reportage, Library of Government College of Art and Craft, Kolkata.*

eye"—that marked tensions within the different "needs" of vision in early twentieth-century India. *How, and from where, must the nation be viewed?* Addressing an exhibition salon, where these contradictory visions seem to collide, the cartoon announces both the transformed subjects of modern art and the inverted values of beauty in art. In this chapter, I focus on artists in Calcutta, those outside the CPI, who confronted this new visuality of hunger, and whose works could have been on display in salons like the one in our opening cartoon, or even in street exhibitions, during the famine years.

The Calcutta Group of artists was formed in 1943 as a response to the famine. It continued, through various shifts in membership, until 1953, traversing a critical transitional decade of decolonization. They represented an early model of artist collectives, which consciously assimilated the purpose of art with an active social address beyond merely representational content, and which, while remaining outside the folds of politics, actively engaged in political dialogues. These artists, and similar groups that followed in Bombay, Madras, and Kashmir, would be called "progressive" artists—a category that was tied to the organic integration of the folk with the modern that we encountered in the art discourse around Jamini Roy, yet was distinct in its rhetoric of combining social realism with modernism. The famine in Bengal triggered this new notion of progressive art in 1943–44, and throughout the Calcutta Group's active period, between 1943 and 1953, this notion of the progressive in visual art would register a new dialectic between realism and modernism. The famine, as we will begin to see here, not only created a conjuncture for such new vectors to emerge but, along the lines of Stuart Hall's reading of the "conjunctural," kept recurring in the visual imagination of artists from the region *long after* the crisis had passed. The Calcutta Group is central to this discursive reading of the famine in the visual art of the region and the nation.

Reflecting on the "dearth of revolutionary content in Bengali painting," Dhurjatiprasad Mukhopadhyay, sociologist, writer, and a significant figure in the left-wing cultural movement in India, observed in his 1938 article "On the Social Background of Contemporary Indian Painting," that "a new type of sympathy" was required in artists in order "to convert visual observation into motives for creating novel forms of art," for technical changes to become real, for art to play its historical role, and for emotional content to fall in line with the environment. No art can progress, he noted, "unless society changes through crisis."[2] Mukhopadhyay was writing for the first volume of *New Indian Literature*, a journal initiated by the Progressive Writers' Association (PWA). Nestled among a mere handful of pieces on visual art from the left's cultural movement before 1943,[3] Mukhopadhay's contribution can be seen to presage here the new vectors of the post-1943 years. His actively political staging of the social purpose of visual art also anticipates new and more pronounced leftist exposés on social realism that the poet Bishnu Dey, for instance, was to write in the mid-1940s, with the Calcutta Group at their center.

Related intrinsically to the transnational flavor of the left-wing cultural activism that was particularly strong during the Popular Front period, social realism has been described as not so much a style as "an attitude towards the role of art in life" that emerged during the mid-1930s.[4] It embodied the politics of association that brought together a wide range of left-leaning artists, regardless of their relation to the Communist Party. In late-colonial Calcutta, social realism in art found its terra firma. Yet readings of social realism as a blanket idiom to cover a broad range of artistic responses to the famine need to be considered with caution, for the implicit homogenizing tendency that they carry. Such readings tend to collapse a spectrum of artworks and artistic subjectivities that, while engendered by the conjunctural terrain of the 1940s, were nonetheless ideologically disparate. By stepping outside narratives of famine representations in art, as well as the generic use of social realism to describe this corpus, I suggest unpacking here both the idea of the "social" in art and that of "realism" as an artistic style. Far from being stable markers of visual art during the 1940s, both of these categories were in fact sites of agendas, anxieties, and contestations throughout the 1920s and 1930s, and this was particularly strong—albeit dispersed—in the 1940s. Tensions around the ideas of the social and of realism during the post-famine years introduced a new, hitherto unregistered dialectic in Indian art—one between the social and the socialist, between form and content, as well as between art and ideology. Seen through such a dialectical lens, the social emerges as a critical question within artistic modernities of the 1940s, invoked as well as resisted by artists and critics in their will to visualize the modern. The social, I argue, was *beyond* the questions of subject and content, and animated multiple understandings *and* confusions around art's political accents. Such multi-layered and often dissonant readings become sharper if we observe that in the 1940s artists and critics, in their respective appraisals of and admonitions around realism in art, were using vocabularies of both social realism and the more ideologically steered communist line of socialist realism (upheld by the CPI since 1943) *interchangeably*.

The difference between critical realism (often associated with the social consciousness of social realism in art) and socialist realism, the Marxist theorist György Lukács has argued, is one of "perspective," not "simply the acceptance of socialism": the critical realist writer, while responding to socialism, still writes "from the outside," while the socialist realist writer writes "from the inside." [5] Such differences of perspective are important for understanding the alliances between critical realism and socialist realism, or as this chapter will pursue, between social and socialist realism. Their ideological overlaps as much as their differences play key roles here, creating an irregular aesthetic and a *vacillating discourse* of partisanship in art. The Calcutta Group, formed at the conjuncture of the grassroots left-wing cultural movement around the famine and the climactic politics of the closing decade of anti-colonial struggle, offers a case in point for teasing out the fixities of social realism and of the generic category of "famine art," and for looking into the dialectic of outside/inside that marked the left's foray into the non-party artistic field. Ideological slippages between notions of the social and the socialist are key in reading the historicity of the Calcutta Group, and more generally, the political history of progressive art during this critical decade of political transition. The idiomatic "wavering" of the Calcutta Group—between folk idioms and modernist abstraction, for instance—has been noted by critics.[6] This vacillation, I argue, was also ideological, and forms a critical modality of what I have called *partisan aesthetics*.

The Calcutta Group is my entry point for understanding the tensions that underlaid the emergence of "art as testimony" during the famine, the left's forays into the non-party art world and the rhetoric of such dialogues, as well as the critical shifts in the understanding of the self and sovereignty, the individual and the collective, that marked the late 1940s and early 1950s. All these dynamics can be seen via the group's arrival in and displacement within narratives of postcolonial Indian modernism. In effect, I read the Calcutta Group as a key site from which to understand not only the beginnings of progressive art collectives in India in the early 1940s, but also the dialectical formations of the history of progressive art—rethinking in the process what is celebrated as the unique aesthetic of secular modernist universalism of the Progressive Artists' Group that arose in Bombay in 1947.[7]

ART AS TESTIMONY

Realism was born in the streets of Calcutta, noted Burhanuddin Khan Jahangir in his biography of Zainul Abedin—one of the first artists to draw famine victims in the city streets.[8] An iconic painter of post-partition East Pakistan (1947–71, now Bangladesh), Abedin was the youngest teacher at the Government School of Art in Calcutta in the early 1940s, and his finesse in drawing established him as one of the most promising academic realists in the city. Since the 1930s, Abedin, along with his fellow academic artists Gobardhan Ash and Abani Sen, had sketched the city's underbelly, such as its industrial stretches. The predominantly urban repertoire in their works developed a grotesque edge in their famine sketches of 1943–44; in these images of hunger, destitution, food queues, and starvation deaths, realism was graduating from naturalism to the grotesque. Throughout 1943 and 1944, Abedin made a series of ink sketches on the famine in the city, his meager resources limiting him to drawing on brown wrapping paper and using common ink. Abedin's figures were iconic in their minimalist starkness, the existential flux of destitution frozen in speedy, active linearity. His destitutes reenact the struggle for survival in the city streets within the pictorial space, jostling with crows and dogs around rubbish bins, their confrontation, shorn of backdrop details, animating upon Abedin's modest papers the violent alienation of destitution in the city. These images were immediately noticed in the city's art circuits, as well as by the journalistic world, when his famine drawings were used to illustrate the activist-journalist Ela Sen's *Darkening Days, Being a Narrative of Famine-Stricken Bengal* in May 1944.[9] They were also among the very first depictions of famine to appear in print, along with those of the CPI artist Chittaprosad, establishing a significant precedent for artists to follow. Chittaprosad himself drew attention to Abedin's famine works in a 1945 article in the Communist Party organ *People's War*, referring also to the high praises Abedin garnered from politicians and critics alike, from the nationalist leader Sarojini Naidu to the noted orientalist art critic O. C. Gangooly (fig. 3.2).[10]

The violent angularities of Abedin's drawings can be contrasted stylistically with the watercolors of Gobardhan Ash, where the famished bodies stand stooping or in disarray beneath the muted veneer of gloom, their presence on canvas deliberately abstracted through skeletal shadows rather than actual corporeal presence. In his distinctly impressionistic renditions of victimhood and deserted landscapes, Ash depicted primarily rural sights of hunger in his native village of Begumpur, not far from Calcutta. Often portraying villagers in the transition of displacement, Ash's landscapes become themselves specters of the fatalism that characterized his human subjects. Ash was a student and associate of the veteran academic artist Atul Bose in the 1930s, and lived with him during the famine years. In 1943–44, Bose, too, made a series of famine sketches with a similar repertoire. *The Birth of Kalki*—an image of childbirth from the womb of a mother dying of starvation—was the magnum opus of this series of separate sketches assembled together. The artist had witnessed this scene near his residence, though in the final canvas he transposed it to a village setting, an instance of hunger becoming a fluid frame in visual art, staging the trauma of the famine across multiple idioms and icons.

The figuration of hunger is critical in the works of these academic naturalists, particularly in connection with the limits to which they pushed academic verisimilitude in order to visualize new anatomies of starvation. Despite an underlying naturalist proclivity, realism operates in their works not in figural exactitude, but rather in their tendency to evoke pathos, the dramatization of realism unfolding in the grotesque staging of human tragedy. Social realism, as a critical idiom, is thus used to describe the famine works of these artists, and many other lesser-known art students and amateurs who had responded to the famine in various media. Collapsing their art into the immediacy of the "event" of the famine, however, tends to overlook a larger commitment to the urban and the social that the famine energized. Engaging

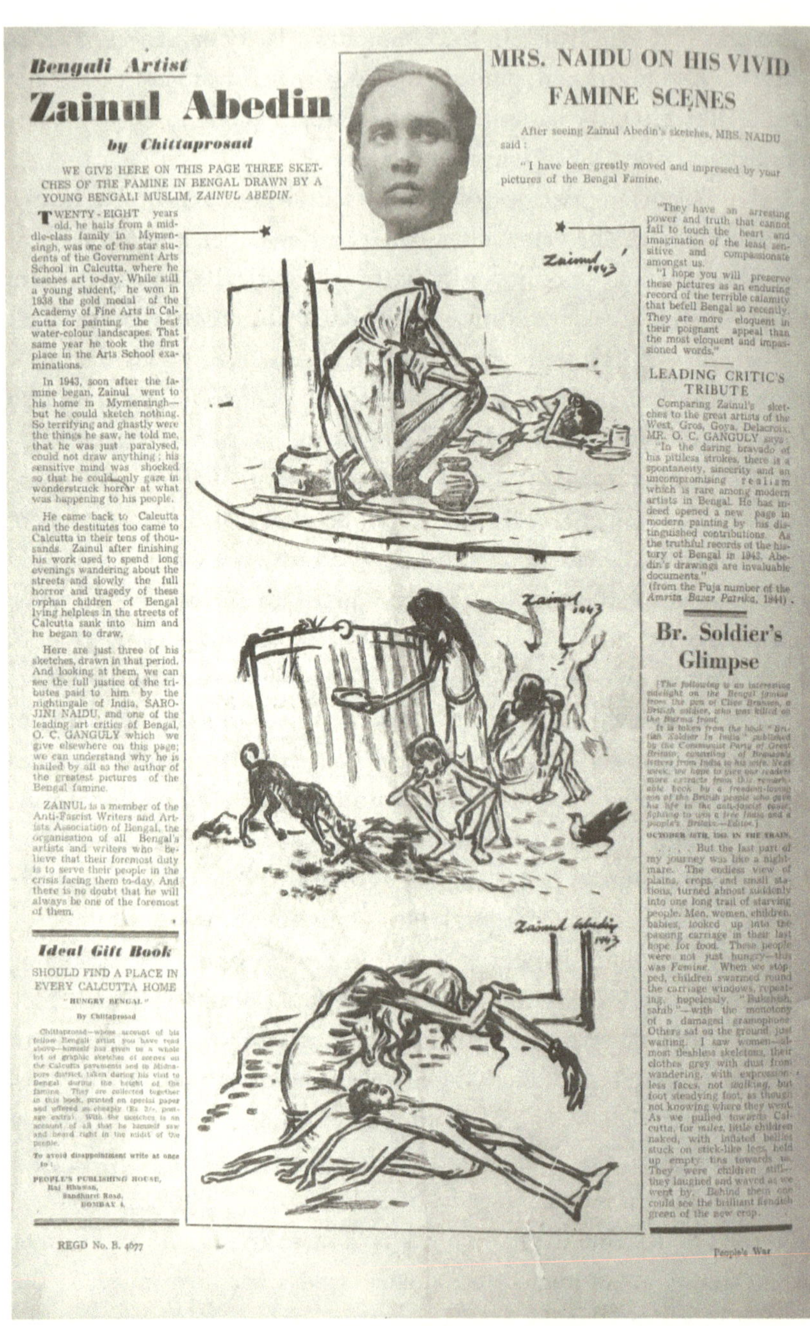

Bengali Artist

Zainul Abedin

by Chittaprosad

WE GIVE HERE ON THIS PAGE THREE SKETCHES OF THE FAMINE IN BENGAL DRAWN BY A YOUNG BENGALI MUSLIM, *ZAINUL ABEDIN.*

TWENTY-EIGHT years old, he hails from a middle-class family in Mymensingh, was one of the star students of the Government Arts School in Calcutta, where he teaches art to-day. While still a young student, he won in 1938 the gold medal of the Academy of Fine Arts in Calcutta for painting the best water-colour landscapes. That same year he took the first place in the Arts School examinations.

In 1943, soon after the famine began, Zainul went to his home in Mymensingh—but he could sketch nothing. So terrifying and ghastly were the things he saw, he told me, that he was just paralysed, could not draw anything; his sensitive mind was shocked so that he could only gaze in wonderstruck horror at what was happening to his people.

He came back to Calcutta and the destitutes too came to Calcutta in their tens of thousands. Zainul after finishing his work used to spend long evenings wandering about the streets and slowly the full horror and tragedy of these orphan children of Bengal lying helpless in the streets of Calcutta sank into him and he began to draw.

Here are just three of his sketches, drawn in that period. And looking at them, we can see the full justice of the tributes paid to him by the nightingale of India, SAROJINI NAIDU, and one of the leading art critics of Bengal, O. C. GANGULY which we give elsewhere on this page; we can understand why he is hailed by all as the author of the greatest pictures of the Bengal famine.

ZAINUL is a member of the Anti-Fascist Writers and Artists Association of Bengal, the organisation of all Bengal's artists and writers who believe that their foremost duty is to serve their people in the crisis facing them to-day. And there is no doubt that he will always be one of the foremost of them.

MRS. NAIDU ON HIS VIVID FAMINE SCENES

After seeing Zainul Abedin's sketches, MRS. NAIDU said:

"I have been greatly moved and impressed by your pictures of the Bengal Famine.

"They have an arresting power and truth that cannot fail to touch the heart and imagination of the least sensitive and compassionate amongst us.

"I hope you will preserve these pictures as an enduring record of the terrible calamity that befell Bengal so recently. They are more eloquent in their poignant appeal than the most eloquent and impassioned words."

LEADING CRITIC'S TRIBUTE

Comparing Zainul's sketches to the great artists of the West, Gros, Goya, Delacroix, MR. O. C. GANGULY says:

"In the daring bravado of his pitiless strokes, there is a spontaneity, sincerity and an uncompromising realism which is rare among modern artists in Bengal. He has indeed opened a new page in modern painting by his distinguished contributions. As the truthful records of the history of Bengal in 1943, Abedin's drawings are invaluable documents."

(from the Puja number of the *Amrita Bazar Patrika*, 1944).

Br. Soldier's Glimpse

[*The following is an interesting sidelight on the Bengal famine from the pen of Clive Branson, a British soldier, who was killed on the Burma front.*

It is taken from the book "British Soldier in India" published by the Communist Party of Great Britain, consisting of Branson's letters from India to his wife. Next week, we hope to give our readers more extracts from this remarkable book by a freedom-loving son of the British people who gave his life in the anti-fascist cause, fighting to win a free India and a people's Britain.—Editor.]

OCTOBER [illegible] IN THE TRAIN.

. . . . But the last part of my journey was like a nightmare. The endless view of plains, crops, and small stations, turned almost suddenly into one long trail of starving people. Men, women, children, babies, looked up into the passing carriage in their last hope for food. These people were not just hungry—this was *Famine*. When we stopped, children swarmed round the carriage windows, repeating, hopelessly, "Bukshish, sahib"—with the monotony of a damaged gramophone. Others sat on the ground just waiting. I saw women—almost fleshless skeletons, their clothes grey with dust from wandering, with expressionless faces, not *walking*, but foot steadying foot, as though not knowing where they went. As we pulled towards Calcutta, for *miles*, little children naked, with inflated bellies stuck on stick-like legs, held up empty tins towards us. They were children still—they laughed and waved as we went by. Behind them one could see the brilliant fiendish green of the new crop.

REGD No. B. 4677

People's War

FIGURE 3.2. *Chittaprosad, "Bengali Artist: Zainul Abedin," People's War, 21 January 1945. Source: P. C. Joshi Collections. Courtesy of Archives on Contemporary History, Dr. B. R. Ambedkar Central Library, JNU, New Delhi.*

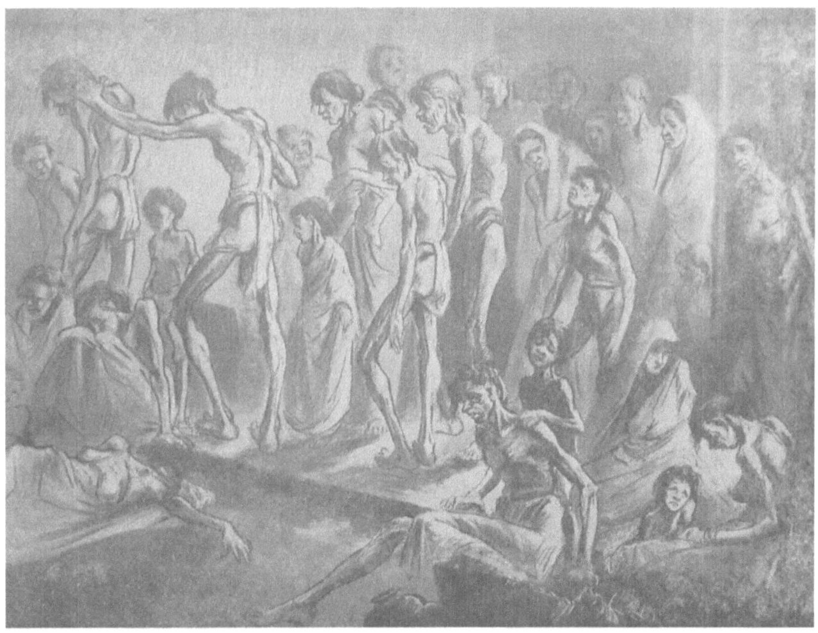

FIGURE 3.3. *Debiprasad Roy Choudhury, When Calcutta Sleeps (1944). Oil. Source: Album, Bengal Painters' Testimony, 1944.*

directly with the corporeality of hunger and destitution, each of these artists abstracted victimhood from the naturalist details, activating once again a tension within academic naturalism. In embodying a new critical vein, works of academic naturalists opened up possibilities for a new critical realism, and generated a dialogue with the urban socio-political context itself, hitherto sparse in Calcutta's art circuits.

Depiction of the famine drew artists from across the board, even Indian-style painters who subscribed to the Bengal School idiom of rarefied mythological and literary painting. While staunchly anti-realist painters like Nandalal Bose painted the famine in allegorical terms by depicting, for instance, a dancing Shiva wreaking destruction on earth while his consort, the goddess Parvati, offers bowls of rice (an image cited and critiqued by Chittaprosad, as discussed in Chapter 2), Debiprasad Roy Choudhury—a realist sculptor who had been associated with the Bengal School—made dark, brooding oil paintings and charcoal sketches of hunger in the city; his *When Calcutta Sleeps* (fig. 3.3) is strongly reminiscent of the works of Käthe Kollwitz. Artistic responses to the famine formed a genre of art as *testimony*—a marker of the artist's patriotic commitment to a nation in distress.

This rhetoric of witnessing and representing crisis dominated the famine exhibitions in Calcutta during 1944–45, as well as the evaluation of these images in later years. The visibility of the famine in the city had made it a direct part of the freedom struggle in a decade marked by mass movements, its documentation by artists differing markedly from the official government commissions or pictorial reviews of famines that had been typical of colonial India in the nineteenth and early twentieth centuries. Depicting the famine was viewed as an act of patriotism, a "homage of love and pity to the vast anonymous legion of hunger stricken and heroic people of Bengal," as described by the eminent nationalist leader Sarojini Naidu in the foreword to the *Bengal Painter's Testimony* (1944), the modest album from the first publicized exhibition of famine art, organized by the Bengal Provincial Students' Federation. The eighth annual conference of the All India Students' Federation (AISF) was presided over by Dhurjatiprasad Mukhopadhyay, with Naidu as the chief guest, and all proceeds of the exhibition were committed to the Famine Relief Fund. Naidu's foreword to the exhibition album exhorted artistic talent to become the "handmaid of human suffering to offer a little amelioration of great distress"; this patriotic tenor carried over to the editors, young artists from the Government School of Art—Arun Das Gupta, Qamrul Hasan, Adinath Mukherji, and Safiuddin Ahmed—who hailed the united action of painters, publishers, and press-workers, Hindus and Muslims, in the patriotic act of dedicating the album to the service of the famished. It is curious, however, that their note did not initiate any dialogue about realism as a tool of social critique, though their own works reflected the famine most vividly, fostering a new exhibiting ethos of displaying sights of social rupture rather than contained rural bounty.

The AISF exhibition, titled *Visions of Bengal*, covered a broad range of artists—from the masters Abanindranath Tagore, Rabindranath Tagore, Nandalal Bose, Debiprasad Roy Choudhury, J. P. Gangooly, and Jamini Roy to the Santiniketan artists Benodebehari Mukherjee and Ramkinkar Baij, as well as the young artists of Calcutta. Though the paintings in the exhibition were not all limited to the famine, it remained the central focus. A wide range of Calcutta artists revealed the variety of representational idioms around this "moment" of socially aware art. The new generation of Calcutta artists included the editors of the album—Qamrul Hasan, Safiuddin Ahmed, and Adinath Mukherji—along with their fellow artists from the art school such as Zainul Abedin and the Communist Party artist Chittaprosad. Among the displays were paintings and sculptures of a set of young artists from the city—Gopal Ghose, Nirode Mazumdar, Prodosh Dasgupta, Subho Tagore, and Rathin Maitra—who had come together in late 1943 to form the Calcutta Group. Distinguishing this collective's work from the other exhibits in the album introduction, the poet Bishnu Dey, by then already a key figure in the left-wing cultural movement, projected a radical agency in their works. These artists, he noted, departed from both the early twentieth-century mythological romanticism of the Bengal School and the earthy paintings of the Santiniketan School, as well as from art school academic naturalism. Their art revealed a change of "values" in art, a conscious quest for form and color, which represented a new spirit of "revolt" in Indian art, a continuation, according to Dey, of the legacy of Jamini Roy and Rabindranath Tagore. Their revolt, he asserted, was not limited to social crisis or to a unilinear artistic sympathy for the downtrodden, but was geared toward a "wide new world, healthy and devoted to the vision of the eye."[11] This was the earliest remark on the formal values in the realist compositions of these artists, a theme that Dey would continue in his sustained writings on the Calcutta Group, drawing them into and supporting them within the left-wing cultural movement of the period.

Group formations by artists in opposition to established canons were not new in the 1940s; precedents can be seen in scattered artists' groups such as the Young Artists' Union and the Art Rebel Centre in the early 1930s. Neither represented a rhetoric of "contexts" or the "everyday": by the early 1940s, Kala Bhavan at Santiniketan under Nandalal Bose and the new generation of artists and art teachers, Benodebehari Mukherjee and Ramkinkar Baij, was exploring new interfaces of art, environment, and modernism. Also, experiments with the languages of international modernism were not a novelty in the 1940s: the works of Rabindranath Tagore, Amrita Sher-Gil, and Jamini Roy had already introduced the formalistic concerns of modernist art, which were reflected also in art discourse.[12] What made the arrival of the Calcutta Group seem radical was precisely their "moment" of inception, which made a language of contemporaneity, contextuality, social signification, and modernist liberation of form all possible within a *singular* analytical frame or field of reference. The group envisaged a fusion of social crisis with a revolutionary departure in form, thus collapsing the social and the formal in art within a consolidated rhetoric of modernist arrival. The famine provided the backdrop for this departure from established canons and, more importantly, determined the frames through which the Calcutta Group would be represented in contemporary cultural discourse.

Despite the origin of the group during the famine, however, it is important to make a methodological separation between the famine works of the academic realist painters and those of the Calcutta Group. This separation is based not on the stylistic lineages of the artists, but rather on the conscious self-positioning and articulations of artistic purpose and method that the group generated, both in their own agenda and in the art discourse generated around them. In the works of the academic realist painters—often art school graduates—the famine had featured variously as narrative, as illustration, or as representation without a wider agenda or a conscious program of artistic rupture; no consolidated artistic action emerged out of the stir created in the art circuits during the famine years until the establishment of the Calcutta Group. When the group was formed in 1943, they were responding to an immediate crisis, in a manner apparently not very different from that of their peers. Yet, in addressing the social context of art, these artists were also trying to grapple with the idiomatic problems generated by the representation of social crisis, rather than simply to produce realistic depictions of trauma. Among the artists of the time, they were in fact coming closest to what Dhurjatiprasad Mukhopadhyay had earlier described as the need for a "new sympathy" to convert "visual observation" into "motives for creating new forms of art." Hence the group needs to be approached beyond frames of artistic pity or art as testimony, and rather read through the dialectics of the social and the formal, of event and the everyday, that beset the discourse around them. The art of the Calcutta Group, I argue, captured a dialectical temper of Indian modernism during the transitional years of decolonization between 1943 and 1953, when a key factor was the dialogues and dissonances around the "social" in art.

THE CALCUTTA GROUP AND THE SOCIAL IMPERATIVE IN ART

The coming together of the Calcutta Group had little to do with shared affinities in style. Nor did the group members form an ideologically cohesive unit; their backgrounds, both social and stylistic, were widely divergent. Among the founding members, sculptors Prodosh Dasgupta and T. Kamala (later Kamala Dasgupta), and painters Gopal Ghose and Paritosh Sen, had at various points in the 1930s received academic naturalist training from the renowned realist sculptor Debiprasad Roy Choudhury at the Government School of Art in Madras. Rathin Maitra and Subho Tagore were also trained in the academic style, at the Government School of Art in Calcutta, Subho Tagore's time there being brief. Nirode Mazumdar and Prankrishna Pal, on the other hand, were trained in the revivalist Indian style at the Indian Society of Oriental Art in Calcutta. Prodosh Dasgupta had left for the Royal Academy in London in 1937 and returned to Calcutta in 1941 to set up his studio at Wellington Square, with a set of students training under him; he was joined by the sculptor T. C. Kamala after their marriage. Paritosh Sen had worked as an art teacher in Indore, and Gopal Ghose, after a prolonged spell as a wandering traveler-artist, finally came to Calcutta in the early 1940s under dire financial straits. As a tenant in a small room at the Indian Society of Oriental Art, he met Nirode Mazumdar and was soon introduced to Prodosh Dasgupta by Paritosh Sen. At various points, Ghosh lodged at Nirode Mazumdar's house and Dasgupta's studio, and it can be assumed that he and Nirode Mazumdar formed the connecting link between Prodosh Dasgupta and Subho Tagore's atelier at S. R. Das Road, which became the collective studio for the new group after its formal beginning in 1943.[13]

When the group was established, almost all of the founding members, except Subho Tagore, were young artists in the early stages of their career, some of them, like Gopal Ghose, struggling to establish a foothold in Calcutta; Rathin Maitra was still a student at the Government School of Art.[14] In the late 1930s, Prodosh Dasgupta and Nirode Mazumdar were displaying their student works at the annual exhibitions of the Academy of Fine Art in Calcutta, Dasgupta's naturalist sculptures like *Burden of Age* and *Opium Eater* bringing him awards in 1936 and 1937.[15] Subho Tagore, a largely untrained artist, had already established himself in the city as a muralist, painter, sculptor, and designer, his exhibitions in 1940–41 winning him accolades from connoisseurs and critics alike for his eye for "primitive" design and crafts.[16] A member of the aristocratic Tagores of Jorasanko, who included stalwarts of Bengal art—Abanindranath Tagore, Rabindranath Tagore, and Gaganendranath Tagore—Subho Tagore projected himself as a rebel, a bohemian radical shunning his aristocratic "blue blood." He traveled widely, and after prolonged spells in Kashmir, Assam, and central India, he returned to Calcutta, basing himself in the southern part of the city, away from the aristocratic milieu of his ancestral home in the north. Here, in his new abode at S. R. Das Road, his neighbors included Nirode Mazumdar and Rathin Maitra, both young artists at that time. Maitra, like Tagore, hailed from an aristocratic landholding family; as a student of the Government Art School, he had met Subho Tagore's brother, Basab Tagore, and thus formed his association with the former.

Largely unknown to one another, the members of the group hence came together by and large through interpersonal associations. The peculiar sociopolitical and cultural currents operating in Calcutta during the Second World War also contributed to their formation. Members of the Allied forces stationed in Calcutta, in particular, supported them with art books and Cahiers d'Art, a showcase of current modernist art in the West, encouraging them in their formulations of a new art opposed to established canons. Some members of the Allied Forces served as sitters for the group artists.[17] The group also received support from Mrs. Maie Casey, the wife of the governor of Bengal, R. G. Casey. Through her initiative, the first informal exhibition of the group was organized in 1944 at Subho Tagore's residence in 5A S. R. Das Road, followed by the first formal exhibition in March 1945 at the Services Art Club in Calcutta.

The works of most of the group members in the 1940s, it has to be remembered, were less formally sophisticated than those they produced after developing their personal styles in the decades following the group's demise. However, in these early stages, the struggle to break out of academic realism can be seen more clearly, often leading to exaggerations of form or a stylized, non-naturalist decorative idiom. An overview of the works of group members during the famine years, 1943–45, reveals their overt engagement with non-naturalist form-making, in minimalistic, simplified contours, flat planes of vivid color, bold linearity, and a conscious attention to mass and volume in sculpture. The somewhat consciously stylized iconography of the artists can be seen to address victimhood, dislocation, and trauma within a strict plasticity of form, deliberately distancing itself from the idealized figuration associated with the Bengal School. The famine dominated their repertoire during this period: Prodosh Dasgupta's sculptural pieces *In Bondage* (1943), *War and Humanity* (1944), *Destitutes* (1944), *Food Queue* (1944), *War*, and *Last Days of Abyssinia* (c. 1945); Rathin Maitra's oils and tempera works *Refugees* (1947) and *Destitute Family* (1944); Nirode Mazumdar's *Orphan* (1944); Prankrishna Pal's *Family* (c. 1944); and Gopal Ghose's minimalistic linear compositions *Back to Her Village* (c. 1944); and Subho Tagore's overtly decorative compositions like *Undefeated* (c. 1943), which suggested a utopian return to the rural in an almost romantic negation of the famine. Most of these works were displayed in the group's early exhibitions, first in 1944 with the *Visions of Bengal* exhibition and in the corresponding album, *Bengal Painters' Testimony*, and twice in 1945, in Calcutta and Bombay, when an exhibition of the group's works was carried by Rathin Maitra alongside the Cultural Squad of the Indian People's Theatre Association.

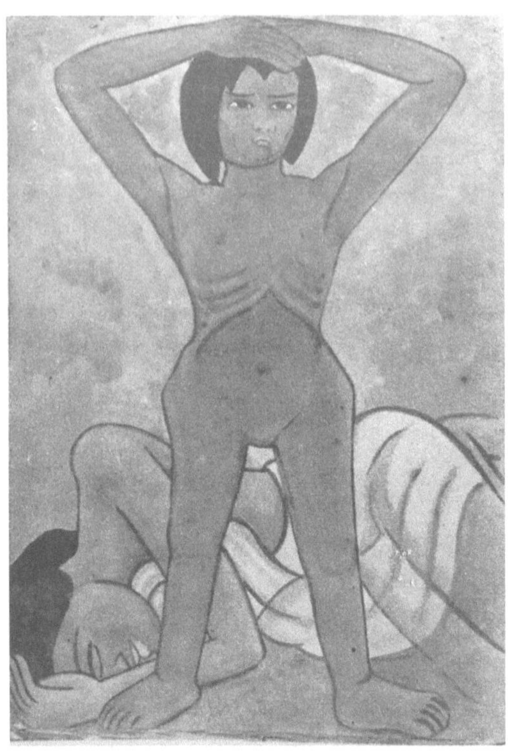

FIGURE 3.4. *Nirode Mazumdar, Orphan (1944). Tempera on board. Oil. Source: Album, Bengal Painters' Testimony, 1944.*

The *Bengal Painters' Testimony* included reproductions of the works of most of the founding members of the group, in a host of styles: for instance, Prodosh Dasgupta's realist sculpture *Food Queue* (1944), Rathin Maitra's oil *Labourers* (c. 1943), Gopal Ghose's minimalist line drawing *Mother and Child* (1944), or Nirode Mazumdar's more modernist rendition *Orphan* (1944, fig. 3.4), as well as Subho Tagore's stylized, angular wooden sculpture, *The Ploughman* (1942), a pictorial version of which he included in his solo exhibition in 1942. The Calcutta exhibition of 1945, held at the Services Arts Club in Calcutta, carried a wider range, including works completely unrelated to the famine, notable examples being Rathin Maitra's *Woman and Child* (c. 1945), *At Tea* (c. 1945), *Paddy-cutters* (c. 1945), Gopal Ghose's ink sketches *Dog and Christ at the Cross* (c. 1945) and impressionistic landscapes, Nirode Mazumdar's portrait studies, as well as head-studies by Prodosh and Kamala Dasgupta.[18] Representative works sent to Bombay as a part of the IPTA tour were again mostly on the famine theme, and had suggestive titles such as Rathin Maitra's *The Hungry Family*, or Prodosh Dasgupta's *Destitute Mother and Child* (c. 1943) and *Food Queue* (1944). However, Dasgupta's *The Last Days of Abyssinia* (c. 1945) was seen as an anti-fascist composition, and Maitra's *Bourgeois Woman* (1946) provided a pointed contrast with his other work.[19] War, recalled Rathin Maitra, was also a driving force in their artistic thought.[20]

The famine works of the group would be exhibited periodically through the 1940s as representative of the signature style of the Calcutta Group, their modernity never dissociated from their roots in social crisis. Some of the artists, like Prodosh Dasgupta, characterized their work on the famine as early experiments, still determined more by "stories" and "emotional excesses bordering on sentimentalism" than by sculptural qualities; he would try to overcome this tendency in his post-famine works between 1946 and 1950, as he writes, when his experiments with mass and volume culminated in the creation of simplified forms—"mostly rounded, cylindrical or ovoid," "a more restrained order of basic forms often instilled with and integrated to themes from everyday life."[21] From the depiction of victimhood, the artists moved on to a parallel yet different iconography of the human condition, which was, however, not entirely disconnected with the basic concerns of their earlier works. In Dasgupta's sculptures, for instance, there was an increasing tendency toward abstract composition, though his subjects remained deeply rooted in the familiar lived realities of everyday life. His sculptures made between 1948 and 1949 brought out these concerns through new experiments with the volume and mass of the material itself, as in works like *Pounding Corn* and *Gossip*. Other group members moved away from famine themes toward a more grounded repertoire of painting labor and leisure, as in the oils and tempera works by Rathin Maitra from the post-1946 period, such as the *Rickshaw Puller*, *Reapers*, *Noonday Siesta*, and *Boat Race Festival*, which show his lasting concern with painting the human condition, using flat earth colors and defined linearity. These were sharp departures from Maitra's primary training

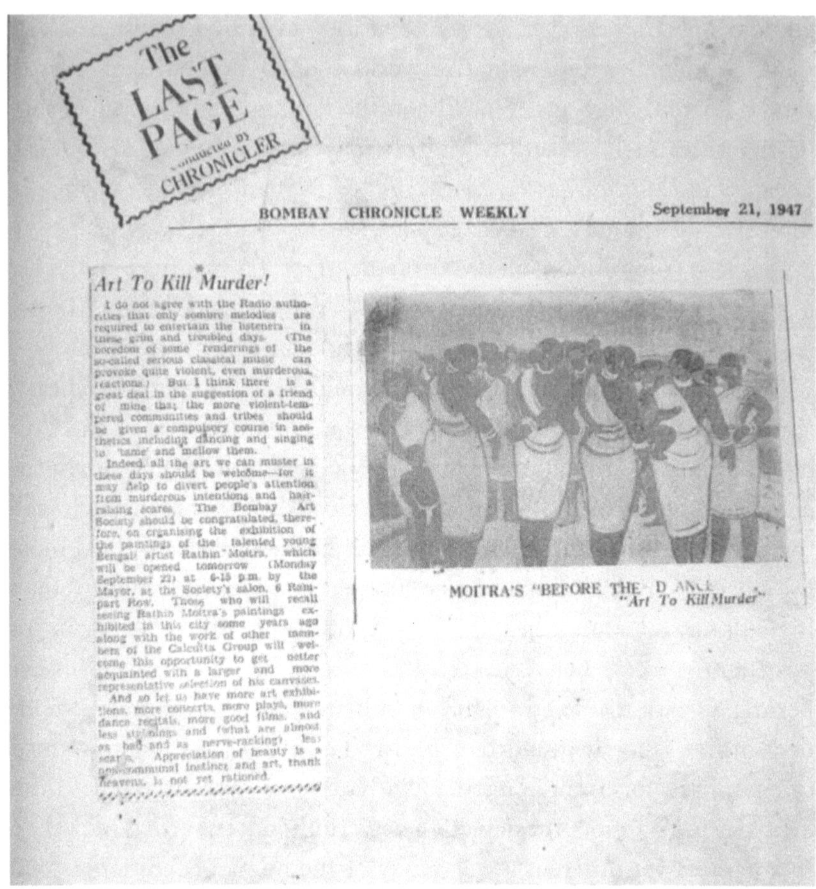

The LAST PAGE conducted by CHRONICLER

BOMBAY CHRONICLE WEEKLY September 21, 1947

Art To Kill Murder!

I do not agree with the Radio authorities that only sombre melodies are required to entertain the listeners in these grim and troubled days. (The boredom of some renderings of the so-called serious classical music can provoke quite violent, even murderous, reactions.) But I think there is a great deal in the suggestion of a friend of mine that the more violent-tempered communities and tribes should be given a compulsory course in aesthetics including dancing and singing to 'tame' and mellow them.

Indeed, all the art we can muster in these days should be welcome—for it may help to divert people's attention from murderous intentions and hair-raising scares. The Bombay Art Society should be congratulated, therefore, on organising the exhibition of the paintings of the talented young Bengali artist Rathin Moitra, which will be opened tomorrow (Monday September 22) at 6-15 p.m. by the Mayor, at the Society's salon, 6 Rampart Row. Those who will recall seeing Rathin Moitra's paintings exhibited in this city some years ago along with the work of other members of the Calcutta Group will welcome this opportunity to get better acquainted with a larger and more representative selection of his canvases.

And so let us have more art exhibitions, more concerts, more plays, more dance recitals, more good films, and less stabbings and (what are almost as bad and as nerve-racking) less scares. Appreciation of beauty is a non-communal instinct and art, thank heavens, is not yet rationed.

MOITRA'S "BEFORE THE DANCE"
"Art To Kill Murder"

FIGURE 3.5. *Rathin Maitra, Before the Dance (1947). Tempera on paper. Reproduced in the Bombay Chronicle Weekly, 21 September 1947. Source: Private papers of Rathin Maitra. Courtesy of artist's son Riten Maitra.*

in academic realism, which he explicitly renounced in 1943. Most significant for him in the 1940s were, however, his works on tribal life, a range of intensely colorful canvasses with stylized, folk-like figuration that he prepared during his stay in the Santhal Parganas. *Before the Dance* (fig. 3.5), *Santhal Folk Dance*, and *At the Beat of the Drum* are some of the paintings associated with his "Dumka period," and when exhibited in Bombay during the riot-stricken hours of September 1947, they were lauded for being "Art to kill murder"—antidotes to "murderous intentions and hair-raising scares."[22]

The Dumka trips, joined also by other group members like Gopal Ghose, Paritosh Sen, and Nirode Mazumdar (who owned a paternal house in the region), were significant in pushing the group members to a new stage in form-making, their move toward primitivistic simplifications of form and use of fiery colors more evident than in their famine period, especially in the works of Maitra and Gopal Ghose. For Maitra, the Dumka period introduced an element of design and a formal sensibility borrowed from folk art. For Gopal Ghose, the Dumka period pushed him from his pre-1946 minimalistic linear drawings toward intense, brooding landscape studies with rich use of color, in paintings such as *Heart Red House* (1946), as well as semi-abstract, expressionistic canvasses of the communal riots in Calcutta in 1946–47, depicting streets and vehicles set aflame.[23] The group's association with Verrier Elwin, an anthropologist and connoisseur of folk art and craft, and the bureaucrat William Archer, who together were documenting tribal arts and songs during this period, as well as the extensive travels undertaken in the central provinces by Rathin Maitra, revealed to them the appeal of the landscape and culture of the tribal belt, which they sought to integrate into their repertoire. Although largely an urban middle-class fascination with the "primitive other," these ventures of the group in the mid-1940s provided another way of accommodating the rhetoric of "the people" in art, beyond a topical, direct response to the immediate social crisis of famines or riots. Most of the Dumka works were displayed at the third annual exhibition of the group held in Calcutta in 1947, along with the works of artists who were new to the group, such as the academic artist Abani Sen.[24]

The primitivistic idiom that entered the group's work after 1945 was already current in the works of Subho Tagore, who had long experimented in tribal motifs and designs, inspired by his travels in the tribal regions of Assam and Central India. His sculptures, executed in angular, stylized forms, some of which were part of the first annual exhibition of the group in 1945, displayed a penchant for the decorative idiom of tribal art with its mask-like faces defined by simplified contours. A richly illustrated volume of Subho Tagore's art up to 1945, with his poems and exhibition reviews, was published in Calcutta in 1945.[25]

It revealed his versatility with medium and his strong sense of design, drawn from handwoven textiles, temple architecture, and Art Deco linear patterns, as well as Chinese and Mexican architectural motifs. The volume contained reproductions of his signature portraits of literary and political figures made through geometrical color planes, his stylized decorative motifs of figure drawings, and bright-hued tempera painting on canvas or wood, as well as primitivistic wooden sculptures and art nouveau playing cards. The binding and layout of the album also reflected Tagore's experience with the design potential of folk art and his sustained interest in textile designs. The album was clearly an expensive publication, and as such, a rare possibility for Calcutta Group artists at this stage, as financial duress generally restricted the group to more-modest catalogues through the 1940s. Subho Tagore had, however, left the group following a disagreement soon after its first annual exhibition in 1945, concentrating thereafter solely on design and collection of art and antiquities. Post-1947, new artists like Abani Sen and his old comrade Gobardhan Ash, and younger artists like Rathin Mitra, Sunil Madhab Sen, Hemanta Mishra, and the much-known Santiniketan artist Ramkinkar Baij, were to join the group, with simultaneous estrangements of some of the founder-members like Rathin Maitra and Gopal Ghose (both left in 1949 to join the Academy of Fine Arts). Nirode Mazumdar and Paritosh Sen were also away, on prolonged stays in Paris, and from the late 1940s, they rarely showed their work in the group exhibitions.

When the group had mounted its first exhibition in Calcutta in 1945, its immediate challenge had been to wrestle out of the Indianness of the tradition that the Bengal School had patronized thus far. The anxieties that the Calcutta Group sparked among advocates of "Indian-ness" in art were not the same critiques of western-style academic art that had dominated disputes between Bengal School artists and their academic naturalist counterparts through the early 1900s. The Calcutta Group offered a distortion of form that brought contemporary European modernism, particularly post-impressionist and expressionist art, to the Indian context, which elicited mixed reviews for the group from the start. The first group exhibition succeeded in ruffling art circuits that had hitherto been largely limited to critiques of either orientalist art or academic naturalism. The patrons of the Indian style were disturbed by the group's complete evasion of Indian-ness and their full-hearted embrace of western modernism, particularly in their affinities to the works of Gauguin and Fauvist art. O. C. Gangooly, the art correspondent for the nationalist daily *Amrita Bazaar Patrika* and a veteran patron of nationalist art, put out a vitriolic review. The new art, he wrote, was just a revolt "borrowed from the West," its thin adherence to linearity bearing the only trace of "Indian pictorialism":

> We are told that this Group has ceased to look back to the past and has outgrown their bourgeois pride in their past history and the petty, if not silly, decorations of their "Indian Art" stage. And though it is categorically denied that these artists are not affected by the dusty wind from distant Europe, their national traditions appear to be submerged full five fathoms deep under the dirt carried by that dubious dusty wind.[26]

Other critics were more encouraging. Shahid Suhrawardy, by then art critic with *The Statesman*, lauded the young artists for their "search for basic form" over "sentimental prettiness and irrelevant details" and their "vigor and authentic artistic intentions." The works, though largely inchoate and inexperienced, still showed promise of developing "personality" and sophistication of artistic technique, which, wrote Suhrawardy, should be the sole standards of judgment: "The standard by which they have to be judged is the same as applies to all art, whether they have been able to realize their conceptions with the help of adequate technique."[27] Suhrawardy's support for modernist styles had first been expressed in his celebrated review of Jamini Roy's works in 1937, which we encountered in Chapter 1; in appraising the first exhibition of the Calcutta Group, Suhrawardy asserted once more the purely artistic criterion of art appreciation. He found in the group's works a completely different order of beauty—"ugly and frightful, and far from the attractive presentation of 'beauty' as ordinarily understood"—that resonated "the expression of the artist's aesthetic excitement."[28] In the works of the Calcutta Group, Suhrawardy noted the influence of European masters like Gauguin, Modigliani, and Matisse.

The most significant anxieties prompted by the group were, however, not around their internationalism, but rather around the social imperative that marked their art. The social content of their works was to remain a bone of contention in their critical appreciation. Suhrawardy's review of the Calcutta exhibition questioned that content, which he felt was "irrelevant to the critical appraisement of works of art."[29] O. C. Gangooly identified the problem more sharply in his review: "A shrewd and subtle attempt is being made by ingratiating flatterers, to rope in our artists to function as cheap propagandists for politics. It is to be hoped that the artists will escape these traps to strangle their spiritual freedom in the name of the political substitute."[30]

Commenting on the introduction provided to the group's first exhibition in Bombay in April 1945, the renowned art critic of the *Times of India*, Rudi von Leyden, questioned the need for art to have any social function at all. The "revolutionary bias" of the group and its claims for the social function of art, he felt, were a "surprisingly negative attitude to take"; realism and the popular in art were only bound to accede to doctrinaire reductionism.[31]

The 1945 text introducing the group to the Bombay audience was written by Bishnu Dey, who became in these years their patron-critic, writing most of the reviews and forewords to their modest exhibition catalogues and introducing them to the wider cultural currents of the 1940s. At the same time, Dey articulated a critical agency for the Calcutta Group in developing a radical aesthetic, a modernity that emanated from the demands of contemporary social crisis. His association with them is significant in understanding the linkages between the plastic arts and the left in these years. More importantly, his writings constitute the earliest corpus of art literature on the group and direct us to the conceptual grids framing the identity, agenda, and politics of their practice. These writings also suggest the underlying tensions in the perceptions around the group, which would become increasingly evident in the late 1940s.

BISHNU DEY AND THE POLITICS OF PROGRESSIVE ART

The arrival of the Calcutta Group, widely noticed in the city's art circuits, was not accompanied by any manifesto, nor did the group members reveal any agenda or ideal in contemporary periodicals or art literature. An almost singular source of ideas and information on the group during its early years (1944–49) was Bishnu Dey, by then a leading figure in the anti-fascist cultural forums—which by 1944 had come under the more pronounced organizational and ideological grip of the Communist Party of India. It has to be remembered, however, that no figure in the Calcutta Group was a card-carrying member of the CPI; the group's association with the party was largely limited to its interactions with protagonists and patrons of the cultural movement, and members of the *Parichoy* circuit.[32]

Rathin Maitra's elder brother Jyotirindra Maitra was a key figure within the IPTA, noted for his composition of revolutionary songs, *Janayuddher Gaan* (*Songs for the People's War*).[33] Rathin Maitra is known to have been the editor of the Fine Arts Sub-Committee of the Anti-Fascist Writers' and Artists' Association,[34] and Nirode Mazumdar made documentary sketches for the annual conferences of the All India Kisan Sabha at Netrakona in 1945.[35] The Calcutta Group was established soon after the formation of the IPTA, and its association with Jyotirindra Maitra and, through him, Bishnu Dey positioned the group in proximity to front organizations of the CPI like the IPTA, the Anti-Fascist Writers' and Artists' Association, and the Friends of the Soviet Union in Bengal. In 1944, soon after the formation of the group, they exhibited their works under the aegis of the Anti-Fascist Writers' and Artists' Association, and in the following year with IPTA's traveling Cultural Squad in Bombay.

Bishnu Dey was closely associated with the group throughout its decade-long tenure. Prodosh Dasgupta recalls him as a regular visitor to the group's haunt at Subho Tagore's studio and as a regular participant in discussions and debates on art. Dey's lasting friendship with Nirode Mazumdar and other group members like Rathin Maitra and Gopal Ghose helped integrate him with the group's public lives.[36] Subho Tagore recalls P. C. Joshi's visiting his studio in 1944, accompanied by Bishnu Dey, Hiren Mukherjee, and Snehangshu Acharya, and being inspired by Joshi's engagement with the artists.[37]

Dey's earliest writings on the artists of the Calcutta Group date from 1944, when he produced the brief but critical introduction to the group's famine exhibits in the *Bengal Painters' Testimony* album, and a short introductory piece on Subho Tagore, "Blue to Red, Subho Tagore Now."[38] Subho Tagore's association with the left and anti-fascist cultural rhetoric was noted in left-wing circuits beginning in 1942, when he organized his one-man exhibition in aid of distressed poets and artists of China, held at the Chinese Consulate of Calcutta. His semi-autobiographical book, *Neel Rakta Laal Hoye Gechhe* (*Blue Blood Turns Red*), published in May 1944 (illustrated by Gopal Ghose and Nirode Mazumdar);[39] his volume of poetry dedicated to May Day, *May Day and Other Poems* (1945); and his cover design for a May Day brochure from 1944 carrying five poems from the "Progressive" poets of Bengal (fig. 3.6)[40] consolidated this association with the progressive movement. For Bishnu Dey, Subho Tagore's bohemian denial of his aristocratic blue blood, his extensive travels among the Garo tribes of Assam and the Gonds of Bastar, and his inspiration from China and the Soviet Union were symbolic of his move toward socialist construction in his artistic repertoire; Tagore's Marxism, Dey hoped, would help him to channel his "remarkable sense of design" into "directions of functional art."[41]

In 1945, Bishnu Dey wrote two extensive pieces on the Calcutta Group, laying out in more concrete terms the social imperative around the group's art. The first, "When Artists Awake . . . Pen-Picture of the Calcutta Group" (fig. 3.7), appeared in *People's War* in April 1945, after the Bombay exhibition of the group. Within the format of an exhibition review, Dey introduced the Calcutta Group as a collective of diverse artistic calibers and lineage, united in a common purpose of developing a fresh visual language in art that sought to depart from both the historicism of the Bengal School and the dominant academic conventions of the art schools. Providing brief notes on each of the found-

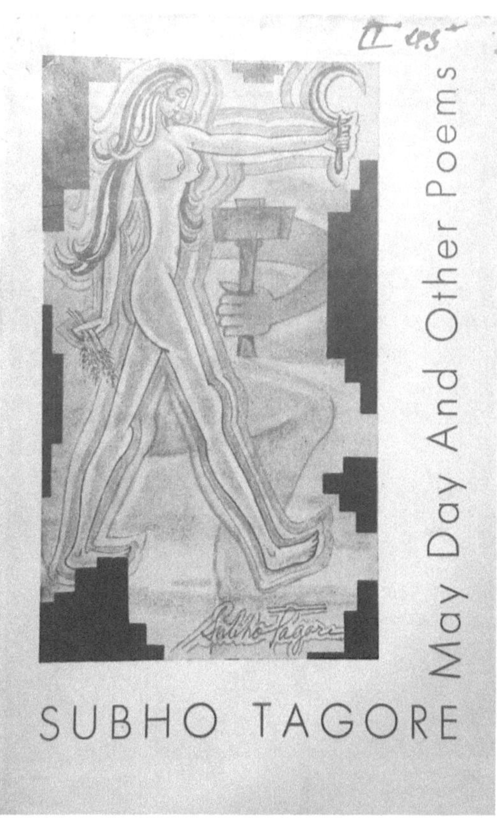

FIGURE 3.6. *Subho Tagore, cover design for May Day brochure from 1944. Source: Private papers of Rathin Maitra. Courtesy of artist's son Romain Maitra.*

ing members of the group, he underscored the principle of "social symbolism" that motivated them, and their will toward "freedom from academic conventions," paralleled by a felt need to "have a vision and social-aesthetic awareness."[42] The group was grounded, he noted, in the fundamental premise that the "supreme value of individuality lies in its social symbolism." The members' works provided an inchoate organic connection with folk art and the attempt to reach out to the people: "Folk-art with its purity of abstract form and conventions, which acquire validity in and through social life has helped the Group in their awareness of the unity, direct or often indirect, between form and content," and "to integrate their work with the lives of the people."

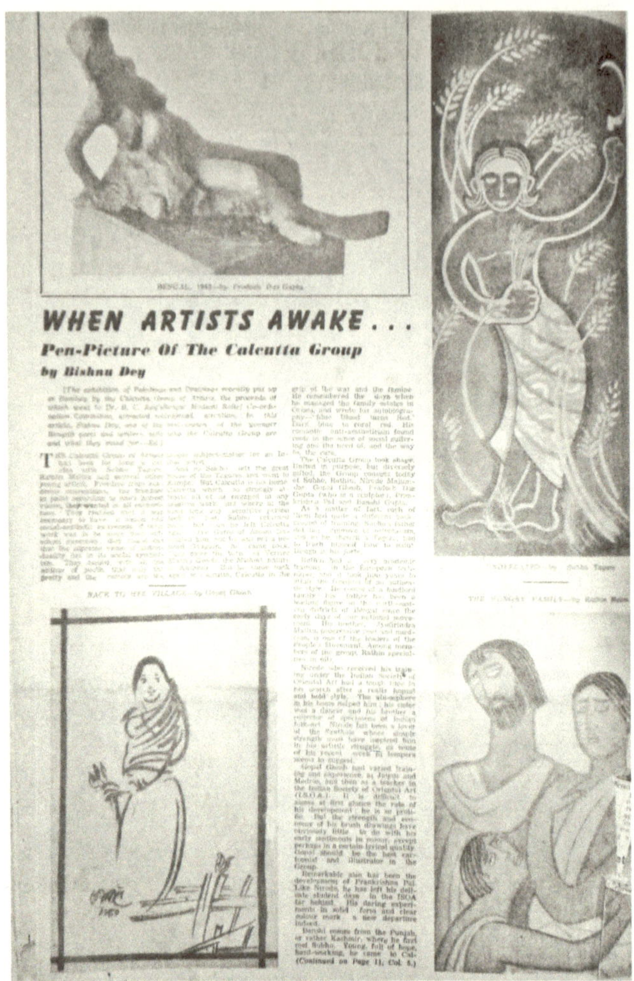

WHEN ARTISTS AWAKE . . .

Pen-Picture Of The Calcutta Group

by Bishnu Dey

FIGURE 3.7. *Bishnu Dey, "When Artists Awake . . . Pen-Picture of the Calcutta Group," People's War, 15 April 1945. Source: P. C. Joshi Collections. Courtesy of Archives on Contemporary History, Dr. B. R. Ambedkar Central Library, JNU, New Delhi.*

To Dey the group represented "the type of the patriot as artist," embodying a commitment to learn, understand, and "feel the life-beat of our people, our kisans and our workers, and to cloak it in the art-form which they have been trained to express."[43] The folk thus became for him a mode of locating social awareness in the works of the group, echoing Dey's writings on Jamini Roy from the same period. His rhetoric of the social symbolism of folk art is similar to the wider notion of the people and the popularization of art that the left was patronizing through the 1940s in India. It also resonated with the larger recovery of folk art by the communist movement internationally during this period, exemplified by the works of the Popular Front critic Sidney Finkelstein, who argued that the continuous tradition of realism is fostered by "the germinating power" of folk art.[44]

Dey's second piece on the group was written as an introductory text accompanying the same Bombay exhibition of 1945, and reprinted as the introduction in a subsequent catalogue of Nirode Mazumdar's paintings published by the group in 1946.[45] Within the short format offered by the piece, Dey developed what can be seen as the earliest manifesto of the group, highlighting the social underpinnings of the group and associating their "visual thinking" with an "immediate social function." Rejecting the alleged western derivations of the group's art, he asserted the contextual specificities in their works. "The experiments in the studios of the Calcutta Group," he wrote, "have a large social justification behind them," and countering the critic O. C. Gangooly's disparagement of the European influences in the group's works, he retorted, "It is not so much the wind from distant Europe but rather the savage reality of our life which [has] informed the spirit of interrogation and revolt in the young artists of Calcutta." The "peculiar reality" of famines, war, and destitution, he felt, imparted to the group's work a "concrete contextuality" that determined their stylistic choices.[46] Dey's piece accorded a definite political edge and class dimension to the group's works in the 1940s, as he remarked that these artists were moving ahead of the "early and upper middle class stage" in Indian art, when Indian nationalism looked to the past to give pictorial shape to nationalist pride in history, to a stage when nationalism had instead found its direction "in and through the people": "It is in the context of political upsurge and growing economic crisis and on the background of recurring floods and famines and chronic epidemics that our young artists seem to turn to a revision of visual thinking."[47] The break with the past, according to Dey, was thus idiomatic as well as ideological, and this disjuncture, he argued, was also a departure from the images of an idealized nation toward concrete artistic interfaces with locality and context—in this case, one ruptured by hunger and displacement.

Dey's writings on the group resonate and run parallel with his own poetic repertoire, with his commitment to the formal and the social values in poetry being carried into his art-critical works. In Dey's poetry, a dialogue between context and structure, between the social and the formal, is evident, with a more pronounced socialist accent after his third book of verse, *Purbalekh* (1936–41), which exactly paralleled the period of the rise of the left-wing cultural movement in India. The social content of his poetic works increased steadily in *Sat Bhai Champa* (1941–44) and *Sandwiper Char* (1943–47), each addressing the sociopolitical flux of the turbulent 1940s, of famine, fascism, communal genocide, and political struggle.[48] This echoed the rising rhetoric of realism and social commitment in art since the late 1930s, and as socialist rhetoric became more pronounced in the mid-1940s, Dey would register these tensions in his interactions with the cultural movement. By the late 1940s, for instance, he faced increasing accusations from the party circuits of being genteel and too modernist for the communist project of the popularization of culture.

Bishnu Dey had never been a member of the Communist Party; rather, he was an ardent fellow-traveler. His friendships with party activists like Hiren Mukherjee and General Secretary P. C. Joshi gave him the freedom to accommodate himself within the collaborative ethics of the anti-fascist cultural resistance, though his relationship with the more conservative faction in the movement remained fraught. Post-1945, after the Nazi defeat, this section of the party became less tolerant toward the earlier demand for a wide ideological front and began crafting a more conservative party rhetoric in cultural criticism, evident in the changed tenor of the critical-review journal *Parichoy* after it was sold by Sudhindranath Datta to cultural workers of the Communist Party in July–August 1944. Dey's differences with the party became more vivid in the post-1946 period, when he expressly participated in cultural debates taking place in the Communist Party in

France. He supported Roger Garaudy's position of the impossibility of any aesthetic theory of the Communist Party. In 1947, Dey had translated Garaudy's original article "Artists without Uniform" as "Urdihin Shilpi," published in the local Communist Party periodical *Arani* (February 28, 1947). In the Garaudy-Aragon debate that ensued within the French Communist Party, widely discussed in the left-wing press in India, Dey sided with Garaudy, while the majority within the Indian left sided with Louis Aragon's support for a Communist aesthetic policy. Post-1947, Dey's distance from the party and the movement itself increased, his Marxist politics now branded as "Trotskyite reaction" and "perverted," most vehemently in the articles against him published in *Parichoy*.[49] By the end of 1947, Dey's dissociation from *Parichoy* was complete.[50] In July 1948, he started *Sahityapatra*, under the editorship of Chanchalkumar Chattopadhyay. In a critical piece titled "Rajay Rajay," published in *Sahityapatra* in 1948–49, he put forward his own position on aesthetics and politics. Referring to Garaudy, he noted that though consciousness is basically a product of social, economic, and organic causes, there is a spontaneity and autonomy in art and literature that identifies an artist or a writer as progressive, the "personal problem of taste of inclination" being an integral part of the judgment.[51]

Dey's increasing isolation within the left's cultural movement coincided with his association with the Calcutta Group. This marginalization became apparent in his vehement advocacy of the group's modernist aesthetic, which he saw as firmly rooted in social signification. His understanding of left-wing aesthetics, evident in his art criticism around the Calcutta Group and his earlier writings on Jamini Roy, went beyond instrumentalism or didacticism. Despite an ideological commitment to the Soviet Union, he was never a patron of mechanistic realism. Instead, in his conceptualization of the Calcutta Group, Dey can be seen to invoke persistently the assimilation and portrayal of a complex contemporary reality through strong formal consciousness, free from ideological determinism.[52] The political and aesthetic potentials of folk forms were key to his conceptualization of modernism, and his trips to Rikhia in the tribal belts of Dumka with Calcutta Group artists through 1945–46 consolidated this dimension, in both his poetry and his art writings. In 1946, he went to Rikhia with his family and group members Nirode Mazumdar, Rathin Maitra, and Gopal Ghose.[53] In April of that year, the artists and Dey gathered at Rikhia once more, this time along with the civil servant and art historian William Archer. The group's association with Archer and the anthropologist Verrier Elwin resulted from their close ties with Bishnu Dey.[54] In 1946, Archer was the deputy commissioner of Dumka, the headquarters of the tribal provinces, and it was at his invitation that Dey, along with Nirode Mazumdar, Gopal Ghose, and Prankrishna Pal, went there, eventually to be joined by Rathin Maitra and Paritosh Sen.[55] This period also reflected Dey's own interest in tribal motifs and songs. The publication of his collection of poems *Sandwiper Char* coincided with the Dumka phase of the Calcutta Group and featured adaptations from folk themes and forms found in the tribal songs of Oraons and Santhals, and folk songs of Chattisgarh.[56]

Dey introduced the artists of the Calcutta Group to Jamini Roy, and in his writings, he continued to uphold Roy as the chief inspiration behind the group's modernist experiments. The very first review of the group, by Shahid Suhrawardy for *The Statesman*, had also ascribed the group's "paternity" to the modernism of Jamini Roy; the will of the young artists to revolt against both academic conventions and blind acceptance of tradition, as well as their efforts at resolving the formal tension between tradition and modernity, were seen as a direct result of Roy's revolt.[57] In Dey's writings, this relationship between the group's social commitment and what he had earlier described as the socialist symbolism in Jamini Roy[58] was defined and expanded. According to some of the group members, however, this view was not entirely accurate; for instance, Prodosh Dasgupta, a founding member of the Calcutta Group and a dedicated chronicler of the group's short career, in his memoirs denies any direct influence from Jamini Roy, asserting the originality of the group artists' own thoughts on form, in contrast to Dey's claims.[59] In fact, Dasgupta's memoirs repeatedly express anxieties about Dey's ideological framing of the group's works, particularly with regard to the association he forged with the left-wing cultural movement, which was sustained in large part through artists Rathin Maitra and Nirode Mazumdar, both of whom, Dasgupta noted, were friends of Dey.[60]

Bishnu Dey's own dissociation with the party carries interesting parallels with the group's increasing distance from party circuits and from the cultural rhetoric of progressive art. Dasgupta's dissonant assertions are significant in tracing its ideological trajectory in the late 1940s. The fifth annual exhibition of the group, in 1949, Dasgupta noted in his memoirs, brought about a decisive break with the left-wing circuits. The exhibition displayed a considerable body of work produced by group members during the period 1943–49, spanning their famine works, the Dumka phase, and the post-1947 works on the riots and refugee influx in the wake of partition, as well as their new treatments of vignettes of everyday life outside of the kind of historical ruptures that increasingly defined their works in 1948–49.

The exhibition also marked a shift within the group, with new artists entering, the old cohesion loosening, and group members moving more toward formal experimentation rather than toward immediate social themes. The exhibition drew renewed attention to the group as a modernist collective in the newly independent nation-state. Their style of "distortion and exaggeration and the choice of arbitrary color schemes of high chromatic values" as well as "their choice of trivial subjects and models," derided by critics like O. C. Gangooly in 1945, were now praised by him for introducing a "new order of beauty," making "innovative, progressive strides" in the pursuit of understanding the basic aesthetics of form, color, harmony, and balance.[61] At the exhibition, Gopal Haldar, the veteran Communist cultural worker, then editor of *Parichoy* and also a friend of the group, is said to have approached Dasgupta, feeling "completely out of sorts after visiting the exhibition," and asked him whether the group was not "going astray from the cherished path of socialist realism"; Dasgupta recalls his answer to Haldar's question, a simple yet emphatic denial of any ideological commitment: "We never took the pledge to follow the path of socialist realism. All we want is to understand life and interpret it in terms of creative art. Indeed we believe in humanism *without any political binding or direction* (emphasis mine)."[62]

This dialogue, Dasgupta recalls in his memoirs, disrupted the relationship with Haldar, but also expressed how, in their aims and achievements, the group felt "progressively enriched."[63] The subtle tensions here between vocabularies of the social and the socialist cannot be missed. It was the collapsing of the notion of social commitment in their works (hitherto upheld by various critics, including Bishnu Dey) with the political value of the socialist that created an ideological crisis for the group in this period. Hence came Dasgupta's vehement rejections of any association with the idiomatic category of realism. Given the backdrop of a wider international formalization of socialist realism as the official art doctrine of the Stalinist Soviet Union, this dialogue between the party critic Haldar and the artist Dasgupta connotes a more structural tension between content and form, realism and modernism, which became increasingly sharply defined in the post-1948 period.

In the art writings from/on the group in post-independence India, a recurrent feature was a language of humanism, shorn of "realist" associations. Gopal Haldar's critique of the apparent eclipse of socialist ideals in the works of the group in 1949 contrasts starkly with Bishnu Dey's review of the Calcutta Group exhibition of January 1949, published in *The People* (May 22, 1949).[64] This piece became a defense of sorts for the modernist art of the Calcutta Group, which, Dey argued, represented the "dialectic" of form and content; the group, Dey exhorted, should not be deterred by the critiques offered by "so-called" Marxist critics paying lip service to progressive criticism. Invoking Francis Jourdain's recent writings in *La Pensée* (no. 21, 1948), Dey foregrounded issues of the social roots of art, particularly ideological determinism. He urged the Calcutta Group to develop artistic form from their deep-rooted subjectivities, beyond the mere surfaces of form or an uncritical realism, and to ground their works in a "dialectical sensibility" of the outside world and artistic consciousness. Their public and their critics, he asserted, ought to be "patient" to appreciate the resolution of this dialectic.[65]

The 1949 exhibition also saw the first articulated manifesto from the group's members, drafted by Prodosh Dasgupta and circulated in the form of a newspaper piece during the exhibition. Dasgupta recalls that fifty copies of this article from the *Republic* were kept at the entrance of the 1949 exhibition, of which many were then sold.[66] The historical significance of the manifesto is noteworthy, particularly since a more widely discussed catalogue text of the Calcutta Group published during their last exhibition in 1953 has subsequently come to be viewed by art historians as the first (rather belated) group manifesto. The 1953 text was actually a modified version of this 1949 text, and its differences, though slight, carry significant ideological resonances that provide insight into the ideological landscapes of the early postcolonial artistic field in India.

IN THE IMAGE OF "MAN"

Between 1947 and 1953, when the final exhibition took place in Delhi, the Calcutta Group exhibited some of their most important works from the 1940s. Throughout this period, their concerns regarding representation of the human condition persisted, albeit often in images of the everyday sights of rural and urban labor and leisure. These concerns can be identified in the 1949 text penned by Prodosh Dasgupta. The period from 1910 through 1943, wrote Dasgupta, was marked by "an increasing secularization of politics and an expansion in the democratic consciousness," a change that was of fundamental importance in providing "new ideals" for modern art. In India, as in the West, these changed ideals were reflected in struggles against classicism and religious bias in art: "The Gods and Goddesses are being pulled down from their lofty pedestals and Man has been enthroned in their place."[67] A significant portion of this text would be reprinted in a revised version for the group's last exhibition.

In the 1953 piece, Dasgupta identified the central principle of the group as humanism, which he defined as art both "international and independent," based on the celebration of "Man." The guiding slogan for the group, he wrote in a distinctly secular tone, was that "Man is supreme, there is none above him." Yet in the 1949 text, the political undercurrents of the group's formation were more prominent, an element absent from the 1953 version. In 1949, Dasgupta acknowledged the need for art to have connections with life; in the early 1940s, he wrote, an increasing number of people were demanding that art be rescued from "the ivory tower," to be connected intimately "with the politics and economics of the country, an art reflecting among other things, the sorrows and sufferings of the people."[68] By the time of the 1953 exhibition, however, this political undertone had been diluted, the revised text declaring at the very outset the arrival of "Man" as the supreme subject of art. This humanist ideal remained with the group, through debates about the primacy of content over form and vice versa, and in spite of the misgivings of some of the founding members and their critics about the political associations of some of the group members. Indeed, humanism as an ideal was evoked in both the 1949 and the 1953 texts as the key concern of the group.

In the 1949 and the 1953 versions, resonances with international modernism were equally pronounced. Both declared as the guiding maxim of the group that art should be "international and independent," that art cannot progress or develop "if we always look back to our past glories and cling to our old traditions at all cost," and that the purity of tradition cannot be maintained in a modern world where art is becoming an international activity. The ideal motivating the Calcutta Group, according to the manifesto, was thus to choose and integrate foreign influences with the national style and tradition, "to understand the spirit of our times and acknowledge the dictates of necessity."[69] The Calcutta Group, Dasgupta stated elsewhere, was "basically tradition-bound," though with a "liberal attitude borrowing from the outside world to enrich ourselves [so as to] express in a better and much fuller way."[70] Hence tradition was to be mediated via a keen appreciation and selection from international art movements and practices. This internationalism was seen as a direct reflection of the "spirit of the times," and as a moment of maturation for Indian modern art.[71]

The language of contemporaneity evoked here is connected to ideas of progress and selfhood, and the moment of the group's arrival is visualized as a beginning point in the search for pure form. The idea of freedom was thus equated both with freedom from the heavy ideological load of tradition and with a modernist subjectivity that aims at a free "progressive synthesis" of internationalism and indigenous tradition. The idea of artistic modernity was collapsed within that of democratic consciousness—the arrival of the "common man" and, more importantly, a progressive "secularization of politics," both of which were conscious ideals of the new Nehruvian nation-state.[72] We might ask if this "man" stands for the rights of pure individualistic autonomy, or if "man" is a representation of the collective, a sort of microcosm for the social at large. The assertions of the supremacy of the "individual," as contained in the professed political modernity of an independent nation-state, appear more in sync with the modernizing aspirations of India in the 1950s, which were furthered by the individualist assertions of the secular man in quest of selfhood. The early 1950s made this shift in the rhetoric around progressive art and the Calcutta Group more clear.

In 1950, the group held a joint exhibition in Calcutta with the Progressive Artists' Group, which had been formed in Bombay in 1947. The exhibition was organized by the Calcutta Group, and carried in its catalogue introduction a brief note on the aims and objectives of the Bombay Progressives. This stated in no uncertain terms that "Art will, as long as it remains, be esoteric. It can be utilitarian, didactic, socialist and religious, but then it is mercenary, pedagogic, political and devotional but never pure intrinsic art."[73] The artists claimed freedom for content and technique, and a desire to arrive at a "vigorous synthesis" of elemental laws of aesthetic order, plastic coordination, and color composition, without any ideological adherence or strict method. This tenor of formal freedom was also prominent in reviews of the Calcutta Group's last show in Delhi in 1953, most notably in the review by Indologist and art historian Klaus Fischer that was published in *Marg*, the most visible art periodical of the time. In his substantial and well-illustrated review, Fischer ascribed a "spiritual" journey to the group—

"from the cataclysm of the famine years to the dawn of a new scientific age—one of factories, dams . . . and the triumph of 'Man.'" The "Human and the Divine" were valuable reference points in the works of the Calcutta Group, Fischer suggested, and the artists strove to capture them in the true spirit of the mechanical age through the rejection of traditional forms and the search for new ones; their art studied "archetypes common to all great civilizations of the past and the present . . . not in the unconscious manner of primitive culture, but with full consciousness."[74] The group, he asserted, was not constrained by any singular style or "ism," nor had they "exchanged the slavery of society or nature with that of fashion or business": their art was thus characterized by "freedom"—"of thought, style and purpose." Fischer saw in the group a "will" to be "good citizens": "They earn their livelihood as art teachers, museum artists, gallery keepers, staff artists or lawyers. They are not forced to 'produce' works of art for pleasing the public and for selling them at any price, especially at the cost of good taste."[75]

In Fischer's text, arguably the first elaborate and widely circulated review to feature each member of the group, the identity of the modern Indian artist was subsumed within the institutional spaces of the new nation-state. With regard to the Calcutta Group, such a claim is perhaps not wholly unfounded; by the mid-1950s, most of the Calcutta Group artists were employed in art institutions—Prodosh Dasgupta was the professor of sculpture at the Government College of Art and Craft, Calcutta, and soon to become the director of the newly established National Gallery of Modern Art, New Delhi; and both Rathin Maitra and Gopal Ghose were employed at the Academy of Fine Arts in Calcutta. Fischer celebrated at once the internationalism and individualism of the Calcutta Group, and tethered both to the ideals of patriotism and citizenship. "How can the contemporary artist best serve his country?" he asked, offering as an answer a curious marriage of the individual and the national: an artist could best serve his nation not by producing "obtrusive works of religious or social contents, but [by] directly devoting himself to art for art's sake, by developing his forms as best as possible and even by departing from the contemporaries' demands, always following his own views and ideas."[76] Fischer's ideas seemed to contain an implicit contradiction between the artist's absolute creative freedom and his "service" to the nation. Yet such conflicts or (at best) dichotomies were liquidated by his valorizing precisely this "pure subjectivity" of modernist art, and wedding it to visions of political modernity in the secular, democratic republic. The idea of art's social commitment, hitherto dominant in the readings of the group, was negated both as purpose and as content, almost as a misfit in the post-independence modernist milieu: "The subjects in the exhibits of the Calcutta artists are of less importance. Indian nature and men, folklore of the different tribes from the Eastern and Northern regions of India. Social subjects (especially 1943–44, when they were "urgent") are only starting points of their artistic ideas."[77]

The gradual transition in art discourse around the Calcutta Group, from the "concrete contextuality" of the mid-1940s to the humanist individualism of the late 1940s and early 1950s, reflects a structural transition of the cultural imperatives of the nation-state and, indeed, a conscious depoliticization of the discursive tenor of art—in particular a marked dissociation from leftist ideologies. For the artists, the 1940s was a critical moment in the enactment of modernism in Indian art, a "moment" that had close connections with trajectories of left-wing cultural imagination. In Bengal, the famine made these connections more concrete, and at the same time more prone to eventual slippages between the values of the social and the socialist. The affiliations and denunciations of the group members also offer an entry into the dilemmas within the left-wing cultural intervention of the 1940s, the members representing the curious mélange of artistic subjectivities that both participated in and differed from the left-wing rhetoric to various degrees, producing thereby a complex array of artistic radicalisms. In its transitions, the group also registered the often-missed negotiations between context and form *within* modern art during these critical transitional years of the late 1940s and the early 1950s.

The group's consistent concern with the social in art, despite internal differences and the eventual dissolution of the group itself, needs to be read against the more general preoccupations of their contemporaries, particularly in the context of the promise of political modernity under the new prime minister of post-independence India, Jawaharlal Nehru. This era introduced into art discourse systematic researches into the nation's local, folk, and craft heritage, and simultaneously consolidated the notion of the new citizen-artist, one who performs his conscious role as artist within the nation by portraying/engaging with the nation's heritage, through its land, labor, and craft. As the 1950s brought about a renewed presence of the nation as the central trope of official ideology and, more importantly, a renewed negotiation of the modern, the new aesthetic of the Nehruvian nation-state consciously and selectively appropriated the national-popular ethos of the 1940s left-wing cultural movement by celebrating the same notion of the "people" that had been repeated since the interwar decades, despite multiple ideological shifts. Yet the Nehruvian aesthetic liquidated the radical oppositional content within the idea of the people that the 1940s had generated. By celebrating the individual with the collective, Nehruvian cultural modernity allowed for the collapsing of individual freedom with formal freedom. The social was now increasingly to be equated with the socialist, which was negatively construed under a growing ideological streamlining during the Cold War. As review literature on the Calcutta Group reveals, radicalism too became reframed as doctrinaire rigidity, while the modern became the call for freedom—for society and, more importantly, for the individual.

The new nation-state built its narrative of the modern by selecting pre-1940s artistic production, whether in the romantic revivalist works of the early Bengal School painters or the ruralist works of the interwar period. The radicalism of the 1940s remains a missing link between these early stages and the new art of the 1950s that the state patronized. With realism discredited in the mid-twentieth century due to its appropriation by Stalinist socialist realism and the cultural orthodoxy of Zhdanovism, the idiomatic and ideological collapsing of the social with the socialist has created in art narratives in India a veritable blind spot in locating the dominant yet ambiguous realism of the 1940s. At most, art in Bengal in the 1940s is captured within the momentous immediacy of the Bengal famine of 1943, and hence the association and dissolution of collectives such as the Calcutta Group remain tied to the narratives of the "moment" of social realism of the mid-1940s, which are rendered invalid in more stable times. The socially rooted modernism of the group also becomes a vernacular art language of fraught locational aesthetics that gets subsumed under the modernist promise of the new post-independence nation-state, as radical artists are (often discursively) transmogrified into good citizens, and critical realism into deradicalized humanism.

Through the 1940s, the Calcutta Group had various degrees of association with the left, although most of its members had avoided the rhetoric of socialist idealism. Yet, they shared a conscious will to portray concrete social reality, irrespective of personal differences, be they ideological or stylistic, as is affirmed in articles they produced during that decade. In the writings of Rathin Maitra, for instance, the element of class consciousness was prominent, registering in his works through the 1940s in his adherence to the trope of laboring bodies. Writing in *Atikrama*, a journal published by the Government School of Art in Calcutta, Maitra called for art to be located within the contemporary demands of mass politics. His article "Bharatiya Silpe Jug Paribartan" ("Paradigm Shift in Indian Art" [translation mine]), though short and not overtly polemical, noted the important shift in the class character of art from the times of Abanindranath Tagore. The contemporary art scene in Calcutta was witnessing the "twilight of the aristocracy and the arrival of the common man"—the "middle classes." The change in the social composition and class content of art, Maitra noted, was symbolized in the person of Jamini Roy, who produced art for the common man, a pictorial idiom shorn of classicism and grounded firmly in earthy tones and the folk motifs of rural India. Maitra's attention to the changing social character of the art world and of the vanguard artists themselves suggests not only the anxieties of a new generation of artists in the city, but also his affinities with a Marxist conception of the dialectics and internal dynamics of the field of practice, as well as the social demands on aesthetic practice itself. The volume, though undated, is evidently from 1944–45, being jointly edited by Subho Tagore and Maitra, who appears as the editor of the visual art section of the art school.[78] Maitra's close association with Bishnu Dey and the left-wing cultural movement, primarily through his brother and IPTA activist Jyotirindranath Maitra, was criticized in later years by other Calcutta Group members such as Prodosh Dasgupta—though Dasgupta's own concerns in portraying labor and leisure were not far removed from a committed social sensibility, which continued in his works until his marked shift toward abstraction beginning in the late 1950s.

A significant concern of the artists since their earliest meetings had been the connection between art and life. The notion of "Man" that highlighted their manifestos of 1949 and 1953 served as the fulcrum for tensions around subjectivity and content, the individual and the collective, as well as questions of commitment and autonomy in art, under changing affiliations with the left-wing cultural movement. While Dasgupta distanced himself from left-wing affiliations, he acknowledged nonetheless the milieu generated by the "cultural revolution" that developed with the Second World War and the Bengal Famine of 1943, wherein all "progressive-minded writers, poets, dramatists, actors and musicians" provided "whole-hearted support" to the Calcutta Group.[79] The group participated in this rhetoric of radicalism despite the occasional discomfort of some of its members, sharing in the wider commitment to art's social imperative that was tied to Bengal's cathartic experiences of famine and genocide during the 1940s. This commitment to locality also allowed them to imagine a socially engaged realist sensibility outside the strict ideological framings of socialist realism that were increasingly upheld by the CPI from the mid-1940s. Even to a dissident like Dasgupta, this social sensibility was the beginning of a progressive art movement that spread to the rest of the country through the next decade.

Between 1943 and 1953, the Calcutta Group was never a stable whole; its membership was in constant flux, particularly after 1947, and very few from the initial core group remained beyond the late 1940s. Internal strife and lack of cohesion are often blamed for the group's eventual dissolution. Subho Tagore had been the first to quit the group, in 1945, while Paritosh Sen and Nirode Mazumdar ceased to feature in the group shows after leaving for Paris in the late 1940s; in 1948, Gopal Ghose and Rathin Maitra left and joined the Academy of Fine Arts, and in the 1950s, Prodosh Dasgupta joined the newly established National Gallery of Modern Art in New Delhi. New members were incorporated in the following years: Rathin Mitra and Sunil Madhab Sen in 1947, Abani Sen and Gobardhan Ash in 1949, and Ramkinkar Baij, the esteemed modernist artist from Kala Bhawan, in 1950. By this time, the group was not integrating young, upcoming artists, but rather those who were already established, in an effort to revive or sustain the critical presence of the group in the artistic field. After the last exhibition, in 1953, the dissolution was complete, although the individual members continued to work successfully in the following decades, some of them producing more mature work than that of their Calcutta Group phase.

The dissolution of the Calcutta Group has historically signified a diminution of their credibility as a collective, or even of the tentative ideas they had sought to engage with, no matter how briefly, in the 1940s. The Calcutta Group features in progressive narratives as just another progressive artist collective formed in the 1940s, along with the Delhi Silpi Chakra in Delhi and the Progressive Groups in Kashmir and Madras, and indeed as marginal to that narrative as well, while art historical attention has continued to be heavily focused on the Bombay Progressives. The Calcutta Group, as group member and noted artist Paritosh Sen noted, despite being the first "progressive group" of the 1940s, and having been involved in the formation of the Bombay Progressives, was not mentioned in the manifesto or other statements of that group.[80] However, in its art, agenda, and anxieties, and even in its inherent weaknesses and contradictions, the Calcutta Group was, it can be argued, the missing link in narratives of the Indian modern during the transitional years of decolonization, where the mantle of modernism tended to pass from the pre-1940s experiments of Gaganendranath Tagore, Rabindranath Tagore, Amrita Sher-Gil, and Jamini Roy to the Bombay Progressives in the 1950s. The challenge, however, lies not in retrieving the muffled voices of an under-represented collective from the dominant narratives, nor in investigating the verities of such claims of marginalization. It is necessary, rather, to follow the mechanisms and languages of "selection" that framed the Calcutta Group under the shifting art-critical values during decolonization, for they reveal not only the aesthetic ideologies of these transitional decades but the production of a hegemonic discourse of postcolonial national-modern identity.

HERE, ON THE THRESHOLD of moving on to the next theme of this book, "Postcolonial Displacements," I would like to make two points.

First, slippages between the social and the socialist during the late 1940s and the early 1950s carry clues to the political unconscious of midcentury Indian modern art. At its core sits the idea of progressive art. The separation of the idea of the progressive from its aesthetic and political lineages stemming from the 1930s, and its consequent "release" into the spaces of modernist aesthetics on the brink of postcolonial "arrival," seem to appear in art writing as an accelerated process—triggered by independence and partition, as well as by the promises of a postcolonial modernity under Jawaharlal Nehru. This process, when slowed down and explored through discursive shifts, makes more visible the rhetorical transformations that were prompted by both a retreating cultural activism within the CPI, and the agendas and anxieties of the new group of modernist artists who were seeking to reframe their art in a new nation-state. The 1950s, hence, carry hidden stories of displacements that lie beneath the more cataclysmic ruptures of partition.

Second, in both the visual reportage of the artist-cadres and the works of the Calcutta Group, there is a critical diffraction of hitherto dominant narratives of art and the nation. After 1943, I will argue, the narrative of the nation was decentered in Indian art for the first time. Locality would now emerge not (only) as the site of a nation materialized, but of a "nation displaced," as the famine in Bengal transformed contextual materiality forever, a rupture that would only be aggravated by the genocide and refugee influx in the years following Indian partition in 1947.

Yet, this decentering of the nation in art by the wartime famine was by no means restricted to the national/local dynamic. It was global—in assimilating the discourse of an international left-wing socialist realist aesthetic within Indian art, and more potently, in revealing a shadow narrative of World War II in the empire.

Part II
POSTCOLONIAL DISPLACEMENTS

CHAPTER 4

"ALL THE MORE REAL FOR NOT BEING PREACHED"

Forms and Futures of Socialist Art in Nehruvian India

THE UNTITLED OPENING IMAGE (fig. 4.1) in this chapter comes from a folio of sketches (ink on scraperboard) that Chittaprosad made around 1953. The etchings were part of a commission that the artist received for an illustrated children's edition of R. P. Dutt's *India Today*, a seminal book on India's anti-imperial struggle written from a Marxist perspective. Dutt, a founding member of the Communist Party of Great Britain and editor of *Labour Monthly*, wrote *India Today* between 1936 and 1939, during the Comintern's Popular Front period. It was published by the Left Book Club in 1940 and was banned soon after by the British Indian government. It was, however, circulated instead among CPI members, chapter by chapter and in small type, in the early 1940s.[1] When the children's edition of *India Today* was being considered in independent India, Dutt is supposed to have personally preferred Chittaprosad to work on the commission, as the artist writes in a June 1953 letter to his friend Murari Gupta.[2]

Images like the one reproduced here accompany a teleological narrative that traces Indian history from precolonial rural plenitude through various stages of colonial oppression, industrialization, labor strikes, peasant resistance, and grassroots mobilization of Communist Party workers. They echo a high socialist realist idiom, with sharp overtones of folk art in their flatness and defined linear composition. They

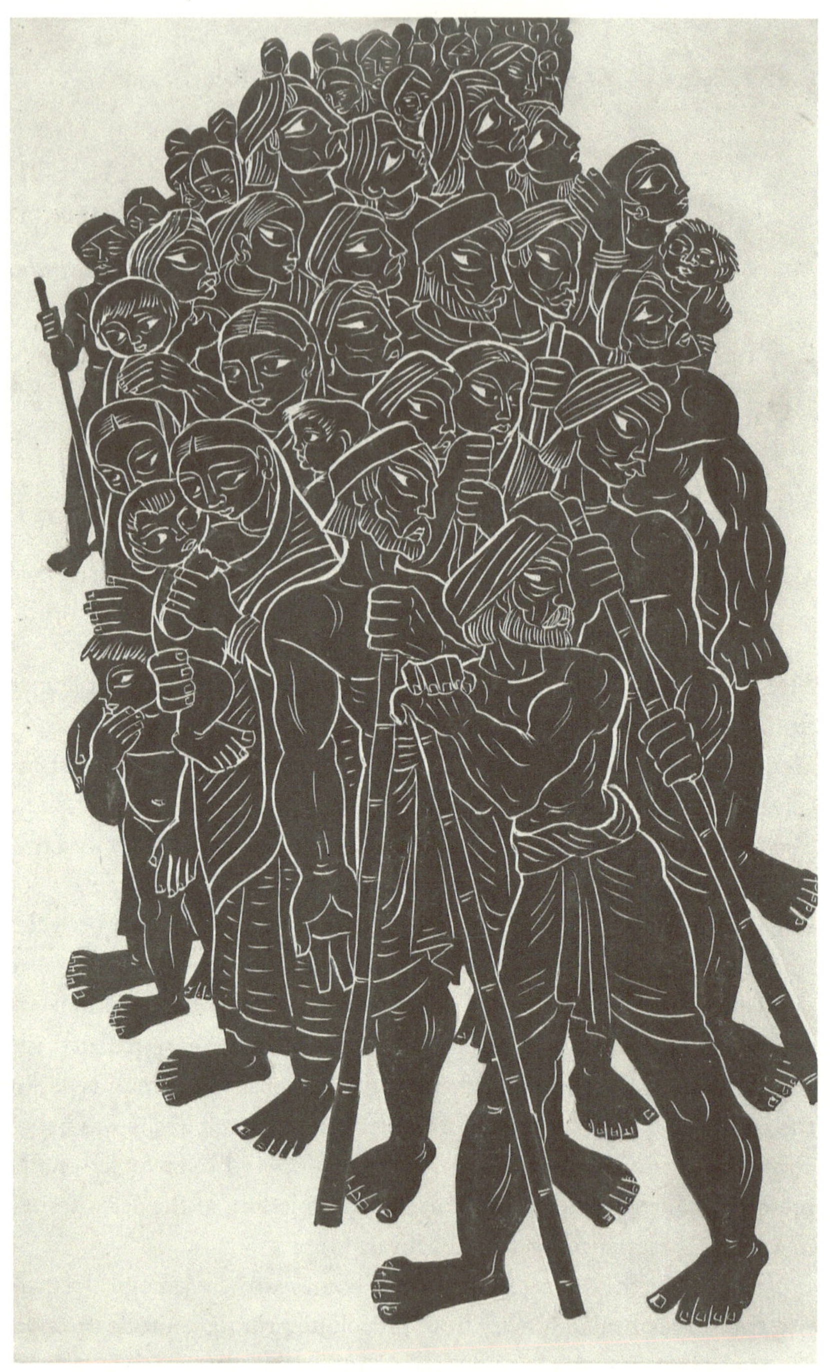

FIGURE 4.1. *Chittaprosad, Untitled (c. 1953). Ink on scraperboard. Courtesy of Delhi Art Gallery (DAG), New Delhi.*

carry Chittaprosad's signature assimilation of the folk with a revolutionary popular imaginary, a style of art known as "agitator and organizer," which he had been developing since the postwar years as an active artist-cadre with the CPI, until his dissociation from the party in the late 1940s. Yet, the formal schemes of this series seem to be new. The artist is not only using stylized laboring bodies with bamboo cudgels, sickles, Communist flags, and drums, as was his repertoire from the postwar period, but seems to transform the emotive address of such images of collectivity through new formal experimentations with black and white, and with the density and linearity of such compositions. The image here, for instance, shows a conscious compression of figures into a singular organic whole that condenses as a collective, a laboring multitude. We see in the constituent figures an air of despondency, yet also an alert, almost poised revolutionary anticipation.

Writing to Murari Gupta in September 1953, Chittaprosad expressed his excitement about experimenting with this new form of "carving or etching on a special kind of board," yet tempered his enthusiasm with financial calculations regarding the cost of material and the slender support available from the People's Publishing House:

> But the process is turning out to be quite expensive. I am doing these in scraper board . . . The boards are 18″ × 20″, four rupees twelve annas each, will need about two dozen of them, which means over a hundred rupees just for the boards, let alone other accessories. From the [Rs.] 200 that P.P.H [People's Publishing House] had given for the materials, [Rs.] 70 to 80 has already been spent for linos.[3]

These anxieties speak to an artist's struggle with resources, not uncommon otherwise. Yet Chittaprosad's unique location—vis-à-vis both the CPI and the post-independence Indian art world, significantly centered in Bombay, where he lived—implicates his struggles within wider histories. His keen illustration in the opening image here activates these multiple histories—of the CPI and its cultural movement, as well as of socialist iconography in postcolonial India. It captures also the shadow histories of the cultural politics of the Cold War, when a socialist aesthetic celebrated since the 1920s and 1930s was increasingly identified with the stultified totalitarian style of socialist realism upheld by the Zhdanovist Soviet Union, but also with the wider Soviet sphere of influence, with which postcolonial India shared a close tie: our opening image, for instance, was part of a folio—a set of approximately 53 images—that were sent to the Warsaw Youth Festival in July 1955.[4] Nehruvian India of the 1950s is a yet understudied period, during which these histories intertwined in often unresolved ways. The particular *afterlife* of the left's cultural movement—*after* its high noon under Party General Secretary P. C. Joshi in the 1940s, and following its dissolution after the Second Party Congress in Calcutta in 1948—is critical here.

The arrival of independence and inauguration of the Nehruvian nation-state coincided with a dissolution of the CPI's active cultural mandate and cultural patronage. This was, however, more textured than a withdrawal of the party from cultural action. Rather, there was a marked dispersion of the cohesion of the cultural front that the party had developed in the 1940s. Party artists like Chittaprosad and his fellow cultural workers negotiated this dissolution while striving to reconfigure their affiliations, affects, art, and politics. Even during the heyday of the cultural movement, a multivalent and ambiguous use of the idea of progressive art by the left had both drawn in *and* eventually alienated, non-party artists, while the party's negligence toward its own artist-cadres like Chittaprosad beyond their journalistic roles arrested possible expansions of a socialist avant-garde in visual art. Manifestos, letters, and autobiographical fragments from the 1950s reveal that as the party stopped fostering cultural patronage as a whole, its artists and cultural workers were negotiating a dialectical cultural politics. At one level, they lamented the residues and ruins of the "golden era" of the 1940s cultural movement, while staking claims, albeit unmet, for rejuvenation of the party's cultural mandate. At another level, they argued for new artistic forms and political destinies of socialist art within a postcolonial cultural field, where competing meanings of "man," the "people," "humanism," and "democratic consciousness" in art were active.

In this chapter, I ask what forms socialist art took in the postcolonial India of the 1950s, when the anti-imperial struggle of the 1940s was transformed and sublimated under the rhetoric of the promise of political modernity in Nehruvian India. Such forms captured the political shifts of late-colonial India and post–World War II transnational politics on the left, and are potential aesthetic formations of what I see as "postcolonial displacements." To trace these shifting grounds and meanings typical of the 1950s, I consider here how the question of form itself became a mode of reconfiguring the filiations and futures of socialist art. I pursue these forms through the journeys and struggles of some of the CPI artist-cadres from the 1940s, through the shifting cultural milieus of Nehruvian India in the 1950s and early 1960s. I elaborate also the ways in which new vocabularies of "democratic consciousness," "citizen-artist," and modernist individualism were being developed in art writing, to produce a new postcolonial humanist aesthetic that sustained a commitment to the progress of "Man" (continuing also the conversation from Chapter 3) while steering away from the socialist connotations of the "people" that had prevailed through the 1930s and 1940s. I am developing here four "forms" through which displacements of the left's socialist aesthetic in early postcolonial India can be understood: *dissolution*, *ambivalence*, *diffraction*, and *transformation*.

DISSOLUTION

The relation of the left with Jawaharlal Nehru's government at the dawn of independence was complex. In June 1947, the CPI under Joshi had pledged support for the national leadership under Nehru,[5] but by the end of the year this would change drastically. After the first Cominform meeting, in September 1947, and the consolidation of the political line of Andrei Zhdanov, secretary of the Central Committee of the Communist Party of the Soviet Union, the CPI took a firm anti-Nehru position, reversing the party line of Joshi.[6] At the Second All-India Party Congress, held in Calcutta in February 1948, the new leadership within the party called for active armed struggle against the new nation-state, vowing to attack the Nehruvian state through a "genuine fighting alliance of the masses."[7] The year 1948 also saw the exit of the Congress Socialist Party from the Indian National Congress, which was now accused by the socialists of being dominated by the interests of finance capitalists.[8] By 1949, the CPI was banned in Bengal, as the new nation-state remained ever cautious about Communist action. For instance, a circular issued by the (post-partition) West Bengal government to the district and police authorities warned district magistrates against the CPI's spreading political propaganda through dramatic performances organized by bodies like the All-India IPTA and the All-India PWA. The circular empowered district magistrates to take action against such performances, under the colonial-era Dramatic Performances Act of 1876.[9]

The Second Party Congress also saw a gradual hardening of the party's cultural line, which had begun resonating increasingly with the Zhdanov Doctrine—the stringent new cultural doctrine that declared "Socialist Realism" as the official aesthetic of the Stalinist Soviet Union. With the exit of P. C. Joshi from the party, the alliance that held cultural workers together across ideological lines within the larger rhetoric of cultural movement was loosened, as the party discarded its active role in cultural patronage. Though party leadership kept shifting during 1949–51, the cohesive cultural vision of the Joshite period was never to return. The CPI's intervention in the visual arts, both focused and limited in the 1940s, was virtually absent in the 1950s, when most of the artists had moved away from any association with the party. Even in the early 1950s, while the party was keen to organize exhibitions of posters, sketches, paintings, and sculptures on topics like "life and culture of the people of each province and the history of IPTA,"[10] no organizational efforts were made to revive the role of artists within the cultural apparatus of the party. Despite a new focus on the peace movement and the beginning of the anti-imperialist Peace Front, the IPTA itself began losing its national character in the late 1950s.[11]

By the late 1940s, Chittaprosad had distanced himself from the party apparatus, while continuing to live in the outskirts of Bombay in Andheri. Sudhi Pradhan noted Chittaprosad's personal "dejection" after the party's Calcutta session, recounting with wry disapproval how the artist, along with his photographer friend and comrade Sunil Janah, "went into the Grand Hotel of Calcutta and drank and saw cabaret as a reaction immediately after the Congress."[12] Even when Chittaprosad reemerged in party circles in 1952, a period that coincides with Joshi's own partial return to the party fold, the party's cultural agenda had shrunk considerably. Chittaprosad's dissociation with the CPI was, however, neither simple nor complete. His letters to his friends and comrades, mostly from this period of the early 1950s, reveal a sense of melancholia that defined not only his very subjective interface with the cultural movement but also the affective *afterlife* that the cultural movement itself took on in the 1950s. This disquiet and melancholia run through Chittaprosad's letters, as he complains time and again about the party's nonchalance and the stifled potential of the cultural movement, while remaining in conscious isolation, half expecting the party to acknowledge his art.[13]

For another CPI artist from the late 1940s, Somnath Hore, adhering to the party line became economically nonviable, though he continued to make posters and woodcut prints for the party and retained his membership till 1956. Although he was active in the late 1940s, by 1950 there were, he recalls in his autobiography, rifts within the party:

> An editorial in the journal *For a Lasting Peace, For a People's Democracy*, published in early-1950 raised a storm in the party. All these years we had obeyed the Party leadership unquestioningly. Now, all of a sudden, we started speaking out; we started finding fault with every aspect of the Party, though it was mainly restricted to those in our cells.[14]

He realized at that time, he noted, that developing creativity would not be possible within the material bounds of party politics, and that the mere opportunity to draw for the party was not enough. In 1956, both Hore and his wife, Reba, renounced their party membership. This was, however, not a denunciation of Marxist politics, he noted, but rather an example of the "yawning gap between socialist philosophies and socialist parties."[15]

Hore's drift was borne out by fellow cultural activists of the left. That this dissolution was not ideological, but triggered by inadequacy, appears most sharply in a thesis, *On the Cultural Front*, written by noted filmmaker and then-activist with the IPTA Ritwik Ghatak. In this document, submitted to the CPI in 1954, Ghatak made a sharp distinction between ideological and organizational dissonances. The "problem of culture," he noted, is a problem of organization, not ideology—"at the levels of the Party, the Platform, and Art."[16] It is curious, Ghatak observed, that no communist artist can be seen working within the progressive cultural sphere, and that no work of "high value" had come from communist cultural workers since the late 1940s. The "use of Culture" to the party is mechanistic, Ghatak noted, either as a "money-making machine" or as a "mobilizer in meetings and conferences to keep the crowd (and not the masses) engaged with whatever the artists can offer."[17] Cultural workers themselves, meanwhile, longed for a return of "Joshi's Golden Period," for "the sake of Culture."[18] Though Ghatak admits that his argument was directed mainly toward what he calls the "collective" arts—such as theater, opera, or ballet—and not "individual" arts like poetry, painting, and crafts, his aim in *On the Cultural Front*, he noted, was to talk about the crisis of cultural patronage in its broadest sense, using specific areas as focus.[19] Ghatak's thesis triggered at first no response, but ultimately resulted in his expulsion from the party.

Ghatak argued that the "troubled waters of controversy are not of the ocean of ideology or Party-line," but "primarily practical questions."[20] Yet the dissolution of the cultural movement, while triggered by disappearing party patronage rather than ideological alienation of its patron-artists, as activists like Hore, Ghatak, and Chittaprosad note, was nonetheless ideological too. This dissolution had begun immediately after the Party Congress at Calcutta in 1948. Integral to it were questions of communist ideology, as well as shifting artistic interfaces with the concept of political and social commitment in art. The shifting political grounds in a transitional India were critical, too; the radical impetus that had sustained the anti-imperialist politics of the 1940s was giving way in the 1950s to a politics of affirmation rather than resistance. The coming of the Nehruvian nation-state and its promises of political modernity influenced the political mood substantially, as the CPI itself began losing its critical cultural voice. The idea of commitment in art opens up the dialectical texture of Indian modernism in this period, as it triggered interesting shifts within one of the left's peculiar contributions to the vocabularies of cultural production, namely the idea of progressive art.

Geeta Kapur has observed in her discussion of progressive art that the Indian left, while integrating "the people" in its cultural radicalism of the 1940s, had produced at the same time "its own conservatism, even an incipient Stalinism." Thus while in the Indian context the left's cultural movement was both modern and avant-garde, its increasing stress on realism and consolidation of the partisan rhetoric of socialist realism, to Kapur, prevented the movement from attempting daring formal experimentations. In the Cold War division between freedom and commitment, Kapur argued, the rhetoric of realism within progressive art separated it from narratives of freedom and hence from the "modern" itself: "For if in the heyday of socialism we do not designate art practice in avant-garde terms, we cannot in postmodern times so readily invent a vanguard discourse that has an appropriate historical import."[21] The material history of progressive art that unfolded in close dialogue with the left-wing cultural movement of the 1940s, however, reveals a more complicated history.

The idea of the progressive in visual art, I will suggest, inhabited not only modes of official allegiances like that of an artist-cadre like Chittaprosad, but also evidenced a characteristic ambiguous affiliation to social commitment in art. Key to understanding the left-wing rhetoric of progressive art are not (simply) its protestations of realism, but the mechanisms of association and assimilation that formed the social texture of radical art practice. Ambiguity around the idea of commitment—at times social, at times political—was well suited to the quasi-political associations on which Joshi's cultural movement was built. While sustaining a collective of young artists committed to party directives, the CPI under Joshi had patronized a politics of assimilation of non-party artists through an expanding discourse of social commitment in art. This not only formed the basis of progressive art criticism but also captured its tensions once the "moment" of the 1940s had passed. A propensity toward dissolution, I argue, was built *into* the very form in which left-wing cultural patronage developed from its earliest moments in the late 1930s.

The party's outreach toward non-party artists is important for understanding the paradoxes of progressive art, rather than solely the party's dissolution. A dichotomous stance, as we have seen in the previous chapters, marked the attitude of the party toward its own artist-cadres, who continued to be seen as "suppliers of raw material" from which artists *outside* the party fold would develop "higher art."[22] This reductive logic with regard to party artists, the burden of which an artist-cadre like Chittaprosad bore, is symptomatic of the paradoxes within the left's cultural project of progressive art. Juxtaposing Chittaprosad with his contemporaries, such as the Calcutta Group, takes us closer to the problem. As I have argued so far, neither a conservative party critic like Gopal Haldar nor more liberal critics like Bishnu Dey wrote on Chittaprosad in the 1940s or 1950s, although Dey did observe the lack of integration between the Calcutta Group and a committed political artist like Chittaprosad.[23] Instead, it was the party that sought to draw in non-party artists from the "progressive groups" like the Calcutta Group or the Progressive Artists' Group in Bombay. But by the late 1940s, these artists began distancing themselves from the communist undertones of progressive art, further dissolving the artistic lineages of the left's cultural movement, as well as the political lineages of modern art from the 1940s.

An inadequate legacy of left-wing rhetoric of progressive art both unites and splinters artists from the 1940s. Artists in both the Calcutta Group and the PAG began their careers with a "progressive" will to portray the poor, marginalized, and downtrodden, as the sociopolitical crisis of the 1940s reinforced the left's cultural imperative of taking art to the people. Some of them, such as Francis Newton Souza of the PAG, had personal ties with CPI activists that were more those of a fellow-traveler than an affiliated CPI member; Souza was a regular at the party office, and the party's organ, *People's War*, carried reviews of his works.[24] In the late 1940s, when this cohesive ethic loosened with the shift of guard within the CPI, most of these artists began actively dissociating from the party as well as from the "tag" of progressive art. While a language of social signification remained with the Calcutta Group through its various mutations, the Bombay Progressives, despite an initial association with the left, had by the late 1940s renounced all associations with the party, as well as with the cultural movement. For Souza, a founding member of the PAG, this denial was clear:

> I do not quite understand now, why we still call our Group 'Progressive.' Not that the most retrogressive institutions call themselves so, but we have changed all the chauvinist ideas and the leftists [*sic*] fanaticism which we had incorporated in our manifesto at the inception of the Group . . . we found this in the course of working an impossibility . . . the gulf between the so-called people and the artists cannot be bridged. . . . Today we paint with absolute freedom for content and technique almost anarchic; save that we are guided by one or two sound elemental and eternal laws, of aesthetic order, plastic co-ordination and colour composition.[25]

Writing years after the dissolution of the Calcutta Group, one of its founding members, the sculptor Prodosh Dasgupta, also sounded distinctly uncomfortable with the group's political associations, and with the constant attributions of realism that the left-wing cultural movement projected on them. Like Souza, Dasgupta expressed discomfort with the group's association with the term "progressive." His rebuff to Gopal Haldar's complaint about the group's art not being socialist enough during the 1949 annual exhibition (as we saw in Chapter 3) is symptomatic of this rejection of leftist associations.[26] The confusion of the *social* with the *socialist*, as I discussed in the preceding chapters, was a conceptual confusion on the part of the left-wing cultural movement. By the late 1940s, artists like Dasgupta and Souza, eager to separate themselves from an increasingly conservative turn with the CPI, would conflate realism with Stalinism and *social* commitment with *socialist* commitment, suggesting an often-missed concrete tension between realism and modernism in Indian art during these critical transitional years.

By the 1950s, even apart from the actual dispersal of artists tied to the progressive groups, this ideological displacement or disowning of the values of progressive art began to be visible. As new values of Nehruvian socialism and state-led developmentalism gained cultural currency, the left's rhetoric of a cultural radicalism both national and popular, which had been developing since the late 1930s, was to undergo a subtle transformation: the new national-popular aesthetic in Nehruvian India would retain the rhetoric of "man" as the subject of art, but sublimate its ideological content to create what can be seen as a deradicalized image of popular hope, resilience, and productivity. New artistic and art-critical values of a depoliticized "new humanism" and "democratic consciousness" were increasingly entering the artistic field. This dissolution of the radical populism of the 1940s in the 1950s, as well as the rejection of art's political address, is the discursive loop within which the question of socialist art in postcolonial India needs to be read.

To access the mutations of the progressive cultural movements within the new political context and ideological parameters of post-independence India, it is necessary not only to be conscious of the dissolution of the critical consciousness and collective culture of the CPI's "Joshite" period but, more importantly, to follow the traces of new and ambivalent artistic vocabularies of the "people" and the "folk" that often developed from within official national patronage. A case in point would be the early anthropological commissions given to a working artist-sculptor like Meera Mukherjee, who, fresh from her art training in Germany, was commissioned by the Anthropological Survey of India in 1956 to document the craft practices of the metal craftsmen of central India; in Mukherjee's art this led to a sustained practice and discourse drawn from folk art and modernist assimilation of the ethos and stylistic vicissitudes of folk craft practices within distinctly individualist depictions of labor and leisure in her series of *cire purdue* (lost-wax method) sculptures from the late 1960s.[27] Similar initiatives were taken up by artists like K. G. Subramanyan and Prabhash Sen, as well as initiatives at the ethnographic museums at Bharat Bhavan conceptualized by Swaminathan in the 1950s and 1960s, where this genre of transmutation of the national-popular in Nehruvian aesthetic can be pursued. Such artists occupy that ambivalent space where a socialist sensibility can be identified *without* echoes of the socialist radicalism that had flashed in the 1940s, but instead a Nehruvian commitment to revival of the national-popular potentials of folk art and rural art and crafts. Conscious of an artist-artisan continuum, artists like Subramanyan and Swaminathan—discussed extensively in the historiography of Indian modernism—introduced fresh techniques and devices in addressing the nation and the everyday, the modern and the folk, by developing formal complexes that would accommodate both social sensibility and modernist consciousness.[28] My focus here, however, remains on the *particular* and *dispersed* afterlives of the socialist art of the 1940s in the new cultural vocabulary in Nehruvian India.

AMBIVALENCE

Reviewing the works of artists of the "transition" period—as the 1950s were called—the artist and critic Jaya Appasamy identified, in a 1954 article in *Marg*, a "new humanism":

> Art today reflects the contemporary vision, which is democratic, questioning, diverse. The artist looks steadily at the man in the street, the children of the street, rural folk and the ordinary artisan. His themes are about them, their life, humour, joys and sorrows. In India this is perhaps the first time that man unglorified is the widespread subject of creative minds. This attitude and the more dynamic nature of the painting is a product of the times, of change and reorientation in ideas and a new humanism which is all the more real for not being preached. Indian painting has been lyrical, grand, ecstatic, edifying: it has now a new quality, it is democratic.[29]

Appasamy's observations are instructive. They suggest not only the new subjects and concerns of artists during the first decade of independence, but also a disposition, toward subject and style as well as toward the ideology of representation. This is the new rhetoric of modern art in the nation-state—"democratic, questioning, diverse," a "new humanism . . . all the more real for not being preached."

This idea of "man" was closely tied to that of freedom. Art criticism published in *Marg*, the most celebrated art journal launched at the dawn of independence in 1947, is indicative here. *Marg* came into print with Mulk Raj Anand as the general editor and a host of cultural personalities whom we have already encountered—many of them left wing—as contributing editors, including Shahid Suhrawardy, Bishnu Dey, John

Irwin, and Karl Khandalavala, among others. Introducing the inaugural volume of *Marg*, Indologist and art historian Hermann Goetz noted: "What modern Indian art needs, is freedom, freedom from outside interference and freedom of character."[30] Freedom was indeed the visual rhetoric that blurred lines between political and aesthetic identities. Freedom called for the rejection of ideological regimentation or motivation. Freedom was tied to the "arrival" of the citizen-artist, a celebratory figure committed to the project of Nehruvian modernity, rather than plodding in its shadows. The rhetoric of "man" as the sovereign subject sits at the core of the national-modern project. *Marg* laced its opening volumes with quotes from the classical poet Chandidas: "Listen. O Brother Man. There is no higher truth than Man," and from Elliot Smith: "Man has the seeing eye, the understanding ear, and the skillful hands to shape his own destiny."[31]

A strong rejection of ideological influence in visual art had existed already in the late 1940s. Reviewers of the PAG exhibition in 1949 had stated emphatically that the group members "do not subscribe to any 'ism': And if at all they do, then it is only individualism."[32] Reviews of the Calcutta Group's shows in the early 1950s had likewise vehemently foregrounded a depoliticized view of the universal "Man"—not broken but celebratory, a national-modern abstracted from sociopolitical ruptures. By the time of the Calcutta Group's last exhibition, the understanding of the progressive itself was being altered, marking a sharp break from its socialist connotations in the 1940s. Klaus Fischer's review of that last exhibition, in 1953, had, as we saw in Chapter 3, affirmed the group's evolution from the crisis decade of the 1940s to a new promised land of independence—one of factories and dams, and the "triumph of 'Man.'" A rhetoric of artists-as-citizens was already emerging in the early 1950s—in Fischer's terms, the "will" to be "good citizens"[33]—that was seeking to generate a cultural consensus that connected artistic individualism with a cultural commitment to the political modernity of the new nation-state. These pieces celebrated the image of "Man" as the universal subject of freedom and the protagonist of global democracy, unmarked by ideology or class war, and delivered out of the memory of struggle.

An iconic image from the mid-1950s that upheld the centrality of this image in the national-modern canon is M. F. Husain's painting titled, rather evidently, *Man* (1951). The pensive figure of "Man" is surrounded by splintered landscapes of color, fragmented figures, and divine pantheons. The chaos is at once formal and existential, like the vortex of history itself, as "Man" sits poised at the center of the canvas. The image suggests convergences of the mythic and the philosophical, of national and individual narratives.[34] It also thrusts forth a fluid simultaneity of past and present, of tradition and modernity, visualizing a sense of timelessness within the national-modern imagination of post-independence India. Not only did the figure of man lie at the heart of this invention of the national-modern subject, it deployed an ambivalent aesthetic that would abstract a sovereign subject from the ideological trappings of the left's rhetoric of the "people." Man, free and composed, was to be the allegorical subject of the nation's sovereignty. In another painting—*Zameen*, meaning "land"—made in 1955 (fig. 4.2), Husain returned to the epic scope of the rural as the metatext of the nation's biography, the painting itself becoming a composite whole of symbols, texts, icons, and the primordial everyday of rural India. In 1955, Husain received a national award for *Zameen* from the newly established Lalit Kala Akademi—the national art academy established in 1954 by the Nehruvian government—reaffirming his status as the leading visualizer of the Nehruvian national-modern aesthetic.

Indian independence, Geeta Kapur noted, placed before postcolonial artists the ontological question "What is at stake in being an Indian?" For the urban middle-class intelligentsia, she argued, identity and authenticity were values desired individually but sought in collectivity: "Even the tasks of subjectivity, so long as they are unresolved, require acts of allegorical exegesis—often via the nation."[35] Kapur's formulation of a progressive aesthetic, at the transitional juncture of the 1950s, is committed to this synchrony between national aspirations and modernist imagination. A "peculiar coincidence occurs between the state's constitutional promise of democratic secularism and the secularizing logic of aesthetic modernism," she has argued elsewhere.[36] Progressive projects, she noted, were mediated via nationalism, albeit in a

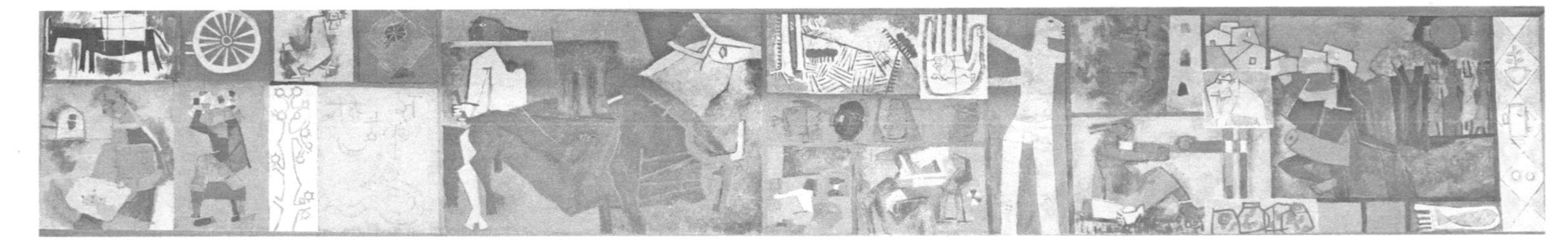

FIGURE 4.2. *M. F. Husain, Zameen (1955). Oil on canvas. Courtesy of National Gallery of Modern Art, New Delhi.*

universalizing modernist schema, and promised in "existential rather than political terms" forms and routes of cultural self-determination. Artists like Husain—who was a founding member of the PAG—symbolized for her a "well-set narrative of modernism," wherein bourgeois artists "first develop a progressive left-wing consciousness and later appropriate its more revolutionary directions into subjective existential language."[37] A socialist aesthetic sits comfortably with Kapur's theorization of the Nehruvian national-modern aesthetic. Husain's modernist reframing of myths and rural subjects and textures, Kapur argued, could also become a "socialist register in the liberal society of post-independence India," where an artist like Husain could become a "peoples' representative."[38] As *the* emblematic progressive, M. F. Husain represents this space of conjunction where the pre- and post-independence national-modern interlock—a syncretic and stable subject-space where socialism and nationalism, the mythic and the secular, the individual and the collective, meet in harmony.[39]

This allegorical presence of the collectivity within artistic subjectivity is the ground for an ambivalent afterlife of socialist aesthetics in postcolonial India, where the persistence of the collective contained layered ideological dissolutions and reconfigurations. Reading Husain's *Zameen* or *Man* with some of Chittaprosad's works from the mid-1950s takes us closer to this ambivalence, which hid a deradicalization of the socialist rhetoric in art. Husain's *Man* is framed by symbols that capture the allegorical presence of the nation-as-epic; as do the many figures in his village series from the 1950s, it reveals a containment of the self *within* the narrative, whether one of rurality or postcolonial subjectivity. In contrast, in a series of linocuts made in the early 1950s, Chittaprosad portrayed a rural India and rural subjects as sites not of composure but of displacement *from* the narrative. These prints (figs. 4.3a and 4.3b) were made for *Do Bigha Zamin*—a film by Bimal Roy that portrayed the destitution of a debt-ridden farmer displaced into the city. Hindi films in the 1950s brought out this subterranean narrative of struggle and the incompleteness of independence, a narrative that slipped out of visual art rather quickly. With many activists of the IPTA now absorbed into the Hindi film industry, film scripts and song

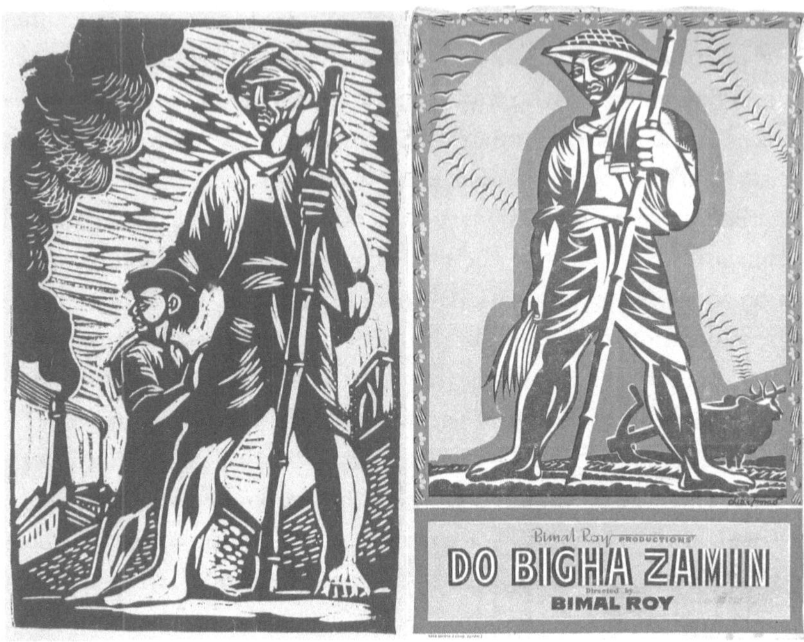

FIGURES 4.3A AND 4.3B. *Chittaprosad, Untitled prints made for the film Do Bigha Zamin (c. 1952–53). Linocuts on paper. Courtesy of DAG, New Delhi.*

lyrics became a site for the continuation of the radical revolutionary content of IPTA.[40] Here there was a persistence of the subject-as-rebel or the underbelly of the nation, a subalterneity that in visual art became appropriated in a celebratory repertoire committed to the promises of the national-modern project of postcolonial India.

This deradicalization of subalterneity lay implicit in the cultural politics of the early 1950s. Art criticism in leading journals like *Marg* reaffirmed the arrival of "humanism" as an aesthetic value, without allusions to the socialist affiliations of some iconographies of man or the human condition. Even when subjects of Mexican socialist murals were discussed in *Marg*, in works of artists like Diego Rivera and David Alfaro Siqueiros, references to radical populism remained conspicuous by their absence. Resistance to "abstract, geometric and surrealist forms" in Mexican art was portrayed as a celebration of "humanistic" art, committed to the "destiny of Man": "All that is most primordial in human life, the struggle for existence, the elemental forces of Nature, the drama of our own days, the liberation of the spirit, the primitive myths of man, the fundamental concepts of justice."[41] When the first Indo-Soviet Exhibition was held across different Indian cities in 1952, displaying a select spread of Soviet socialist realist paintings for the first time in India, this ambivalence around a depoliticized idea of man became more visible, alongside the shifts around notions of art's social, political, and formal dimensions. In his opening speech at the Soviet Fine Arts Exhibition in New Delhi in 1952, for instance, education minister Maulana Abul Kalam Azad quoted Lenin to assert: "Art belongs to the people. It must be lodged with its deepest roots in the very thick of the broad masses and loved by them. It must unite the feelings, thoughts and will of these masses and elevate them. It must awaken and develop the artist in them."[42] Ironically, Azad saw in the work of Soviet artists the possibility of reconciliation between "Art for Art's Sake and Art for the People," as he noted that the conflict between these two "formulations," was "more apparent than real," since they had in common the "manifestation of the human spirit"; one celebrated the individual's "likes and dislikes," and the other promoted those of society at large. For Azad, the shared ground between them was the idea of "abiding social values."[43]

Reviews and responses to this exhibition of socialist realist art registered the ideological dissonances that marked the national-modern aesthetic during these transitional decades of decolonization. While the official voice, captured here by Azad, hailed the universal human spirit in art, for noted art critics in Bombay like Karl Khandalavala, the Soviet exhibition showed nothing more than the "masochistic servility" of socialist realism.[44] Modern painting, Khandalvala noted later that year, was inevitably "socially significant," birthed by crisis and technological advancement, but "Art does not become revolutionary by depicting factories, chimneys, hammers"; "true progress" lay not in subject matter but in the "actual handling of paint and canvas" that gives "spirit to bodies."[45] This tension between content and form echoed Cold War polarities between freedom and ideology. The rhetoric of man and freedom, while claiming to transcend ideological binds, seems to resonate with the future non-alignment politics of Nehru—a conscious middle ground between commitments to the community and to the individual.

Commenting on the fate of social art in the United States during the Cold War, art historian Andrew Hemingway has pointed out that the iconography of class struggle was replaced in the 1950s by a more symbolic imagery of the "human condition," "an imagery more specific and figurative than that offered by Abstract Expressionism . . . but often allegorical and sometimes obscure."[46] Humanism in the 1950s, he argued, offered key stakes for communists and liberals alike. For the former, humanism represented the progressive forces of history, an antithesis to the "absence of human content" identified with the formalism and the perceived dehumanization of abstract art. For liberals, a prewar progressive rhetoric was soon overshadowed by the "bleaker tenor" of Cold War liberalism, matched with "an utter scepticism towards the USSR and acceptance of bourgeois democracy as the best social model available."[47] Despite fundamental differences from the particularities of the Indian context, this characterization of postwar humanism in visual art is fairly telling in understanding the celebratory rhetoric of "man" in the national-modern aesthetic of Nehruvian India. A clue can be found in the ideology of the famous *Family of Man* exhibition of the Museum of Modern Art in the United States in 1955, which sought to capture a very Nehruvian idea: "unity of mankind within its diversity."[48] The exhibition traveled to India soon after, in June 1956. Dedicated to the "dignity of Man,"[49] it highlighted the timelessness and universalism of contained labor—"the families of the world engage in the same basic tasks."[50] Visualized as "an epic woven of fun, mystery, holiness,"[51] such meta-narratives of the universalism of the human condition would mark Nehruvian aesthetics significantly.

The mid-1950s formed the transitional period when formal elements in art were taking over the sociopolitical accent of the left from the 1940s, producing in the process a universal humanity in art. Appasamy chronicles this transitional phase aptly in a 1967 *Marg* article. The "painters of transition," as Appasamy called them—artists like K. K. Hebbar, N. S. Bendre, Bhabesh Sanyal, Gopal Ghose, Rathin Maitra, K. C. S. Panicker, Sankho Chaudhury, and Chintamoni Kar—all began their careers with a "poeticisation of proletarian themes," a dominant tendency of the 1940s, which continued into the early 1950s in depictions of a social everyday in art. However, from the late 1950s, Appasamy noted, a shifting trend toward abstraction subsumed the remnants of social critique in art, with the space of content shrinking significantly. There was a gradual indigenization of content, which would result in a complete absorption in abstract, totemic compositions, effecting a final disjuncture with the radical aesthetic of the preceding decade. By this time, Appasamy writes, there was an increasing shift toward an abstraction of the subject into texture, arriving at a "kind of action painting" ; even pastoral themes were formalized, she writes, as in the case of M. F. Husain, whose dominant repertoire of rural subjects in the 1950s was in fact less the actual theme of his works than "the slabs of colour, their juxtaposition, contrasts, depths and surface variations."[52]

The gradual dissociation of artists from radical social intent was matched by critics who denounced art's sociopolitical address. For instance, in the art criticism of Richard Bartholomew, artist Ram Kumar's patron-critic, there was a shift toward supplanting the tenor of "middle-class tragedy" in Kumar's works with the more universal language of "human tragedy." Kumar had been tied to the Communist Party during his stay in Paris and, after his return to India in 1951, to the Cultural Committee of the CPI. These were the years when Kumar, like Chittaprosad, worked with the World Peace Movement and painted themes of urban poverty. Following a trajectory similar to that of Hore, Kumar dissociated himself from the party in the mid-1950s. In his works, radical content was seen to shift toward a more expressionistic handling of the urban subject. Writing on Kumar in 1955, Bartholomew lauded the artist's exit from the CPI, noting that, as a gifted artist, Kumar could not "fake."[53] More importantly, the social address that persisted in Kumar's works despite his rift with the party was universal—"beyond time and space," an "urban predicament" distilled from the political textures of Indian society.[54] This stress on existential iconography under the wider rubric of humanism was a mode of universalization of the material content, context, and ideology. By 1959, Bartholomew was writing that the "slogan-mongering and the stiltedness of a half-hearted socialist realism" had been replaced in Kumar's art by something like the "song of a sinner."[55]

When *Lalit Kala Contemporary*, the first modern art journal from the Lalit Kala Akademi (established in 1954), was released in 1965, it visualized the new postcolonial national-modern aesthetic:

> Contemporary art is characterised by an immense freedom. The artist has outgrown the past and now works according to those principles which are purely painterly and which have rejected the dominance of subject matter. . . . The content of this art is the temperament of the artist himself, and he, as a sensitive instrument, does not fail to mirror the tensions and problems and hopes of our day. . . . There is no clear subject matter—though, except in the case of abstract painters, there is no complete rejection of it either. Indeed the *position of the subject is ambiguous and non-committal* (emphasis mine).[56]

This ambiguity and deradicalization—a noncommittal humanism "all the more real for not being preached"—is the political unconscious of the national-modern aesthetic of Nehruvian India.

Reacting to the Soviet exhibition in 1952, the left had revealed a splintered and complex position. The exhibition drew effusive praise from cultural critics tied to the cultural movement of the 1940s, like Bishnu Dey and Gopal Haldar in Bengal, who by then were in opposing positions within the left-wing cultural movement. Yet while both hailed the triumphant images of man from the Soviet Union, Bishnu Dey's review was significant in drawing attention to the "incomplete realism" in Soviet socialist art, one that still awaited an "*integrated consciousness of form and contemporaneity* (emphasis mine)."[57] In his autobiography, Somnath Hore speaks of being fascinated with the Soviet exhibition of 1952. But "questions arose as soon as the initial fascination passed," he recalls: "What sort of art was this? Either the meticulous representation of the individual, or the context was of consequence; both aesthetics as well as technique seemed to be downplayed."[58] "It was clear," he writes, "that the appeal of a picture could not be contained by the limitations of the camera . . . rather it manifested itself through the passionate and creative life of the artist."[59] This consciousness of form, or an artistic subjectivity that stretched beyond questions of political commitment or ideological streamlining, was increasingly visible in the works of communist artists like Chittaprosad and Hore through the 1950s. These specific interfaces with new ideas of artistic form, I argue, need to be traced not only as individual artistic directions but as an overall aesthetic disposition, shaped by the frustrations around the need for creative expression, a dilution of radical ideological import of art, as well as by the difficulties and inadequacies of party-political patronage that Ghatak had laid out, for instance, in *On the Cultural Front*. To understand the directions of socialist forms in the works of these former artist-cadres once the left-wing cultural movement hit the wall post-1948, I use the idea of "diffraction"—forms of continuities that develop from the forms of obstacles.[60]

DIFFRACTION

Chittaprosad's works from the 1950s and 1960s show the artist grappling with formal possibilities within pressing limitations of resource. Post-1947, he seems to carry on the socialist realist subjects—resistance, resilience, and solidarities—that marked the CPI's postwar shift toward a politics of mass resistance.[61] Yet works of this period are also undeniably marked by a fast-disappearing patronage, which was particularly stifling for an artist living hand-to-mouth, while both resolutely anti-market and in deep rejection of the new party high command under incoming General Secretary B. T. Ranadive. Most of his cartoons in the early 1950s were made for the leftist journal *Crossroads*. He was still getting weekly commissions from the party, but often without pay.[62] These difficulties—of patronage, affiliation, and sustenance—shaped Chittaprosad's post-1948 directions. Such difficulties produced obstructions that streamlined both the directions that socialist artists from the 1940s took or had to abandon and the specific forms that socialist iconography adopted as a result. Indeed, the question of form is the organic field where these ideological and artistic negotiations around the dissolving moment of the left's cultural movement gained materiality. To understand the forms and futures of socialist art of the 1940s in postcolonial India, we need to rethink questions of continuity and afterlives. As party patronage dissolved, socialist aesthetics persisted in diffractions—in dispersed, diffused directions and forms—that were *shaped by difficulties* as much as by the new possibilities available in national or transnational forums.

By early 1947, as party-political negotiations punctuated India's fraught arrival into an independence marred by partition and genocide, Chittaprosad's cartoons pictorialized decolonization as a complex battlefield—of people and state, class and capital. Here workers, peasants, Hindus, and Muslims tower over hacked territories, dueling politicians, and unholy ententes of capitalists, princes, and bureaucrats; the tenuous nationalism of a *khadi*-clad (*khadi,* the fabric patronized by the Gandhian movement) politician gleams on the axe of the Public Safety Bill that he wields over protestors demanding food, clothing, and housing, as British and Indian capitalists steamroll their bodies; and a monumental barricade of Indians, Turks, Arabs, Vietnamese, and Chinese fighters towers over scorched lands, thwarting stealthy Anglo-American forces with a triumphant flag of "Quit Asia." A chuckling Uncle Sam becomes the new Statue of Liberty in another cartoon, crowned with daggers and dangling the atom bomb while his pet vultures seem to guard burning books of Goethe, Paine, and Gorky piled at his feet; values of truth, freedom, or progress burn too, while fresh supplies of crime, terror, spies, filth, and lies are marshaled (fig. 4.4).

India's prime minister, Jawaharlal Nehru, is a staple of many of these cartoons, which mocked the moral assumptions of Nehruvian non-alignment, showing him repeatedly as a dithering statesman in the crafts of the Cold War. For instance, in an undated cartoon probably from 1950, Nehru is shown rising over the globe with a garland held in open arms to welcome a battered Uncle Sam, who hides a dagger behind a beaming sack of dollars while being kicked out of China by a leviathan-like Chinese peasant. Unlike the cartoons of Shankar, whose protagonist, the "Common Man," shadowed Nehru's trails and policies with satirical bafflement,[63] Chittaprosad's work shows Nehru as the eager victim of U.S. imperialism, a pawn in postwar neocolonialism. Anti-imperialism assumes a defined socialist realist aura in Chit-

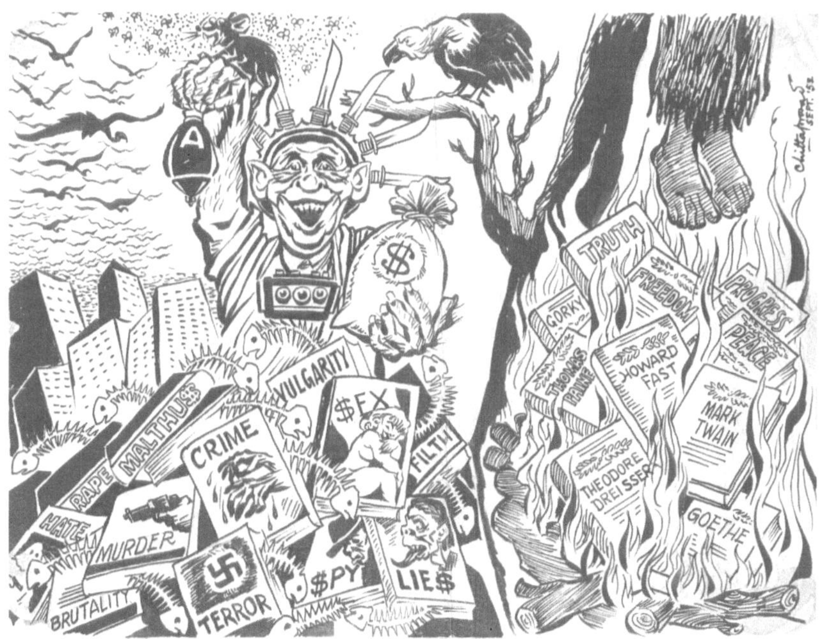

FIGURE 4.4. *Chittaprosad, American Imperialism (1952). Brush and ink on paper. Courtesy of DAG, New Delhi.*

taprosad's posters for the World Peace Council (WPC), his pet engagement in the early 1950s. His peace posters from 1951 and 1952 reflect the party's initiatives from the All-India Peace Convention held in Bombay in May 1951, which urged the Nehru government to invite Asian powers to work toward the withdrawal of all foreign troops from Asia[64] and initiated concrete critiques of Anglo-American financial imperialism (fig. 4.5). Indeed, against the backdrop of waning party enthusiasm for cultural activism, these posters gave Chittaprosad a purpose to sustain a socialist cause, and are pointers toward a political subjectivity that remained deeply ideological, bordering on the dogmatic at various points. His support for a Stalinist USSR, even in the early 1950s, is noteworthy, as he writes to his friend and comrade Somnath Hore with great pride of his prints being published in *Ogonyok*, one of the Soviet Union's oldest illustrated weekly magazines.[65] Under the shadow of the Cold War, these posters for the World Peace Council made between

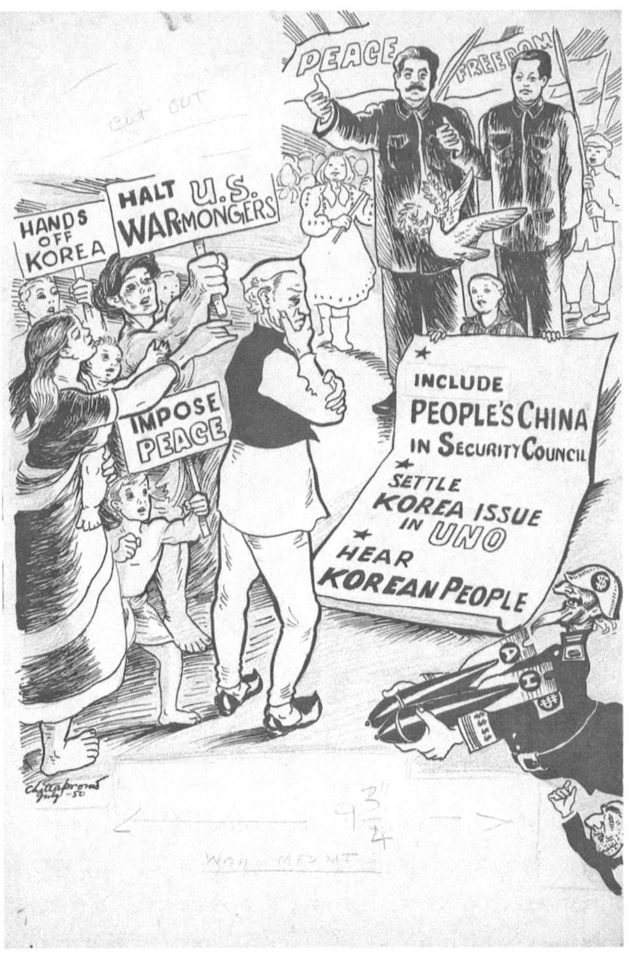

FIGURE 4.5. *Chittaprosad, Sketch for peace poster (1952). Brush and ink on tracing paper. Courtesy of DAG, New Delhi.*

1949 and 1955 invoked the visual rhetoric of the anti-fascist cultural resistance of the Popular Front period.[66]

When the exhibition of socialist realist art from the USSR came to Bombay in 1952, Viktor Klimashin, the Soviet watercolorist and chief artist for *Ogonyok*, visited Chittaprosad (photographs of this visit appear in the collection of the Delhi Art Gallery) and collected Chittaprosad's pastels and gouache works of peasant women singing during the Bezwada conference of the Kisan Sabha of 1944.[67] These were also the years when Chittaprosad was developing close ties with what was then Czechoslovakia, a connection he would continue to nurture through friends like F. Salaba, the Indologist Dr. Miloslav Krasa, and the filmmaker Pavel Hobl.[68] These new friendships, and his works for the WPC, fostered his visibility in the socialist world, despite his own lack of travel—what Simone Wille, following Edward Said, has called "imaginative geographies" of Chittaprosad's socialist internationalism.[69] In one of the linocuts he made during this period, the artist shows himself with works of Nâzım Hikmet and Pablo Neruda, a staging of his own ideological and affective affiliations with the transnational left-wing cultural movement during the Cold War. Pavel Hobl's 1972 documentary on Chittaprosad, *Confessions*, received a special award at the World Peace Council. Writing in the *Daily Worker* in 1955, Sidney Finkelstein noted the monumentality of Chittaprosad's linocuts.[70]

Despite his disenchantment with the party, socialist imagery persists in Chittaprosad's work, and gains in fact a critical stance that the party itself was unwilling to sanction. His tool was the theme of labor, which he used as a prism for activating multiple planes of political address, such as displacement, struggle, solidarity, and precariousness. From the early 1950s, Chittaprosad returned to that theme—which had been a favorite subject in his postwar commissions for the *People's Age*—yet with a difference in address. From his earlier focus on the everyday lives of mill workers and vignettes from working-class neighborhoods of Bombay, he turned toward capturing the struggles of labor under the shadow of industrialization. In a series of linocuts on children, childhood, pavements, and construction sites, Chittaprosad not only shifted away from the grand subjects of political modernity, but displaced, more importantly, the allegorical traces of the nation in art. Labor as theme opens up his visualization of precarious living. Child labor in various forms dominates this period. In works like *The Bidi Workers*, *Newspaper Boys*, and the iconic *Gone Mad* (linocut on paper, 1952)—which shows a street urchin snatching food from crows over a dustbin heap with the city skyline looming in the background—street children fight on the edge of lunacy or labor in *bidi* (tobacco) facto-

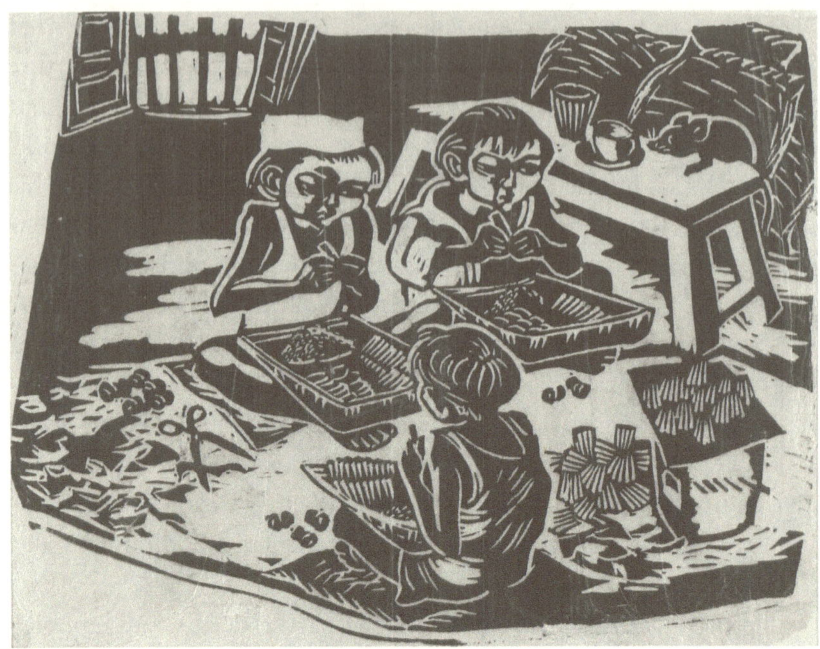

FIGURE 4.6. *Chittaprosad, Bidi Workers, from Angels without Fairy Tales (1952). Linocut on tracing paper pasted on mountboard. Courtesy of DAG, New Delhi.*

ries while mice nibble at their morsels (fig. 4.6) or work as newspaper vendors in the frozen monotony of daily toil, or sleep by the wayside as traffic crushes past. Crows, mice, roosters, and rushing vehicles inhabit these linocuts, thrusting themselves into the living spaces of destitutes. In another series showing rural displacement, parts of which were illustrations for Bimal Roy's *Do Bigha Zamin*, suburbia's industrial landscapes capture a grinding social disintegration that feeds urban poverty. The utopic frame of labor that was common in the 1940s is ironically displaced into a new narrative of the subaltern, where the subject of art is not only the oppressed classes of society but also the underbelly of the national-modern project itself.

Labor was also an aspect of Chittaprosad's own activist subjectivity, impelling him to return to the famine-struck districts of Maharashtra for months, documenting hunger and destitution in much the same tenor as his famine works of 1943 did. In the early 1950s, he can be seen as continuing the impulses that drove artist-cadres like him in the 1940s. In 1953, for instance, while documenting famine and flood in the poorest of quarters in Maharashtra, he wrote to Murari Gupta about Nehru's visit to famine-affected areas:

> I have returned roasted and half-dead on the 1st of May. Nehru had visited Mangi that very morning. Barely 7 to 10 minutes. He was impressed by the self-help efforts of the farmers. After a convoluted introduction, he briefly summed up his duty of claiming that none would henceforth remain hungry. A thousand rupees were spent to prepare the metaled road for his grand arrival, another thousand for the podium. He posed for the camera in near-dance poses, threw garland-bouquets brought from Pune-Bombay to the women of the peasant families, uttered a Jai Hind and climbed up to his jeep. From 11 am the *khadi*-clad locals had parrot-trained the crowd to say Pandit Nehru *zindabad*; Pandit left on his jeep, the crowd remained silent. The next day it's an uproar in all newspapers.[71]

Chittaprosad returned from Mangi with 70 sketches and more than 650 photos, hoping that the party would exhibit his works. He was met instead with a dithering party response, which to him revealed more than financial backtracking on exhibition costs: "[And] even if it were possible," he noted, referring to the promised exhibition, "I doubt whether it would serve its purpose because it amounts to challenging Nehru. Had there been a support from the Kisan Sabha it could have been successful."[72] Even the annual conference of the IPTA, where he hoped to show his works, had become, he noted, "merely a dance-of-the-ghosts," "people's theatre minus the people." His personal exhaustion merges with his disillusionment with the party and the Nehruvian state, and questions the residues of the social commitment of artists. "The route to an artist's link with his country, in this land and these times," he noted, lamenting the failure of Mangi famine drawings to draw patronage, "is so unfathomably far that it fails my sight, energy and intellect."[73]

This sense of despondency also marked Chittaprosad's commission for the children's edition of R. P. Dutt's *India Today*, a rough work with which I opened this chapter. In these illustrations, he strove to connect lineages of subaltern struggles, from the tribal resistance of the colonial period like the Santhal Rebellion to new protest landscapes of strikes and community mobilization under the clarion call of the Communist worker and the party flag. Indeed, these images can be seen as an attempt to return to socialist realism's myth-making tropes by narrativizing working-class struggle in British India, in an entirely new style of using ink on scraperboard. Laboring bodies—embedded in industrial landscapes, or welded together in concrete collectives—seem alert, active, and poised in revolutionary anticipation. The socialist idiom is complex here, combining two contesting, albeit typical, qualities of socialist realist imagery: one that wants to "shock people out of complacency" and another that is "reflective and introspective," envisioning a projected future and the promise of a socialist society.[74] Social and socialist realism intertwine here, mixing trauma and pastoral harmony in a singular artistic narrative. It seems to disturb, almost consciously, a very similar idiom of labor used in Nehruvian imagery, where celebration of rural plenitude was a way of marking the hegemonic imagination of postcolonial promise.[75]

Monumentality—a typical socialist realist idiom used to create larger-than-life projections of labor and resistance—is active in some of these images, whether in the figures of the destitute child snatching morsels from the food-bin against the backdrop of an industrial city, the rickshaw-puller hand-pulling hefty, sneering customers, or uprooted villagers poised in grave doubt before fuming factories. Linocuts were particularly suited for the emergence of this dark, nocturnal landscape or for bringing out the expressionistic rupture of displacement itself, as for instance in the works on drought and flood victims that Chittaprosad did in 1953. Throughout the 1950s, he frequently sought assistance to further his political project of creating art for the people—"legends of the country on a national scale, even on a global scale, which is impossible with paintings that are part of an exhibition-patron circuit or the journal dependent black-and-whites." But "linocuts too require assistance," as he noted in a letter to Murari

Gupta, "from mass organizations, progressive printing presses, implying mainly that there is no art-consciousness in a party." [76]

From the late 1950s until his illness and return to Calcutta, Chittaprosad dedicated himself to making puppets and puppetry shows for local slum children. Writing to Gupta on July 31, 1957, he mentions his Czech friend Salaba gifting him money for a puppet project—100 rupees each month for a period of six months. Salaba also gifted him a puppet stage.[77] He writes about composing plays to be staged for puppet shows. He had named his puppetry theater group "Khelaghar":

> One of the members is an engineer. He is preparing the torso of the puppets, trunks with legs, in the factory following the Czech technique, I will supply the heads. I have already produced some five such whole figures. . . . Since I am still under the spell of foreign prototypes, the puppets continue to follow a naturalistic schema. But other fresh plans are filling my imagination; intend to "puppetise" the folk wood and terracotta toys.[78]

His puppetry was picking up momentum, his letters brimming with excitement around "a new kind of life . . . centred around the puppet performance," with new enthusiasts, even the "ruling authority" being drawn to his puppets. Yet his rejection of "the world of exchange" persisted,[79] even while monetary support remained paltry. While traveling puppetry troupes from Czechoslovakia—the Radost—paid visits to his performances, Khelaghar dwindled by the late 1950s.[80] In a letter to Murari Gupta from November 1958, Chittaprosad mentions shutting it down.

Despite his marginal living in post-independence Bombay—uninvited to join either the city's celebrated Progressive Artists' Group or even the Calcutta Group of artists—Chittaprosad made an interesting appearance in *Marg*. Mulk Raj Anand, founding editor of *Marg* and architect of the Nehruvian national-modern aesthetic, published some of Chittaprosad's linocuts of folk dance, akin to his sketches of IPTA ballets of the 1940s, to illustrate a report on the All India Folk Dance festival of August 5, 1954. As one of the founding members of the Progressive Writers' Association—the formation of which inaugurated the rhetoric of critical realism and left-wing cultural radicalism in India—Anand would have been thoroughly aware of Chittaprosad's lineage and the political import of such national-popular visualizations of folk art. Yet the feature carried no discussion or note on Chittaprosad. When Anand introduced him in a foreword accompanying a later portfolio of his linocuts, he portrayed Chittaprosad as a carrier of the legacies of the Bengal Schools, imbued with a "great deal of folk feeling":

> In fact the drawings, linocuts and woodcuts of this highly talented artist may easily be mistaken for the work of the village artisan if we did not know that the vitality of his line derives from the conscious alliance, by a trained draughtsman, with survivals of folk-tradition in the villages, particularly of Bengal.[81]

The fact that the portfolio was meant for an American audience does not justify a complete erasure of the artist's radical use of graphic art, even if his Communist identity appeared to be taboo. This tepid lacing of Chittaprosad's prints is indeed a subtle displacement of meaning and frames from the left-wing national-popular art of the 1940s to a deradicalized folk footprint under the meta-frame of Nehruvian modernity. Chittaprosad's letters to his mother reveal his own discomfort regarding his early friendship with Anand, who offered to send him money by selling his prints to publications in India and abroad; while keeping "innumerable works" of the artist, Anand is known to have paid Chittaprosad the paltry sum of Rs. 35 for the *Marg* prints and, moreover, to have disenfranchised him entirely while circulating such prints in both *Marg* and the American magazine.[82]

This episode also points toward the ways in which the (in)visibilities of a political artist like Chittaprosad became institutional. Nothing concrete was written on him until the 1990s, except the occasional published letter in vernacular periodicals like *Parichoy* and various little magazines in Bengal. His former comrades cite him in their memoirs, almost as a symbol or fragment of a past lost—of the CPI, and of a certain ethos of cultural resistance during decolonization.[83] Even in Sudhi Pradhan's meticulous three-volume documentation of the cultural movement, Chittaprosad's presence remains slender, in what is a tertiary reference to visual arts within the larger scope of the leftist cultural movement.[84] While the dissipation of the left's cultural-political project in independent India can explain these erasures, the blind spots and appropriations of the postcolonial national-modern aesthetic compel historical attention. Writing on Chittaprosad, then, requires listening to multiple scales of exclusion as well as exile. What we have in Chittaprosad is, indeed, a mesh of personal disillusionment and structural erasure that reveals the displacements of socialist art in postcolonial India.

Unlike Chittaprosad, who persisted in the margins, his fellow artist-cadre from the 1940s Somnath Hore followed a different path in the 1950s. In the mid-1950s, Hore was converting his documentary sketches of the Tebhaga movement from 1946 into woodcuts. Hore's woodcut prints of Tebhaga from the early 1950s reveal a formal crystallization. Still rooted in narrative, they allow for a deepening of fissures in the bodies on the canvas, bringing out the expressionistic potential of the drawings. Akin to Chittaprosad's works from the same period, Hore's prints from this time collect the dark recesses of urban Calcutta—refugee camps, pavements, beggars, and destitution. Hunger and displacement dominate some of these works as much as the collective action of the Tebhaga, entering a raw form beyond the immediacy of the drawings in his *Tebhaga Diary*. This is a transitional point in Hore's career, one that took him out of sketching and into explorations of new formal treatments of the stories of the 1940s. The theme of hunger and destitution would recur in his works over the next three decades, but each time with a formal difference.

For Hore, negotiations around form reveal a narrative more embedded—within both the CPI and the post-independence art world—than that of Chittaprosad. In 1954, he had already accepted a teaching position at the Indian Art School set up by Atul Bose, to develop a print department at the college. Bose had been one of Hore's teachers at the Government School of Art. In the late 1940s, Hore had already begun to be noted for his "political art," which was, until then, tied to the party's demands—"subjects such as the teachers' movement, communal harmony, the tea garden-workers' movement, the strike by the workers of the *Amrita Bazar Patrika* and so on."[85] This was also the time when he began to realize the limitations on artistic form that party work entailed: "I became acutely aware that merely ornamenting the subject matter through the various techniques and stylistics of art was by no means sufficient to create the desired emotional reactions. There was a powerful requirement to transcend the subject. . . . Sentimentality creates a barrier to the delineation of the emotional theme."[86] In 2011, a series of Hore's prints and socialist posters from the 1950s was exhibited that revealed his peak period as a party artist in the 1950s, before he consciously dissociated himself to pursue a more sustained artistic career as a printmaker and sculptor.[87] When he left the CPI in 1956, he moved into the interiors of the post-independence art circuits, holding on to socialist imagery in its various mutations. In 1958, he went on to take a teaching position at Delhi Polytechnic (renamed Delhi Art College in 1964) and became, as he admits in his autobiography, more concerned with the formal possibilities of art.[88]

TRANSFORMATION

In his thesis to the CPI, Ritwik Ghatak had called for an active engagement with the present and future of left-wing art, rather than a pursuit of nostalgia. "We are not seeking a 'golden period', but a proper place in the body of the Party, and our share in Party rights and responsibilities," he wrote.[89] This denial of cultural nostalgia is striking, Ghatak's thrust toward the urgency of transformation overtaking his commitment to revolutionary romanticism: "Drop the idea that Revolution is round the corner. It is not. Forget about that former previous 'elation', former 'enthusiasm', and that romantic feeling of Revolutionary 'zeal'—in a word, all that guided us up to at least 1950."[90] This impatience with the past is the crux of the transformational imperative that left-wing aesthetics underwent in early postcolonial India.

Early in *On the Cultural Front*, Ghatak sounds a clarion call for transforming the past into the future of socialist art: "Reshape the past, hammer the present and forge the future."[91] This call for transformation and malleability marks the left's interface with modernist formalism, as artists from within the folds of the left stepped over into the domains of artistic modernism that were expanding in Nehruvian India. The metaphor of malleability also arises in the writings of Somnath Hore. In his diary from the late 1980s, Hore rejected the consistencies of ideological or formal purity: "We are all a certain kind of alloy, beaten into shape from a mix of many metals. This may do away with purity but it does instil in us strength."[92] The malleability of communist artists like him is also a temper of dialogue, and the simultaneity of being open to futures and a persisting presence of the past. This habitation of the past is not one of nostalgia, or what Walter Benjamin had called a "left-wing melancholy,"[93] but an unrelenting commitment to the dialectic of past and future. The question of "form" in socialist art was to be negotiated through this dialectical aesthetic, a transformation through praxis. To understand form, Ghatak insisted, a communist artist was supposed to study the past with scrupulous care and learn from its experiments and achievements. This aesthetic labor, he warned his comrades, was not to be done hastily: "It means learning the whole process; from the inception of 'theme-content', through stages of development, to the final product."[94] Neither was it going to be steeped in sloganeering: "Slow, methodical, tenacious work is what is necessary."[95]

Such aesthetic work also required participation—with artists outside the context of the left. Ghatak called for solidarities built on professional concerns and issues of form and creativity. The communist artiste's task, he noted, was to "*mobilize* and *guide* the masses through creation and through physical participation."[96] The physical aspect, as described by Ghatak, is critical to understanding the question of form—both artistic form and forms of cultural participation. "Our physical responsibility," he argued, "is primarily to the others of our same trade, the same specialized profession, who are never a *mass*, never."[97] Serving the profession meant cooperating with "specialized persons and groups with the objective to create art and *thereby* serve people."[98] Ghatak's stress on form and the values of "Bourgeois culture" is telling: "We have to take all that is good in that culture . . . to reshape that culture, reshape to achieve our goals, and to harness it to our purpose."[99] Transformation—of form and politics in socialist art—is at the core of Ghatak's argument: "Our comrades must creatively work among these artistes in order to learn their 'melody and speech' and 'method of their utterances'; that is, to learn *their form, their mode of handling philosophic content.*"[100] Art, he argued, is not a "mass-organization where problems are of a general nature"; only artistes can execute this collectivity, as "Communist artistes *are* the organizers."

If Ghatak's voice is applied to the careers of both Chittaprosad and Somnath Hore through the 1950s and 1960s, the problem of platforms and collaborations reveals anxieties of belonging, as well as dialogues, with each of these artists negotiating participation and rejection in his own way. Both of them grappled with questions not only of form and subjectivity, but of their own transformations through journeys from the CPI's cultural movement and its futures as well. In Chittaprosad's case, the journey was complex—retirement and denial of participation, and a turn away from the familiar grids of meaning. After Khelaghar shut down, Chittaprosad reinvented the investments in book illustrations and works on childhood that he had begun in the early 1950s. He began illustrating Indian epics like the *Ramayana* and folk tales. By the late 1960s, he had come to be known specifically as an illustrator of childhood, combining folk iconography with the humor and whimsy of children's books. The linocuts of child labor that he had made already in 1952–53 were finally published by UNICEF as *Angels without Fairy Tales*, a part of the International Conference in Defence of Children held in Vienna in April 1952.

Throughout the 1960s, Chittaprosad continued to have visions of reinventing popular art. In November 1960, he wrote about his idealized plans for touring Bengal on foot to write a history of Bengal in pictures. He sought to reinvent illustration, he wrote, by using "new source materials," like Ashok Mitra's *Census Report of Bengal*—not "an academic history-in-pictures" but one based on walking through Bengal "on foot as far as possible—for two years." His letter details his plans, reminiscent of his tours through Bengal's famine-struck districts in 1943–44:

> The tour programme will be prepared from textual references in advance. Then I will bring back photographs of historic Bengal from my tour in cities-villages-open terrain—a glimpse of the past as seen through my contemporary vision. . . . It isn't essential to make use of pictures as the saddle-horse of history. At least I don't intend to do that—pictures won't merely be a supplement to the text. Had my famine sketches not been supported by reportage, even then the pictures would have spoken for themselves. What is essential is that the life-rhythm of the pictures maintain a connection with the flux of history, and that is precisely why I must tour Bengal on foot.[101]

While Chittaprosad's ideals remained committed to tuning art with the "flux of history," the artist himself resisted participating in the impulses and economies of the art world in postcolonial India. In his works from the 1960s, there was a retreat from political art altogether, a transformation of socialist aesthetics from revolutionary imagery to the romanticism of folk imagery. For Chittaprosad, even after Khelaghar, puppetry continued in his illustrations of children's books, childhood itself allowing him an abstraction from his despair around poverty—his own, and that of the party from which he sought recognition. This absorption in book illustrations in the 1960s revealed his euphoric commitment to a renewed folk iconography and its potentials. The illustrations punctuated also the artist's longing for a failed project of socialist art, which he had held on to throughout the 1950s, despite difficulties. In a letter to Chittaprosad in 1967, the Marxist poet and Chittaprosad's former comrade-in-arms Jyotirindranath Moitra, wrote: "*Bhule jao byarthata-r nesha*," which can be roughly translated to "Abandon your obsession of failure."[102] Failure, however, is in itself a form of participation. As a new analytical drift within art history suggests, failure carries a tension between "non-fulfilment and expectation" and is, therefore, a complex form with "connotation, symbolic charges and cultural roles, which are often diverse and contradictory."[103] These contradictions drove the transformation of socialist art in the post-colony.

Desire and despair were as much a part of the dialectical aesthetics of the postcolonial left as were the new artistic negotiations between socialist commitment and modernist experimentation.

In Somnath Hore's career after his dissociation from the CPI in 1956, this dialectic can be charted through his journeys—from Calcutta to Delhi, then back to Calcutta, and eventually to Santiniketan—which were triggered by his refusals and returns, journeys that shaped his artistic material and method. These travels are key to Hore's art of abstraction—the journey away from context, event, violence, and rupture, and the return to temporal distance and memory as a way of reconstructing the past. Hore's Delhi years saw him go as far from the "subject" as he could. His color intaglios from the early 1960s reveal the play of surfaces and color, almost totemic patterns, both luminescent and dense. This phase of his work is the only time that he explores bright colors, though the shadow of the "subject" is never far away. *The Ninth Symphony*, a print collage from 1962, exemplifies this play of values—light and darkness, subject and texture interlock. The subject continues to creep back during the late 1960s; bodies materialize out of color and forms, almost rupturing abstract compositions from their core. The deep etchings from 1966, like *The Weary*, and *Child* are similarly telling. By the end of the 1960s, figures return fully in his works, in lithographs soaked in red with minimalistic figures. The abstraction of body into form is almost complete.

Yet it is interesting to see the persistence of dissatisfaction in this artist. "During my stay in Delhi," Hore wrote, "I tried to free myself of subject matter but The Subject never let go of me." Without a conscious pursuit of the subject, he writes, the "wounds" of the famine of 1943, of war and the communal riots of 1946, kept "inscribing themselves" into his "techniques of drawing":

> One would work without any preconceived notions as I chiselled the wood for my woodcuts, as I marked the metal with acid. Later, however, all those innumerable cuts and marks would bring intimations of only one subject matter—the helpless around us, the rejected, the hungry. The chalk that had

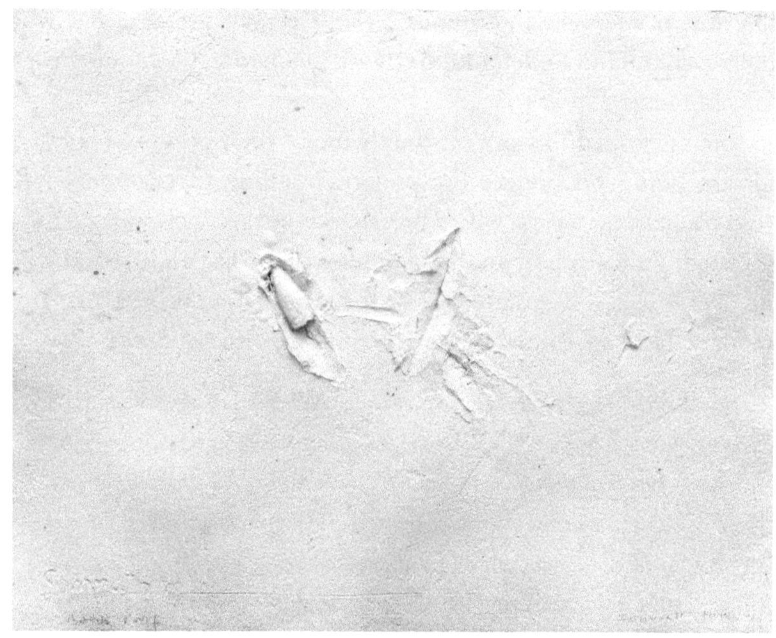

FIGURE 4.7. *Somnath Hore, Wounds (c. 1977). Paper pulp print. Courtesy of Akar Prakar Gallery, Kolkata. © Artist's Estate.*

> crossed my fingers to reach my heart when I sketched the victims of famine left a wound that would not heal.[104]

In 1967, Hore suddenly resigned from his Delhi job and returned to Calcutta, and in mid-1969, he moved to Santiniketan.

Between 1971 and 1979, Somnath Hore made the series of paper-pulp prints with which I began this book, and which forms the cover itself. The *Wounds* carried white-on-white compositions dramatized with sudden ruptures and incisions, often with red paint trickling along pierced or scraped and gouged surfaces (fig. 4.7). The molds were first made on clay or wax sheets, then transferred to cement matrices on which paper pulp was poured, to create a highly textured surface with undulations, freckles, pores, and fissures. The surface was then gashed or split open with a knife, or scarred with a scorching rod, burning or melting the wax. These were extensions of Hore's intaglio prints from engravings done on acid-lacerated metal plates, where he made sharp and skeletal figures with geometrical contours bearing marks of hunger.

Hore continued to work on the theme of the wound in his famous sculpture series on hunger (he preferred calling these *Bronzes*) that would come in the 1980s, where he created concave, hollow figurines—emaciated, limp animals and human forms—by suspending and wrapping over one another flattened, warped, or gashed wax sheets. In an interview, Hore explained the idea behind his *Wounds Series*:

> I am all the time involved in one concern. What I call the Wounds. Social wounds you may call it. Whether it is famine or refugees, or the riots, or whatever it is. For this concept I don't have to think, it is there inside me. I don't have to think in terms of the material . . . I remember seeing the metal plate in nitric acid, and the bubbles of anger, making wounds on the metal. I thought this was a most appropriate means to express my own ideas, by this etching process.[105]

Hore's *Wounds* thrust forth an aesthetic of loss, violence, and ruins. While the postcolonial national-modern aesthetic picked up the image of the contained rural quotidian, providing vignettes of an India poised between tradition and modernity, in the works of former artist-cadres like Somnath Hore, art took on an imagery of rupture. What is important here is the process of *abstraction*—a radical simplification of form, whereby the artist distances himself from the factual tangibility of lived experience, the abstraction of form capturing within itself an "affective dynamic" of history itself.[106] Yet, the wound is a call for corporeality. It makes the body itself a vulnerable text of ruptures, dissolving into material—metaphorical skin, streets, and histories. Though "wound" as a theme became explicitly articulated in Hore's works only in the 1960s, it can be read in fact as an allegory for his own journey. This abstraction was, in essence, his political dialogue with subject itself.

The "transformation of memory," writes Pierre Nora, "implies a decisive shift from the historical to the psychological, from the social to the individual, from the objective message to its subjective reception, from repetition to rememoration."[107] This journey from memory to metaphor is active in Hore's *Wounds Series*. Memory is objectified through the erasure of situational details; the material form captures the essence of malady and anguish. The nature of the abstraction arrived at thus—the silent presence of the wounds in the understanding of modernism in Indian art—requires much more critical art historical scrutiny than it has so far received.

The persistence of the "subject" is Hore's subjective encounter with the dialectical aesthetics of left-wing artists. At the close of his autobiography, *Amar Silpakatha* (*My Thoughts on Art*), Hore staged this dialectic in an interesting question-and-answer format:

> - What is the relationship between politics and art?
> Real art cannot be a vehicle for politics when it has turned into party politics. Art may well reflect social consciousness; however, that is of small consequence. It is clear from one's own experience that ill-considered politics goes far beyond poorly visualized art. . . .
> - Is there a connection between socialism and art?
> Socialism is the social consciousness earned by the exercise of one's innate cognition. Artistry on the other hand is the special ability that one is born with. Socialism may well encourage an artist to create works of art, but it can never make him an artist.[108]

For Chittaprosad, a transformation of artistic idiom and voice occurred within his often self-staged distancing from the art world, as well as in the political potentialities of his folk imageries. Speaking to Pavl Hobl, Chittaprosad asserted: "It is not enough, however, for the Indian artist merely to sympathize with the peasant or to borrow from Indian folklore. We must give the Indian peasant our moral and political backing and create an art that will serve the Indian peasant not only as a source of inspiration, but an art of which he will be the main consumer and patron."[109]

He wrote profusely throughout the 1960s, mainly children's editions of epics, poems, and short stories. Many of these remained in manuscript form and eventually were lost when his property shifted hands during family conflicts in the 1980s.[110] A collection of three poems written by Chittaprosad alongside thirty illustrations was published in the Netherlands in 1982, edited by the Dutch poet Ad van Rijsewijk. A review of this volume appearing in the journal *New Perspectives* printed a fragment from one of his last poems, *Night Cactus*—an echo, I would like to argue, of an aesthetic of melancholia that became a form of socialist artistic subjectivity in a communist artist like Chittaprosad:

> Like you, I am greatly surprised,
> I do not know where I've been,
> I do not know how I came here . . .
> [. . .] Did I know what happened,
> And from what beginnings,
> It started to happen?
> Even now, do I know? [. . .][111]

TRANSFORMATION OF THE socialist idiom through the 1950s and 1960s paralleled shifting iconographic and art-critical concerns in the artistic field of post-independence India. Writing in 1967, Jaya Appasamy delineated three kinds of transformation in artistic values and styles: first, a shift from "local nationalistic idioms to a world international language," even "folkish" styles becoming more divorced from life and context; second, a "diminishing interest in subject," leading to a "disintegration of the figure into texture, panels and planes," moving from the figurative and the romantic toward abstraction, formal distortion, and intellectualism; and third, a sense of the "autonomy" of art, "freed from description and message." "One of the problems resolved in the 1950s," she noted, "was that of being Indian within quotes."[112]

Such a reading misses, however, a politics of *difference*—between the national imaginary and sub-national cultural imaginations, where the asymmetrical trails and trials of decolonization were more visible. Such differences, as much as the less-spectacular histories of cultural transformation that I have discussed here, produce the fragmented narratives that are often displaced in pursuits of postcolonial modernism and its affirmations.

In Chapter 5, the closing chapter of this book, I will explore what peculiar resonances the displacements of decolonization—both the famine of 1943 and the partition in 1947—had on the art of the "locality," here post-partition Calcutta.

CHAPTER 5

"REVOLUTION IN THE TROPICS, LOVE IN THE TROPICS"

Arts of Displacement in the Post-colony

> Perspiration. The odour of it. A dilapidated CSTC bus emitting a morbid trail of black smoke. Burnt-out grass, dead grass, butts of crushed cigarettes, rags, pieces of paper, a quiet coexistence inside the two parallel lines of the tram tracks [. . .]
> [. . .] Revolutionary truth on the wall. Or at least a version of it. Beggars. A leper and his comely wife. Suddenly a tree, about twenty feet tall, thin branches all over, blushing with flowers [. . .]
> [. . .] A newspaper kiosk, poetry magazines by the dozen, more revolutionary truth. Revolution in the tropics, love in the tropics, insipid poetry in the tropics. The red triangle, the vulgar society, ethos travelling down from New Delhi [. . .]
> [. . .] Political parties who couldn't care less, incapable of caring more, the books speak of situations in Russia or China or Cuba, no clue to Calcutta 1969. Clenched fists, Mao's Red Book, violence in the air, to be met by matching violence, vapour, the meaning of meaning [. . .]
> [. . .] Dusk, whining drizzle of rain, slush, mud and smoke. Is it hopelessness, or the lull before insurrection, maybe again an equipose.
>
> (Asok Mitra, "Calcutta Everyday," *Calcutta Diary*)[1]

ASOK MITRA'S "Calcutta Everyday" is very consciously a text of fragments. Now a part of his seminal book of essays, *Calcutta Diary*, this piece was written in 1969 for the noted left-wing periodical *Frontier*, edited by the Marxist poet Samar Sen, with whom Mitra shared a long association going back to the *Parichoy* circle of the 1930s.[2] The milieu of the piece was the political acceleration of the late 1960s and the early 1970s, when post-independence Calcutta was battling visceral far-left political unrest, fanning out from a grassroots peasant movement in the remote quarters of Naxalbari in northern Bengal. The city was already a ruptured space, a process that had begun back in 1943, when millions of refugees from famine-ravaged rural Bengal poured into the city, transforming its visuality radically. The hunger, destitution, and death, as well as the resilience that Calcutta seemed to embody, had since then been aggravated by the communal genocide and refugee influx at the fraught arrival of independence over partition in 1947. Through the 1950s and 1960s, the city absorbed waves of displaced refugees, brewing in an economy of shortages, political agitation, and social disintegration. The promise of independence seemed less visible here. Despite national enthusiasm for planning and progress, this eastern metropolis, Partha Chatterjee writes, resonated with "voices of disenchantment."[3]

In Mitra's "Calcutta Everyday," a fragmented city becomes *textual form*, unmoored from a *singular* narrative harness. People, streets, meanings, and the nation itself appear as fragments, entering the essay as a rolling film of visual stills. Each phrase, each sentence captures in its drift the marks and edges of the city's streets: pavements clogged with poverty, walls plastered in layers of political graffiti, structures on the brink of dissolution; there are echoes of a revolutionary internationalism, even as the city itself seems to be out of sync. Almost abstracted from its own chaotic density, the city, as Mitra noted, seems suspended in indifference: Mitra's "equipoise" suggests a city precariously poised on the brink of disintegration. In politics and poverty, the post-colony seen from the fragmented textual scape of Mitra's "Calcutta Everyday" seems to be a dialectical site where past and present interlock, and future itself seems displaced. An aesthetic of combat seems to sustain it, as struggle and resilience, decay and creation entangle.

For artists in the city, displacement, degeneration, and struggle were persistent subjects, as much as was their shared will to seek artistic forms that would make sense of such locational pulls. The Naxalbari movement from the late 1960s accelerated this imagery, with political graffiti and posters merging with new artistic visualizations of the city itself *as* a political canvas—featuring not only resistance, but repression, instability, and an almost embodied visceral form of the *city-as-rupture*. This binding of form and location was in itself a dialectical one. The art of postcolonial Calcutta is not (only) a narrative of the "representation" of refugees of partition or of political protest. The idea of representation itself needs to be loosened here from its mimetic echo of "reflection," and read as practices and strategies that "emerge out of a radicalizing context": as Moinak Biswas argued in the context of an iconic "refugee film" of the late 1940s and early 1950s—*Chinnamul* (Uprooted); made in 1948–49, and released in 1951)—Calcutta offered in the post-independence decades "a context where the very urgency of the real, and the instability of the categorical difference between event and form, experience and expression, create the scope for a capture, a portrayal that can be directly related to the life of the object." Artists in the city, thus, were not only "representing" the city they lived in, but were themselves protagonists and witnesses to the "present *as* the city."[4] Such "presentness" in the city was an accumulation of three decades, not merely a singular rupture of the partition of 1947. In the film, for instance, as in many paintings to come from the city, dialogues (or images, metaphors in painting) would refer back to the famine of 1943, a déjà vu that displaces the singularity of 1947 in both predating it and continuing long after, in quotidian "minor" displacements as refugee flows persisted. In films like *Chinnamul*, the city itself emerges as a protagonist, as Biswas points out, invoking a *form*, and the question of the "referent" itself thus calls for reconsideration.[5]

Art in postcolonial Calcutta saw not the modernist promise of the nation-state, but a slump in organized art activity and patronage, and a dearth of art galleries. What was vital in post-independence art practice in Calcutta is, perhaps, not to be found in stable institutional sites or sustained patronage, but in new collectives of expelled art college students, in diffused street exhibitions, and in images of depletion and rupture rather than promise. The Calcutta Group had disintegrated in 1953, and its members had dispersed, much like those of the Progressive Artists' Group in Bombay, most of them either leaving India or joining new art institutions. While Santiniketan remained a center for a modernist imagination (albeit with persisting negotiations with a ruralist vision), its narratives were still separate from the trajectories of post-partition imaginaries in Calcutta. This lull of the 1950s was nonetheless significant. It begins to unravel once the questions are altered. Instead of looking for a modernist imaginary that would capture the promise of freedom, or lend itself to the nation-form, I would like to ask here, *What makes post-partition Calcutta different?* My intent is not to seek a uniquely regional exclusivity, or even to expand (yet again) the canon of Indian modernism into its regional eclecticism. Indeed, stories of modernity in Indian art are stories of various regional formations—whether that be at Kala Bhavan at Santiniketan, or at M. S. University in Baroda, or in the postcolonial formations in Madras or even New Delhi. What interests me here are the questions that are posed by such *differences* that postcolonial Calcutta was marked by, and what such questions mean for our expanding understandings of postcolonial modernisms. The city presents, I will argue, sites of multiple displacements—not only one structured by refugee influx and sinking economic containment, but also a displacement from the narratives of the nation-state. The arts of displacement at play here thrust forth the regional or the locational as a "partisan" dynamic that is its own form, and has to be read as such.

Rather than pursuing idioms and figures of postcolonial modernism, I am interested in thinking about what obsessed artists from the region, what they struggled with, or what their possible locations might be—vis-à-vis their national counterparts and the national narratives that write them in and out in curious ways. I pursue these questions in four segments that seek to understand postcolonial displacements as both content and form in the art emerging from Calcutta—shaping in their turn, historiography of postcolonial modernism itself. The chapter—as does the rest of the book so far—stops in the years preceding the declaration of national Emergency in 1975 under Prime Minister Indira Gandhi, and thereby foregrounds the dynamics of the political in Indian modern art *before* the development of a more active political consciousness among artists at the national scale since the mid-1970s.[6]

CALCUTTA, "UNCONFINED CITY"

To visitors to the city through the 1950s and 1960s, Calcutta appeared to be a "shock" that seemed to assault composure and arrest the very possibility of (aesthetic) abstraction. When the artist A. Ramachandran visited in 1957 from his native Kerala, he was struck by what he later recalled as an image of man, both unreal and viscerally real:

> In July 1957, I landed at Sealdah station, Calcutta. The impression of the platform with thousands of refugees is still vivid in my mind. An entire family consisting of parents and children with pots and pans as well as stray dogs shared an area of six feet by six feet. Within this area the whole cycle of procreation, birth, disease, decay and death [was] enacted.[7]

"In the gutter," he writes, "I saw my first Christ-like image, stretched out naked, drinking the murky water of the sewage." He particularly remembers the ironic image of a "haggard old woman," destitute amid the grimy city streets, "kicking a worn out timepiece and abusing it saying: 'You have cheated me.'" Such images remained in his works as "major motif[s]," perhaps prefiguring the diabolical friezes of convoluted bodies in suspension that he was to create soon after: "My first image of man," Ramachandran admits, "I developed in the streets of Calcutta."[8]

When the Italian auteur Pier Paolo Pasolini visited India in the 1960s, the city appeared to him as "the unconfined city where every human pain and suffering touches the extreme limit, and life is carried out like a funeral ballet."[9] To the poet Allen Ginsberg, who stayed in the city at various points through the 1960s, Calcutta seemed "filled with newspapers and war and burning trams by railroad stations where soldiers wave from trains at homeless lepers sleeping months on huge concrete floors."[10] The city failed to make sense, time and again, to its visitors. Günter Grass, writing in the 1980s, would grapple thus with this cacophony of meanings: "Write a poem called 'Calcutta' and stop taking planes to far-off places. Get a composer to set all the projects for cleaning up Calcutta to music and have the resulting oratorio (sung by a Bach society) open in Calcutta. Develop a new dialectic from Calcutta's contradictions. Transfer the UN to Calcutta." His final line, "Let's not waste another word on Calcutta. Delete Calcutta from all guidebooks," becomes a paradoxical tribute to the refusal of stable meanings the city seemed to be hinged on.[11]

The city was "unconfined" in ways both plural and paradoxical. Unconfinement was literal when it came to the crisis of space: the spilling over of the refugee exodus into a stretched city space had been raw since the famine of 1943, and the partition of 1947 brought a fresh surge of large-scale refugee influx, which continued persistently thereafter into the 1970s. By the end of 1951, the number of refugees in West Bengal was estimated to be almost 2.5 million, climbing to 3.5 million in 1956, and 6 million in 1973. However, unlike the western borders of India, which had seen a high of 15 million refugees arriving just between August and December 1947, the patterns of "settlement" in the east were distinctly different—with more destitution and urban squalor. Already in 1951, West Bengal's 2.51 million refugees were more than the 2.4 million in Punjab, for instance. The population of the state grew at a faster pace than that of the rest of the country, from 20 million in 1947 to 35 million in 1961, with a whopping 33 percent population increase between 1951 and 1961, during which period the national percentage was 21.5 percent. As late as 1973, the rates of refugee settlement in West Bengal were "the same as they had been in 1951 and 1961"[12]—the liberation war in post-partition East Pakistan, leading to the formation of Bangladesh in 1971, had added a fresh spurt of refugees pouring into the city.

The political tenor of the city was unconfined too, reverberating in the streets in persistent protests, rallies, and strikes. During the 1950s, Calcutta saw a steady rise in agitational politics, spearheaded by the Communist Party of India. While the Indian National Congress had remained a dominant political force, holding itself as a "party of order" harnessed to a nationalist prerogative and the promise of the "Nehruvian consensus," the CPI made significant political gains in the assembly elections of 1957.[13] The splits within the Communist Party—first in 1964, into the CPI and the CPI-Marxist (CPI-M) and then in 1967, into the new far-left CPI-Marxist-Leninist (CPI-ML)[14]—and ideological polarization along Soviet, Chinese, or centrist lines exposed the region to locational, national, and global tensions around Communist politics.[15] By the late 1960s, far-left politics gripped the city, transforming the cityscape into a site of visceral class war.[16] Spreading from its beginnings in the Naxalbari grassroots peasant movement, political resistance cut through urban Calcutta, to be met with violent suppression.[17] "Spring Thunder Breaks over India," proclaimed the Chinese radio broadcasts in July 1968, at the beginning of the Naxalite insurgency.[18] When the Naxalite movement burst out in Calcutta in April 1970—with the force of a "cultural revolution"—it had, however, a limited spell, coming at the end of the Naxalite struggles that had raged through the countryside before being exposed to severe state repression. In the city, Naxalite resistance accelerated the political undercurrents that had been simmering since the 1940s. As the city became an active site for imagining revolution, its visualities seemed to activate afterlives of the left-wing cultural resistance of the 1940s, with images of peasant guerrilla fights on city walls echoing the failed movements and resilient histories of that period. A striking image of such graffiti appears in Pablo Bartholomew's photographs on 1970s Calcutta, and on the cover page of his 2012 album, *The Calcutta Diaries.*[19]

Students formed the crux of the battleground in the city, developing a form that was peculiar to urban resistance: re-inscriptions of public spaces with active (dis)locations of political icons. In the early 1970s, international reviewers described Calcutta as overwhelmed by "Mao-quoting, bomb-throwing extremists [who] organised peasant guerrilla war-fare, . . . robbed banks, murdered policemen, and beat up rival Communist leaders."[20] Observing the city of the late 1960s in his 1971 book, *Calcutta*, Geoffrey Moorhouse describes the entanglement of far-left ideology with the city's spatial and social fabric itself:

> Frequently they would converge upon the Soviet Consulate or the Soviet Information Centre, bearing their placards of Mao Tse Tung, shouting their slogans, which lumped Russian and American imperialism together. When Durga Puja arrived, they set up their propaganda stalls among all the other *pandals* around the Maidan and hoisted portraits of Mao alongside posters advising the people to take the path of armed struggle.[21]

The university was the hotbed of resistance. Sumanta Banerjee describes Calcutta University as being under siege: "As files and records, question papers and answer scripts, chairs and tables went up in flames, stencilled portraits of Mao Tsetung gazed down approvingly from the school and college walls which shrieked out in loud letters: 'political power grows out of the barrel of a gun.'"[22]

A particular form of iconoclastic "statue-smashing" formed the cornerstone of Naxalite violence in Calcutta in 1970—attacks on institutions and property, and the bashing, blackening, and vandalizing of public statues and portraits of celebrated cultural and nationalist icons. While condemned even by activists within the CPI-ML, such attacks were described as "absurdist actions" with "the symbolic value" of exposing the absurdity of Indian society—and keeping alive in the process "the possibility of revolt."[23] Such protests were also read as "unconscious and primitive" forms of attacking a political culture that had betrayed the cause of revolutionary movements and peasant struggles that had constituted the anti-colonial movement but had been underplayed or erased in "official" narratives of twentieth-century India.[24] Statue-smashing, Sanjay Seth has argued, was indeed a kind of "icon-breaking" and formed a peculiar modality of uncontained annihilation that marked the "cultural revolution." Following historian Ranajit Guha, Seth noted that these were rejections of "a whole history of what it meant to be on and of the Left" in a "backward country."[25] Read in "context," such defacements were more than "negative actions"; they revealed potentially alternative rationalities that sought to *literally* dismantle a progressive culture that was perceived as being erected on a feudal society.[26] The indiscriminate smashing of icons of both progressive modernists and traditionalists revealed a revolutionary subversion of both the left-wing politics of the CPI-M and the narrative of nationalist politics. It drew its idioms and mechanics from Maoist thought and valorized the peasantry as the vanguard of revolution.

What questions of postcolonial modernity emerge from this "uncontainment" of statue-smashing? Visuality, Nicholas Mirzoeff argued, has a contradiction built into it: it can be a mode of representing hegemonic or iconic visual culture and, at the same time, "a mode for resisting it by means of reverse appropriation."[27] Visuality, he noted, carries a dialectical bind between authoritarian modes of picturing, and potential subversions and appropriations of such visual tropes by subaltern groups and subcultures. He designates the latter "Visuality 2," resonating with what Dipesh Chakraborty has called "History 2"—subaltern or counter-hegemonic appropriations of the "totalising thrusts" of a universalistic meta-modality of "History 1."[28] This historical agency of Visuality 2 thus opens up a potential field of minor sights/sites and actions/interventions that displace canonical modes of art, aesthetics, and political being, through a "*relation of difference* that is always deferred" (emphasis mine)[29] and thus attuned to revolutionary disruptions of consensus—political, social, and cultural.

The question of "shock" that I noted at the outset of this chapter needs to be read in relation to these strategies of disruption and difference—conscious or otherwise. Shock, in Benjaminian terms, dislocates and (re)activates the city dweller.[30] In dialogue with the use of interruption, montage, and juxtaposition in Brechtian plays, the formal resonances of which can be found in Benjamin's works, shock, it is argued, "shatters perception, exposing the discontinuities of history."[31] Calcutta seems to be a striking case study in such ruptures of the "homogeneous empty time" of the imagined communities of "nations,"[32] sustaining itself as a site of fragmented, heterogeneous temporalities[33] *within* meta-narratives of postcolonial sovereignty. The refugees in postcolonial Calcutta not only disrupted urban topography along new lines of excess and tenuous containment, which became a battleground for the poor, homeless, and destitute; there was also, as Sudipta Kaviraj has noted, "a plebianisation of public space," at once "a consequence of democracy" and a subaltern rejection of the abstraction of the "nation" or its historical struggles—"the lower middle classes' mode of living in history." Filth, as the material embodiment of the "excess" of displacement in postcolonial Calcutta, "is not just a material thing but a conceptual entity," Kaviraj argued,[34] as are these modes of political excess, which are chaotic, unresolved, and persistent.

Calcutta in the early 1970s, wrecked by a Maoist political resistance, created a visuality that resisted the idealized imagery of a national-modern art. Art in Calcutta through the 1960s and 1970s—the high noon of abstraction in international and Indian modern art—had remained primarily figurative. In the works of Calcutta artists from the late 1950s and through the 1960s and 1970s, the fate of the city seemed to skew the form of the subject. This created an urban idiom that ran through the works of artists in the city, invoking the ridiculous, the sinister, and the fantastic.[35]

In Calcutta, the social realist iconography of the 1940s gave way to new experimentations with the grotesque, the surreal, and the existential. The 1940s had introduced, through progressive art circles and the work of artist-cadres, a visual vocabulary of unrest, conflict, and resistance; in the works of the new generation of artists, this unrest would appear as individual angst in a city ruptured. The city itself provided idioms of catharsis in the works of most of the artists working there; the organic form they explored became emblematic of the chaos they lived in. Satire was evoked through caricature and fantastic exaggerations of the human form in the works of artists like Paritosh Sen and Jogen Chowdhury to capture both the ridiculous and the sinister, while in Somnath Hore's work, the abstract form—of the "Wound," for instance—became the visual text for the ruptured corporeality of the city *lived.* For artists who grew up in Calcutta *as* refugees, the unconfined city and its quotidian struggles were deeply personal. The noted artist Jogen Chowdhury, for instance, recounts his experience as a refugee in the city, his early drawings of the refugees and refugee camps still raw with the immediacy of displaced habitation. His recollections also point toward the direct conversation between displacement and style in the works of his contemporaries, at least in their early works from the 1950s and 1960s. Noting in particular the "depressive" qualities in his early refugee drawings, he recalls: "The themes were depressive, this was both due to the social scene and our family situation"[36]:

> I was greatly disturbed by the general state of despair around me. In my schooldays, I even had the experience of going without food for days. . . . We did not have electricity in our house, and I had to read by the hurricane lantern. I had to fall back on black and white because we did not have enough

> light. . . . We had [a] miserable state of living when we came to Kolkata as refugees. Our plight, both physical and mental, must have also affected my use of colours. The criss-crossing lines, too, may be carrying traces of the environmental complications of the time.[37]

To artists visiting the city, Calcutta seemed monstrous and epic, a phantasmagoria at once debilitating and cathartic. The early works of the artist Ramachandran, who visited the city in the 1950s, were triggered, for instance, by this encounter, and reveal *via form* a colossal tragedy and the struggle for space in the city of displacements. Throughout the 1960s and 1970s, Ramachandran explored a critical realist idiom in his mammoth canvasses, which he described, quoting Dostoevsky, as "extending into the fantastic."[38] His figures in these gigantic canvasses are headless, male and female, lumped together against dead space, and compressed into distortion, disease, and pestilence, offering a "grim ontology of human existence."[39] When he showed the images to his mentor, the celebrated artist of modernist social realism Ramkinkar Baij, based at Santiniketan, the master, he recalls, was aghast at the "pessimism" in his work:

> Poor man, he was sorry that he had created a monster out of me! All my monstrosities started from just one devastating sculpture of his, "The Famine". I am not sorry to be a monster even though my teacher felt so. Indian aesthetics attributes three qualities. Sattvik, Rajasik and Tamasik. The Tamasik is the quality attributed to monsters.[40]

The *tamashik* is the aesthetic trope—a tragic consciousness—that runs through the affective imaginations of postcolonial Calcutta. The urban space is the dominant motif, the fate of the subject being inescapably skewed by the frames of the city.

A "TAMASHIK" AESTHETIC

A modest album published in 1970—*Drawings by Fourteen Contemporary Artists in Bengal*[41]—is a cue to investigate how artists working in Bengal in the 1950s and 1960s understood their practice. The album was published by a set of artists, most of whom came from two artists' groups formed in Calcutta during 1960–64: The Society of Contemporary Artists (1960), and soon after, the Calcutta Painters (1964).[42] They were mostly from the first generation of post-partition artists, who would have witnessed the accelerated political and cultural resistance of the 1940s and the transformation of the city through the 1950s. Artists like Rabin Mondal, Nikhil Biswas, Bijan Choudhury, Gopal Sanyal, or Bikash Bhattacharjee would have grappled with the post-partition art world in Calcutta in the 1950s, while Somnath Hore, also represented in the volume, was by then a veteran in the genres of socially committed art, having been a part of the socialist realist turn in the 1940s, as both a participant and later, a critic. The volume stands out particularly for its staging of images with texts from the artists themselves, almost as a manifesto for an undefined aesthetic agenda. The point of convergence among the painters was a certain commitment to the dialectic between form and content. Not all the artists from the two groups contributed, but those who did revealed this commitment in briefs attached to the images. Let us hear them.

The artist Nikhil Biswas, posthumously represented in the volume, raised the question of "dehumanisation": "I should like to dissect everything connected with a 'human being'—his blood and muscles, his morbidity and sexuality. . . . The problem today, as I feel, revolves around our inner existence. . . . Yes, it is the problem of dehumanisation that confronts us."[43] The album's editor, the artist Rabin Mondal, who by then had developed his own idiom of the displacement and alienation of refugees in the city, upheld the "physically mutilated figure of Christ" as an aesthetic ideal suited to the times:

> Man today is being forced to undergo a restless existence. Incoherence, disappointment, a sense of maladjustment produce a feeling of insecurity in our mind. But I am not an escapist, desirous of seeking refuge in a dream-world away from the dirt and squalor of modern life. I dislike forcible idealization. And with its merits and demerits, I am in love with the contemporary language of modern visual at through which alone I can express myself. (Mondal, *Broken Image*, 1969)

In the works of Bijan Choudhury, the idiom of struggle becomes a celebration of resilience and victory, of "Man, fortified with a strong will-force":

> I want to create a dynamic realism in my approach. . . . It will be sheer foolishness on our part to neglect reality and run after abstract art in a country [that] is still in the grip of poverty, illiteracy and prejudice. Man, fortified with a strong will-force and always at war with antagonistic forces, has inspired me to paint the subtleties of his personality. (Chowdhury, *War*, 1968)

Somnath Hore, who by then had already made a mark in Delhi, before returning to Calcutta, and Santiniketan, had often spoken of the impossibility of "escaping the subject" in his own works. In the album, he noted the enduring entanglement of pictorial values and human values:

> I paint with an ache in my heart. Pictorial values in my paintings are most important though they are tinged with pain. In the dazzle of modern art, many things look confusing, but the brilliance itself is a sign of strength and vitality which forge ahead. Thus my drawing depicts human values being pierced and trampled upon—a parting kick of the dying society. (Hore, *Fallen*, 1970)

What comes up time and again in the volume is not a negation of the importance of form, but a persistence of context or the locational, in ways often unresolved. The artists' commitment to the human figure is consistent, both as subject and as the site of experimentation. Multiple existential tropes weave into this encounter with the human figure—from Biswas's "confrontation," Mondal's "incoherence," and Hore's "pain," to Chowdhury's rejection of "abstraction."

Gopal Sanyal, whose *Towards Heaven* (fig. 5.1) is reproduced here from the *Drawings by Fourteen Contemporary Artists in Bengal* album, grapples in his work with the horrors of refugee destitution. In Sanyal's drawings of refugees, dense backgrounds in black charcoal foreground the figures as hollow, almost evacuated forms.[44] This frontal staging of the human subject with writhing, twisted, furrowed bodies echoed also in the paintings of the artist Rabin Mondal, whose works from the late 1960s develop figural distortions as (and with) totemic symbols[45]

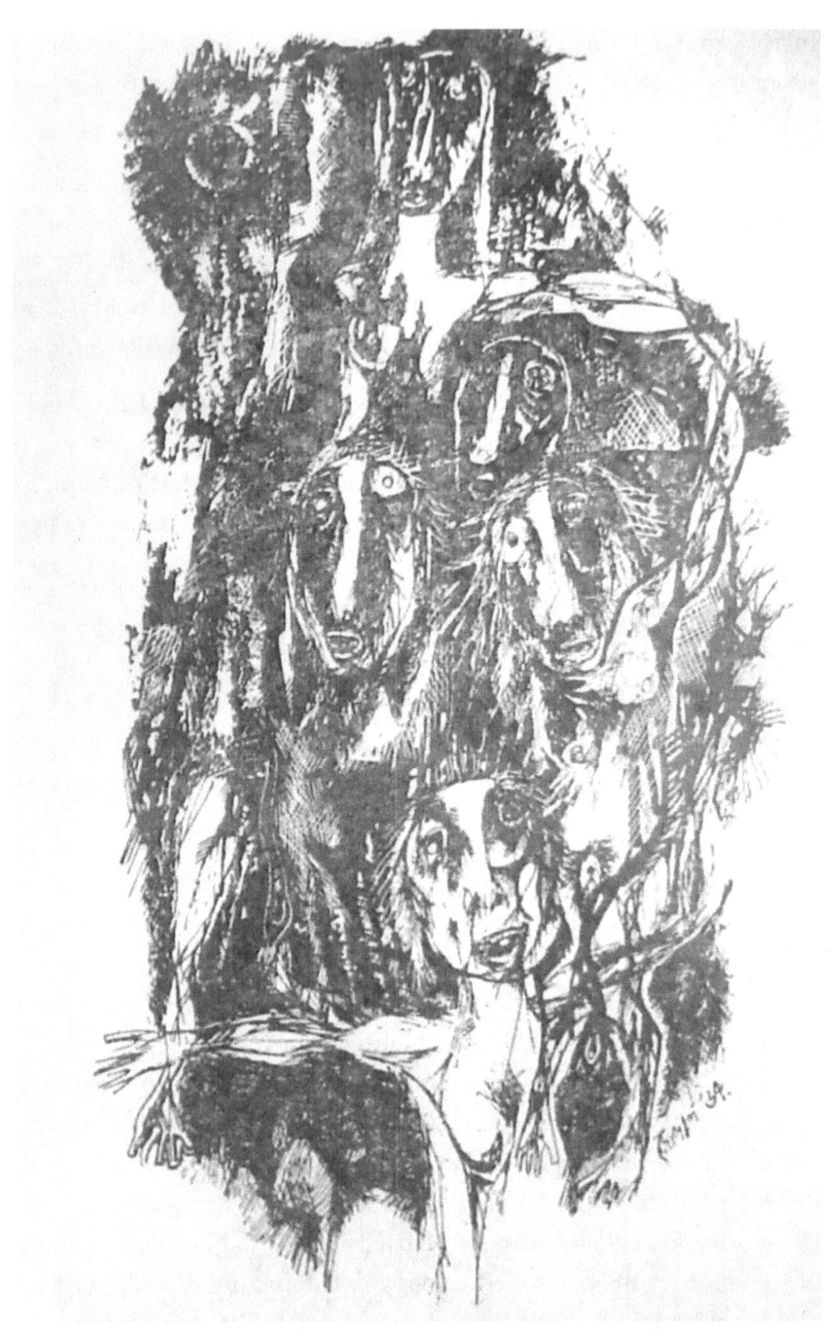

FIGURE 5.1. *Gopal Sanyal, Towards Heaven (1969). Ink drawing. Source: Album, Drawings by Fourteen Contemporary Artists in Bengal. Private papers of Rabin Mondal. Courtesy of Rabin Mondal.*

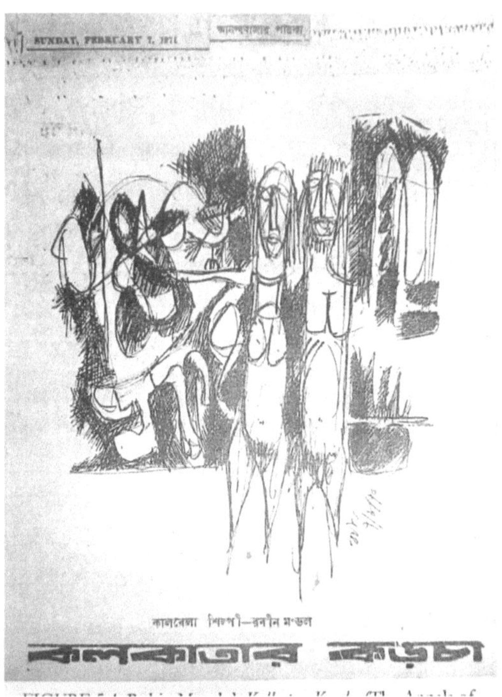

FIGURE 5.2. *Rabin Mondal, Kolkata-r Karcha (The Annals of Kolkata), Anandabazar Patrika, 2 February 1971. Source: Private papers of Rabin Mondal. Courtesy of Rabin Mondal.*

to capture figurations at once abstract and deeply social. Mondal's inspirations lay in tribal folk motifs as much as expressionistic and cubist figuration, most active in his *Brothel Series*. We find resonances already, of artists like the Sudanese painter Ibrahim El-Salahi working with similar idioms at the same period. In Mondal's drawing reproduced here, *Kolkata-r Karcha*—the city logs (fig. 5.2)—the clustered yet fractured human images become signifiers of the refugee destitutes' tenuous everyday lives. The imagery of the family repeats across iconic forms that seem caught up in ruptured scales and labyrinths. The "King" recurs in these works, as a symbol "of power, decadence, the will to rule" with an undercurrent of weakness and desolation, what Mondal's friend and reviewer Pritish Nandy would later note as the "apodal, obscure, inactive" figures that seemed frozen in dislocation on canvas.[46]

In the works of another artist, Bijan Choudhury, the city and its subjects were the site of an epic struggle, a text for political resistance. Choudhury had been associated with the then-illegal Communist Party in independent India in the late 1940s. In the early 1950s, in a tense political atmosphere of anti–food shortage protests, Choudhury and his fellow artists Nikhil Biswas, Prakash Karmakar, and Shyamal Dutta Ray were expelled from the Government College of Art and Craft (formerly the Government School of Art in colonial Calcutta) for protesting the visit of Governor Kailashnath Katju to inaugurate the art school exhibition. In 1950 Choudhury went to Dhaka to attend a literary convention and had to stay on at the art institute there, sheltered by his former teacher in Calcutta, Zainul Abedin, who since his migration to post-partition East Pakistan in 1947 had become the principal of the art institute in Dhaka. When Choudhury came back to Calcutta in 1960, his first solo exhibition at the Arts and Prints Gallery in Calcutta inaugurated a new active urban imagery that was chaotic and cacophonous—whether in combining mythic images of war and triumph or in creating dense labyrinths for myth, habitation, and confrontation, as in his works on the urban underbelly in his *Kalighat Series*. In Choudhury's canvasses, critic Sandip Sarkar noted "migrant hordes" who arrived in the city "as strangers and toilers": "They were hungry, dirty, and the very image of disinherited. Their counterparts were the Fallen Heroes and the Black Christs, a host of victims, from Lulumba to Martin Luther King."[47] Throughout the 1960s, strikes, processions, and political agitation entered Choudhury's visual imagery, as evident in his *War* for the *Drawings* album (fig. 5.3). This visualization was distinctly transnational, inspired by movements of decolonization as much as a surging Maoist politics, recalling Vietnam, Cuba, Chile, and Algeria. These imageries, as his reviewer J. F. Maure, the director of the French Cultural Centre in Calcutta, noted in the early 1970s, revealed "the values of figurative art" that addressed "the mystery of evil in those paintings by an artist who is at once fascinated and horrified."[48]

In the ink drawings and charcoal sketches of Nikhil Biswas, a new aesthetic of "combat" emerges around foregrounded figures caught in

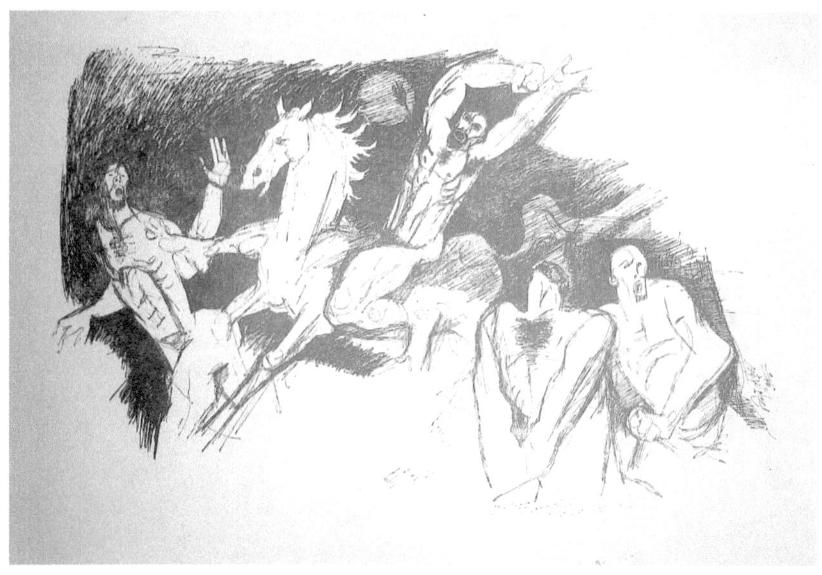

FIGURE 5.3. *Bijan Choudhury, War (1968). Pen and ink drawing. Source: Album, Drawings by Fourteen Contemporary Artists in Bengal. Private papers of Rabin Mondal. Courtesy of Rabin Mondal.*

mythic struggles. For Biswas, the contortion of lines into dense figures became a mode of seeking pictorial metaphors of power and struggle. In his *Combat Series* from the early 1960s, figures, often conjured through dense webs of bristling lines, suggest bodies that bend, stretch, collide, or cave in. In his *Clown Series* from the same period, clowns or harlequins emerge as images of vulnerability amidst their quotidian performances. Biswas's watercolors and charcoals on cheap brown paper, or drawings and paintings of the bull, the horse, and other animals in violent movement, often made on newspapers and unprimed weak fabric, or even on cement walls—reveal a commitment to visualize "the tragedy of the human condition,"[49] often on an epic visual scale on large canvasses. Going through Biswas's diaries (fig. 5.4) that he kept for both his *Combat Series* and his *Clown Series* during the 1960s until his untimely death in 1966, one can visualize the artist's intellectual negotiations with form and struggle. His reminder that it is "dehumanisation" that the contemporary world is struggling against emerges in

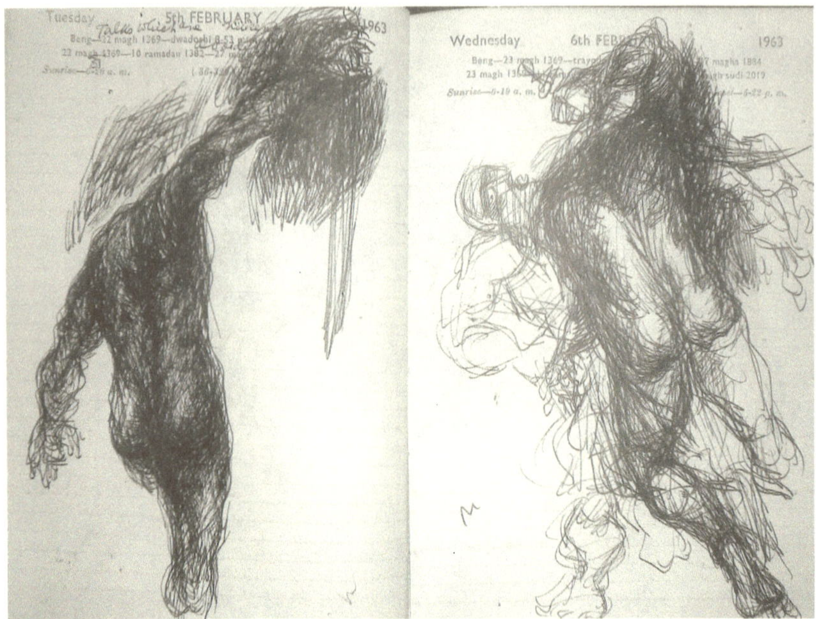

FIGURE 5.4. *Page from Nikhil Biswas's diary on his Combat Series. Courtesy of Debabrata Biswas.*

his drawings around the struggles of the human figure itself.[50] Critics commented on his obsession with the subjective idea of a heroic struggle against death and the "element of the macabre" in his art—"His huge drawings were ideographs," they noted, "Writhing figures of human beings and anthropomorphic bulls and horses brought to the fore strong statements of agony and suffering."[51] In Biswas's "convulsive, grappling lines" that "billow out centrifugally, struggling to reach out to a better beyond," critics in later years saw the "the brutalisation caused by urban anarchy."[52] This figuration is very similar to contemporaneous work being done by artists in apartheid Africa like Dumile Feni or Julian Motau, in whose works figuration itself was the formal text of the existential struggle to survive within and vis-à-vis the dehumanizing externality of the townships. The body becomes here the site for the formal play of horror, suspension, and depletion. Often through frontal framing, a body foregrounded becomes a nodal organism that receives and enacts existential forces—of society outside, as well as of form within the canvas.

Biswas's clowns echo in the play of angst and humor in the satirical paintings of city subjects by Paritosh Sen (the veteran painter from the erstwhile Calcutta Group) and Jogen Chowdhury's works from the 1970s. In the 1970s, new motifs were emerging. Shyamal Dutta Ray's watercolor *Broken Bowl Series*, for instance, would metonymically symbolize the hunger around, and also cite the history of hunger and destitution that the city carried.[53] The broken bowl image, the artist would recall later, had its roots in the dismal financial state out of which he and his friends had grown.[54] The historian and critic Nihar Ranjan Ray saw in the series the birth of a "new icon"—a symbol and a sign, a connecting link between art and the depraved, hungry masses as well as the bleak future.[55] In Bikash Bhattacharjee's photorealist oils, the motif of a "doll"—left on deserted curfewed street corners, lying across bloodstained papers and clothes, or hanging out from drawers in ransacked domestic interiors (fig. 5.5)—developed in his iconic *Doll Series* of the early 1970s, echoes the eerie disquiet of the Naxalite era in Calcutta. In Bhattacharjee's works, the figurative is combined with the dramatic juxtaposition of the surreal, conjuring a sense of the uncanny. The city emerges as a "crowded jungle of asphalt, brick, mortar and steel"[56] where the street itself is the site of dramatic ruptures—whether in throwing up skeletons of the buried dead, or carrying ruins animated.

Comparing the "expressiveness of the young Calcutta painters" and the "expressionism" of the Progressive Artists' Group of Bombay, art historian Ratan Parimoo made an interesting distinction of visual imagination hinged to the question of "location." The Bombay Progressives, he wrote, used figural distortions, thick impastos, or the fracturing of pictorial space, maintaining a controlled treatment of formal stylistics and emotional communiqué. Their formal idioms drew heavily on German Expressionism, keeping plasticity of form and style preponderant over the dramatic social content. In contrast, in the works of the Calcutta artists he saw "the image and the environs in which

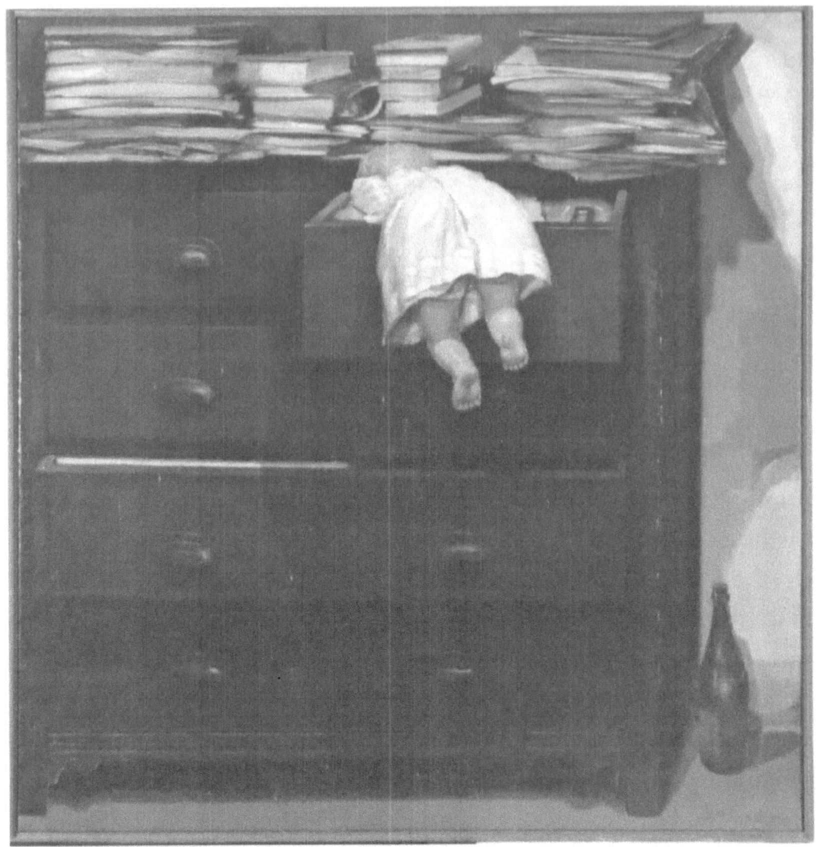

FIGURE 5.5. *Bikash Bhattacharjee, Doll Series (1971). Oil. Courtesy of National Gallery of Modern Art, New Delhi.*

it is placed" evoking "uncanny effects"; thus Abstract Expressionism or Surrealism were more serviceable here as pictorial devices.[57] While the postcolonial city was shared content in art in the 1960s in both Bombay and Calcutta, for artists in Bombay, the dynamic cityscape allowed a playful aesthetic of pastiche and kitsch, a whimsical "corruption and contamination" of forms from the Bombay everyday itself, as Sonal Khullar has noted.[58] In Calcutta, however, the persistence of rupture and the uncanny produced in most instances an art of the city embroiled in conflict and excess, almost unable to allow exteriority or gaze.

The political element in the art of region—the repertoires of struggle and disintegration that ran through the Calcutta artists' works—was active both as art's subject or content and as the very conditions of art-making itself. Artists and critics in Calcutta seemed acutely aware of the structural dislocations and socioeconomic stagnation that kept the city out of what Hore called the "dazzle" of modern art on national art circuits. In his autobiography, Rabin Mondal argued that "economic imbalance, refugees, unemployment and consequent political unrest are strikingly different from those of other states. . . . Due to these factors patronage to fine art in the field of social activities has not registered any significant increase, which directly or indirectly influences an artist's life."[59] Artists like Biswas struggled with patronage, a theme that continues in the works of many artists working in Calcutta during this period. Some of them, like Biswas, used material like packing paper or cemented walls as easels,[60] while others, like Mondal, battled day jobs and hours of power cuts to sustain painting as a profession.

Galleries and forums for pictorial journalism remained limited in Calcutta—undoubtedly a sign of the dearth of private capital. In the absence of a periodical like the *Illustrated Weekly* of Bombay, or of patron critics like Charles Fabri (for the Delhi Shilpi Chakra in Delhi) or Karl Khandalavala and Kekoo Gandhy (for artists in Bombay), artists in the city failed to articulate a discursive turn. *Sundaram,* a Bengali periodical dedicated to visual art in Calcutta, was the only forum, and a short-lived one at that. Started by Subho Tagore, one of the founder members of the Calcutta Group, *Sundaram* remained a lonely voice of art criticism and image circulation. Its editorials, humorously composed by Tagore in the manner of third-person commentary, encapsulated time and again the differential status of Calcutta, and its marginality within the national patronage of modern art.[61] While the Academy of Fine Arts, established earlier, in 1933, gradually consolidated itself through government grants,[62] no national gallery or national academy was planned, and provisions of grants and fellowships remained meager. In 1952, the Chemould Art Gallery—one of the first private galleries (and framing shops) in the city, set up by

Kekoo Gandhy on Park Street—became a primary site for exhibiting the works of the new generation of artists in the 1960s. Other important galleries exhibiting these works were the Alliance Française Gallery, Artistry House, the Arts and Prints Gallery, and by the late 1960s, the Birla Academy of Art and Culture. The formation of new artists' groups in the early 1960s like the Society of Contemporary Artists and the Calcutta Painters gave artists from the city some visibility in Delhi, in both group and solo exhibitions and at the national exhibitions. Artists received patronage, though often not in economically viable terms, from new critics like Ahibhushan Malik and Sandip Sarkar, the art critic for *Anandabazar Patrika* and its magazine, *Desh*.[63] Samar Sen, the editor of the radical left-wing journal *Frontier*, and Asok Mitra, with whom we began, were also patrons, as were left-wing intellectuals like Robi Sen.[64]

The manifesto of the Calcutta Painters is significant for its foregrounding of questions of struggle and patronage over those of formal pursuits. It reflects the particular sociocultural fabric of postcolonial Calcutta, where young artists had to battle financial hardship and the acute apathy of the state and the public toward visual artists. Signed by all of the group's founding members—Rabin Mondal, Nikhil Biswas, Gopal Sanyal, Ranjan Rudra, Bijan Choudhury, and Prakash Karmakar, all of them young artists and novices in the city's art world—the manifesto acknowledged the pessimism and anxiety of the practice itself:

> Our society today does not care for us-artists. Writers are relatively fortunate because their creations go to thousands through periodicals and publications. Thus they have a contact with the society. Musicians have audience. But we painters are isolated. Paints and canvasses are frighteningly expensive, and in order to paint some of us have to half-starve often. The money spent in paints could have given milk to our children. Some of us have to deprive our wives and children of even proper clothing in order to be able to paint. We do not think it is romantic. We think it is grim.[65]

For noted critics in Calcutta during this period, such as Sandip Sarkar, Calcutta seemed to have been "black-listed by present-day art historians and critics who have their seats in Bombay and Delhi." The possible reasons Sarkar gives for this situation are interesting:

> One reason might be that critics concentrate on successful artists only—that is artists who sell. It is, of course, common knowledge that, comparatively speaking, artists of Calcutta do not sell. While Bombay has the "younger generation of businessmen and executives" who want to buy paintings, Delhi has "political bigwigs, the consulates, the private and public money for institutional buying". The Calcutta artists do not have any of these facilities. The successful ones are moderately successful compare[d] to the Delhi-Bombay standards. Most of the time they fight to survive.[66]

The signature of Calcutta's context and locational particularity thus echoed displacement on multiple planes, ranging from the artistic subject of the displaced refugees and the destitute to the outdated (by the late 1960s in India) idiom of realism or content-driven "social" art, to infrastructural displacement from the structures of the national art world, as well as what one could argue to be a historiographical displacement from the narratives of postcolonial modernity itself. Marked indeed by the sparse visibilities of art from the city at national scales, such displacements are interesting *historically*, not for their potential restorations within the narratives of Indian modernism, but to see more closely what space displacements have occupied in the modernity visualized by early postcolonial art.

NATION AND DISPLACEMENT

In the 1960s, while artists in Calcutta struggled with visual forms and figurations that would make sense of the displacements and destitution in the post-partition city, the national art discourse remained largely inattentive. A critical factor in this schism was a wider dominance of the idiom of the rural everyday and folk-modern repertoire that was being patronized by the national art academies. In Delhi, while national academies formed in the mid-1950s—like the Lalit Kala Akademi for fine arts (founded in 1954)—continued to streamline the artistic field, controlling the "style" and "content" of artworks to be shown at the annual National Exhibitions, started in 1955, new collectives began to question this rationale. Although Jawaharlal Nehru, in his inaugural speech at the first National Exhibition, had asserted the need to move beyond older models and to encourage new artists,[67] the Selection Committee judges, in their guidelines for the prospective participants, patronizingly opposed "undigested influences" and "derivative strains," encouraging folk themes and pastoral works in a bid to reflect national traditions.[68] It is therefore not surprising that art from Delhi remained overtly occupied with folk themes and rural scenes, even while that rurality was being reframed in modernist figurations and use of textures. The conservatism of the nation's new art academy was reflected also in its promotion of scholarship in art and art publications, with an overt stress on ancient Indian art and classical traditions, and little interest or investment in contemporary artists. Even noted artists recall, for instance, that post-independence India had "no role for the urban, contemporary artist, the man who would fabricate and comment upon the present, and who would not necessarily continue with folk and classical forms."[69] It was only in 1962 that the *Lalit Kala Contemporary*, the Akademi's journal for "contemporary" artists, could be launched to expand the purview of the more conservative classical orientation of the earlier journal *Lalit Kala*.[70]

Yet throughout the 1950s, new modes and sites of resistance were being formed that effectively challenged the dominance of art societies dating from the colonial period, and sought to refurbish the standards of national academies like the Lalit Kala by active participation in art administration. The Delhi Shilpi Chakra, for instance, pioneered by artist Bhabesh Sanyal—a refugee from Lahore himself—developed a sound social base of patrons by drawing the support of middle-class intellectuals like schoolteachers, university professors, doctors, lawyers, writers, actors, and musicians; the Chakra also drew state commissions from the government, as well as steady patronage from the embassies located in the city. This was itself an offshoot of a new national-popular aesthetic that developed in the capital with a conscious move toward making a national idiom in art accessible for popular consumption and aesthetic appreciation. This new aesthetic was reflected, for instance, in the discourse around "new humanism" and "democratic" consciousness in art that emerged in Delhi during this period, as discussed in Chapter 4.

For refugee artists from Lahore who settled in Delhi, images of refugees and beggars dominated the early works of the 1950s; examples from this genre are Bhabesh Sanyal's series *Beggars, My Neighbours*, Satish Gujral's paintings of refugee displacement, and Ram Kumar's series on urban destitution, where the theme of humanity under the impact of social violence and neglect finds eloquent expression. Bhabesh Sanyal's reminiscences are illustrative of the concerns of artists in Delhi who, like him, were refugees from the newly formed West Pakistan:

> I took to sketching a lot. I did not have to go far to seek out subjects. Life around me pulsated with the activities of the displaced and the destitute. From my studio windows I could watch the cobblers at rest or at work, the hawkers and the peddlers in action, and the patient behaviour of the commuters at the bus stand. Moreover, the tragedy of the uprooted mass of humanity hung heavy on my mind.[71]

Social realism was a palpable concept in the early 1950s. For instance, the second anniversary exhibition of the Delhi Shilpi Chakra in April 1951 included the Critics Forum—a joint forum for artists and critics—where the critic Charles Fabri is known to have launched a discussion titled "Modernism in Indian Art": a "very explosive subject," the "fitting finale" of which was the artist Bhabesh Sanyal's "spirited plea for social realism."[72] Early exhibition reviews of the artists of the Delhi Shilpi Chakra, of which Sanyal was a founding member, note this stress on "humanity in distress, pain and labour," and the social consciousness in the works of member artists like Sanyal, Ram Kumar, and Satish Gujral.[73]

The theme of partition, the artist Satish Gujral noted, dominated his works between 1947 and 1952, a period during which, he recalls, he inevitably depicted what he saw and felt as a refugee himself. The influence of Mexican muralists appeared in his art most prominently following his stay and training in Mexico between 1952 and 1955, when he apprenticed with the muralists Diego Rivera and David Alfaro Sequiros. During that time he developed figurations of twisted, strained, crouching forms depicted in bold, sweeping brushstrokes, using massive anatomical forms and heightened expression to convey a sense of the frozen agony of the uprooted, and accompanying the figures with an entire symbolist apparatus of chains, skulls, serpents, extinct volcanoes, and ruined columns. His larger-than-life, brooding expressionist figures in charcoal or oils—such as *Mourning En-masse* (1947–48), *Despair* (1954), *Days of Glory* (1952), *Snare of Memory* (1954), and *Shrine* (1956)—took on a grotesque, almost surreal edge, marking the beginning of his quest for a modernism that could accommodate the experience of trauma. Commenting on his partition paintings, Gujral described his art as "an expression of conflict, of man against fate, of the individual against his environment or even against his own being."[74] Yet, in the 1950s, Gujral recalls, while some artists in Delhi like Prannath Mago and Bhabesh Sanyal were in their way "trying to depict village life or scenes with 'native' colour," "art with social commitment was totally unknown."[75]

In Bombay, partition imagery was more marginal than in Delhi; in some rare exceptions, however, such as the works of Tyeb Mehta, partition did enter the abstract potentialities of figural art, with play of *in-canvas* displacements of planes and forms. Mehta's large oils in the *Diagonal Series* from the 1970s, for instance, featured flat surfaces, arranged in controlled suspension; his figures collide, split, and entangle, disrupted at times by a fissure across the canvas, rupturing as well as containing the colliding figures in a grand symmetry. A completely different arrangement of displacement *within* pictorial space emerges here; whether in his *Falling Figure Series* or in works like *The Gesture*, the persistence of dislocation and collision would become a hallmark of Mehta's art, representing, as he would note, a "cosmic tragedy."[76] Mehta's split surfaces and figures, while remaining essentially minimalist, grapple with the memory of partition and conflict, with the artist's conscious and continuing quest for a monumental "metaphor" of violence.[77] His recurring motifs of the trussed bull, the falling figure, or the rickshaw puller were to him both "compulsive" and "mutable," attuned to capturing the "many levels of violence" in society, while remaining rooted in formal devices: "Between me and the image," he noted, "the image itself has its own connotation. And the way I structure the painting, there is so much mutation that when it reaches the viewer, it has another power totally."[78]

Despite these early works by a select few, however, there remained a surprising dearth of partition imagery in the works of post-independence artists. The noted artist Ghulam Mohammed Sheikh made this stark observation in 1973:

> The fact that the contemporary Indian artist who has witnessed the struggle for Independence, the agony and horror of partition and the changing society of the post-Independence era oscillating between moods of apathy and unrest, has scarcely portrayed these—and never effectively—shows that he has not found it necessary or important to be part of a history he is living in, or evolve an idiom that would relate his art to this history. Rather he has jealously guarded the purity of his art from such "extraneous" involvements.[79]

The social reference of the progressive artists in Bombay was short-lived, Sheikh observed, as most of the noted members of the Progressive Artists' Group left India, while the ones who stayed, "despite their excellent performance in the international art arena were, nonetheless bound to their 'invocation of the image of India'": "This being ambiguous and their involvement with local Indian environment being marginal or remote, what they portrayed of India was either subtle or peripheral and in certain cases, superficial . . . even those—like Husain, Souza and Ram Kumar—who derived inspiration for much of their early work from local environment and people eventually turned toward the projection of a personal style."[80] Satish Gujral, Sheikh noted, while being "*the only artist* [emphasis mine] to paint agonies of partition" would not succeed in portraying it effectively, because "his interpretation of pathos was so literal that he could not escape mannerisms of melodramatic gestures and expressions."[81]

The persistence of the figurative in the works of artists from Bengal was noted at various points by reviewers in national art periodicals like *Marg* or, from the mid-1960s, *Lalit Kala Contemporary.* Artists from the city, critics noted, were "products of the city, with its turmoil, pain and uncertainty."[82] Critics writing in these journals, particularly those from Calcutta, noted time and again a peculiar kind of heightened figurative art emerging from a city paralyzed by "strikes, *gheraos*, processions, burning of trams,"[83] and exhibitions characterized by "that distinct, Calcutta art feature of focusing attention on assertively lively images of man and/or other beings placed in an ambiguous environmental situation."[84] Commenting on Nikhil Biswas's 1966 posthumous exhibition in the German Democratic Republic, reviewers noted the persistence of the figurative:

> In the midst of the abstract wave, which is influencing art of India in the 1960s, Nikhil's art proclaims humanistic ethics. His pictures are filled with the dramatic gesture of struggle and pain, the rebellion against suffering and force, and the search for light. . . . He wants to free himself from the decorative and sketchy basic tendency in contemporary Indian art. . . . He is very serious in his desire to create a realistic art with its roots in national and social life.[85]

Testimonials of artists from both the Calcutta Painters and the Society of Contemporary Artists point toward the social as an active component shaping the art of the period, bringing the notion of contemporaneity back to the center of artistic production, as it had been during the 1940s. Writing for the 25th anniversary of the Society of Contemporary Artists (from which the Calcutta Painters had emerged as a splinter group), Pranab Ranjan Ray, member and patron of the society, observed the "conceptual consensus" among the artists, despite individual differences:

> The Society's name came to be associated with a new kind of Indian contemporary art, which is responsive to the here-and-now reality and reacts to the reality. It is an art [that] depends upon the image of the phenomenal world, more or less figurative, often allegorically narrative, often lyrical and quite iconoclastic. Or should we say, that by the closing decade of the Sixties, through pressure of events in West Bengal and through our own exchange of ideas and experiences some kind of conceptual consensus about the relation between art and the here-and-now reality had slowly emerged, which *al-*

though not an articulate ideology was nonetheless a loose kind of a unified concept [emphasis mine].[86]

The society was a forum for the exhibition of some of the most significant works from the 1960s and 1970s that we have been discussing here—including Dutta Ray's *Broken Bowl Series*, Hore's *Wounds Series*, and Bhattacharjee's *Doll Series*—with artists in the group trying time and again to give "form" to the chaos of the city within which they were embedded. The serial cover page of the group's annual exhibition catalogue, for instance, bears this entanglement of the group's artists with the life of the city itself, with the singular question in Bengali—*Ki Chai?* ("What do you want?" or "What is desired?") sprouting out from the chaos (fig. 5.6).[87] The group (still active in current Kolkata) was also significant for the space given to important women artists from the city—the most notable being Shyamashree Ghosh, Anita Roy Chowdhury, Arundhuti Roy Chowdhury, and Uma Siddhanta—and for developing print technology for supporting some of the most highly regarded graphic art from the city.

Reviewing the works of Calcutta artists in Delhi in *Lalit Kala Contemporary*, Pranab Ranjan Ray argued that they combined images of "topical interest" with a "sense of humanity": "The eleven Calcutta painters now exhibiting at the Lalit Kala Gallery are truly provincial as logically as the Baroda painter is provincial in relation to his New York contemporary. Not that they lack vision or intellectual vitality; but they are less defiant, less innovative than the Baroda painter."[88] Another way of putting it, he said, was that these artists lacked "historical sensibilities"—"that is to say one cannot locate their works inside of art history as neatly as one does [those] of a Baroda painter."[89] Yet the very notion of historical sensibility seems misplaced in this reading, since history for these artists was not a resource but a dialectical *present*, the very location of the form. The generational aspect in Calcutta painters was also strong; commenting on the paintings of Rabin Mondal, critic Pritish Nandy wrote, "It is the language of the generation he belongs to and speaks for. A generation that has amidst the uncertainty and incoherence of our times, dared to speak."[90] Such paintings, Nandy noted

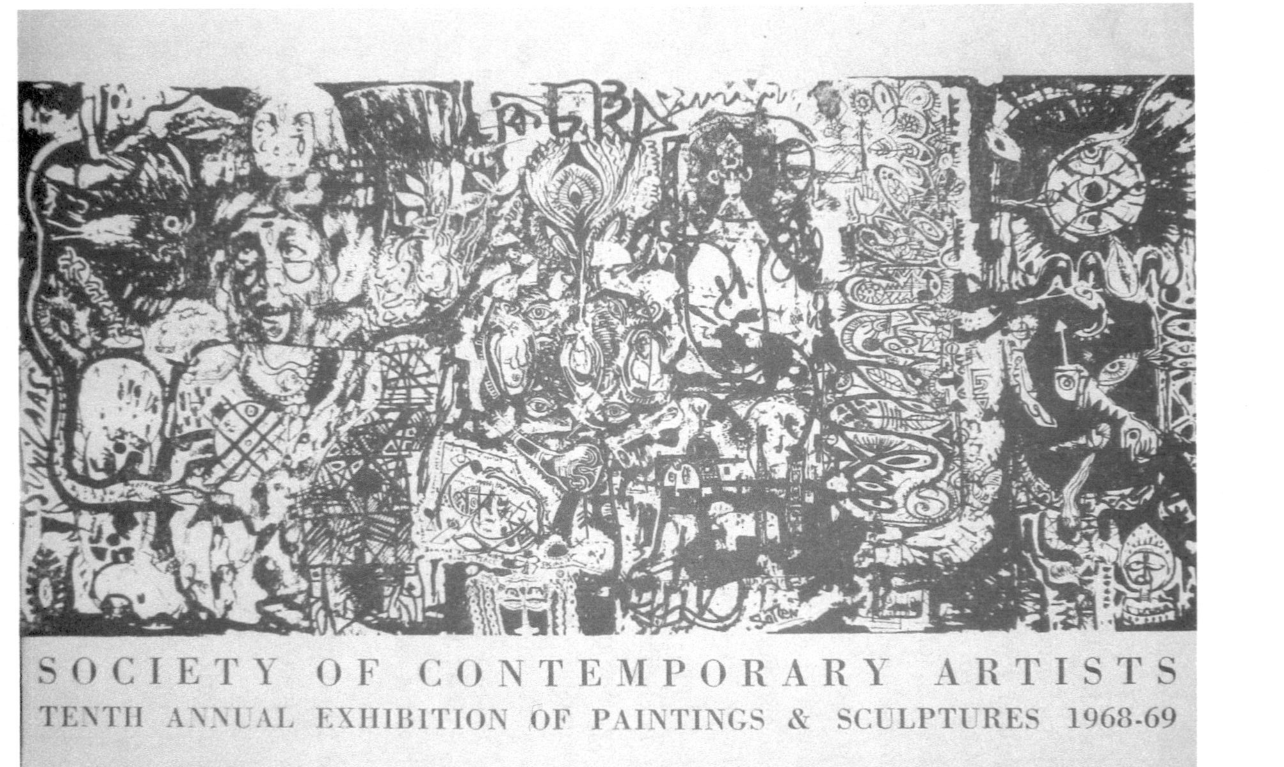

FIGURE 5.6. *Serial cover page, Society for Contemporary Artists, Tenth Annual Exhibition of Paintings and Sculptures 1968–69. Source: Archives of the Society for Contemporary Artists.*

elsewhere, were "smoke signals. Perhaps even omens. Like this city, Calcutta. Mortal, guilty, but for us the entirely beautiful." [91]

For artists working in Calcutta, the sociopolitical inscriptions of art, drawn out by the content *becoming* form, were not separable from the peculiar marks of the city itself. Writing his "Reflections" in *Lalit Kala Contemporary* in 1968, Paritosh Sen, long a partisan to art's social address, would note:

> All art is conditioned by time and the chemistry of the soil on which it is processed. It invariably reflects the human condition in so far as it corresponds to the ideas and aspirations, the needs and hopes of a given historical situation, and within it the art is also capable of promising constant development, although I do not feel it is the business of the artist to be engaged in a clinical description of reality.[92]

Thus, commitment to figurative art did not in itself suggest the impossibility of abstraction; rather, it carried the persistence of the materiality of the location and context of the city. Sen noted that he desired his images to occupy "that twilight zone of ambiguity which is midway between figuration and non-figuration": "I want an element of plastic violence, of rich saturation of colour."[93]

In a 1962 painting titled *Abstraction*, artist Bikash Bhattacharjee seems to make an ironic allusion to the city-form of Calcutta. His female protagonist—displaced, pauperized, emaciated—sits with her hands tied and a mirror between her toes. The background appears to be a textured empty space, making the protagonist at the center all the more iconic. It is not clear if the mirror is held out for the viewer or if the protagonist is trying to see herself. She seems distracted; a distant and detached gaze seems to belie her firm grip on the mirror and her frontal staging within the canvas. She is destitute, possibly a refugee, a street dweller, begging to make a living. Her hunger-ridden, fissured, hollowed-out body is both a testimony to the contemporary visuality of Calcutta in these years and an echo from the visualities of the famine years. The mirror stands out as an interface—both as a reflection of the interiority of the protagonist and as a suggested question for the viewer to navigate: *what are the scopes of abstraction amid lives so concrete?* Bhattacharjee's titling of the image makes this double coding active, posing an ironic challenge to the very mechanism of abstraction.

While the politically charged binaries between abstraction and realism do not sit squarely within Indian art, and artists have consciously refused to operate within the terms set by such "global" polarities,[94] there remains an often-muted tension between the contextual/locational and the national. As the radicalism of the 1940s—with its waves of displacement and genocide—dissolved or was diluted under the hegemonic repertoire of Nehruvian modernist imaginaries, modern art in India in the 1950s and 1960s, as we have seen, celebrated the citizen-artist and the *arrival* of the nation rather than its fault lines. Realism and the social, however, echoing time and again the memory and ruptures of the 1940s, recurred in the art of the *locality*, generating a heterogeneous temporality *within* (narratives of) postcolonial modernism.

PLACES OF THE POLITICAL

In contrast to the 1950s and the 1960s, when art writing from the postcolonial art capitals eclipsed the political in art beyond generic affirmations of "democratic consciousness" and "citizen-artists" (as we saw in Chapter 4), in the 1970s political intent resurfaced—in both artistic form and art criticism. In 1975, Prime Minister Indira Gandhi declared the Emergency, suspending democratic rights for the first time in postcolonial India. As political crisis captured the national imagination, extending beyond regional political instabilities, visual art in centers of national-modern aesthetics—Delhi, Bombay, and Baroda—saw returns to and retellings of the political in art, with fresh visual and discursive vocabularies. Emergency laid bare the fissures in the postcolonial state, striking at the root of the modernist dream of sovereignty. In the works of artists like Gieve Patel, Vivan Sundaram, Sudhir Patwardhan, and Bhupen Khakhar—artists born in late-colonial India and entering the artistic field in the late 1960s—the crisis prompted new satirical, grotesque, and expressionistic figurations. In bids to reclaim democracy, they sought to retrieve in art the space for the narrative and radical figurative art, couched in relative obscurity by the late 1960s under the wider predominance of folkish idioms and totemistic abstract art—a point we heard from the critic Jaya Appasamy's 1967 notes in Chapter 4. To the critic Geeta Kapur, friend and patron-critic of this new generation of artists from Baroda, the shifting political rubric of India in the 1970s was a new historical conjuncture that served as a catalyst for new political impulses within art practice. The Emergency, Kapur recalls, "re-defined and also degraded the role of the nation-state," triggering thereby "mixed agendas for a national culture." As the left grappled with "a new and protective role towards the disintegrating nation," in the cultural field, artists and critics "tried to place the *national* in reaction to the *modern* and arrived at the hyphenated term *national-modern* to keep the cultural question sufficiently dialectical."[95] Kapur's telling of the political consciousness of Indian national-modern art is critical, both for the archival signature that her writings from the period carry and for the historical theorization of art that she developed since the 1970s.

During the 1960s, as M. S. University in Baroda was emerging as the center for counter-institutional modernist art, generating new forums for artistic experimentation and discourse, the journal *Vrishchik*, with Kapur's own writings at its forefront, was providing a dynamic site for new narrative and discursive mobilizations around postcolonial modernism. *Vrishchik*, and briefly the journal *Contra'66*—both modeled after the style of handcrafted "little magazines" based in Baroda—would carry a new "dissenting voice of the artist as an editorial signature" and cultivate a new political consciousness by critically evaluating questions of tradition, identity, and indigenism.[96] While counter-institutional in its critiques of the stultified mores of the national art academy in Delhi, a new Baroda-Delhi axis of artists and art writing would develop through the 1970s, the culmination of which can be seen in the *Place for People* exhibition in 1981, curated by Geeta Kapur.

Kapur's art writings from the 1970s chart her growing conceptualization of art's political consciousness. Introducing *Vrishchik*'s special issue "The Social Context of Contemporary Indian Art" in 1973, Kapur wrote, for instance, that the artist's true significance lies not in conscious concern or participation in social problems or in their solutions, but in "the unity within him, of conscience and memory—a conscience which sees into the heart of things" and "a memory that carries within it, the accretions of culture." [97] Echoing Arnold Hauser, Kapur in *Contemporary Indian Artists*, written in 1978, would describe the work of art as the "nodal point of several different causal lines: psychological, sociological and stylistic,"[98] highlighting an aesthetic need to avoid "dilution" of the history and memory of early twentieth-century struggles into "novel concoctions."[99] In the essays of this critical volume, Kapur argued for the urgent need for an aesthetic rootedness in "reality" in a twofold scheme: on a subjective level, "as a state of being and consciousness" and on a social experiential level, "as a changing fact of history."[100] The question of "authenticity," she would argue, was resolved not simply in the "subjective sincerity" of the artist but also in its "social significance"—an aesthetic sensibility rooted in the artist's location in and dialogue with history and the present.[101] Kapur's understanding of historical memory also seems to nuance the possibility of a locational politics. "For the creative artists," she argued, "tradition takes the form of memory; the memory of experiences imbibed as well as lived. Correspondingly, reality too—the concrete lived reality of a given place and time—must transform itself in the imagination before it can be 'realized' in art."[102]

When Kapur curated and introduced *Place for People* in 1981, with new narrative works by artists from the Baroda/Delhi axis—Bhupen Khakhar, Nalini Malini, Sudhir Patwardhan, Gulamohammed Sheikh, Vivan Sundaram, and Jogen Chowdhury (who had relocated from Calcutta to Delhi via Madras/now Chennai), her catalogue introduction, titled "Partisan Views about the Human Figure" read as a "manifesto" of a new "narrative turn" in Indian modern art. It opened with the assertion of a present that can cut across "conventional polarities of Indian and Western" in Indian art and bring "new options" of "sensibility and ideology."[103] The "subject of the human figure," Kapur noted, "can provide this point for the polemic and I mean to use it"—as she would in laying out the artists' works on the city and its labyrinths, the body as landscape, and questions of habitation and palimpsests. Surveying hallmarks of twentieth-century Euro-American expressionistic figurative art alongside readings of classical Indian narrative imagery, Kapur's text was exquisite. It invoked, through citations of Walter Benjamin and Herbert Marcuse, a "historical materialism" and an "affirmation" in the artist that would mean "comprehending, by an act of generosity, the anarchy of life," and developing via "fierce acts of imagination" "utopian alignments with ongoing history."[104]

While Kapur's voice is art critical, and partisan in itself (insofar as she is committed to speaking for and to the art movement with which she herself was aligned, her persisting commitment to aligning art with "history"—whether as memory or as experience—raises the curious question of the historicity of the artistic form that she was championing, almost as a paradigm shift—the "human form" itself, and its political potentialities. To opt out of the polarities of "Indian and Western" via the political form of an embodied people in art, while richly aligned with twentieth-century Euro-American movements, surely would have carried in 1980 the recent visualities of mid-twentieth-century radical figuration in India itself—one that was entangled with history as much as it was a victim of it. The rise and dispersal of the left's cultural movement, to which Kapur herself was alert, would have provided an ideal lineage to cite and nuance; so would the works grappling with political and social ruptures in Calcutta itself or, for that matter, instances of radical figuration from the margins of the nation-state itself—even if such works carried unstable locations with the spaces of "high art." What seems missing in Kapur's *Place for People* manifesto, ironically, is the very idea of the "people"—a *historical consciousness*, in other words, of either place or people, in all the contradictions of their recent histories. The importance of this omission is not a matter of "representation" (simply of *other* artists, for instance), but a discursive one, particularly so given the historiographical significance that this exhibition and Kapur's art-critical voice itself have come to carry in the past decade. The implications for historiography, and theory, are many. As I close this book, I will raise a couple of them.

Even as contemporary scholarship has begun questioning, among other things, the essentially urban middle-class "gaze" over the subaltern in Kapur's (and the artists') portrayal of "the people" in the exhibition,[105] what stands out, particularly along the drift of the histories that have emerged so far in this book, is the question of the *political* itself. What is the political in histories of twentieth-century Indian art? More specifically, can this political be disentangled from, or at least read in *contra-diction* to, the hegemonic presence of the "nation-form"? Are *other* modes of political aesthetics or political subjectivities possible?

Neither "people" nor "place" was a radical novelty in Indian art in the 1980s, nor were these vocabularies ideological *tabula rasas*; rather they were entangled with heterogeneous political values that formed what I have called partisan aesthetics during India's long decolonization. The disjuncture between the national and the modern—or the dialectical bind of "national-modern" that Kapur visualizes in the post-Emergency 1970s—had *longue durée* histories dating back to the 1940s, when the visualization of the nation itself and the category of "people" were being brought into question, and given a revolutionary potentiality. It is this national-popular aesthetic that was reconfigured in Nehruvian India under the wider celebration (cultural and discursive) of "citizen artist, secular art." The radical potentiality of the "people" in art persisted in the margins of postcolonial national-modern imagery; it eluded, however, spaces of high art and centers of postcolonial modernist imaginaries. The question of "place" itself calls for a radical rethinking, not only to affirm—along the lines of the postcolonial valorizations of "locational" traditions and idioms—the local and the contextual, but to ask if and how such sites might be in contradictory relations to a national imaginary. What remains *outside*, for instance, emerging dominant narratives of postcolonial modernism? Must the locational fit into a meta-frame of the national? Does allegory in the post-colony remain inevitably harnessed to the nation?[106]

Kapur saw "locational ideologies" in "archaic and mock-ironic forms of ancestor worship," "institutionalized" in Calcutta and Santiniketan, in Cholamandalam and Kerala in the South, or in Baroda, where artists provided radical reuses of mythology and located tradition to "create chinks in the armour of modernism." Her Indian modern appears to carry a syncretic elasticity that allows for a national-modern framework capable of accommodating a broad set of locational interventions:

"Indigenist genres make for located knowledge, and this in Gramscian terms, is the source for the strategy of interference. Anthropologists and cultural theorists will now privilege such interventions in order to argue in favour of partisanship on the homeground of culture and politics."[107] This elasticity of postcolonial modernism, when read strictly from within the discursive structures of graphic and plastic art (and not collapsed with films and theater, for instance), seems to generate its own universalizing impulse—one that is alert to difference but committed to a national-modern inertia of harnessing the locational to the national *anyway*. For Kapur, partisan discourse in Indian art is a self-definitional mechanism that operates as the "subject enters history." The national allegory, to her, is this interface of "entering," regardless of whether such an encounter generates synchrony or dissonance (as in the case of Kapur's discussion of partition trilogy of the auteur Ritwik Ghatak).[108] While Kapur acknowledges that a typical left-wing radicalism in parts of the country (in Kerala and in West Bengal, for instance) does provide an "alternative culture"—"more radical art practice than we may acknowledge in the normal course of recounting our national modern"[109]—in her theorization, the locational remains lost.

Expanding the political scope (and bite) of Kapur's argument, I will argue that locational ideologies are not (only) vernacular uses/subversions of past/tradition or a "fierce sense of identification with a mythologized land and its people,"[110] but also material entanglements with the textures of a "located present." If and when the narrative logic of the postcolonial "time" is displaced *as well*—beyond *just* the universalizing temporality of a national or a global modern—the idea and intent of what is "locational" opens up radically. Freed from the syncretic elasticity of a national-modern symbiosis, locational ideologies can then allow for spaces of contra-national and sub-national imaginations, while creating room for transnational imaginations that are not *necessarily* driven by the logic of modernist internationalism.

Subsumed under the still more spectacular tragedy of partition in 1947, the scouring trails of the Bengal famine remained tied to the history of the locality, rather than to that of the nation. In postcolonial Calcutta, where the famine echoed right into the 1970s in fresh metaphors of the wound, the begging bowl, and the fragmented city-form, the notions of "place" and "people" carried meanings very different from those of the national narrative. The entanglement of the artists with the locations and histories they inhabited also carried a different dialectical weight. The arts of displacement in the post-colony are thus potential partisan interventions into thinking about sub-national, locationally rooted visual art that might or might not have been either alert to counter-hegemonic imagination or successful in resolving the dialectic of form and content. The locational, I will suggest, need not be solely an oppositional category, poised *contra* the national or the global. Rather, it needs to be salvaged from its merely relational dynamics to be viewed as a new site for the radical materialities and temporalities of decolonization. The locational is a structural rubric for intellectual histories of twentieth-century aesthetics in the post-colonies, and as such it is a dynamic ingredient in comprehending the *extra*-national, even the transnational. Displacements triggered by decolonization are always bound *by* and *to* the materialities of localities, not the abstractions of nation-states or national-modern art. So are transnational solidarities that are *beyond* the rhetoric of the "flow" of global agents and art funds, but lie in locational modes of cosmopolitanism, affiliations, or partisanship, as I noted at the start of this book.

The fissured socioeconomic fabric and political dissonance in postcolonial Bengal wedges an aesthetics of difference between the nation and the region, the national and the vernacular, which characterized the dialectical modernisms in the new Third World during decolonization. Such "difference" seems to put pressure on notions of "national allegory" that have come to signify cultural production in the Third World.[111] Geoffrey Moorhouse's historical staging of post-partition Calcutta in his book *Calcutta* (1971) can act as a useful pointer to the epistemic questions that can be asked *from* the location and historicities of the city:

> In a sense, the story of Calcutta is the story of India and the story of the so-called Third World in miniature. It is the story of how and why Empire was created and what happened when Empire finished. It is the story of people

> turning violently to Communism for salvation. It is also the story of Industrial Revolution. The imperial residue of Calcutta, a generation after Empire ended, is both a monstrous and a marvelous city.[112]

Calcutta appears here as both clue and symptom, as residue as well as epic. As "imperial residue," the city seemed to carry peculiar historical materialities that emerged at the dialectical interfaces of the "retreat" of empire and the "progress" of the nation-state, each with its own momentum. Yet the city also reveals the mechanisms of *becoming marginal*, a positionality that is shaped by both the spectacular and the corrosive, *longue durée* histories of decolonization.

THE HETEROGENEOUS TIME of the post-colony resides in the elasticity of the idea of the locational and of marginality itself. Like categories of the subaltern or the vernacular, marginality, I will propose here, is relational, mutable, and transformational. A location central to the national imaginary until the 1940s—Bengal—can become as marginal as the perceived geopolitical margins of the postcolonial Indian nation-state—whether that be the northeast, the south, or the contested frontiers in Kashmir—once we start unpacking the hegemonic national-modern imagination that tends to dominate narratives of postcolonial modernity and its modernism too. At the least, marginality can become a dialogical field—a partisan site—where a heterogeneous temporality of decolonization can be negotiated, where rationalities and the syncretic logic of the "center" can be questioned. If not in aesthetics—in habitation, imaginations, ethics, and form, even if non-spectacular or non-modernist—where else might alternative belongings in the post-colony manifest? For while *continued* political struggles at such perceived margins remain prone to constant structural control, displacements, appropriations, or simply inattention, partisan aesthetics of and from these shifting margins carry shadow lines that are sites of both difference *and* persistence—keeping open ever new potentialities of modernist realignments of people with place.

POSTSCRIPT

TOWARD AN AESTHETICS OF DECOLONIZATION

IN *PARTISAN AESTHETICS*, I have tried to put forward a set of propositions that, while drawn from the locational histories and politics of post/colonial (West) Bengal, seeks to *speak to* (as opposed to *speaking for*) both national and transnational aesthetics of the mid-twentieth century. These propositions can be summarized as follows:

First, in its early stages in the 1930s, cultural rhetoric of the Indian left developed in dialogue with modernist thoughts on form and its (potentially) organic ties to society and with the involvement of fellow travelers rather than committed communists.

Second, socialist realism in the late-colony, as developed by the CPI artist-cadres under the shadow of the famine and anti-colonial populism of the 1940s, "provincialized" the idealizing gaze of classical Soviet Socialist Realism to develop a socialist expressionism—both realist and utopian, anti-colonial and anti-imperialist.

Third, foundational to the radical socialist cultural front of the Indian left was the production of an ambiguous discourse of "progressive art"—one that deliberately erased ideological lines between the social and the socialist in art, to draw in artists from outside the party fold.

Fourth, this ambiguity in itself made the left's socialist iconography susceptible, in postcolonial times, to deradicalizations and appropriations, particularly under the patronage of a Nehruvian political modernity that assimilated and reconfigured the left's radical iconography of a revolutionary "popular" *within* the affirmative rhetoric of democratic "national-popular" art and the citizen-artist.

And finally, displacement—foundational to the locational aesthetics of twentieth-century frontier states like Bengal (as well as the northeastern and northwestern frontiers), but marginal to narratives of postcolonial modernism in India—is both a historical and an analytical lens through which new *uncontained* and *dialectical* histories of art and decolonization can be written.

Such propositions emerge from what I have called "partisan aesthetics"—a participatory field of visual art, the left, and decolonization in late-colonial and early postcolonial India that both produces and disperses forms of politicality in midcentury aesthetics in the post/colony. These propositions have sought to nuance, in particular, the meanings and historicities of the political and of modernity in art—via questions, for instance, of history, memory, affiliation, and location. A focus on visual art, mainly the plastic arts—and not a holistic reading of the left's cultural movement in literature, performance, films, and photography—has been my conscious strategy to historicize "form" via its ideologies, and modernism itself via its dialectical histories. The question of the left and its cultural footprints across the twentieth century runs through the book as both an agent and a shadow—marking the trajectories of artistic form, as well as modes of artistic obsession, alienation, and nostalgia.

The 1970s accelerated political activism in art, triggered by both far-left Naxalite agitation and the imposition of Emergency in 1975. In a way, the 1970s reactivated the conjunctural moment of the 1940s, when art and politics intertwined on a national as well as a locational scale. A return to the political post-Emergency, as I noted in Chapter 5, was marked by exhibitions such as *Place for People*, as well as a national leftward turn in cultural discourse. Seminars such as "Marxism and Aesthetics," held at Kasauli in 1979, discussed for the first time realism/modernism dialectics along the lines of the Brecht-Lukács debate of the 1930s[1] (although echoes of these issues were active in the art discourse in India in the 1930s and 1940s), and new journals like the *Jour-*

nal of Arts and Ideas were initiated by critic-activists like Geeta Kapur to theorize cultural politics.[2] It was also between the late 1970s and early 1980s that Sudhi Pradhan, a cultural activist of the left's cultural movement of the 1940s, brought out the collected documents of the cultural movement in three volumes, describing it as the "Marxist cultural movement."

By the 1990s, as India was turning increasingly toward a right-wing politics, left-wing nostalgia became in itself a mode of recalling and citing a socialist cultural past—one in which celebrating a unified vision of a national "progressive" socialist culture became more urgent—more so, for instance, than investigating the political contradictions and irregularities *within* that cultural past. In contemporary times, histories of the left are being celebrated in scholarship, as global politics turns increasingly toward right-wing populism. This shift matches a curatorial and historiographical engagement with writing and displaying cultural forms of twentieth-century transnational left and the arts of decolonization: recent academic-curatorial collaborations like the exhibitions on "postwar," "postcolonial," and "postcommunist" art,[3] or ruptures of decolonization—like partition—read as "productive acts"[4] mark these turns.

Yet, the project in *Partisan Aesthetics* has not been one of (left-wing) nostalgia or celebrations of a postcolonial modern; rather it has been an archival treatment of "irregular histories." As Asok Mitra aptly noted in his review of Pradhan's first volume of *Marxist Cultural Movement* in 1979, while recording significant phases of political movements, it is critical to extract and separate "the wheat of history . . . as far as possible . . . from the chaff of nostalgia." Mitra maintained, however, that the cultural movement, with all its "inner tensions," could no longer be ignored, particularly "the contribution of the cultural front to the strengthening of the movement as a whole": "The front was a luminous part of the whole, a part which influenced to a major extent the morphology and metabolism of the whole in the thirties and the forties."[5]

Such irregular histories of art on the left, in their contradictions, invoke, as I have proposed in this book, the peculiar temporalities and cultural trails of decolonization itself: intertwined in such histories are stories of locational and sub-national differences, dialectical understandings of postcolonial freedom, and sociopolitical affiliations that exceed the rationalities of postcolonial nation-states. I have foregrounded ideological textures *within* the postcolonial modern via the locational and the politics of marginality that it can activate, to refract and subvert hegemonic national-modern impulses. Two potential directions in scholarship can emerge from here.

One such direction is the writing of new trans-border histories of artistic modernities in postcolonial South Asia. Bengal in itself is a site that can be read closely to reveal patterns of locational consciousness and obsessions with the memories of the 1940s that echo on both sides of post-partition Bengal. Iconic examples of this can be seen in the recurring idioms and narratives of hunger, struggle, and labor in the works of artists like Zainul Abedin, who after partition in 1947 was forced to migrate to Dhaka, the new capital of post-partition East Pakistan (eastern wing of post-1947 Pakistan), becoming the key artist-pedagogue there. One of the major architects of social realism during the 1930s and the famine years of 1943–44, Abedin would become foundational to the cultural movement for self-determination as East Pakistan fought recurring battles against West Pakistan, leading up to the Liberation War of 1971, which birthed independent Bangladesh. In his works the famine persisted as what I have called elsewhere "shadow lines" of the 1940s, as he drew—via images of exile and return, sowing and reaping— a nation on the brink of selfhood in 1971.[6]

As the birth of current Bangladesh marked the *second arrival* into independence of colonial eastern Bengal, unfinished struggles from the 1940s were rehashed, affective ties to land, locality, and nation realigned, cities reinscribed, and memories reconfigured. Such migratory modalities of the displacements of decolonization—for artists and idioms, as well as for memories of rupture—offer new entry points for visualizing an "aesthetics of decolonization"—in its incomplete, *longue durée* forms and its regional cross-border histories.[7] While scholarship is now exploring cross-border solidarities in art—the Liberation War inspiring artists in India including, for instance, both Chittaprosad and Somnath Hore[8]—a wider trans-regional modality of thinking about twentieth-century aesthetics in South Asia still needs to be initiated: art histories *from* the Global South, in other words, need to (re)imagine the "South" *beyond* the merely political or nation-statist rationalities of decolonization or the postcolonial nation-modern imaginary itself.

A second, related direction is around potential transnational and connected histories of decolonization. Driving questions that emerge here could be: Can decolonization have an aesthetic form that is unmoored from the narratives of national "arrivals" or "promises"? If we pursue instead the forms and fragments of displacement that a retreating empire produced, or disenchantments despite independence, what transnational narratives and aesthetic forms might decolonization take? From Southeast Asia to African and Arab contexts, (postcolonial) freedom had as its dialectical other, displacement—in both climactic ruptures like partition and quotidian struggles that continued as its afterlives. Such displacements are tied to experiences of hunger, genocide, and refugee influx, but also to the fragmentation of political and cultural solidarities. In art, this was often reflected in an aesthetic rooted in expressionistic figuration and a surrealistic iconography grounded in a fractured urban space, inventing time and again metaphors for thrusting the social into the formal and negotiating memory within modernism. These were also sites where artists remained alert both to the rise of abstraction as a global modernist currency and to its dehistoricizing impulses, against which they sought to articulate their own formal engagements with context. To write such histories, not only do we need to attend to dreams and utopias as much as failure and loss, but we also need to loosen national boundaries to ask how histories, memories, and artistic forms themselves percolated across political frontiers and imaginaries that had been splintered by the trails of twentieth-century decolonization. Such conversations, when read in dialogue with similar imageries of trauma and dislocation being explored in the wider postwar, decolonizing world, promise potentials for alternative global aesthetics of decolonization. This alternative is one that would destabilize the nation-state as a frame—not (only) in scalar terms, but as an often-defining, organizing rationality, and hence method, in thinking about cultural modernities of the postcolonial or "non-western" world.

Partisan Aesthetics has been an effort to understand aesthetics in dialogue with the politics and displacements of decolonization. In closing, I will pose an open-ended question, one that can be picked up for other localities, nations, or regions: What histories emerge if postcolonial modernisms are pursued through their irregularities and marginalities *within* nation-states? *Partisan Aesthetics* is only one of many potential answers to this question.

NOTES

INTRODUCTION

1. All quotes here are from a 2009 translation of Somnath Hore's original *Amar Chitrabhabana* (1992), recommissioned by Seagull Books after its first 1992 English translation, which accompanied Hore's *Wounds* exhibition at the Seagull Foundation. See Hore, *My Concept of Art*, 25–26.

2. Hore, *My Concept of Art*, 29–31.

3. Hore, Santiniketan, 1/11/1991, *My Concept of Art*, 61–63.

4. See Pradhan, *Marxist Cultural Movement in India*.

5. See, for instance, Ginwala, "So Many Hungers."

6. Greenough, *Prosperity and Misery in Modern Bengal*.

7. Amartya Sen, *Poverty and Famines*; Amartya Sen, *The Political Economy of Hunger*.

8. Stephens, *Monsoon Morning*, 178.

9. Stephens, *Monsoon Morning*, 184.

10. Issues of *Anandabazar Patrika* and *Amrita Bazaar Patrika* between July and October 1943. Srimanjari, *Through War and Famine*; Janam Mukherjee, *Hungry Bengal*.

11. Weisenfeld, *Imaging Disaster*, 5.

12. See Kali Charan Ghosh, *Famines in Bengal, 1770–1943*; Bhowani Sen, *Rural Bengal in Ruins*; Ela Sen, *Darkening Days*; Tarakchandra Das, *Bengal Famine (1943)*.

13. *First Bulletin of the Indian People's Theatre Association*, reprinted in Pradhan, *Marxist Cultural Movement in India*, 147.

14. On expanding the "chronology of famine," see Janam Mukherjee, *Hungry Bengal*, 11.

15. Amartya Sen, *Poverty and Famines*, 200–15.

16. See Madhushree Mukherjee, *Churchill's Secret War*; Khan, *The Raj at War*.

17. Suranjan Das, *Communal Riots in Bengal, 1905–1947*, 74.

18. Janam Mukherjee, *Hungry Bengal*, 18.

19. See Chilka Ghosh, *Chhobir Bishoy, Bishoyer Chhobi*, which translates roughly as "Content of Art, Art of Content"; see also Sandipan Bhattacharya, *Chhobir Rajniti, Rajniti-r Chhabi* ("Politics of Art, Art of Politics"); and more recently, a chapter on visual art and the left in Anuradha Roy, *Cultural Communism in Bengal*.

20. See Som, "Bangla-r Chitrakala o Bhashkarje Pragati Chetana-r Dhara," 353–74; Sripantha, *Daya* ; Nikhil Sarkar, *A Matter of Conscience*; Nercam, *Peindre au Bengale (1939–1977)* ; Mallik, "Social Realism in the Visual Arts."

21. See Ghosh, *Chhabir Bishoy*; also Chilka Ghosh, "The Sight/Site of Woman in the Art of the Forties," 22–29; Anuradha Roy, *Cultural Communism in Bengal.*

22. Gramsci, *Selections from Prison Notebooks*, 178.

23. Stuart Hall and Doreen Massey in conversation. See Hall and Massey, "Interpreting the Crisis," 57–58.

24. Janam Mukherjee, *Hungry Bengal*, 12.

25. Hall, "Black Diaspora Artists in Britain," 3.

26. Traverso, *Left-Wing Melancholia*, xiv–xv.

27. McLean, *The Event and Its Terrors*, 2.

28. Bourdieu, "The Field of Cultural Production, or: The Economic World Reversed," in Bourdieu, *The Field of Cultural Production*, 34.

29. Bourdieu, "The Production of Belief: Contribution to an Economy of Symbolic Goods," in Bourdieu, *The Field of Cultural Production*, 106.

30. Sontag, "On Style," in *Against Interpretation and Other Essays*, 18.

31. Koselleck, *Futures Past*, 258–59.

32. For a detailed discussion of Reinhart Koselleck and Paul Ricoeur around historical experience and imagination, see Boven, "Metaphor and Metamorphosis," 152.

33. See the Orientalist critic O. C. Gangooly's attacks on academic realist sculptor Fanindranath Bose in "Art of a Bengali Sculptor."

34. Asit Haldar, "Twenty-five Years of Contemporary Indian Painting," in *Art and Tradition*, 64.

35. Percy Brown, *Indian Painting*, 66.

36. Atul Bose, *Bangla-i Chitrakala o Rajniti-r Eksho Bochor*, 33.

37. As noted in Asit Haldar's letter to Atul Bose, rejecting cooperation for the latter's proposed Academy of Fine Arts in Calcutta. Personal correspondence of Atul Bose, courtesy of artist's son, Sanjib Bose.

38. Coomaraswamy, *Essays in National Idealism*, i.

39. Reviews of Indian-style art in Berlin, in "The Indian Exhibition," 80–81.

40. Guha-Thakurta, *The Making of a New "Indian" Art*, 7; see also Mitter, *Art and Nationalism in Colonial India, 1850–1922.*

41. Mitter, *The Triumph of Modernism.*

42. Rabindranath Tagore, "The Centre of Indian Culture," 30.

43. See Mandal, *Bharatsilpi Nandalal*, 1:176–83; Guha-Thakurta, "Visualizing the Nation."

44. See Siva Kumar, *Santiniketan*; also see Chakraborty, Kumar, and Nag, *The Santiniketan Murals.*

45. Nandalal Bose, "What Is Art?," in *Vision and Creation*, 35.

46. Casey, *Getting Back into Place*, 31.

47. For continuities and departures between the Bengal School and Nandalal Bose's art pedagogy, see Benodebehari Mukherjee, "The Santiniketan School of Art," 87; see also Benodebehari Mukherjee, *Adhunik Shilpashiksha* .

48. For the middle-class and elite cultural tendency toward romanticization of

tribal lives via an *abstraction* of "the concrete and immediate reality" and into a rarefied idealistic "space of Culture," see Prathama Banerjee, *Politics of Time*.

49. Benodebehari Mukherjee, *Chitrakar*, 46. See also Nandalal Bose's letter to Indulekha Bose, 11.5.42, reproduced in Bose, *Vision and Creation*, 248–52; Bose's critique of realism, even in the works of his student and colleague in the 1940s, the iconic artist of Kala Bhavan, Ramkinkar Baij, was reflected in his conversation with biographer Mandal. See Mandal, *Bharatsilpi Nandalal*, 4:526.

50. For close analysis of iconic academic realist artists like Atul Bose, Debiprasad Roy Choudhury, or Hemendranath Mazumdar, see Mitter, "Naturalists in the Age of Moderism," in *The Triumph of Modernism*, 123–76.

51. See, for instance, volumes of short-lived initiatives like the journals *Indian Academy of Art* (early 1920s) and *Shilpi* (late 1920s) started by Hemendranath Mazumdar; also see Hemendranath Mazumdar, *Chhabi-r Chasma*.

52. *1933 Guide: Art Rebel Centre Exhibition* (private papers of Gobardhan Ash). Courtesy of Nirban Ash.

53. A brief review of the exhibition was published in "Nana Katha/Miscellaneous," *Bichitra* Year VII, vol. 1, no. 1 (Sraban 1340/1933): 133–34.

54. Kumarsinha, "Modern Movement of Indian Art," 67.

55. Sri Prabodh Basu, "Bangla-r citrasilper dhara," *Bichitra*, Year X, vol. 2, no. 1 (Magh 1343 BS/1936), 51–63.

56. Gobardhan Ash's Diary, 43.

57. Jaminikanta Sen, "Adhunik Chitrakala-i Bangla Desh," *Bichitra*, Year XII, vol. 1, no. 1 (Sraban 1345 BS/1938), 42–47.

58. Kaviraj, "The Art of Despair," 272–74.

59. Pulinbehari Sen, "Kolikata-r Silpa Pradarsani," 550.

60. Nirad C. Chaudhuri, "An Exhibition of the Paintings of Manindra Bhusan Gupta," 209–10.

61. Chaudhuri, "Manindra Bhusan Gupta," 210.

62. Dipesh Chakraborty, *Provincializing Europe*, 149–50.

63. Ellman, *The Hunger Artists*, 7; see also Kelleher, *The Feminization of Famine*.

64. Mouffe, *On the Political*, 8–9; see also Laclau, *Emancipations*.

65. Aston, "Artists and Politics," 4.

66. Terracciano, *Art and Emergency*.

67. Aston, "Artists and Politics," 80.

68. Marcuse, *The Aesthetic Dimension*, 8.

69. Marcuse, *The Aesthetic Dimension*, 53.

70. Marcuse, "Art as Form of Reality," in *Art and Liberation*, 4:146.

71. See Gandhi, Speech at Faizpur, "A Villagers' Exhibition," *Harijan*, 2 January 1937; "Haripura Notes III," *Harijan*, 5 March 1938; Jaya Appasamy, introduction to *Six Haripura Panels*, by Nandalal Bose.

72. Bertolt Brecht, in Theodor Adorno et al., *Aesthetics and Politics*, 76.

73. Badiou et al., *What Is a People?*, 15.

74. Rancière, *Staging the People*, 15.

75. Badiou et al., *What Is a People?*, 12.

76. *People's War*, 12 March 1944.

77. See Degras, *The Communist International, 1919–1943*.

78. Roberts, *Philosophizing the Everyday*, 4–5.

79. Vials, *Realism for the Masses*, xxix.

80. Williams, "Lecture on Realism."

81. David Forgacs, "National-Popular: Genealogy of a Concept," in *The Cultural Studies Reader*, ed. Simon During, 182.

82. A point rarely addressed, even in works like Lahusen and Dobrenko, *Socialist Realism without Shores*.

83. Manjapra, "Communist Internationalism and Transcolonial Recognition," 159.

84. Manjapra, "Communist Internationalism and Transcolonial Recognition," 160.

85. Schmitt, *The Theory of the Partisan*, 6–11.

86. Schmitt, *The Theory of the Partisan*, 10.

87. Schmitt, *The Theory of the Partisan*, 13.

88. Hauser, "Propaganda, Ideology, and Art," 131.

89. Ghatak, *I Strode My Road*.

90. See Pinney, *Photos of the Gods*; Jain, *Gods in the Bazaar*; see also Sumatri Ramaswamy, *Beyond Appearances?*

91. For critical work on this exhibition, see Zitzewitz, *Aesthetics of Secularism*; Khullar, *Worldly Affiliations*.

92. Kapur, *Place for People*.

93. Kapur, *When Was Modernism*, 181.

94. Kapur, "Partisan Modernity," 28–42.

95. Kapur, *When Was Modernism*, 294.

96. Kapur, *When Was Modernism*, 226.

97. In Sudhi Pradhan's meticulous three-volume documentation of the cultural movement, only two articles were devoted to painting: the first by art critic Arun Sen, written in the late 1970s, and the second, a 1938 essay by Dhurjatiprasad Mukhopadhyay—writer, sociologist, and an associate of the Progressive Writers'Association, along with some select images circulated among left-wing groups in the 1940s. Pradhan, *Marxist Cultural Movement*, vol. 2.

98. Foucault, *Archaeology of Knowledge and Discourse on Language*, 128–29.

99. See Guha-Thakurta, *The Making of a New "Indian" Art*; Mitter, *Art and Nationalism in Colonial India*; Mitter, *The Triumph of Modernism*; Rebecca Brown, *Art for a Modern India, 1947–1980*; Zitzewitz, *The Art of Secularism*; Khullar, *Worldly Affiliations*; Terracciano, *Art and Emergency*.

100. I have benefited from extensive works in Bengali by scholars and art critics like Sovon Som, Mrinal Ghosh, and Prasanta Daw, as well as a rich body of little magazines that have chronicled artists in the region.

101. See, for instance, the series of edited volumes: Dhananjay Das, ed., *Marx-*

badi Sahitya Bitarka, vol. 2; Susnata Das, *Fascibad-birodhi Sangrame Abibhakta Bangla*; Dhananjay Das, *Bangla Sanskritite Marxbadi Chetana-r Dhara*; *Chhobir Rajniti, Rajnitir Chhobi*; Anuradha Roy, *Challish Dashaker Bangla-i Ganasangeet Andolan*.

102. Martins, "Failure as Art and Art History as Failure."

103. Mitter, "Interventions," 544.

104. Mitter, "Interventions," 541.

105. Rebecca Brown, "Response," 555–57.

106. Khullar, *Worldly Affiliations*, 14.

107. Khullar, *Worldly Affiliations*, 24.

108. Dadi, *Modernism and the Art of Muslim South Asia*, 4–10.

109. Huyssen, "Geographies of Modernism," 191–92.

110. Huyssen, "Geographies of Modernism," 200.

111. Appadurai, *Modernity at Large*, 178.

112. Saskia Sassen, foreword to Kahn, *Framing the Global*, 9.

113. See Harney, *In Senghor's Shadow*; Kane, *The Politics of Art in Modern Egypt*; Feldman, *From a Nation Torn*; Okeke-Agulu, *Postcolonial Modernism*.

114. Bandopadhyay, *Decolonization in South Asia*, 6.

115. Bandopadhyay, *Decolonization in South Asia*, 4–6.

116. Mitchell, "The Stage of Modernity," 8.

117. Timothy Brennan, "The National Longing for Form," in Bhaba, *Nation and Narration*, 47.

118. Bhaba, introduction to *Nation and Narration*, 4.

119. Samuel, *Island Stories*, ix.

120. Raymond Williams, "When Was Modernism?" in Pinkney, *The Politics of Modernism*, 34–35.

121. Duara, *Decolonization*, 1.

122. Chakrabarty, Majumdar, and Sartori, *From the Colonial to the Postcolonial*, 3.

123. Kaviraj, *The Imaginary Institution of India*.

124. See Anderson, *Imagined Communities*, and Partha Chatterjee, "The Nation in Heterogeneous Time"; see also Partha Chatterjee, *The Politics of the Governed*.

125. Partha Chatterjee, *The Nation and Its Fragments*, xi.

126. Pandey, "In Defense of the Fragment," 29.

127. Jain, *Gods in the Bazaar*, 14–15.

128. Jain, *Gods in the Bazaar*, 14–15.

129. Dipesh Chakraborty, *Provincializing Europe*, xvii.

130. Brzyski, *Partisan Canons*, 7.

131. Harney, "The Densities of Modernism," 479.

CHAPTER 1

1. *Amrita Bazar Patrika*, undated, from September 1937, album of newspaper reports. Courtesy of Archives of the Indian Society of Oriental Art, Calcutta.

2. Gandhi's inauguration speech, Report on the Lucknow Congress, "A Unique Exhibition," *Harijan*, 4 April 1936.

3. Mandal, *Bharatsilpi Nandalal*, 1:488, 4:554. See also Benodebehari Mukherjee, *Adhunik Silpasiksha*, 82–88.

4. See Mukul Dey, foreword to *Exhibition of Drawings and Paintings by Jamini Roy.*

5. Sachin Sengupta, "Jamini Ray-er Silpa Pradarshani," *Anandabazar Patrika*, undated, possibly from September 1937, album of newspaper reports. Courtesy of Archives of the Indian Society of Oriental Art, Calcutta.

6. Suhrawardy, *Prefaces.*

7. Sudhindranath Datta, *The World of Twilight.* For references to the album and the essay, see Shyamal Krishna Ghosh, *Parichoy-er Adda.*

8. Bishnu Dey and John Irwin, *Jamini Roy.*

9. Reprinted in Pradhan, *Marxist Cultural Movement in India*, vol. 2.

10. Bishnu Dey, "Art of Jamini Roy," *Sahityapatra*, November 1948, and "Jamini Ray o Tar Silpabichar."

11. See Banerjee, *Politics of Time.*

12. Jamini Roy in conversation with Bishnu Dey (broadcast from All India Radio), reproduced in Bishnu Dey, "Jamini Ray-er Katha," in *Jamini Ray*, 14.

13. Dey, "Jamini Ray-er Katha," in *Jamini Ray*, 17.

14. Dey, "Jamini Ray-er Katha," in *Jamini Ray*, 17.

15. Dey, "Jamini Ray-er Katha," in *Jamini Ray*, 65.

16. Brief newspaper report on the ISOA exhibition of August 1930, source unknown. Courtesy of Newspaper Reports album of ISOA, Calcutta.

17. Brief newspaper report.

18. Brief newspaper report.

19. Brief newspaper report.

20. Devi, "Silpi Srijukta Jamini Ray-er Pradarsani."

21. Mitter, *Triumph of Modernism*, 100–106.

22. Reprinted in Gurusaday Dutt, *Folk Arts and Crafts of Bengal*, xviii–xix.

23. Benodebehari Mukherjee, "Jamini Roy and His Art," *Ananda Bazar Patrika*, 18 February 1945, *Archer Papers*, mss. F. 236/165. Oriental and India Office Collections, British Library.

24. Bishnu Dey, "Jamini Ray-er Katha," in *Jamini Ray*, 21.

25. For Jamini Roy's new patronage among urban left-wing intellectuals, see Ratnaboli Chatterjee, "'The Original Jamini Roy.'"

26. Detailed documentation of the events and discussions of these gatherings can be found in the diary kept by Shyamal Krishna Ghosh, writer and regular at *Parichoy*, published as a series in the 1980s in the magazine, and as a book, *Parichoy-er Adda.*

27. Bishnu Dey, *Jamini Ray*, 58–59.

28. *Parichoy* 2, no. 2, Kartik 1339BS/1932.

29. Amiya Dev, *Sudhindranath Datta*, 29.

30. Quoted in Shils, introduction to Datta, *The World of Twilight*, xvi–xvii.

31. Dev, *Sudhindranath*, 33.

32. Dey and Irwin, *Jamini Roy*, 32.

33. Buddhadeb Bose, *Amader Kabita Bhaban*.
34. Bishnu Dey, "Jamini Ray-er Katha," *Jamini Ray*, 63.
35. Mitra, *Three Score and Ten*, 96.
36. Williams, *Politics of Modernism*, 175.
37. Denning, *The Cultural Front*, xix.
38. Suhrawardy, *Prefaces*, 116.
39. Suhrawardy, *Prefaces*, 132–33.
40. Suhrawardy, *Prefaces*, 135.
41. Suhrawardy, *Prefaces*, 118.
42. Suhrawardy, *Prefaces*, 137.
43. Suhrawardy, *Prefaces*, 137.
44. Suhrawardy, *Prefaces*, 120.
45. Suhrawardy, *Prefaces*, 120.
46. Shyamal Krishna Ghosh, *Parichoy-er Adda*, 119–20.
47. Diary entry of 20 May 1938, Ghosh, *Parichoy-er Adda*, 84–85.
48. Ghosh, *Parichoy-er Adda*, 86–90.
49. Suhrawardy, *Prefaces*, 116.
50. Thistlewood, "Herbert Read's Organic Aesthetic [I] 1918–1950," 215.
51. Edward Shils, introduction to Datta, *The World of Twilight*, xvi–xvii.
52. Datta, "Jamini Roy and the Tradition of Painting in Bengal," in *The World of Twilight*, 96.
53. Datta, "Jamini Roy," 106–7.
54. Datta, "Jamini Roy," 104.
55. Datta, "Jamini Roy," 101.
56. Datta, "Jamini Roy," 107.
57. Datta, "Jamini Roy," 107–9.
58. Datta, "Jamini Roy," 113.
59. Datta, "Jamini Roy," 119.
60. Datta, "Jamini Roy," 115.
61. Datta, "Emancipation of Poetry," reproduced in *The World of Twilight*, 126. [First published in Bengali as "Kabyer Mukti," in *Parichoy* 1, no. 1 (1931)].
62. Datta, "Emancipation of Poetry," 127.
63. Sudhindranath Datta, "Whiggism, Radicalism, and Treason in Bengal" (address to the Second All-India conference of the PWA), reproduced in Pradhan, *Marxist Cultural Movement*, 1:86.
64. Datta, "Whiggism," in Pradhan, *Marxist Cultural Movement*, 1:87–88.
65. Datta, "Whiggism," in Pradhan, *Marxist Cultural Movement*, 1:87–88.
66. See Arun Sen, *Sudhindranath/Bishnu De*.
67. The collected English translations of the letters were published by Visva-Bharati in 1960.
68. Gorky's popularity in Bengal in the 1930s is confirmed by a series of translations of his works since the 1920s. See Mitra, *Three Score and Ten*, 59. See also Sarkar and Das, *Bangalir Samyabad Charcha*.

69. See Pradhan, *Marxist Cultural Movement*, vol. 2.

70. Mukherjee, *Towards Progressive Literature*; Maxim Gorky, Speech at the Soviet Writers' Congress, 1934.

71. Surendranath Goswamy and Hiren Mukherjee, *Pragati.*

72. Dhurjatiprasad Mukhopadhyay, "On the Social Background of Contemporary Indian Painting," 46.

73. Dey and Irwin, *Jamini Roy*, 3–5.

74. Dey and Irwin, *Jamini Roy*, 25.

75. Dey and Irwin, *Jamini Roy*, 25.

76. Dey and Irwin, *Jamini Roy*, 28.

77. Dey and Irwin, *Jamini Roy*, 29–30.

78. Dey and Irwin, *Jamini Roy*, 29–30.

79. Anand, "Recollections," 52–53.

80. Anand, "Recollections," 56.

81. Anand, "Recollections," 56.

82. See Margolies, *Writing the Revolution*; Anand, *Conversations in Bloomsbury*; Croft, *Comrade at Heart.*

83. Read, "What Is Revolutionary Art?" 12–22.

84. Jamini Roy, in conversation with Mary E. Milford, in Milford, "A Modern Primitive."

85. Mulk Raj Anand, "On the Progressive Writers' Movement," in Pradhan, *Marxist Cultural Movement*, 1:12.

86. Anand, "On the Progressive Writers' Movement," 1:13.

87. Datta, "Jamini Roy," in *The World of Twilight*, 120–21.

88. Datta, "Jamini Roy," 121.

89. Datta, "Jamini Roy," 121.

90. Dey and Irwin, *Jamini Roy*, 35.

91. Shyamal Krishna Ghosh, "Parichoy-er Partham Jug," 22.

92. Shyamal Krishna Ghosh, Diary entry, 30 December 1938, *Parichoy-er Adda*, 120.

93. "Review of the recent Communist activities in India," compiled by the DIB, Secret: Intelligence Bureau (Home Department), Home/Poll/1937, F 7/7, as reproduced in Subodh Roy, *Communism in India*, 84–85.

94. Roy, *Communism in India*, 82–83.

95. Hiren Mukherjee, *Us/A People's Symposium*, v–vii.

96. XYZ, "On Progressive Criticism," in Mukherjee, *Us/A People's Symposium*, 13.

97. *First Bulletin of Indian People's Theatre Association*, reprinted in Pradhan, *Marxist Cultural Movement*, 1:147.

98. Arun Sen, *Sudhindranath/Bishnu De*, 38.

99. See Hiren Mukherjee, *Tari Hote Tir*, 365.

100. Dev, *Sudhindranath Datta*, 33.

101. A detailed list of the regulars was prepared by Hiran Kumar Sanyal in *Parichoy-er Kuri Bochor o Ananyo Smritichitra* (Calcutta: Papyrus, 1975).

102. A point noted in the context of the PWA, by Gopal, *Literary Radicalism in India*, 27. See also Anjaria, *Realism in the Twentieth-Century Indian Novel.*

103. Chinmohan Shehanobis, "Report on Bengal Progressive Writers and Artists Association, 1945–46," reprinted in Pradhan, *Marxist Cultural Movement*, 1:349.

104. Gopal Haldar, "Jamini Roy o Jatiya Chetana," 313–15.

105. Caute, *The Fellow-Travellers*, 4.

106. Caute, *The Fellow-Travellers*, 3.

107. Anand, "On the Progressive Writers' Movement," *Marxist Cultural Movement*, 1:15.

108. Anand, "On the Progressive Writers' Movement," 1:22–24.

109. Anand, "On the Progressive Writers' Movement," 1:25.

110. Arun Sen, *Bishnu Dey*, 25.

111. Sen, *Bishnu Dey*, 33.

112. Hiren Mukherjee, *Tari Hote Tir*, 380.

113. Datta, *The World of Twilight*, 121.

114. Dey, "Art of Jamini Roy," *Sahityapatra*, November 1948, 70–74.

CHAPTER 2

1. Chittaprosad, "Chhobi-r Sankat." I am grateful to Arun Ghosh at the Bhupesh Bhawan Library, Calcutta, for making available extremely rare volumes of *Arani.*

2. The phrase, attributed to Joseph Stalin, was used by A. Zhdanov at the Soviet Writers' Congress in 1934 and cited repeatedly to describe the aesthetic of socialist realism. See A. Zhdanov, *Speech at the Soviet Writers' Congress*, 1934, 21.

3. Excerpts from Chittaprosad's typed autobiography (mss. 14–15), reproduced in Prodyot Ghosh, *Chittaprosad* , 15.

4. Prodyot Ghosh, *Chittaprosad*, 15

5. Evocative here are Frans Masereel's early twentieth-century wordless woodcut novels *Arise Ye Dead* (1917), *The Dead Speak* (1917), and *The Passion of a Man* (1918). See Masereel, *Passionate Journey.*

6. For Si Lewen's 1957 works, see Spiegelman, *Si Lewen's Parade.*

7. Prodyot Ghosh, *Chittaprosad*, 14.

8. James, *Soviet Socialist Realism*, 1. For formulations of tendentious art in Marx and Engels, and later Lenin, see Baxandall and Morawski, *Marx and Engels on Literature and Art*; Solomon, *Marxism and Art*; Lukács, *Writer and Critic and Other Essays.*

9. Lukács, "Critical Realism and Socialist Realism," 93–135.

10. James, *Soviet Socialist Realism*, 91.

11. Constitution of the Union of Writers, quoted in James, *Soviet Socialist Realism*, ix.

12. Lahusen and Dobrenko, *Socialist Realism without Shores.*

13. Koselleck, *Futures Past*, 258–59.

14. According to the Intelligence Bureau Report of 1944, the Communist Party was continuing its policy of "obstructive cooperation." Quoted in Srimanjari, *Through War and Famine*, 130–33.

15. Joshi, *Indian Communist Party.*

16. The unpopularity of the People's War line, even among Communist cadres and grassroots workers, has been widely noted. See Manikuntala Sen, *Shediner Katha*, 61. See also Overstreet and Windmiller, *Communist Party of India.*

17. Sumit Sarkar, *Modern India, 1887–1947*, 353.

18. See Srimanjari, *Through War and Famine*, 129.

19. The Chittagong Armoury Raid of April 1934 was an attempt by revolutionary freedom fighters to raid the armoury of police and auxiliary forces at Chittagong in East Bengal (now Bangladesh).

20. Prodyot Ghosh, *Chittaprosad*, 7.

21. Prodyot Ghosh, *Chittaprosad*, 7.

22. Prodyot Ghosh, *Chittaprosad*, 8.

23. Prodyot Ghosh, *Chittaprosad*, 8.

24. *Janayuddha*, 14 April 1943.

25. Anuradha Roy, in conversation with Chinmohan Sehanobish, in Roy, *Cultural Communism in Bengal*, 332.

26. "Introducing Chitta," *People's War*, 28 November 1943.

27. Hore, *Amar Chitrabhabana*, 8–12.

28. Hore, *Wounds*, 12.

29. The *Tebhaga Diary* was documented in 1946 during Hore's stay with the Bengal Provincial Kisan Sabha activists in course of the struggle, and published in the Bengali little magazine *Ekshan* in 1956.

30. Brief references on these artists can be found in Kamal Sarkar, *Bharater Bhaskar o Chitrashilpi.*

31. The artist's interview, "Jibon, Silpa o Rajneeti-r Bibhinno Bishoy," in Sandipan Bhattacharya, *Chhobi-r Rajneeti, Rajneeti-r Chhobi*, 277–78. See also Satya Sen, "Interview with Debabrata Mukhopadhyay," 71.

32. *Janayuddha* 2, no. 11 (9 July 1943).

33. Lahiri, *Collected Writings*, 2:8.

34. Pranab Ranjan Ray, "The Political in Art," 69. Ray refers here to the memoirs of the poet Subhash Mukhopadhyay, who was asked as a party worker to travel to North Bengal and write about his experiences of the movement in an "emotively didactic manner." The product of this assignment was his famous elegy to the toilers in his much-known text, *Amar Bangla* (1951).

35. *People's War*, 22 October 1944.

36. See Roychodhury, "Documentary Photography, Decolonization, and the Making of 'Secular Icons'"; Terracciano, *Art and Emergency*; Rahman, *Sunil Janah*; Janah, *Photographing India.*

37. See articles on Zainul Abedin in *People's War*, no. 30, 21 January 1945, and on Rathin Moitra and the Calcutta Group of artists in *People's Age*, 25 February 1945 and 23 September 1945.

38. Chittaprosad, "Zainul Abedin," *People's War*, no. 30 (21 January 1945), 12.

39. As recalled by Gouri Bhattacharya, the artist's sister, in Chittaprosad, *Kshudartho Bangla.*

40. Chittaprosad, *Hungry Bengal*, 1.

41. A collection of these reverse side images is kept at the Delhi Art Gallery, New Delhi.

42. *Hungry Bengal* was a part of a large amount of famine literature produced by the CPI, including Somnath Lahiri, *Queues of Death*; P. C. Joshi, *Who Lives If Bengal Dies?*; and Krishna Benode Roy, *Bengal Famine and the Problems of Rehabilitation.* Party literature on the famine also included series of pamphlets and posters for mobilizing funds and support from the urban and rural masses.

43. Chittaprosad, "The Riches Piled Here."

44. Prodyot Ghosh, *Chittaprosad*, 22.

45. Prodyot Ghosh, *Chittaprosad*, 9.

46. Joshi, *The New Situation and Our Tasks*, 3–5.

47. Joshi, *The New Situation and Our Tasks*, 5.

48. Dhanagare, *Peasant Movement in India*, 155.

49. See Sunil Sen, *Agrarian Struggle in Bengal, 1946–47*, 61–63.

50. In 2009 the complete album was published for the first time by Seagull Books. It records the movement until the mid-1930s, though it is unclear when Hore went or where these images were circulated, if at all. See Hore, *The Tea-Garden Journal.*

51. Mao Zhedong, *Problems of Art and Literature*, 17–18. While Mao's Yenan speech was being circulated in the mid-1940s through reports, the first full translation was published by the People's Publishing House in India only in 1950.

52. See Sunderason, "Framing Margins," 67–87.

53. Prodyot Ghosh, *Chittaprosad*, 9–10.

54. Prodyot Ghosh, *Chittaprosad*, 9–10.

55. Prodyot Ghosh, *Chittaprosad*, 9–10.

56. Mallik, *A Sketchbook of 30 Portraits.*

57. Constitution of the Union of Writers, quoted in James, *Soviet Socialist Realism*, ix.

58. *People's Age*, 6 January 1946.

59. *People's War*, 21 January 1945.

60. *First Bulletin of IPTA*, 2.

61. *People's War*, Independence Day, no. 21 January 1945.

62. James, *Soviet Socialist Realism*, 1.

63. Ahmad Ali, "Progressive Views of Art," in Pradhan, *Marxist Cultural Movement*, 1:61.

64. Raghupati Firaq, "The Indian Renaissance at the Parting of Ways," in Pradhan, *Marxist Cultural Movement*, 1:48–49.

65. The phrase was famously used by Joseph Stalin: "socialist in content and national in form." See Stalin, *Marxism and the National-Colonial Question.*

66. *People's Age*, 21 January 1946.

67. *People's War*, 2 September 1945, 7.

68. *Janayuddha*, 17 June 1942.

69. Report on the Ninth All India Kisan Sabha Conference, *People's War*, 6 May 1945, 1.

70. For instance, see Gopal Haldar's review of the Friends of the Soviet Union exhibition of Soviet posters at the Indian Art School, *Parichoy*, Jaishtha 1352 (BS)/1945.

71. *Janayuddha*, 7 July 1943.

72. Prodyot Ghosh, *Chittaprosad*, 23–24.

73. Chinmohan Shehanobish, "Sanskriti Sammelan-e," *Arani*, 2 July 1943, 786.

74. Resolutions adopted at the conference of the Anti-Fascist Writers' and Artists' Association, *People's War*, 4 February 1944.

75. "The Bhooka Bengal Exhibition," *People's War*, 9 January 1944. The article also carried Chittaprosad's sketch of a stream of visitors queuing up at the exhibition.

76. "Bhooka Bengal Exhibition."

77. *People's War*, 22 October 1944, 9.

78. "Maharashtrians of All Walks Aid Bengal." 12.

79. "Report of the Anti-Fascist Writers' and Artists' Association," January–June 1944. The sales figures can be seen in the advertisement of the Cultural Cell of the CPI in *People's War*, 17 November 1944.

80. Rasul, *History of the Kisan Sabha*, 110.

81. *People's War*, 26 March 1944. From brochure of the Bezwada Congress. Source: P. C. Joshi Collections. Courtesy of Archives on Contemporary History, Dr. B. R. Ambedkar Central Library, JNU, New Delhi.

82. *People's War*, 18 April 1944.

83. Rasul, *History of the Kisan Sabha*, 114.

84. *People's War*, 10 April 1945.

85. Anuradha Roy, *Cultural Communism in Bengal*, 320.

86. *Janayuddha*, 16 February 1944.

87. See Mukhopadhyay's interview with Satya Sen, in *Mukhar, Debabrata Mukhopadhyay Volume.*

88. *People's War*, 22 June 1944, 7.

89. Chittaprosad, "Chhobi-r Sankat."

90. Chittaprosad, "Chhobi-r Sankat."

91. Rea, *On Revolutionary Art.*

92. Gopal Haldar, ed., *Revolutionary Art.* I am grateful to the late Arun Ghosh, Bhupesh Gupta Bhawan Library, for drawing my attention to this rare volume.

93. Haldar, *Revolutionary Art.*

94. Gopal Haldar, "Culture O Communist Dwaityo" [Culture and Communist Responsibility], was published in October 1944 as a directive to the CPI cadres. It was reprinted in 1947 in a collection of Haldar's essays on culture, *Bangali Sanskriti-r Rup* [Character of Bengali Culture]. I have accessed the subsequent reprint in Dr. Debipada Bhattacharya, Dr. Aruna Haldar, and Dr. Amiya Dhar, eds., *Sanskritir Biswarup, Gopal Haldar* (Calcutta: Manisha, 1986), 22.

95. Gopal Haldar, "Culture O Communist Dwaityo," 23–24.

96. K. N. Panikkar, "Left Cultural Intervention," 761–62.

CHAPTER 3

1. I encountered the album, in a rather serendipitous manner, in "Almirah 8" at the library of the Government College of Art and Craft, Calcutta.

2. Dhurjatiprasad Mukhopadhyay, "On the Social Background of Contemporary Indian Painting."

3. Pradhan's meticulous documentation of the cultural movement included only two articles devoted to painting—one by art critic Arun Sen, written in the late 1970s, and the other a 1938 essay by Dhurjatiprasad Mukhopadhyay.

4. Hills, "Art and Politics in the Popular Front," 181.

5. Lukács, "Critical Realism and Socialist Realism," 93.

6. Pranab Ranjan Ray, "To carry the roots in the veins," 8–15.

7. See the exhaustive work of Zehra Jumabhoy and Boon Hoi Tan in the exhibition and catalogue *The Progressive Revolution: Modern Art for a New India.* See also Dalmia, *The Making of Modern Indian Art.*

8. Jahangir, *The Quest of Zainul Abedin*, 32.

9. Ela Sen, *Darkening Days.*

10. *People's War* 30 (21 January 1945), 12.

11. Bishnu Dey, introduction to Arun Dasgupta et al., *Bengal Painters' Testimony*, 4.

12. For an overview of these artists, see Archer, *India and Modern Art.*

13. Prodosh Dasgupta's quasi-autobiography and memoirs, *Smritikatha Silpakatha*, 96.

14. Gopal Ghose, "Atmakatha" in *Saradiya Pratikshan* (private papers of Gopal Ghose, undated).

15. Catalogue and Price List from Exhibition Catalogues of Third (December 21) and Fourth Annual Exhibitions (December 22, 1936 to January 10, 1937) of the Academy of Fine Arts (private collection of Atul Bose).

16. Home, *The Art of Subho Tagore.* I am grateful to the family of art writer and collector Nikhil Sarkar for providing me access to the album.

17. References to these appear among the private papers of Rathin Maitra, as well as in the reflections of Calcutta Group artists spread across biographical material and interviews. See also recollections on Bishnu Dey from Calcutta Group artists, mainly Rathin Maitra, Gopal Ghose, and Nirode Mazumdar, in the commemorative volume *Smriti or Sattay Bishnu Dey*, edited by Sujit Ghosh.

18. For display information from the 1945 exhibitions, I have relied on reviews of the Calcutta exhibition by Shahid Suhrawardy for *The Statesman* (26 March 1945) and by O. C. Gangooly for *Amrita Bazaar Patrika* (27 March 1945).

19. Most of these works from the forties are accessible only in the form of reproductions in contemporary periodicals, though some are not accessible at all.

20. Som, "Fascibirodhi Chitrakala o Calcutta Group," in Susnata Das, ed., *Fasci-*

bad-birodhi Sangrame Abibhakta Bangla. See also Som, "Calcutta Group"; and Mrinal Ghosh, "Calcutta Group o Challish-er Silpakala: Pariprekshita."

21. Prodosh Dasgupta, *My Sculpture*, 20.

22. "Art to Kill Murder," exhibition review of Rathin Maitra, *Bombay Chronicle Weekly*, 21 September 1947 (private papers of Rathin Maitra). Courtesy of the artist's son Riten Maitra.

23. Gopal Ghose, *Pre-Independence Years* (exhibition presented by Anuradha Bose at Birla Academy of Art and Culture, 12–17 August 1997). Courtesy of the artist's daughter, Deepa Bose.

24. Catalogue of the Third Annual Exhibition of Paintings and Sculptures, 24 May–1 June 1947. I am grateful to Rathin Maitra's sons, Romain Maitra and Riten Maitra, for providing me invaluable access to the artist's vast private papers in multiple locations.

25. Home, *The Art of Subho Tagore*.

26. "Exhibition of the Calcutta Group," *Amrita Bazar Patrika*, 27 March 1945 (private papers of Prodosh Dasgupta).

27. Shahid Suhrawardy, "Calcutta Group: Promising Works by Young Artists," *The Statesman*, 26 March 1945 (private papers of Prodosh Dasgupta).

28. Suhrawardy, "Calcutta Group."

29. Suhrawardy, "Calcutta Group."

30. *Amrita Bazar Patrika*, 25 March 1945. Courtesy of the artist's son, Pradeep Dasgupta.

31. von Leyden, "City Exhibition of Paintings, Calcutta Group's Work." Leyden, an Austrian émigré in Bombay, was one of the most important patrons of the Progressive Artists' Group.

32. Dasgupta, "The Calcutta Group—Its Aims and Achievements"; see also Dasgupta's quasi-autobiography, *Smritikatha Silpikatha*.

33. Anuradha Roy, *Challish Dashaker Bangla-i Ganasangeet Andolan*; Damodaran, *The Radical Impulse*.

34. The *Half-Yearly Report*, January–June 1944, of the AFWAA, details three subcommittees: the IPTA subcommittee, the Fine Arts subcommittee, and the Publication subcommittee (private papers of Rathin Maitra).

35. "Kisan o Shilpi-r sammelan," Report on the Kisan Sabha conference at Netrakona, *Parichoy*, Baishakh 1352 (BS)/1945.

36. *Bishnu Dey: Shilpa-karma, Shilpa-samgraha, Shilpa-bhabana*, exhibition organized at the Bangiya Sahitya Parishat, 18–31 July 2005. I am indebted to Deepa Bose, daughter of the Calcutta Group painter Gopal Ghose, for drawing my attention to this modest volume.

37. See Subho Tagore on P. C. Joshi in *Saradiya Anustup* (c. 1984), reproduced in Sarkar and Das, *Banglalir Samyabad Charcha*, 491–95.

38. Bishnu Dey, "Blue to Red, Subho Tagore Now," in Home, *The Art of Subho Tagore*.

39. A rare copy of the first edition is in the collection of Rathin Maitra's family.

40. The brochure cover "May Day MCMXLIV, Dedicated to My Comrades who are Fighting against Aggression," reproduced in *The Art of Subho Tagore*. The entire proceedings from the sales of the folder were donated to the Russian Red Cross.

41. Bishnu Dey, "Blue to Red."

42. Dey, "When Artists Awake . . . ," 12.

43. Dey, "When Artists Awake . . . ," 11.

44. See Finkelstein, *Art and Society*.

45. Bishnu Dey, introduction to *Calcutta Group Presents 8 Monochrome Reproductions of Nirode Mazumdar's Paintings*, W. G. Archer Papers, mss. Eur. F236/156, OIOC. The catalogue can be approximately dated to 1946, as Bishnu Dey's biographer, Arun Sen, remarks on Dey's article after their Dumka trip of 1946. See Arun Sen, *Bishnu Dey*, 55–57. That the 1946 piece was already available during the 1945 exhibition of the Calcutta Group in Bombay is evident in Rudi von Leyden's review of the Bombay exhibition, in which he seemed to critique some of Dey's propositions.

46. Dey, "Introduction." Dey is referring here to O. C. Gangooly's comments on the Calcutta Group's 1945 exhibition in *Amrita Bazaar Patrika*, March 27, 1945. See earlier section of this chapter for the reference to this review.

47. Dey, "Introduction."

48. Bishnu Dey, *Kabitasamagra*.

49. See articles by Manik Bandopadhyay, *Parichoy*, Paus1354/1948. The same volume contained Dey's responses to the critiques and his protest against the sectarianism of the party line in literature.

50. See Samar Sen, *Babubrittanto o Prasangik*, 250–51.

51. See Arun Sen, *Bishnu Dey*, 66; Arun Sen, "Bishnu Dey Rachanapanji," *Parichoy*, Baishakh 1386 (May–June 1979): 154–59.

52. Asok Sen, "Poet of Human Fulfilment" (article originally written in 1966), in Bishnu Dey, *Water My Roots*, 26.

53. Arun Sen, *Bishnu Dey*, 55.

54. See Elwin, *The Tribal World of Verrier Elwin*. A set of photographs of the works done by artists like Rathin Maitra and Gopal Ghose during their stay at Dumka is kept in the collection of William Archer's private papers. Mss. Eur. F236/155. OIOC, British Library.

55. Arun Sen, *Bishnu Dey*, 56. Dey's correspondence with William Archer refers to a series of trips to Dumka undertaken between 1945 and 1946 (W. G. Archer Papers, Mss. Eur. F236/156, OIOC).

56. In 1947 Bishnu Dey reviewed Verrier Elwin's *Folk Songs of Chattisgarh*, with contributions from W. G. Archer. Reproduced in Bishnu Dey, *In the Sun and the Rain*.

57. Shahid Suhrawardy's review of the Calcutta exhibition of the Calcutta Group, *The Statesman*, 26 March 1945. See also Bishnu Dey, introduction to *Calcutta Group Presents 8 Monochrome Reproductions*.

58. Dey and Irwin, *Jamini Roy*.

59. Prodosh Dasgupta, *Smritikatha Silpakatha*, 48.

60. Prodosh Dasgupta, *Smritikatha Silpakatha*, 53–54, 89–90.

61. Gangooly, "Interpreters of New Order of Beauty."

62. Prodosh Dasgupta, "The Calcutta Group: Its Aims and Achievements," *Lalit Kala Contemporary* 31 (April 1981): 10.

63. Prodosh Dasgupta, "The Calcutta Group," 10.

64. Reproduced in Bishnu Dey's collection of essays, *Prabandha Sangraha*, 1: 176–78.

65. Dey, *Prabandha Sangraha*, 1:176–79.

66. See Dasgupta, *Smritikatha Silpakatha*, 46, 151.

67. Prodosh Dasgupta, "The Calcutta Group," *The Republic*, 27 August 1949, unpaginated.

68. Dasgupta, "The Calcutta Group" (1949).

69. Dasgupta, "The Calcutta Group."

70. Dasgupta, "The Calcutta Group."

71. Dasgupta, "The Calcutta Group."

72. Dasgupta, "The Calcutta Group."

73. Introduction to the joint exhibition of the Calcutta Group and the Bombay Progressives, written by H. Gage, a founding member of PAG (private papers of Gobardhan Ash). Courtesy of the artist's son, Nirban Ash.

74. Klaus Fischer, "The *Calcutta Group*," 60–61.

75. Fischer, "The *Calcutta Group*," 61.

76. Fischer, "The *Calcutta Group*," 71.

77. Fischer, "The *Calcutta Group*," 64.

78. The periodical was short-lived and only scattered portions can be found. Archer Papers, Mss. Eur. F236/156. Oriental and India Office Collection, British Library.

79. Prodosh Dasgupta, "Essays on Art."

80. Paritosh Sen, *Rong Tuli-r Baire*, 99–100.

CHAPTER 4

1. P. C. Joshi, "R. P. Dutt and Indian Communists," originally published in *Indian Left Review* 1, no. 4 (July 1971); reprinted in Chakravartty, *People's Warrior*, 322.

2. Mallik, *Yours Chitta*, 13. Some of these letters were first published in the Bengali review journal *Parichoy*. See "Chittaprosad-er Chithi o Chhara."

3. Chittaprosad, Letter to Murari Gupta, 26 September 1953, in Mallik, *Yours Chitta*, 17.

4. Collected papers of and on Chittaprosad. Courtesy of Delhi Art Gallery Archives and Documentation Centre.

5. "Statement of Policy," *People's Age* (29 June 1947): 6–7.

6. *Communist Statement of Policy*.

7. *People's Age* (14 and 21 March 1948).

8. Zachariah, *Nehru*, 181–83.

9. Pradhan, *Marxist Cultural Movement*, 2:54.

10. Suggestions made for preparing the Seventh All-India IPTA conference held

in March 1953, drafted by Niranjan Sen and published originally in the IPTA organ *Unity* (December 1952); reprinted in Pradhan, *Marxist Cultural Movement*, 2:104–8.

11. Suggestions, for documents and resolutions of this last all-India conference.

12. Sudhi Pradhan, "Chitta Prasad," in Mallik, *Chittaprosad*, 1:215.

13. Chittaprosad's letters to his former comrades like Sunil Janah and Somnath Hore, and close associates like Samar Sen, reproduced in *Kshudarto Bangla* and *Anustup Special Volume on Samar Sen* (Kolkata: Anustup, 2017).

14. Hore, *My Concept of Art*, 16.

15. Hore, *My Concept of Art*, 17.

16. Ghatak, *On the Cultural Front*, 15.

17. Ghatak, *On the Cultural Front*, 14.

18. Ghatak, *On the Cultural Front*, 13.

19. Ghatak, *On the Cultural Front*, 47.

20. Ghatak, *On the Cultural Front*, 24.

21. Geeta Kapur, *When Was Modernism*, 302.

22. See Chapter 2 for Gopal Haldar, "Culture O Communist Dwaityo."

23. Bishnu Dey, "Calcutta Group," in *Sahityer Bhabishyat*; reprinted in Bishnu Dey, *Prabandha Sangraha*, 1:176.

24. *People's War* (4 August 1946): 10. See also Francis Newton Souza in conversation with Yashodhara Dalmia in Dalmia, *The Making of Modern Indian Art*, 42.

25. F. N. Souza, "Progressive Artists' Group," *Patriot Magazine*, 12 February 1984, quoted in Dalmia, *The Making of Modern Indian Art*, 43.

26. See Chapter 3 for details, Dasgupta, "Calcutta Group" (1981).

27. Meera Mukherjee's own writings are the best guides to understanding this artist-artisan continuum that she consciously developed and practiced. Portions of her published diaries, *Chach-er Gabheer Theke*, are informative, as are her documentary works "Gharuas"; *Folk Metal Craft of Eastern India*; and *Metalcraftsmen of India*. Mukherjee was the senior research fellow at the Anthropological Survey of India during 1961–64.

28. For discussions of the works of K. G. Subramanyan and Swaminathan, see Kapur, *When Was Modernism*; Rebecca Brown, *Art for a Modern India*; and Khullar, *Worldly Affiliations*.

29. Jaya Appaswamy, "Some Contemporary Painters in Delhi," 52. Appaswamy's focus here is on the painters of the Dilli Shilpi Chakra, founded by artists like Bhabesh Sanyal, Kanwal Krishna, Biren De, K. S. Kulkarni, Dinkar Kaushik, Prannath Mago, Dhanraj Bhagat, et al., who were based in Delhi.

30. Goetz, "Whither Indian Art," 88.

31. *Marg* 1, no. 1 (August 1947).

32. JM, reviews of the "Exhibition of the Progressive Artists' Group," *Marg* 3, no. 3 (1949).

33. Fischer, "The Calcutta Group," 60–61.

34. For extensive discussions on Husain's national-modern aesthetic from this pe-

riod, see Kapur, "Modernist Myths and the Exile of Maqbool Fida Husain"; also Khullar, *Worldly Affiliations*.

35. Kapur, *When Was Modernism*, 298.

36. Kapur, "Secular Artist, Citizen Artist," 425.

37. Kapur, *When Was Modernism*, 272–73.

38. Kapur, *When Was Modernism*, 366.

39. Kapur, *When Was Modernism*, 366.

40. See, for instance, Dass, "Cinetopia"; Prasad, *Ideology of the Hindi Film*; Vasudevan, "Dislocations."

41. Contreras, "A Survey of Modern Mexican Art," 39.

42. Maulana Azad, opening speech, Soviet Fine Arts Exhibition, New Delhi, 3 May 1952, Document 41, in *Selected Works of Maulana Abul Kalam Azad*, vol. 6, *1951–1952*, ed. Ravinder Kumar (New Delhi: Atlantic Publishers and Distributors, 1992), 225.

43. *Selected Works of Maulana Abul Kalam Azad*, 226.

44. Khandalavala, "Art Chronicle," 1st Quarter of 1952, 100.

45. Khandalavala, "Art Chronicle," 3rd Quarter of 1952, 47–48.

46. Hemingway, *Artists on the Left*, 226.

47. Hemingway, *Artists on the Left*, 238.

48. *UNESCO Courier*, February 1956.

49. MOMA Press Release for *Family of Man*, 1.

50. MOMA Press Release, 2.

51. MOMA Press Release, 4.

52. Appasamy, "Contemporary Indian Art—1950's," 12.

53. Richard Bartholomew, "The Paintings of Ram Kumar," *Hindustan Times*, 23 October 1955, reproduced in Richard Bartholomew and Geeta Kapur, *Richard Bartholomew: The Art Critic*.

54. Bartholomew, "A Painter of Urban Predicament," *Design*, December 1957, reproduced in *Richard Bartholomew: The Art Critic*.

55. Bartholomew, introduction to *Catalogue: Exhibition at Kumar Art Gallery*, New Delhi, 1959, reproduced in *Richard Bartholomew: The Art Critic*.

56. Bartholomew, introduction to *Catalogue*.

57. Bishnu Dey, "Soviet Shilpa Pradarshani (1952)," in Bishnu Dey, *Prabandha Sangraha*, 1:179–83; Gopal Haldar, "Bangli Sanskriti Prasange," in *Gopal Haldar Rachanasamagra*, vol. 1.

58. Hore, *My Concept of Art*, 17–18.

59. Hore, *My Concept of Art*, 18.

60. I borrow this conceptualization of "diffraction" from Anne Laura Stoler's talk on the tensile and fluid formations of colonialism, "Diffracted Histories and Colonial Recursions in These Times," delivered at Leiden University, May 2016, as a part of the Global Asia Scholar Series.

61. This was a sharp turn away from the trauma and tragedy that characterized Chittaprosad's wartime famine works, which shadowed the party's support for the

Allied war effort under its "People's War" line. For the shifting registers of Chittaprosad's works before and after 1945, see Sunderason, "'As Agitator and Organiser.'"

62. Chittaprosad, Letter to Somnath Hore, 31 October 1952, in *Kshudarto Bangla*, 183. Reprinted in English translation in Mallik, *Yours Chitta*.

63. For Shankar's cartoons, see Khanduri, *Caricaturing Culture in India*.

64. *Unity*, June 1951. Courtesy of Bhupesh Gupta Bhawan, Calcutta.

65. Chittaprosad, *Kshudartho Bangla*, 181–82.

66. The WPC, though apparently non-aligned, was itself Soviet-dominated. See Wernicke, "The Unity of Peace and Socialism?"

67. Chittaprosad, *Kshudarto Bangla*, 181–82.

68. "Chittaprosad and Czechoslovakia," (author name not mentioned) essay from Orbit Press Agency, reproduced in Mallik, *Chittaprosad*, 1:159–61.

69. Wille, "A Modernist Transnational Socialist Solidarity."

70. Sidney Finkelstein, "Chittaprosad," *New York Daily Worker*, November 16, 1955, quoted in Prodyot Ghosh, *Chittaprosad*, 17.

71. Original letter in Bengali published in *Parichoy*, reprinted in English translation in Mallik, *Yours Chitta*, 10.

72. Mallik, *Yours Chitta*, 11.

73. Chittaprosad, Letter to Murari Gupta, 26 June 1953, in Mallik, *Yours Chitta*, 14.

74. Hung, "Two Images of Socialism," 52.

75. For a discussion of this genre of imagery, see Srirupa Roy, *Beyond Belief*, and Freitag, "Consumption and Identity."

76. Chittaprosad, Letter to Murari Gupta, 26 June 1953, in Mallik, *Yours Chitta*, 15.

77. Chittaprosad, Letter to Murari Gupta, 31 July 1957, in Mallik, *Yours Chitta*, 9.

78. Chittaprosad, Letter to Murari Gupta, 31 July 1957, in Mallik, *Yours Chitta*, 21.

79. Chittaprosad, Letter to Murari Gupta, 25 April 1958, in Mallik, *Yours Chitta*, 24.

80. Chittaprosad, Letter to Murari Gupta, 22 September 1958, in Mallik, *Yours Chitta*, 27.

81. Mulk Raj Anand, "Introducing Chittaprosad," 1955, unpaginated (accessed from the private papers of Chittaprosad, Delhi Art Gallery). The note would have accompanied a portfolio on the artist published in an American magazine.

82. Chittaprosad's letter to his mother, 26 July 1963, in Mallik, *Yours Chitta*, 65–66.

83. Artists Prabas Sen and Somnath Hore, for instance, wrote on Chittaprosad in the artist monograph series of the Lalit Kala Akademi, *Chittaprosad*.

84. See Pradhan, *Marxist Cultural Movement*.

85. Hore, *My Concept of Art*, 22–23.

86. Hore, *My Concept of Art*, 25.

87. See *Somnath Hore: Prints, Drawings, Posters*.

88. Hore, *My Concept of Art*, 25.

89. Ghatak, *On the Cultural Front*, 15.

90. Ghatak, 65.

91. Ghatak, 13.

92. Hore, *Until the Rain*, 14.

93. Benjamin, "Left-Wing Melancholy."

94. Ghatak, *On the Cultural Front*, 16.

95. Ghatak, 17.

96. Ghatak, 24.

97. Ghatak, 24.

98. Ghatak, 39.

99. Ghatak, 13.

100. Ghatak, 16.

101. Chittaprosad, Letter to Murari Gupta, 20 November 1960, in Mallik, *Yours Chitta*, 31.

102. Letter to Chittaprosad from "Batuk-da" (a name by which the poet Jyotirindranath Maitra was known), reproduced in Mallik, *Chittaprosad*, 1:207.

103. Martins, "Failure as Art and Art History as Failure."

104. Hore, *My Concept of Art*, 25–26.

105. Somnath Hore, in conversation with Neville Tuli, reproduced in Tuli, *The Flamed Mosaic*, 308.

106. Bennett, *Empathic Vision*, 1.

107. Nora, "Between Memory and History," 15.

108. Hore, *My Concept of Art*, 53–54.

109. Miloslav Krása, "Chittaprosad," *New Orient*, 37. Courtesy of DAG Archives and Documentation Centre.

110. The artist's sister details the loss of typed manuscripts of stories, illustration projects, and poems. See Gouri Bhattacharya, "Nihsanga Paribrajak" [A Lonely Traveler], in *Kshudarto Bangla*, 41.

111. "Remembering Chittaprosad—Indian Artist and Poet," review of *Chittaprosad: A Lifetime in India—Linocuts and Poems*, ed. Ad van Rijsewijk, *New Perspectives* 6: 32. Reprinted in Mallik, *Chittaprosad*, 1:176.

112. *Lalit Kala Contemporary* 3 (1965): 4–5.

CHAPTER 5

Parts of this chapter have appeared in S. Sunderason, "Making Art 'Modern': Revisiting Artistic Modernism in India," in *Modern Makeovers: A Handbook of Modernity in South Asia*, ed. Saurabh Dube (New Delhi: Oxford University Press, 2011), and S. Sunderason, "Framing Margins: Mao and Visuality in Twentieth-Century India," in *Art, Global Maoism, and the Chinese Cultural Revolution*, ed. Jacopo Galimberti, Noemi de Haro-Garcia, and Victoria H. F. Scott (Manchester: Manchester University Press, 2019).

1. Mitra, "Calcutta Every Day," in *Calcutta Diary*, 3–5.

2. See Mitra, *Three Score and Ten*; Samar Sen, *Babubrittanto o Prasangik* [The annals of the Babu and relevant writings].

3. See Partha Chatterjee, "The Political Culture of Calcutta," 188.

4. Biswas, "The City and the Real," 49–50.

5. Biswas, "The City and the Real," 55.

6. For sustained discussions of art during and post-Emergency, see Geeta Kapur, *When Was Modernism*, as well as her works as discussed in this chapter; Terracciano, *Art and Emergency*; Khullar, *Worldly Affiliations*; Zitzewitz, *The Art of Secularism.*

7. Ramachandran, "Notes from the Underground," 23.

8. Ramachandran, "Notes from the Underground," 23.

9. Pasolini, *The Scent of India*, 47.

10. Ginsberg, *Indian Journals*, 135.

11. Grass, *The Flounder.*

12. See Ramola Sanyal, "Contesting Refugeehood"; Pranati Chaudhuri, "Refugees in West Bengal"; Samaddar, *The Marginal Nation*; Joya Chatterji, *Spoils of Partition*, 109–59; Uditi Sen, *Citizen Refugee.*

13. See Partha Chatterjee, "The Political Culture of Calcutta," and recent empirical works like Sengupta, Sengupta, and Banerjee, "People, Politics, and Protests."

14. For histories of the splits within the CPI, see Partha Chatterjee, "The Political Culture of Calcutta"; Brass and Franda, *Radical Politics in South Asia*; Ahmad, *Lineages of the Present.*

15. See Wilson and Connery, *The WO R L D I N G Project*; Cook, *Mao's Little Red Book*; Seth, "Indian Maoism," 289–313; Kang, "Maoism."

16. For growing left-wing activism and refugees in West Bengal, see Prafulla Chakrabarti, *The Marginal Men.*

17. See Sumanta Banerjee, *India's Simmering Revolution*; Pradip Basu, *Towards Naxalbari (1953–1967).*

18. "Spring Thunder Breaks over India," *People's Daily*, 5 July 1967, reprinted in Seth, "Indian Maoism," 291.

19. Pablo Bartholomew, *The Calcutta Diaries.* See http://calcutta.pablobartholomew.com (accessed 4 December 2019) for details on the image and the project. The image could not be procured to be published in this book despite extended negotiations with the photographer.

20. "CALCUTTA," *Chicago Tribune*, March 31, 1974, http://www.chicagotribune.com/archive (online May 15, 2017).

21. Moorhouse, *Calcutta*, 337.

22. Sumanta Banerjee, *India's Simmering Revolution*, 178.

23. Asok Rudra, "Naxalite Fireworks," *Frontier*, May 30, 1970, quoted in Seth, "Smashing Statues, Dancing Sivas," 43–44.

24. Guha, "The Politics of Statues," *Frontier*, November 28, 1970, quoted in Seth, "Smashing Statues, Dancing Sivas," 44.

25. Seth, "Indian Maoism," 290.

26. Seth, "Indian Maoism," 307.

27. Mirzoeff, "On Visuality," 54.

28. See Dipesh Chakraborty, *Provincializing Europe.*

29. Mirzoeff, "On Visuality," 66.

30. Benjamin points to the play of "shock" in the city, which breaks the numb-

ness in city dwellers and engages them in critical interfaces with and understandings of situations with new radical sensibilities, thus producing new potential political aesthetics. See Walter Benjamin, "On Some Motifs in Baudelaire," 172.

31. See, for instance, Ezcurra, "On 'Shock.'" Use of Brechtian mechanisms of shock was active in theater productions in Calcutta in the 1950s–70s. See, for instance, Utpal Dutt, *Towards a Revolutionary Theatre.* In the context of artists working in Bombay in the late 1980s, Karin Zitzewitz has used the Benjaminian notion of shock in the city to describe artistic interfaces with urban streets and poverty. See Zitzewist, "The Moral Economy of the Street."

32. Anderson, *Imagined Communities.*

33. Partha Chatterjee, "Whose Imagined Community?" in Chatterjee, *The Nation and Its Fragments*; see also Chatterjee, "The Nation in Heterogeneous Time."

34. Kaviraj, "Filth and the Public Sphere."

35. I am drawing my arguments here from a previously published article, Sunderason, "Making Art 'Modern.'"

36. Kumar, "Images of Experience," 61.

37. Jogen Chowdhury, *Enigmatic Visions*, 52; see also Manas Ray, "Growing Up Refugee," 163–99.

38. See R. Siva Kumar, *Ramachandran*, 1:72. Classic compositions from this period include monumental paintings like *The Cells* (1964), *Indian Resurrection* (1965), *Encounter* (1967), and *Vision of War* (1977).

39. Kumar, *Ramachandran*, 1:79–80.

40. Ramachandran, "Notes from the Underground," 24.

41. *Drawings by Fourteen Contemporary Artists of Bengal.*

42. Works of these artists at a national level are next to none, beyond locally produced overview pieces. See, for instance, Rudrangshu Mukherjee, *Art of Bengal*, and Sinha, *Call of the Real.* In-depth biographical and analytical work has been done in Bengali; see Mrinal Ghosh, *Pashchimbang-er Chitrakala-i 1960-r Dashak ebong Doshjon Shilpi.* Some of the recent artist catalogues with biographical monographs of significance are Sandip Sarkar, *Kolkata*; Santo Datta and Rubina Karode, *After the Fall*; Majumdar, *Close to Events*; and Sandip Sarkar, *The Passion of Nikhil Biswas*, among others.

43. Adapted and translated from an article by Nikhil Biswas published in *Sambitti*, a Bengali monthly. *Drawings by Fourteen Contemporary Artists of Bengal.*

44. Sandip Sarkar, "Bijan Choudhury and Gopal Sanyal."

45. For El Salahi's use of calligraphic figuration, see Dadi, "Ibrahim El Salahi and Calligraphic Modernism."

46. Nandy, *Calcutta Painters Presents.*

47. Sandip Sarkar, "Bijan Choudhury: An Appreciation."

48. The Alliance Francaise Calcutta Presents "A Retrospective Exhibition of Paintings and Drawings by Bijan Choudhury, 14 –20 February 1977" (private collection of Bijan Choudhury).

49. Sankar Ray, "The Art of Nikhil Biswas."

50. I am grateful to the artist's son, Debabrata Biswas, and Prakash Kejriwal of Chitrakoot Gallery in Calcutta for allowing me access to Biswas's works and the diaries he kept during the early 1960s.

51. *Lalit Kala Contemporary* 6 (1967): 51.

52. Ella Datta, "Nikhil Biswas," 106.

53. Shyamal Dutta Ray, "In Muted Colours," *Illustrated Weekly of India*, October 22–28, 1989, 29 (private papers of Shyamal Dutta Ray). Courtesy of the artist's family.

54. See artist's interview in *The Statesman*, 28 September 2001 (private papers of Shyamal Dutta Ray). Courtesy of the artist's family.

55. Artist's interview in *Ananda Bazar Patrika*, 16 December 1995 (private papers of Shyamal Dutta Ray). Courtesy of the artist's family.

56. Pranab Ranjan Ray, "To carry the roots in the veins," 13–14.

57. Parimoo, *Studies in Modern Indian Art*, 98.

58. Khullar, "'We Were Looking for Our Violins,'" 112.

59. Rabin Mondal, "A Glimpse of Realities," in Mukul Dey, *Amar Katha*, as reproduced also in Datta and Karode, *After the Fall*, 256–57.

60. Sankar Ray, "The Art of Nikhil Biswas."

61. I am grateful to Asim Dasgupta at the National Library, Calcutta, for making available rare issues of *Sundaram*.

62. Kamal Sarkar, "Fifty Years of the Academy of Fine Arts," and Lady Ranu Mookerji, "Reminiscences," in *The Academy of Fine Arts, Golden Jubilee*, 1–4.

63. Malik is known to have taken the exhibition of these artists' work to the Jehangir Art Gallery in Bombay, after which the Society of Contemporary Artists was established with a group of eleven member artists. The secretary was the artist Nikhil Biswas, the other members being Malik himself, Shyamal Dutta Ray, Prakash Karmakar, Anil Baran Saha, Sanat Kar, Bijan Choudhury, Arun Bose, Kamala Roy Chowdury, Sailen Maitra, and Somnath Hore. In 1964, some of the artists splintered off from the group to form the Calcutta Painters, its founding members being Prakash Karmakar, Nikhil Biswas, and Bijan Choudhury from the Society of Contemporary Artists, with the additional members being Rabin Mondal, Gopal Sanyal, and Ranjan Rudra.

64. Rabin Mondal, *Shilpabhabona*, 75–76.

65. *Manifesto of the Calcutta Painters.*

66. Sandip Sarkar, "Artists of West Bengal," *Frontier*, 14 July 1973, 9–10. I am thankful to Sandip Sarkar for providing old *Frontier* issues.

67. Speech of Jawaharlal Nehru, First National Exhibition, 4 March 1955. Catalogues of the National Exhibition accessed at the archives of the Lalit Kala Akademi, New Delhi.

68. The Report of the Selection and Judging Committee, National Exhibition, 1956. Lalit Kala Akademi archives, New Delhi.

69. Patel, "To pick up a brush."

70. Bhabesh Sanyal, *The Vertical Woman*, 2:25–26.

71. Sanyal, *The Vertical Woman*, 2.
72. "Art Chronicle," *Marg*, 2nd and 3rd quarters 1951, 83.
73. For reviews of 1951–58 exhibitions, see *Delhi Shilpi Chakra: The Early Years*.
74. The artist in conversation with Uma Vasudev, in *Satish Gujral*, iv.
75. Alkazi, "Gujral Speaks," 51.
76. The artist, quoting Kandinsky, in Kapur, *Pictorial Space*.
77. Shoumini Sengupta, "Indian Artist Enjoys His World Audience."
78. Dalmia, "Interview with Tyeb Mehta."
79. Sheikh, "Tradition and Modernity."
80. Sheikh, "Tradition and Modernity."
81. Sheikh, "Tradition and Modernity."
82. *Lalit Kala Contemporary* 17 (April 1974): 53.
83. "Art Chronicle," *Lalit Kala Contemporary* 7 and 8 (April 1968): 67.
84. *Lalit Kala Contemporary* 22 (September 1976): 38.
85. Karl-Erich Muller and Dieter Schmid, introduction to Nikhil Biswas exhibition at the GDR in 1966 (private papers of Nikhil Biswas). Courtesy of Delhi Art Gallery.
86. Pranab Ranjan Ray, "25 Years of the Society of Contemporary Artists," unpaginated. I thank the author for allowing me to copy this rare commemoration volume, now out of print.
87. I am thankful to the Society of Contemporary Artists for giving me access to their group studio and archives in Calcutta, and providing me with a copy of the group's exhibition catalogue.
88. Pranab Ranjan Ray, "Art Chronicle," 50.
89. Ray, "Art Chronicle," 50.
90. Pritish Nandy, *Rabin Mondal: Recent Paintings at the Gallery Chemould*, 1–14 January 1971, Calcutta (private papers of Rabin Mondal). Courtesy of the artist.
91. Nandy, *Calcutta Painters Presents an Exhibition of Paintings by Rabin Mondal* (private papers of Rabin Mondal). Courtesy of the artist.
92. Paritosh Sen, "Reflections," 32.
93. Paritosh Sen, "Reflections," 32.
94. When the American critic Clement Greenberg visited India in 1967 with the *Two Decades of American Painting* exhibition, the artist Gieve Patel noted: "The American Statement seemed too complete in its own context, and offered an impassive façade" for artists in India. See Patel, "The Decades and the Seminar," 6. For reports on the exhibition, see "Two Decades of American Paintings," *The Patriot* (New Delhi), 2 March 1967. For a discussion of Greenberg's India tour, see Gupta, "In a Postcolonial Diction."
95. Kapur, "Signatures of Dissent"; see also Saloni Mathur's book on the Kapur-Sundaram archive, *A Fragile Inheritance*.
96. Kapur, "Signatures of Dissent." For issues of *Vrishchik* and *Contra'66*, I have used the digitized archives of the artist Gholammohammad Sheikh. Courtesy of Asia Art Archive, Hong Kong.

97. Kapur, "Introduction," *Vrishchik*.
98. Kapur, *Contemporary Indian Artists*, xix.
99. Kapur, *Contemporary Indian Artists*, x.
100. Kapur, *Contemporary Indian Artists*, x.
101. Kapur, *Contemporary Indian Artists*, xi.
102. Kapur, *Contemporary Indian Artists*, xi.
103. Kapur, *Place for People*, 1981.
104. Kapur, *Place for People*.
105. See, for instance, Luis, "What Is the 'People' in 'Place for People'?"
106. In India, Shivaji Panikkar has addressed this as a "need of the elite mainstream, and its assertion of authority" while discussing the Radical Group active in Kerala between 1985 and 1989. See S. K. Panikkar, "From Trivandrum to Baroda and Back"; see also S. K. Panikkar, "Indian Radical Painters and Sculptors."
107. Kapur, *When Was Modernism*, 293.
108. Kapur, *When Was Modernism*, 294.
109. Kapur, *When Was Modernism*, 333–34.
110. Kapur, *When Was Modernism*, 291.
111. Fredric Jameson, for instance, places on "Third World literature" the burden of allegory, an argument rebuffed famously by Aijaz Ahmad as a "sweeping hypothesis" akin to "First Worldism." See Jameson, "Third World Literature in the Age of Multinational Capital"; Ahmad, "Jameson's Rhetoric of Otherness and the 'National Allegory.'"
112. Moorhouse, *Calcutta*, unpaginated.

POSTSCRIPT

1. The collected papers were published in *Social Scientist* 8, nos. 5/6 [Marxism and Aesthetics] (December 1979–January 1980).
2. Kapur, "Signatures of Dissent," 81.
3. A significant recent initiative has been the exhibition *Postwar—Art between the Pacific and the Atlantic, 1945–1965*, organized by Haus der Kunst in Munich in 2016.
4. Nasar, "Lines of Control," in Dadi and Nasar, *Lines of Control*, 10.
5. Mitra, "Milestones and Ignominies," 1840.
6. See, for instance, Sunderason, "Shadow Lines."
7. Further to a European Commission Marie Curie project, Aesthetics of Decolonisation: Artists, Modernisms and Nation-States in India, West and East Pakistan, 1947–71 (2013–2017), I have elaborated on the idea in Sunderason, "Aesthetics of Decolonisation in South Asia."
8. See, for instance, Singh, "Indian Art and the Bangladesh War."

BIBLIOGRAPHY

BOOKS AND ARTICLES IN ENGLISH

Adorno, Theodor, Walter Benjamin, Ernst Bloch, Bertolt Brecht, and Georg Lukács. *Aesthetics and Politics: The Key Texts of the Classic Debate within German Marxism.* Afterword by Fredric Jameson. London: NLB, 1977. Reprinted, London: Verso, 1990.

Ahmad, Aijaz. "Jameson's Rhetoric of Otherness and the 'National Allegory.'" *Social Text* 19 (Fall 1987): 3–25.

———. *Lineages of the Present: Ideology and Politics in Contemporary South Asia.* London: Verso, 2002.

An Album of Nandalal Bose: With a Biographical Note. Calcutta: Santiniketan Asramik Sangha, 1956.

Alkazi, E. "Gujral Speaks." *Art Heritage* 6 (1986–87): 50–61.

Anand, Mulk Raj. *Conversations in Bloomsbury.* Edited by Saros Cowasjee. London: Wildwood House, 1981.

———. "Recollections on Jamini Roy" (1944). First published in *Our Time* (April 1946). Reprinted in *Lines Written to an Indian Air.* Bombay: Nalanda Publications, 1947.

Anderson, Benedict. *Imagined Communities: Reflections on the Origin and Spread of Nationalism.* 2nd ed. London: Verso, 2006.

Anjaria, Ulka. *Realism in the Twentieth-Century Indian Novel: Colonial Difference and Literary Form.* New York: Cambridge University Press, 2012.

Appadurai, Arjun. *Modernity at Large: Cultural Dimensions of Globalization.* Minneapolis: University of Minnesota Press, 1996.

Appasamy, Jaya. "Contemporary Indian Art—1950's." *Marg* 21, no. 1 (December 1967): supplement, unpaginated.

———. Introduction to *Six Haripura Panels,* by Nandalal Bose. New Delhi: Lalit Kala Akademi, 1984.

———. "Some Contemporary Painters in Delhi." *Marg* 7, no. 4 (September 1954): 47–61.

———, ed. *Twenty-five Years of Indian Art: Paintings, Sculpture, and Graphics in the Post-independence Era.* New Delhi: Lalit Kala Akademi, 1972.

Archer, W. G. *India and Modern Art.* London: Allen and Unwin, 1959.

Aston, Dore. "Artists and Politics, Politics and Art." *Social Text* 12 (Autumn 1985): 71–83. https://doi.org/10.2307/466605.

Badiou, Alain, Pierre Bourdieu, Judith Butler, Georges Didi-Huberman, Sadri Khiari, Jacques Rancière, Bruno Bosteels, Kevin Olson, and Jody Gladding. *What Is a People? New Directions in Critical Theory*. New York: Columbia University Press, 2016.

Bagal, Jogesh Chandra. *History of the Government College of Arts and Crafts, 1864–1964*. Calcutta, 1966.

Bandopadhyay, Sekhar. *Decolonization in South Asia: Meanings of Freedom in Post-independence West Bengal, 1947–52*. London: Routledge, 2009.

Banerjee, Prathama. *Politics of Time: "Primitives" and History-Writing in a Colonial Society*. New York: Oxford University Press, 2006.

Banerjee, Sumanta. *India's Simmering Revolution: The Naxalite Uprising*. London: Zed Press, 1984.

Bartholomew, Pablo. *The Calcutta Diaries*. New Delhi: Art Heritage Gallery, 2012.

Bartholomew, Richard, and Geeta Kapur. *Richard Bartholomew: The Art Critic*. Edited by Carmen Kagal, Pablo Bartholomew, and Rati Bartholomew. Noida: BART, 2012.

Basu, Pradip. *Towards Naxalbari (1953–1967): An Account of Inner-Party Ideological Struggle*. Calcutta: Progressive Publishers, 2000.

Baxandall, Lee, and Stefan Morawski, eds. *Marx and Engels on Literature and Art: A Selection of Writings*. With an introduction by Stefan Morawski. New York: International, 1973.

Bayly, Chris. *Empire and Information*. Cambridge: Cambridge University Press, 1996.

Benjamin, Walter. "Left-Wing Melancholy." In *The Weimer Republic Sourcebook*, edited by A. Kaes, M. Jay, and E. Dimendberg, 304–6. Berkeley: University of California Press, 1994.

———. "On Some Motifs in Baudelaire." In *The Writer of Modern Life: Essays on Charles Baudelaire*, edited by Michael W. Jennings. Cambridge, MA: Harvard University Press, 2006.

Bennett, Jill. *Empathic Vision: Affect, Trauma, and Contemporary Art*. Stanford: Stanford University Press, 2005.

Bhaba, Hilary E., ed. *Framing the Global: Entry Points for Research*. Bloomington: Indiana University Press, 2014.

Bhaba, Homi, ed. *Nation and Narration*. New York: Routledge, 1990.

"The Bhooka Bengal Exhibition." *People's War*, 9 January 1944.

Biswas, Moinak. "The City and the Real: *Chinnamul* and the Left Cultural Movement in the 1940s." In *City Flicks: Indian Cinema and the Urban Experience*, edited by Preben Kaarsholm, 40–59. London, Calcutta, and New York: Seagull, 2007.

Bose, Atul. *Bangla-i Chitrakala o Rajniti-r Eksho Bochor*. Calcutta: Ananda Publishers, 1993.

Bose, Nandalal. *Vision and Creation*. Translated from the Bengali original *Dristi o Sristi* by K. G. Subramanyan. Nandalal Bose Birth Centenary Publication Series. Calcutta: Visva-Bharati Publication Division, 1999.

Bose, Sugata, and Kris Manjapra, eds. *Cosmopolitan Thought Zones.* London: Palgrave Macmillan, 2010.

Bourdieu, Pierre. *The Field of Cultural Production: Essays on Art and Literature.* Edited and with an introduction by Randall Johnson. New York: Columbia University Press, 1993.

Boven, Martijn. "Metaphor and Metamorphosis: Paul Ricoeur and Gilles Deleuze on the Emergence of Novelty." PhD diss., University of Groningen, 2016.

Brass, Paul R., and Marcus F. Franda, eds. *Radical Politics in South Asia.* Cambridge: MIT Press, 1973.

Brown, Percy. *Indian Painting.* Heritage of India Series. 2nd ed. Calcutta: Associated Press Y.M.C.A. Publishing House, and London: Oxford University Press, 1917.

Brown, Rebecca. *Art for a Modern India, 1947–1980.* Durham, NC: Duke University Press, 2009.

———. "Response: Provincializing Modernity: From Derivative to Foundational." *Art Bulletin* 90, no. 4 (December 2008): 555–57.

Brzyski, Anna, ed. *Partisan Canons.* Durham, NC: Duke University Press, 2007.

"CALCUTTA." *Chicago Tribune,* March 31, 1974. http://www.chicagotribune.com/archive.

Calcutta Group. *Handbook/Catalogue,* 1953.

Carritt, Michael. *A Mole in the Crown: Memories of a British Official in India Who Worked with the Communist Underground in the 1930s.* Hove: Michael Carritt, 1985.

Casey, Edward. *Getting Back into Place.* Bloomington: Indiana University Press, 1993.

Caute, David. The Fellow-Travellers: A Postscript to the Enlightenment. London: Weidenfeld and Nicolson, 1973.

Chakrabarti, Prafulla. *The Marginal Men: The Refugees and the Left Political Syndrome in West Bengal.* Calcutta: Lumiére Books, 1990.

Chakraborty, Dipesh. *Provincializing Europe: Postcolonial Thought and Historical Difference.* Princeton Studies in Culture/Power/History. 2nd ed. Princeton, NJ: Princeton University Press, 2000.

Chakraborty, Dipesh, Rochona Majumdar, and Andrew Sartori, eds. *From the Colonial to the Postcolonial: India and Pakistan in Transition.* New Delhi: Oxford University Press, 2007.

Chakraborty, Jayanta, R. Siva Kumar, and Arun Nag, eds. *The Santiniketan Murals.* Calcutta: Seagull Books in association with Visva-Bharati, 1995.

Chakravartty, Gargi, ed. *People's Warrior: Words and Worlds of P. C. Joshi.* New Delhi: Tulika Books, 2014.

Chatterjee, Partha. *The Nation and Its Fragments.* Princeton, NJ: Princeton University Press, 1993.

———. "The Nation in Heterogeneous Time." *Indian Economic and Social History Review* 38, no. 4 (2001): 399–418. https://doi.org/10.1177/001946460103800403.

———. "The Political Culture of Calcutta." In *The Present History of West Bengal: Essays in Political Criticism.* Delhi: Oxford University Press, 1997.

———. *The Politics of the Governed: Reflections on Popular Politics.* New Delhi: Permanent Black, 2004.

Chatterjee, Ratnaboli. "'The Original Jamini Roy': A Study in the Consumerism of Art." *Social Scientist* 15, no. 1 (January 1987): 3–18.

Chatterji, Joya. *Spoils of Partition: Bengal 1947–1967.* Cambridge: Cambridge University Press, 2007.

Chatterji, R. "Rathin Moitra." *Marg* 3, no. 2 (1949): 44–46.

Chaudhuri, John. *Philosophizing the Everyday: Revolutionary Praxis and the Fate of Cultural Theory.* London: Pluto Press, 2006.

Chaudhuri, Nirad C. "An Exhibition of the Paintings of Manindra Bhushan Gupta." *Modern Review* 63, no. 2 (February 1938): 209–10.

Chaudhuri, Pramatha. "The Art Movement in Bengal." *Indian Academy of Art* 1, no. 1 (January 1920): 3–4.

Chaudhuri, Pranati. "Refugees in West Bengal: A Study of the Growth and Distribution of Refugee Settlements within CMD." Occasional Paper No. 55, Centre for Studies in Social Sciences, Calcutta, 1983.

Chittaprosad. *Hungry Bengal: A Tour through Midnapore District by Chittaprosad, in November 1943.* Bombay: New Age Printing Press, 1944.

———. "The Riches Piled Here: An Insult to Hungry Thousands Around—Painful Sights in Shayamaprosad's Hooghly Home-Village." *People's War*, 6 August 1944.

———. "Zainul Abedin." *People's War*, 21 January 1945.

Chowdhury, Jogen. *Enigmatic Visions.* Glenbarra Art Museum, 2005.

Communist Statement of Policy: For the Struggle for Full Independence and People's Democracy. Bombay: People's Publishing House, 1947.

Contreras, Guillermo Garces. "A Survey of Modern Mexican Art." *Marg* 6, no. 3 (1952): 39.

Cook, Alexander C., ed. *Mao's Little Red Book: A Global History.* Cambridge: Cambridge University Press, 2014.

Coomaraswamy, Ananda. *Essays in National Idealism.* Madras: Natesan, 1909.

Croft, Andy. *Comrade at Heart: A Life of Randall Swingler.* Manchester: Manchester University Press, 2003.

Dadi, Iftikhar. "Ibrahim El Salahi and Calligraphic Modernism in a Comparative Perspective." *South Atlantic Quarterly* 109, no. 3 (Summer 2010).

———. *Modernism and the Art of Muslim South Asia.* Chapel Hill: University of North Carolina Press, 2010.

Dadi, Iftikhar, and Hammad Nasar, eds. *Lines of Control: Partition as a Productive Space.* A Green Cardamom Project. Ithaca, NY: Herbert F. Johnson Museum of Art, Cornell University, 2012.

Dalmia, Yashodhara. "Interview with Tyeb Mehta." *Art Heritage* 9 (1989–90): 76–85.

———. *The Making of Modern Indian Art: The Progressives.* New Delhi: Oxford University Press, 2001.

Damodaran, Sumangala. *The Radical Impulse: Music in the Tradition of the Indian People's Theatre Association.* New Delhi: Tulika Books, 2017.

Das, Sisir Kumar, ed. *The English Writings of Rabindranath Tagore*. Vol. 3. New Delhi: Sahitya Akademi, 1996.

Das, Suranjan. *Communal Riots in Bengal, 1905–1947*. New York: Oxford University Press, 1991.

Das, Tarakchandra. *Bengal Famine (1943): As Revealed in a Survey of Destitutes in Calcutta*. Calcutta: Calcutta University Press, 1949.

Dasgupta, Arun, Qamrul Hasan, Adinath Mukherji, and Safiuddin Ahmed, eds. *Bengal Painters' Testimony: An Album of Reproduction of Paintings and Sculptures* [plates]. With an introduction by Bishnu Dey. Exhibition organized at the Eighth Annual Session of the All India Students' Federation, Calcutta, December 1944.

Dasgupta, Prodosh. "The Calcutta Group." *The Republic* (27 August 1949). Private papers of Prodosh Dasgupta. Courtesy of the artist's son, Pradeep Dasgupta.

———. "The Calcutta Group: Its Aims and Achievements." *Lalit Kala Contemporary* 31 (April 1981).

———. "Essays on Art." Review of K. G. Subramanyan, *Moving Focus*. Lalit Kala Academi, New Delhi, 1978. *Hindustan Times Weekly*, 8 April 1979.

———. *My Sculpture*. Calcutta: Oxford Book and Stationery Co., 1955.

———. *Smritikatha Shilpakatha*. Calcutta: Pratikshan Publications, 1986.

Dass, Manishita. "Cinetopia: Leftist Street Theatre and the Musical Production of the Metropolis in 1950s Bombay Cinema." *Positions* 25, no. 1 (2017): 101–24. https://doi.org/10.1215/10679847-3710353.

Datta, Ella. "Nikhil Biswas: Clowns and Martyrs." *Art Heritage* 8 (1988–89): 105–6.

Datta, Santo, and Rubina Karode, eds. *After the Fall: Time, Life, and Art of Rabin Mondal*. New Delhi: Delhi Art Gallery, 2005.

Datta, Sudhindranath. *The World of Twilight: Essays and Poems, and Other Essays*. Bombay: Oxford University Press, 1970.

Degras, Jane, ed. *The Communist International, 1919–1943. Documents. Volume 3, 1929–1943*. 2nd ed. London and New York: Routledge, 1971. First published Oxford, 1965.

Delhi Shilpi Chakra, The Early Years. Catalogue of exhibition curated by Pran Nath Mago, 4 December 1997 to 11 January 1998. New Delhi: National Gallery of Modern Art, 1998. Private papers of Bhabesh Sanyal. Courtesy of the artist's daughter, Amba Sanyal.

Denning, Michael. *The Cultural Front: The Laboring of American Culture in the Twentieth Century*. London: Verso, 1997.

Dev, Amiya. *Sudhindranath Datta*. New Delhi: Sahitya Akademi, 1982.

Dey, Bishnu. "Art of Jamini Roy." *Sahityapatra* (November 1948).

———. *In the Sun and the Rain: Essays on Aesthetics*. New Delhi: People's Publishing House, 1972.

———. Introduction to *Calcutta Group Presents 8 Monochrome Reproductions of Nirode Mazumdar's Paintings*. Modern Art Publication, vol. 1, no. 2. Calcutta: The Book Emporium Limited, undated (c. 1946).

———. *Jamini Ray: Tnar Shilpachinta o Shilpakarma Bishaye Kayekti Chinta.* Calcutta: Asha Prakasani, 1977.

———. *Water My Roots: Essays by and on Bishnu Dey.* Edited by Samir Dasgupta. Calcutta: Writers' Workshop, 1973.

———. "When Artists Awake . . . Pen-Picture of the Calcutta Group." *People's War,* 15 April 1945.

Dey, Bishnu, and John Irwin. *Jamini Roy.* Catalogue of Indian Society of Oriental Art, 1944.

Dey, Mukul. Foreword to *Exhibition of Drawings and Paintings by Jamini Roy.* Government School of Art, Calcutta, 30 September–7 October 1929. Courtesy of the Archive of the Indian Society of Oriental Art, Calcutta.

Dhanagare, D. N. *Peasant Movement in India, 1920–50.* New Delhi: Oxford University Press, 1983.

Drawings by Fourteen Contemporary Artists of Bengal. With an introduction by Nirode Mazumdar. Privately published by Priti Mukherjee and Bhawani Mullick. Calcutta, 1970.

Duara, Prasenjit, ed. *Decolonization: Perspectives from Now and Then.* London: Routledge, 2004.

During, Simon, ed. *The Cultural Studies Reader.* London: Routledge, 1993.

Dutt, Gurusaday. "Art of Bengal." *Modern Review* (May 1932).

———. *Folk Arts and Crafts of Bengal: Gurusaday Dutt Collected Papers.* Calcutta: Seagull Books, 1990.

Dutt, Utpal. *Towards a Revolutionary Theatre.* Calcutta: M. C. Sarkar, 1982.

Ellman, Maud. *The Hunger Artists: Starving, Writing, and Imprisonment.* Cambridge, MA: Harvard University Press, 1993.

Elwin, Verrier. *The Tribal World of Verrier Elwin.* New Delhi: Oxford University Press, 1964.

Enwezor, Okwui. "Modernity and Postcolonial Ambivalence." *South Atlantic Quarterly* 109, no. 3 (Summer 2010): 595–620.

Enwezor, Okwui, Katy Siegel, and Ulrich Wilmes. *Postwar: Art between the Pacific and the Atlantic, 1945–1965.* Munich: Haus der Kunst, 2016.

Ezcurra, Mara Polgovsky. "On 'Shock': The Artistic Imagination of Benjamin and Brecht." *Contemporary Aesthetics* 10 (2012). Accessed February 2017. http://www.contempaesthetics.org/newvolume/pages/article.php?articleID=659.

Feldman, Hannah. *From a Nation Torn: Decolonizing Art and Representation in France, 1945–1962.* Durham, NC: Duke University Press, 2014.

Finkelstein, Sidney. *Art and Society.* New York: International Publishers, 1947.

Fischer, Klaus. "The Calcutta Group." *Marg* 6, no. 4 (1953).

Foucault, Michel. *Archaeology of Knowledge and Discourse on Language.* Translated by A. M. Sheridan Smith. New York: Pantheon Books, 1972.

Freitag, Sandria B. "Consumption and Identity: Imagining 'Everyday Life' through Popular Visual Culture." In *Tasveer Ghar: A Digital Archive of South Asian Popular Visual Culture,* 2010. Accessed 20 April 2016.

Gandhi. Speech at Faizpur, "A Villagers' Exhibition." *Harijan*, 2 January 1937.

Gangooly, O. C. "Art of a Bengali Sculptor." *Modern Review* (May 1921).

———. "Interpreters of New Order of Beauty, Calcutta Group, Revolt against Traditional Art Forms." *Nation* (17 January 1949).

Garimela, Annapurna, ed. *Mulk Raj Anand: Shaping the Indian Modern*. Mumbai: Marg Publications, 2005.

Ghatak, Ritwik. *I Strode My Road: Montage of a Mind.* Translated by Sudipta Chakraborty. Calcutta: Monfakira, 2013.

———. *On the Cultural Front.* A thesis submitted by Ritwik Ghatak to the Communist Party of India in 1954. Calcutta: Ritwik Memorial Trust, 2000.

Ghose, Gopal. *Gopal Ghose.* Text by Dwijendra Maitra. Edited by Jaya Appaswamy. Lalit Kala Academi Monograph Series, Contemporary Indian Art. New Delhi: Lalit Kala Akademi, 1966.

Ghosh, Chilka. "The Sight/Site of Woman in the Art of the Forties: Reality, Realism, and Representation." *Social Scientist* 28, nos. 3–4 (March–April 2000). https://doi.org/10.2307/3518187.

Ghosh, Kali Charan. *Famines in Bengal, 1770–1943*. Calcutta: Indian Associated Publishing, 1944.

Ghosh, Prodyot. *Chittaprosad: A Doyen of Indian Art.* Calcutta: Shilpayan Artists' Society, 1995.

Ginsberg, Allen. *Indian Journals.* San Francisco: Dave Haselwood Books and City Lights Books, 1970.

Ginwala, Natasha. "So Many Hungers." *South Magazine*, no. 8 (documenta 14, no. 3). Accessed 6 April 2019. https://www.documenta14.de/en/south/888_so_many_hungers.

"Gobardhan Ash's Diary." *Oitihashik* 10, nos. 1–2 (February 2002).

Goetz, Hermann. "Whither Indian Art." *Marg* 1, no. 2 (January 1947): 88.

Goodway, D., ed. *Herbert Read Reassessed.* Liverpool: Liverpool University Press, 1998.

Gopal, Priyamvada. *Literary Radicalism in India: Gender, Nation, and the Transition to Independence.* London: Routledge, 2005.

Gorky, Maxim. Speech at the Soviet Writers' Congress. Reproduced in *Soviet Writers' Congress 1934: The Debate on Socialist Realism and Modernism in the Soviet Union.* London: Lawrence and Wishart, 1977. Originally published in *Problems of Soviet Literature.* London: Martin Lawrence, 1935.

Gramsci, Antonio. *Selections from Prison Notebooks.* Edited and translated by Quintin Hoare and Geoffrey Nowell-Smith. London: Lawrence and Wishart, 1971.

Grass, Günter. *The Flounder.* Translated by Ralph Mannheim. Harmondsworth, UK: Penguin, 1979.

Greenough, Paul R. *Prosperity and Misery in Modern Bengal: The Bengal Famine of 1943–44*. New York: Oxford University Press, 1977.

Guha, Moni. "The Politics of Statues." *Frontier*, 28 November 1970.

Guha-Thakurta, Tapati. *The Making of a New "Indian" Art: Artists, Aesthetics, and Nationalism in Bengal, c. 1850–1920*. Cambridge: Cambridge University Press, 1992.

———. "Visualizing the Nation: The Iconography of a 'National Art' in Modern India." *Journal of Arts and Ideas*. Special issue on Modern Indian Art, nos. 27–28 (March 1995): 7–41.

Gupta, Atreyee. "In a Postcolonial Diction: Postwar Abstraction and the Aesthetics of Modernization." *Art Journal* 72, no. 3 (2013).

Haldar, Asit. *Art and Tradition*. Lucknow, 1938. Reprint, Lucknow: Universal Publishers, 1952.

Haldar, Gopal, ed. *Revolutionary Art: A Symposium*. Unpaginated. Calcutta: Progressive Book Forum, 1944.

Hall, Stuart. "Black Diaspora Artists in Britain: Three 'Moments' in Post-war History." *History Workshop Journal* 61, no. 1 (2006): 3. https://doi.org/10.1093/hwj/dbi074.

Hall, Stuart, and Doreen Massey. "Interpreting the Crisis." *Soundings: A Journal of Politics and Culture* 44 (Spring 2010): 57–71.

"Haripura Notes III." *Harijan*, 5 March 1938.

Harney, Elizabeth. "The Densities of Modernism." *South Atlantic Quarterly* 109, no. 3 (Summer 2010): 475–503. https://doi.org/10.1215/00382876-2010-002.

———. *In Senghor's Shadow: Art, Politics, and the Avant-Garde in Senegal, 1960–1995*. Durham, NC: Duke University Press, 2004.

Hauser, Arnold. "Propaganda, Ideology, and Art." In *Aspects of History and Class Consciousness*, edited by István Mészáros and T. B. Bottomore. New York: Routledge and Kegan Paul, 1971.

Hemingway, Andrew. *Artists on the Left: American Artists and the Communist Movement, 1926–56*. New Haven, CT: Yale University Press, 2002.

Hills, Patricia. "Art and Politics in the Popular Front: The Union Work and Social Realism of Philip Evergood." In *The Social and the Real: Political Art in the 1930s in the Western Hemisphere*, edited by Alejandro Anreus, Diana L. Linden, and Jonathan Weinberg. University Park, PA: Penn State University Press, 2006.

Home, Amal, ed. *The Art of Subho Tagore*. Calcutta: Art and Letters India Publishers, 1945.

Hore, Somnath. *My Concept of Art*. Translated by Somnath Zutshi. Calcutta: Seagull Books, 2009.

———. *The Tea-Garden Journal*. Calcutta: Seagull Books, 2009.

———. *Until the Rain: Fragments from an Artist's Life*. Calcutta: Seagull Books, 2008.

———. *Wounds*. Booklet published to coincide with an exhibition of sculptures and works on paper (1992).

Hung, Chai-tai. "Two Images of Socialism: Woodcuts in Chinese Communist Politics." *Comparative Studies in Society and History* 39, no. 1 (January 1997): 34–60.

Huyssen, Andreas. "Geographies of Modernism in a Globalizing World." *New German Critique* 100 (Winter 2007): 189–207.

"The Indian Exhibition: Cuttings from the German Press." *Rupam* (July–December 1923): 80–81.

Indian People's Theatre Association. Bulletin no. 1 (July 1943).

Jahangir, Burhunuddinkhan. *The Quest of Zainul Abedin*. Dhaka: International Centre for Bengal Studies, 1993.

Jain, Kajri. *Gods in the Bazaar: The Economies of Indian Calendar Art*. Durham, NC: Duke University Press, 2010.

James, C. Vaughan. *Soviet Socialist Realism: Origins and Theory*. London: Macmillan, 1973.

Jameson, Fredric. "Third World Literature in the Age of Multinational Capital." *Social Text* 15 (Fall 1986): 65–88.

Janah, Sunil. *Photographing India*. New Delhi: Oxford University Press, 2013.

Joshi, P. C. *Indian Communist Party: Its Policy and Work in the War of Liberation*. With an introduction by Harry Pollitt. London: Communist Party of Great Britain, 1942.

———. *The New Situation and Our Tasks*. Resolution of the Central Committee of the Communist Party of India, passed at its meeting in December 1945. Bombay: New Age Printing Press for the Communist Party of India, 1945.

———. *Who Lives If Bengal Dies?* Bombay: People's Publishing House, November 1943.

Jumabhoy, Zehra, and Boon Hoi Tan. *The Progressive Revolution: Modern Art for a New India*. Asia Society Museum, New York, 14 September 2018 to 20 January 2019.

Kane, Patrick. *The Politics of Art in Modern Egypt: Aesthetics, Ideology, and Nation-building*. London: I. B. Tauris, 2013.

Kang, Liu. "Maoism: Revolutionary Globalism for the Third World Revisited." *Comparative Literature Studies* 52, no. 1 (2015): 12–28.

Kapur, Geeta. "Art and Internationalism." *Economic and Political Weekly* 13, no. 19 (13 sMay 1978), 802.

———. "Art in These Dark Times." *Economic and Political Weekly* 12, no. 11 (12 March 1977): 450–51.

———. *Contemporary Indian Artists*. New Delhi: Vikash Publications, 1978.

———. "Introduction." *Vrishchik* 4, no. 4 (December 1973).

———. "Modernist Myths and the Exile of Maqbool Fida Husain." In *Barefoot across the Nation: Maqbool Fida Husain and the Idea of India*, edited by Sumathi Ramaswamy. London, New York: Routledge, 2011.

———. "Partisan Modernity." In *Mulk Raj Anand: Shaping the Indian Modern*, edited by Annapurna Garimella. Mumbai: Marg Publications, 2005.

———. *Pictorial Space: A Point of View on Contemporary Indian Art*. Catalogue of exhibition curated by Geeta Kapur. Rabindra Bhawan Galleries, 14 December 1977–3 January 1978. New Delhi: Lalit Kala Akademi, 1979.

———. *Place for People: An Exhibition of Paintings by Jogen Chowdhury, Bhupen Khakhar, Nalini Malani, Sudhir Patwardhan, Gulam Mohammed Sheikh, Vivian Sundaram*. Jehangir Art Gallery, Bombay. 9–15 November 1981 and Rabindra Bhavan, New Delhi, 21 November–3 December 1981.

———. "Realism and Modernism: A Polemic for Present-Day Art." *Social Scientist* 8 [Marxism and Aesthetics], nos. 5–6 (December 1979–January 1980): 91–100.

———. "Secular Artist, Citizen Artist." In *Art and Social Change: A Reader*, edited by Will Bradley and Charles Esche. London: Tate Publishing in association with Afterall, 2007.

———. "Signatures of Dissent." *Art News Magazine of India* 6, no. 2 (2001): 80–81; reproduced in *Another Life: the Digitized Personal Archive of Geeta Kapur and Vivan Sundaram*. Courtesy of Asia Art Archive, Hong Kong. Accessed online April 14, 2017.

———. *When Was Modernism: Essays on Contemporary Cultural Practice in India*. New Delhi: Tulika, 2000.

Kaviraj, Sudipta. "The Art of Despair: The Sense of the City." In *The Invention of Private Life*. New Delhi: Permanent Black, 2014.

———. "Filth and the Public Sphere: Concepts and Practices about Space in Calcutta." *Public Culture* 10, no. 1 (1997): 108–9.

———. *The Imaginary Institution of India: Politics and Ideas*. New York: Columbia University Press, 2010.

Kelleher, Margaret. *The Feminization of Famine: Expressions of the Inexpressible?* Durham, NC: Duke University Press, 1997.

Khan, Yasmin. *The Raj at War: A People's History of India's Second World War*. New Delhi: Penguin, 2016.

Khandalavala, Karl. "Art Chronicle." 1st quarter of 1952. *Marg* 5 (1952).

———. "Art Chronicle." 3rd quarter of 1952. *Marg* 5 (1952).

Khanduri, Ritu. *Caricaturing Culture in India: Cartoons and History in the Modern World on Shankar*. Cambridge: Cambridge University Press, 2014.

Khullar, Sonal. "'We Were Looking for Our Violins': The Bombay Painters and Poets, c. 1965–1976." *Archives of Asian Art* 68, no. 2 (October 2018): 111–32.

———. *Worldly Affiliations: Artistic Practice, National Identity, and Modernism in India, 1930–1990*. Berkeley: University of California Press, 2015.

Koselleck, Reinhart. *Futures Past: On the Semantics of Historical Time*. Translated and with an introduction by Keith Tribe. New York: Columbia University Press, 2004.

Kumar, R. Siva. "Images of Experience. An Interview with Jogen Chowdhury." *Nandimukh*. Special issue on Jogen Chowdhury (January 2003).

———. *Ramachandran*. Vol. 1. New Delhi: Vadehra Art Gallery, 2003.

Kumarsinha. "Modern Movement of Indian Art." *Four Arts Annual* (1935).

Laclau, Ernesto. *Emancipations*. London and New York: Verso, 1996.

Lahiri, Somnath. *Collected Writings*. Vol. 2, *1933–47*. Calcutta: Manisha, 1986.

———. *Queues of Death*. Bombay: People's Publishing House, 1944.

Lahusen, Thomas, and Evgeny Dobrenko, eds. *Socialist Realism without Shores*. Durham, NC: Duke University Press, 1997.

Leyden, Rudi von. "City Exhibition of Paintings, Calcutta Group's Work." *Times of India*, 30 April 1945.

Luis, Sandip. K. "What Is the 'People' in 'Place for People'?" *The Baroda Pamphlet*, no. 5 (August–September, 2013). Accessed online May 10, 2017.

Lukács, György. "Critical Realism and Socialist Realism." In *The Meaning of Contemporary Realism*, translated by John and Necke Mander. London: Merlin, 1963.

———. *Writer and Critic and Other Essays*. Edited and translated by Arthur Kahn. Lincoln: iUniverse, Inc., and Authors Guild Backinprint.com Edition, 2005. Originally published by Pontypool, Wales: Merlin Press, 1970.

"Maharashtrians of All Walks Aid Bengal." *People's War*, 2 July 1944.

Majumdar, Manashij. *Close to Events: Works of Bikash Bhattacharya*. New Delhi: Niyogi Books, 2007.

Mallik, Sanjoy. *Chittaprosad*. Vols. 1 and 2. New Delhi: Delhi Art Gallery, 2011.

———, ed. *A Sketchbook of 30 Portraits by Chittaprosad*. New Delhi: Delhi Art Gallery, 2011.

———. "Social Realism in the Visual Arts: 'Man-Made' Famine and Political Ferment, Bengal 1943–46." In *Art and Visual Culture in India, 1947–2007*, edited by Gayatri Sinha. Bombay: Marg Publications, 2009.

———. *Yours Chitta: Translated Excerpts from Select Letters of Chittaprosad*. New Delhi: Delhi Art Gallery, 2011.

Manifesto of the Calcutta Painters, reproduced in 25th Anniversary Exhibition of the Calcutta Painters 1–10 March 1990. Birla Academy of Art and Culture, Calcutta. Private papers of Rabin Mondal. Courtesy of the artist.

Manjapra, Kris. "Communist Internationalism and Transcolonial Recognition." In *Cosmopolitan Thought Zones*, edited by Sugata Bose and Kris Manjapra. London: Palgrave Macmillan, 2010.

Marcuse, Herbert. *The Aesthetic Dimension: Toward a Critique of Marxist Aesthetics*. New York: Beacon Press, 1979. Originally published in 1977.

———. *Art and Liberation: Collected Papers of Herbert Marcuse*. Vol. 4. New York: Routledge, 2007.

Margolies, David, ed. *Writing the Revolution: Cultural Criticism from Left Review*. London: Pluto Press, 1998.

Martins, Susana S. "Failure as Art and Art History as Failure." *Third Text*, online, no. 2 (August 2015). Accessed 18 May 2016. http://thirdtext.org/Failure-As-Art.

Masereel, Frans. *Passionate Journey: A Vision in Woodcuts*. New York: Dover Publications, 2007.

Mathur, Saloni. *A Fragile Inheritance: Radical Stakes in Contemporary Indian Art*. Durham, NC: Duke University Press, 2019.

———. "Response: Belonging to Modernism." *Art Bulletin* 90, no. 4 (December 2008): 558–60.

McLean, Stuart. *The Event and Its Terrors: Ireland, Famine, Modernity*. Stanford: Stanford University Press, 2004.

Milford, Mary E. "A Modern Primitive." *Horizon* 10, no. 59 (November 1944).

Mirzoeff, Nicholas. "On Visuality." *Journal of Visual Culture* 5, no. 1 (2006): 53–79.

Mitchell, Timothy. "The Stage of Modernity." In *Questions of Modernity*, edited by Timothy Mitchell. Minneapolis: University of Minnesota Press, 2000.

Mitra, Asok. *Calcutta Diary*. London: Frank Cass, 1977. Reprint, Calcutta: Paranjoy Guha-Thakurta, 2014.

———. "Milestones and Ignominies." Review of *Marxist Cultural Movement in India: Chronicles and Documents (1936–47)*, compiled and edited by Sudhi Pradhan; distributors: National Book Agency, Calcutta. *Economic and Political Weekly* 14, no. 45 (10 November 1979).

———. *Three Score and Ten*. Calcutta: Mandira, 1987.

Mitter, Partha. *Art and Nationalism in Colonial India, 1850–1922: Occidental Orientations*. Cambridge: Cambridge University Press, 1994.

———."Interventions: Decentering Modernism: Art History and Avant-Garde Art from the Periphery." *Art Bulletin* 90, no. 4 (December 2008), 531–48.

———. *The Triumph of Modernism: India's Artists and the Avant-garde, 1922–47*. London: Reaktion Books, 2007.

MOMA Press Release for *Family of Man*.

Moorhouse, Geoffrey. *Calcutta*. London: Weidenfeld and Nicolson, 1971.

Mouffe, Chantal. *On the Political*. New York: Routledge, 2005.

Mukherjee, Benodebehari. "The Santiniketan School of Art." *Visva-Bharati Quarterly*, n.s. (May 1935): 86–97.

Mukherjee, Hiren, ed. *Us/A People's Symposium*, published on behalf of the Anti-Fascist Writers' and Artists' Association. Calcutta, 1943.

———. *Tari Hote Tir*. Calcutta: Manisha Granthalaya, 1974.

———, ed. *Towards Progressive Literature*. Calcutta, 1936.

Mukherjee, Janam. *Hungry Bengal: War, Famine, and the End of Empire*. London: Hurst, 2015.

Mukherjee, Madhushree. *Churchill's Secret War: The British Empire and the Ravaging of India during World War II*. New York: Basic Books, 2010.

Mukherjee, Meera. *Folk Metal Craft of Eastern India*. New Delhi: All India Handicrafts Board, Ministry of Commerce, Government of India, and Publications Division, Ministry of Information and Broadcasting, Government of India, 1977.

———. "Gharuas: A Metal Artisan Group and Their Art," *Man in India* 54, no. 4 (1973).

———. *Metalcraftsmen of India*. Calcutta: Anthropological Survey of India, Government of India, 1978.

Mukherjee, Rudrangshu. *Art of Bengal: A Vision Defined, 1955–1975*. Calcutta: Centre of International Modern Art, 2003.

Mukhopadhyay, Dhurjatiprasad. "The Crisis in Bengali Culture." *Four Arts Annual*, 1935.

———. "On the Social Background of Contemporary Indian Painting (with particular reference to Bengal)." *New Indian Literature* 1, no. 1 (1938).

Nehru, Jawaharlal. *Selected Works of Jawaharlal Nehru*. New Delhi: Orient Longman, 1975.

Nercam, Nicolas. *Peindre au Bengale (1939–1977): Contribution à Une Lecture Plurielle de la Modernité*. Paris: L'Harmattan, 2005.

Nora, Pierre. "Between Memory and History: *Les Lieux de Mémoire*." *Representations* 26 (Spring 1989).

Okeke-Agulu, Chika. *Postcolonial Modernism: Art and Decolonization in Twentieth-Century Nigeria*. Durham, NC: Duke University Press, 2015.

Overstreet, Gene, and Marshall Windmiller. *Communist Party of India, Miscellaneous Pamphlets*. Berkeley and Los Angeles: University of California Press, 1959.

Pandey, Gyanendra. "In Defense of the Fragment: Writing about Hindu-Muslim Riots in India Today." *Representations* 37 (Winter 1992). Special issue, *Imperial Fantasies and Postcolonial Histories*, 27–55. https://doi.org 10.2307/2928653.

———. *Remembering Partition: Violence, Nationalism, and Independence in India*. Cambridge: Cambridge University Press, 2001.

Panikkar, K. N. "Left Cultural Intervention: Perspectives and Practice." *Economic and Political Weekly* 32, no. 15 (April 12–18, 1997).

Panikkar, S. K. "From Trivandrum to Baroda and Back: A Re-Reading." *Nandan* 26 (2006).

———. "Indian Radical Painters and Sculptors: Crisis of Political Art in Contemporary India." In *Creative Arts in Modern India: Essays in Comparative Criticism*, vol. 2, edited by Ratan Parimoo. New Delhi: Books and Books, 1995.

Parimoo, Ratan. *Studies in Modern Indian Art: A Collection of Essays*. New Delhi: Kanak, 1975.

Pasolini, Pier Paolo. *The Scent of India*. Translated by David Clive Price. London: Olive Press, 1984.

Patel, Gieve. "The Decades and the Seminar." *Contra '66*, nos. 5–6 (1967).

———. "To pick up a brush." *Third Text*. Special issue, *Partitions* 31, nos. 2–3 (November 2017): 289–300. Originally published in *Contemporary Indian Art*. New York: Grey Art Gallery, New York University, 1985.

Pinkney, Tony, ed. *The Politics of Modernism: Against the New Conformists*. London: Verso, 2007.

Pinney, Christopher. *Photos of the Gods*. London: Reaktion, 2010.

Polgovsky, Mara Ezcurra. "On 'Shock': The Artistic Imagination of Benjamin and Brecht." *Contemporary Aesthetics* 10 (2012).

Postwar—Art between the Pacific and the Atlantic, 1945–1965. Organized by Haus der Kunst in collaboration with Tate Modern, London; the Institut für Kunstgeschichte, Ludwig-Maximilians-Universität; and the Zentralinstitut für Kunstgeschichte, Munich.

Pradhan, Sudhi, ed. *Marxist Cultural Movement in India: Chronicles and Documents*. Vol. 1, Calcutta: Pustak Bipani, 1979; Vols. 2 and 3, Calcutta: Nabanna, 1982.

Prasad, M. Madhava. *Ideology of the Hindi Film: A Historical Construction*. New Delhi: Oxford University Press, 1998. *Marg* 3, no. 3 (1949).

Rahman, Ram. *Sunil Janah: Photographs 1939–1971*. New York: Gallery 678, 1998.

Ramachandran, A. "Notes from the Underground." *Art Heritage* 6 (1986–87).

Ramaswamy, Sumathi, ed. *Barefoot across the Nation: Maqbool Fida Husain and the Idea of India*. London and New York: Routledge, 2011.

———. *Beyond Appearances? Visual Practices and Ideologies in Modern Art*. New Delhi; Thousand Oaks, CA: Sage, 2003.

Rancière, Jacques. *Figures of History*. Translated by Julie Rose. London: Polity Press, 2014.

———. *Staging the People: The Proletarian and His Double*. London: Verso, 2011.

Rasul, Abdul. *History of the Kisan Sabha*. Calcutta: National Book Agency, 1974.

Ray, Manas. "Growing Up Refugee: On Memory and Locality." In *Refugees in West Bengal: Institutional Practices and Contested Identities*, edited by Pradip Kumar Bose. Calcutta: Mahanirban Calcutta Research Group, 2000.

Ray, Pranab Ranjan. "Art Chronicle." *Lalit Kala Contemporary* 2 (1962): 50.

———. "The Political in Art: A Review of Somnath Hore, *Tebhaga: An Artist's Diary and Sketchbook*." *Journal of Arts and Ideas*, no. 22 (April 1992): 65–80.

———. "Somnath Hore and the Wounds." Introduction to *Somnath Hore*. New Delhi: Lalit Kala Akademi, undated.

———. "To carry the roots in the veins." *Lalit Kala Contemporary* 24–25 (September 1977–April 1978).

Ray, Sankar. "The Art of Nikhil Biswas." *Patriot* (29 October 1967). Private papers of Nikhil Biswas. Courtesy of Delhi Art Gallery.

Read, Herbert. "What Is Revolutionary Art?" In *On Revolutionary Art*, edited by Betty Rea. London: Wishart, 1935.

Report on the Lucknow Congress. "A Unique Exhibition." *Harijan* 4 (April 1936).

Rodgers, Daniel T. "Cultures in Motion: An Introduction." In *Cultures in Motion*, edited by Daniel T. Rodgers, Bhavani Raman, and Helmut Reimitz. Princeton, NJ: Princeton University Press, 2013.

Roy, Anuradha. *Cultural Communism in Bengal*. New Delhi: Primus, 2018.

Roy, Srirupa. *Beyond Belief: India and the Politics of Postcolonial Nationalism*. Durham, NC: Duke University Press, 2007.

Roy, Subodh, ed. *Communism in India: Unpublished Documents, 1935–45*. Calcutta: Ganashakti Printers, 1976.

Roychodhury, Ranu. "Documentary Photography, Decolonization, and the Making of 'Secular Icons': Reading Sunil Janah's Photographs from the 1940s through the 1950s." *BioScope* 8, no. 1: 46–80.

Samaddar, Ranabir. *The Marginal Nation: Transborder Migration from Bangladesh to West Bengal*. Calcutta: Sage, 1999.

Samuel, Raphael. *Island Stories: Unravelling Britain*. Vol. 2 of *Theatres of Memory*, edited by Alison Light, with Sally Alexander and Gareth Stedman Jones. London, New York: Verso, 1998.

Santhal Family: Positions around an Indian Sculpture. Curated by Anshuman Dasgupta, Grant Watson, and Monica Szewczyk. Antwerp: Museum van Hedendaagse, 2008.

Sanyal, Bhabesh. *The Vertical Woman: Reminiscences of B. C. Sanyal, from 1947 to the Present*. Vol. 2. New Delhi: National Gallery of Modern Art, 1992.

Sanyal, Ramola. "Contesting Refugeehood: Squatting as Survival in Post-Partition Calcutta." *Social Identities: Journal for the Study of Race, Nation, and Culture* 15, no. 1 (January 2009).

Sarkar, Kamal. *The Academy of Fine Arts, Golden Jubilee: A Commemoration, 1933–1983*. Calcutta: Academy of Fine Arts, 1983.

Sarkar, Nikhil. *A Matter of Conscience: Artists Bear Witness to the Great Bengal Famine of 1943*. Translated by Satyabrata Dutta. Foreword by Amartya Sen. Calcutta: Punascha, 1998.

Sarkar, Sandip. "Artists of West Bengal." *Frontier*, 14 July 1973.

———. "Bijan Choudhury: An Appreciation." *Art Heritage* 6 (1986–87): 35–37.

———. "Bijan Choudhury and Gopal Sanyal." *Lalit Kala Contemporary* 22 (September 1976): 18–20.

———. *Kolkata: Through the Paintings of Prakash Karmakar*. Calcutta: Pratikshan, 2004.

———. *The Passion of Nikhil Biswas*. Ahmedabad: Mapin, 2010.

Sarkar, Sumit. *Modern India, 1887–1947*. New Delhi: Macmillan, 1983.

Schmitt, Carl. *The Theory of the Partisan: A Commentary/Remark on the Concept of the Political*. Berlin: Dunker and Humblot, 1963. English translation © Michigan State University Press, 2004.

Sen, Amartya. *The Political Economy of Hunger*. Vol. 1, *Entitlement and Well-being*. Oxford: Clarendon Press, 1990.

———. *Poverty and Famines: An Essay on Entitlement and Deprivation*. Delhi: Oxford University Press, 1981.

Sen, Arun. *Bishnu Dey*. New Delhi: Sahitya Akademi, 1993.

———. *Sudhindranath/Bishnu De: Ei Maitri, Ei Manantar*. Calcutta: Asha Prakasani, 1977.

Sen, Bhowani. *Rural Bengal in Ruins*. Bombay: People's Publishing House, 1945.

Sen, Ela. *Darkening Days, Being a Narrative of Famine-Stricken Bengal*. Drawings from life by Zainul Abedin. 1st ed. Calcutta: Sushil Gupta, May 1944.

Sen, Paritosh. "Reflections." *Lalit Kala Contemporary* 9 (September 1968).

———. *Rong Tuli-r Baire*. Kolkata: Bhashabinyash, 2008.

Sen, Prabas. *Chittaprosad*. New Delhi: Lalit Kala Akademi, 1993.

Sen, Satya. *Mukhar, Debabrata Mukhopadhyay Volume*, December 1981–March 1982.

Sen, Srichandra. *The Art of Subho Tagore*. Calcutta: Thacker Spink, 1950.

Sen, Sunil. *Agrarian Struggle in Bengal, 1946–47*. Foreword by Bhawani Sen. New Delhi: People's Publishing House, 1972.

Sen, Uditi. *Citizen Refugee: Forging the Indian Nation after Partition*. Cambridge: Cambridge University Press, 2018.

Sengupta, Anwesha, Sucharita Sengupta, and Paula Banerjee. *People, Politics, and Protests I: Calcutta and West Bengal, 1950s–1960s*. Politics and Practices Series. Calcutta: Mahanirban Calcutta Research Group, 2016.

Sengupta, Shoumini. "Indian Artist Enjoys His World Audience." *New York Times*, 24 January 2006.

Seth, Sanjay. "Indian Maoism: The Significance of Naxalbari." In *Critical Perspectives on Media and Society*, edited by R. Avery and D. Easton. New York: Guilford Press, 1991.

———. "Smashing Statues, Dancing Sivas." *Humanities Research* 11, no. 1 (2004): 42–53.

Sheikh, Gulammohammed. "Tradition and Modernity: Towards a More Relevant Art." *Vrishchik*, Special Volume, "Social Context of Contemporary Indian Art" 4, no. 4 (December 1973), unpaginated.

Singh, Devika. "Indian Art and the Bangladesh War." *Third Text*. Special issue, *Partitions* 31, nos. 2–3 (November 2017): 459–76. https://doi,org 10.1080/09528822.2017.1395161.

Sinha, Modhurima. *Call of the Real*. Ahmedabad: Mapin, 2003.

Siva Kumar, R. *Santiniketan: The Making of a Contextual Modernism*. New Delhi: National Gallery of Modern Art, 1992.

Six Haripura Panels/Nandalal Bose. New Delhi: Lalit Kala Akademi, 1984.

Solomon, Maynard, ed. *Marxism and Art: Essays Classic and Contemporary*. New York: Knopf, 1973.

Somnath Hore: Prints, Drawings, Posters. Exhibition held at Kala Bhavan, Santiniketan, and Seagull Foundation for the Arts, Calcutta, 17 February–1 March 2011.

Sontag, Susan. "On Style." In *Against Interpretation and Other Essays*. London: Penguin Books, 2005. First published in 1966.

Soon, Simon. "What Is Left of Art?: The Spatio-Visual Practice of Political Art in Indonesia, Singapore, Thailand, and the Philippines, 1950s–1970s." PhD diss., University of Sydney, 2015.

Spiegelman, Art, ed. *Si Lewen's Parade: An Artist's Odyssey*. New York: Abrams Comicart, 2016.

Srimanjari. *Through War and Famine: Bengal 1939–45*. New Delhi: Orient Blackswan, 2010.

Sripantha. *Daya*. Calcutta: Nayak Sandeep, 1994.

Stalin, Joseph. *Marxism and the National-Colonial Question: A Collection of Articles and Speeches* (1934). London: Lawrence and Wishart, 1936.

Stephens, Ian. *Monsoon Morning: A Picture of India in 1942–44*. London: Ernst Benn, 1966.

Subramanyan, K. G. *Moving Focus: Essays on Indian Art*. Reprint, Calcutta: Seagull, 2006.

Suhrawardy, Shahid. "Calcutta Group, Promising Works by Young Artists." *The Statesman*, 26 March 1945.

———. *Prefaces: Lectures on Art Subjects*. Calcutta: University Press, 1938.

Sunderason, Sanjukta. "Aesthetics of Decolonisation in South Asia." In *Oxford Research Encyclopedia of Asian History*, edited by David Ludden. Oxford: Oxford University Press, forthcoming.

———. "'As Agitator and Organiser': Chittaprosad and the Art for the Communist Party of India." *Object*, no. 13 (2010): 75–95.

———. "Framing Margins: Mao and Visuality in Twentieth-Century India." In *Art, Global Maoism, and the Chinese Cultural Revolution,* edited by Jacopo Galimberti, Noemi de Haro-García, and Victoria H. F. Scott. Manchester: Manchester University Press, 2019.

———. "Making Art 'Modern': Revisiting Artistic Modernism in India." In *Modern Makeovers: A Handbook of Modernity in South Asia*, edited by Saurabh Dube. New Delhi: Oxford University Press, 2011.

———. "Shadow Lines: Zainul Abedin and the Afterlives of the Bengal Famine of 1943." *Third Text.* Special issue, *Partitions* 31, nos. 2–3 (November 2017): 239–59.

Tagore. "The Centre of Indian Culture: Visva-Bharati." Speech introducing Visva-Bharati, at the Society for Promotion of National Education, Adyar, Madras, 1921. First published in 1919.

———. *Letters from Russia* (1931). Reprint, Calcutta: Visva-Bharati Granthana Vibhaga, 1960.

Terracciano, Emilia. *Art and Emergency*. London: I. B. Tauris, 2017.

Thistlewood, David. "Herbert Read's Organic Aesthetic [I] 1918–1950." In *Herbert Read Reassessed*, edited by David Goodway. Liverpool: Liverpool University Press, 1998.

Traverso, Enzo. *Left-Wing Melancholia: Marxism, History, and Memory.* New York: Columbia University Press, 2016.

Tuli, Neville, ed. *The Flamed Mosaic: Indian Contemporary Painting.* New Delhi: Heart, Mapin, 1997.

———, ed. *Masterpieces and Museum-Quality Indian Modern and Contemporary Paintings.* Curated by Neville Tuli. Bombay: Osian's, December 2002.

———, ed. *Masterpieces and Museum-Quality III, Indian Contemporary Paintings with Rare Books and Vintage Film Memorabilia.* Bombay: Osian's, March 2004.

UNESCO Courier, February 1956.

Vasudev, Uma. *Satish Gujral.* Lalit Kala Series of Contemporary Indian Art. New Delhi, 1970.

Vasudevan, Ravi. "Dislocations: The Cinematic Imagining of a New Society in 1950s India." *Oxford Literary Review* 16, nos. 1–2, *On India: Writing History, Culture, Post-Coloniality* (1994), 93–124.

Vials, Chris. *Realism for the Masses: Aesthetics, Popular Front Pluralism, and U S. Culture, 1935–1947.* Jackson: University of Mississippi Press, 2009.

Weisenfeld, Gennifer. *Imaging Disaster: Tokyo and the Visual Culture of Japan's Great Earthquake of 1923.* Berkeley: University of California Press, 2012.

Wernicke, Günter. "The Unity of Peace and Socialism? The World Peace Council on a Cold War Tightrope between the Peace Struggle and Intrasystemic Communist Conflicts." *Peace and Change* 26 (2001): 332–51.

Wille, Simone. "A Modernist Transnational Socialist Solidarity: Chittaprosad's Prague Connection." *Stedelijk Studies* 9 (2019).

Williams, Raymond. "Lecture on Realism." *Screen* 18, no. 1 (Spring 1977). Reprinted in *Afterall: A Journal of Art, Context, and Enquiry*, no. 5 (2002): 106–15.

———. *The Politics of Modernism: Against the New Conformists.* Edited by Tony Pinkney.London: Verso, 2007.

Wilson, Rob, and Christopher Leigh Connery, eds. *The WO R L D I N G Project: Doing Cultural Studies in the Era of Globalization.* Berkeley: North Atlantic Books, 2007.

Zachariah, Benjamin. *Nehru.* London: Routledge, 2004.

Zhdanov, A. *Speech at the Soviet Writers' Congress*, 1934. London: Lawrence and Wishart, 1977.

Zhedong, Mao. *Problems of Art and Literature.* New York: International Publishers, 1950.

Zitzewitz, Karin. *The Art of Secularism: The Cultural Politics of Modernist Art in Contemporary India.* London: Hurst, 2014.

———. "The Moral Economy of the Street: The Bombay Paintings of Gieve Patel and Sudhir Patwardhan." *Third Text* 23, no. 2 (2009): 151–63.

BOOKS AND ARTICLES IN BENGALI

Ash, Gobardhan. "Amar chhelebela o silpijibon." *Oitihashi* 2, nos. 1–2.

———. *Samagra Gobardhan Ash.* Edited by Santi Nath. Calcutta: Raktakarabi, 2005.

Basu, Sri Prabodh. "Bangla-r citrasilper dhara." *Bichitra,* Magh 1343/1936.

Bhattacharya, Sandipan, ed. *Chhobi-r Rajneeti, Rajneeti-r Chhobi.* Calcutta: Deepayan, 1990.

Bishnu Dey: Shilpa-karma, Shilpa-samgraha, Shilpa-bhabana. Exhibition organized at the Bangiya Sahitya Parishat, 18–31 July 2005.

Bose, Buddhadeb. *Amader Kabita Bhaban.* Calcutta, 1974.

Chakraborty, Rathin. *Rajnoitik Andolon, Sanskriti o Sanskritik Front.* Calcutta: Pustak Bipani, 1988.

Chittaprosad. "Chhobi-r Sankat." *Arani.* Saradiya, 1943.

———. "Chittaprosad-er Chithi o Chhara." *Parichoy* (Saradiya, 1994): 14–27.

———. *Kshudartho Bangla* (Hungry Bengal). Calcutta: Seriban, 1993.

Das, Dhananjay, ed. *Bangla Sanskritite Marxbadi Chetana-r Dhara*, Anustup special issue. Calcutta: Anustup, 1991.

———, ed. *Marxbadi Sahitya Bitarka.* Vol. 2. Calcutta: Notun Poribesh Prakasani, 1976.

Das, Susnata, ed. *Fascibad-birodhi Sangrame Abibhakta Bangla.* Calcutta: Prima Publications, 1989.

Dasgupta, Prodosh. *Smritikatha Shilpakatha/Calcutta Group.* Calcutta: Pratikshan Publications, 1986.

Devi, Santa. "Silpi Srijukta Jamini Ray-er Pradarsani" (The Exhibition of the Artist Jamini Roy). *Prabasi*, Baisakh 1339/1932.

Dey, Bishnu. *Jamini Ray: Tnar Shilpachinta o Shilpakarma Bishaye Kayekti Chinta.* Calcutta: Asha Prakasani, 1977.

———. "Jamini Ray o Tar Silpabichar." *Parichoy*, Poush 1362/1955.

———. *Kabitasamagra.* Calcutta: Ananda Publishers, 1996).

———. *Prabandha Sangraha*. 2 vols. Edited by Dhrubakumar Mukhopadhyay. Calcutta: Dey Publishing, 1997.

Dey, Mukul. *Amar Katha*. Calcutta: Visva-Bharati Granthana Vibhaga, 1995.

Gangopadhyay, Upendranath. "Academy of Fine Arts-er Bhobishyat." *Bichitra*, Sraban 1341/1934.

Ghosh, Chilka. *Chhobir Bishoy, Bishoyer Chhobi: Pratibad o Pratirodh*. Calcutta: N. I. Publishers, 2005.

Ghosh, Mrinal. "Calcutta Group o Challish-er Silpakala: Pariprekshita." *Paricboy Saradiya* 1393/1986.

———. *Pashchimbang-er Chitrakala-i 1960-r Dashak ebong Doshjon Shilpi*. Calcutta: Pratikshan, 1999; 2nd ed., 2006.

Ghosh, Shyamal Krishna. *Parichoy-er Adda*. Calcutta: K. P. Bagchi and Co., 1990.

———.. "Parichoy-er Partham Jug." *Parichoy*, Kartik 1388/1981.

Ghosh, Sujit, ed. *Smriti or Sattay Bishnu Dey*. Calcutta: Utthwak Prakashani, 1992.

Goswamy, Surendranath, and Hiren Mukherjee, eds. *Pragati*. Originally published 1937; rare volume reprinted by little magazines in 1991. Calcutta: Unthak Prakasani, 1991.

Haldar, Asit. *Rabitirthe*. Calcutta: Indian Publishing House, 1958.

Haldar, Gopal. "Culture O Communist Dwaityo." In *Sanskritir Biswarup, Gopal Haldar*, edited by Dr. Debipada Bhattacharya, Dr. Aruna Haldar, and Dr. Amiya Dhar. Calcutta: Manisha, 1986.

———. *Gopal Haldar Rachanasamagra*. Vol. 1. Calcutta: A. Mukherjee and Co. Pvt., Ltd., 1997.

———. "Jamini Roy o Jatiya Chetana." *Parichoy*, Phalgun 1351 (February–March 1944): 313–15.

———. "Soviet Prachir-Chitra Pradarshani." *Parichay*, Jaishtha 1352/1945.

Hore, Somnath. *Amar Chitrabhabana* . Calcutta: Seagull Books, 1992.

Mandal, Panchanan. *Bharatsilpi Nandalal*. 4 vols. Bolpur: Rarh Gabeshana Parishad, 1993.

Mazumdar, Hemendranath. *Chhabi-r Chasma*. Calcutta: Ananda Publishers, 1991.

Mondal, Rabin. *Shilpabhabona*. Calcutta: Banishilpa, 2007.

Mukherjee, Benodebehari. *Adhunik Shilpashiksha*. Calcutta: Visva-Bharati Granthana Vibhaga, 1972.

———. *Chitrakar*. Calcutta: Aruna Prakasani, 1978.

———. "The Santiniketan School of Art." *Visva-Bharati Quarterly*, n.s., May 1935.

Mukherjee, Hiren. *Tari Hote Tir*. Calcutta: Manisha Granthalaya, 1974.

Mukherjee, Meera. *Chach-er Gabheer Theke*. Calcutta: Graffiti, 1997.

Nath, Santi. *Durbhikkher Chitramalay Gobardhan Ash*. Calcutta: Raktakarabi, 2005.

Roy, Anuradha, comp. and ed. *Challish Dashaker Bangla-i Ganasangeet Andolan*. Calcutta: Anustup, 1992.

Roy, Krishna Benode. *Bengal Famine and the Problems of Rehabilitation*. A Memorandum on Rehabilitation submitted to the Government of Bengal by the Bengal Provincial Kisan Sabha. Bombay, 1945.

Sanyal, Hiran Kumar. *Parichoy-er kuri Bochor o Ananyo Smritichitra.* Calcutta: Papyrus, 1975.

Sarkar, Kamal. *Bharater Bhaskar o Chitrashilpi.* Calcutta: Shyamali Ghosh, 1984.

Sarkar, Shipra, and Anamitra Das, eds. *Banglalir Samyabad Charcha.* Calcutta: Ananda Publishers, 1998.

Sehanobish, Chinmohan. "Sanskriti Andolon-er Nutan Dhara." *Janayuddha* , 28 April 1943.

———. "Sanskriti Sammelan-e." *Arani*, 2 July 1943.

Sehanobish, Chinmohon, and Arun Ghosh, eds. *46 No. Ekti Sanskritik Andolon Prashange.* Calcutta: Research India Publications, 1986.

Sen, Arun. *Bishnu Dey-r Katha.* Calcutta: Pratikshan, 1990.

Sen, Jaminikanta. "Adhunik Chitrakala-i Bangla Desh." *Bichitra* 1, no. 1, Sraban 1345/1938.

Sen, Manikuntala. *Shediner Katha.* Calcutta: Nabaparta Prakashan, 1982.

Sen, Paritosh. *Rong Tuli-r Baire.* Calcutta: Bhashabinyash, 2008.

Sen, Pulinbehari. "Kolikata-r Silpa Pradarsani." *Prabasi*, Magh 1342/1935.

Sen, Samar. *Babubrittanto o Prasangik* [The annals of the babu and relevant writings]. Calcutta: Dey Publishing, 2004.

Sen, Satya. "Interview with Debabrata Mukhopadhyay." *Mukhar*, Debabrata Mukhopadhyay Volume, December 1981–March 1982.

"Shibpur Shilpa Pradarsani." *Bichitra*, Jaistha 1343/1936.

"Silpa Pradarsani, Third Annual Exhibition of the Society of Fine Arts." *Sachitra Sisir*, Poush 1330/1924.

Som, Sovon. "Bangla-r Chitrakala o Bhashkarje Pragati Chetana-r Dhara." In *Bangla Sanskritite Marxbadi Chetana-r Dhara, Anustup.* Special issue, edited by Dhananjay Das. Calcutta: Anustup, 1991.

———."Calcutta Group: Uddeshya, Karmapantha o Parinam." *Anustup* 18, no. 1. Calcutta 1390 (1983).

———.*Shilpi, Shilpa o Samaj.* Calcutta: Anustup, 1981.

Tagore, Abanindranath. *Bageswari Silpa Prabandhabali.* Calcutta: University of Calcutta, 1941. Reprint, Calcutta: Rupa, 1962.

Tagore, Rabindranath. *Ashramer Rup O Bikash.* Calcutta: Visva-Bharati Granthana Vibhaga, 1941.

———. "Kala Vidya." *Santiniketan Patrika* 1, no. 8, 1326/1919.

INDEX

Page numbers in italics indicate figures.

ALSO PUBLISHED IN THE SOUTH ASIA IN MOTION SERIES

Dying to Serve: Militarism, Affect, and the Politics of Sacrifice in the Pakistan Army
Maria Rashid (2020)

In the Name of the Nation: India and Its Northeast
Sanjib Baruah (2020)

Faithful Fighters: Identity and Power in the British Indian Army
Kate Imy (2019)

Paradoxes of the Popular: Crowd Politics in Bangladesh
Nusrat Sabina Chowdhury (2019)

The Ethics of Staying: Social Movements and Land Rights Politics in Pakistan
Mubbashir A. Rizvi (2019)

Mafia Raj: The Rule of Bosses in South Asia
Lucia Michelutti, Ashraf Hoque, Nicolas Martin, David Picherit, Paul Rollier, Arild Ruud, and Clarinda Still (2018)

Elusive Lives: Gender, Autobiography, and the Self in Muslim South Asia
Siobhan Lambert-Hurley (2018)

Financializing Poverty: Labor and Risk in Indian Microfinance
Sohini Kar (2018)

Jinnealogy: Time, Islam, and Ecological Thought in the Medieval Ruins of Delhi
Anand Vivek Taneja (2017)

Uprising of the Fools: Pilgrimage as Moral Protest in Contemporary India
Vikash Singh (2017)

The Slow Boil: Street Food, Rights, and Public Space in Mumbai
Jonathan Shapiro Anjaria (2016)

The Demands of Recognition: State Anthropology and Ethnopolitics vin Darjeeling
Townsend Middleton (2015)

The South African Gandhi: Stretcher-Bearer of Empire
Ashwin Desai and Goolam Vahed (2015)

The authorized representative in the EU for product safety and compliance is:
Mare Nostrum Group
B.V Doelen 72
4831 GR Breda
The Netherlands

www.ingramcontent.com/pod-product-compliance
Lightning Source LLC
LaVergne TN
LVHW041109080826
845145LV00007B/1743

* 9 7 8 1 5 0 3 6 1 2 9 9 0 *